| | |
|---|---|
| C. Apply self-awareness and self-regulation to manage of personal biases and values in working with divers constituencies | |
| Competency 3: Advance Human Rights and Social, Economic, and Environmental Justice | |
| A. Apply their understanding of social, economic, and environmental justice to advocate for human rights at the individual and system levels | **2, 3, 4, 6, 7, 8, 9, 11, 13, 14** |
| B. Engage in practices that advance social, economic, and environmental justice | **2, 4, 7, 8, 9, 10, 13** |
| Competency 4: Engage in Practice-informed Research and Research-informed Practice | |
| A. Use practice experience and theory to inform scientific inquiry and research | **10, 11, 13** |
| B. Apply critical thinking to engage in analysis of quantitative and qualitative research methods and research findings | **7, 9, 10** |
| C. Use and translate research evidence to inform and improve practice, policy, and service delivery | **9, 10, 12** |
| Competency 5: Engage in Policy Practice | |
| A. Identify social policy at the local, state, and federal level that impacts well-being, service delivery, and access to social services | **3, 6, 8, 9** |
| B. Assess how social welfare and economic policies impact the delivery of and access to social services | **2, 4, 5, 6, 9, 10, 12** |
| C. Apply critical thinking to analyze, formulate, and advocate policies that advance human rights and social, economic, and environmental justice | **1, 2, 4, 5, 7, 8, 9, 13** |
| Competency 6: Engage with Individuals, Families, Groups, Organizations, and Communities | |
| A. Apply knowledge of human behavior and the social environment, person-in-environment, and other multidisciplinary theoretical frameworks to engage with clients and constituencies | **1, 2, 4, 5, 6, 8, 9** |
| B. Use empathy, reflection, and interpersonal skills to effectively engage diverse clients and constituencies | **1, 5, 6, 7, 9, 10, 14** |
| Competency 7: Assess Individuals, Families, Groups, Organizations, and Communities | |
| A. Collect and organize data, and apply critical thinking to interpret information from clients and constituencies | **5, 7, 10, 14** |

| | |
|---|---|
| B. Apply knowledge of human behavior and the social environment, person-in-environment, and other multidisciplinary theoretical frameworks in the analysis of assessment data from clients and constituencies | **1, 2, 3, 4, 5, 6, 7, 9, 12** |
| C. Develop mutually agreed-on intervention goals and objectives based on the critical assessment of strengths, needs, and challenges within clients and constituencies | **4, 5, 6, 9** |
| D. Select appropriate intervention strategies based on the assessment, research knowledge, and values and preferences of clients and constituencies | **4, 6, 7, 9, 10** |

| Competency 8: Intervene with Individuals, Families, Groups, Organizations, and Communities | |
|---|---|
| A. Critically choose and implement interventions to achieve practice goals and enhance capacities of clients and constituencies | **3, 4, 5, 6, 7, 8, 11, 13** |
| B. Apply knowledge of human behavior and the social environment, person-in-environment, and other multidisciplinary theoretical frameworks in interventions with clients and constituencies | **2, 4, 5, 6, 8** |
| C. Use inter-professional collaboration as appropriate to achieve beneficial practice outcomes | **1, 2, 6, 8** |
| D. Negotiate, mediate, and advocate with and on behalf of diverse clients and constituencies | **1, 4, 6, 7, 8, 9, 13** |
| E. Facilitate effective transitions and endings that advance mutually agreed-on goals | **5, 6, 8** |

| Competency 9: Evaluate Practice with Individuals, Families, Groups, Organizations, and Communities | |
|---|---|
| A. Select and use appropriate methods for evaluation of outcomes | **10** |
| B. Apply knowledge of human behavior and the social environment, person-in-environment, and other multidisciplinary theoretical frameworks in the evaluation of outcomes | **1, 2, 4, 5, 6, 8, 9** |
| C. Critically analyze, monitor, and evaluate intervention and program processes and outcomes | **5, 6, 8, 12** |
| D. Apply evaluation findings to improve practice effectiveness at the micro, mezzo, and macro levels | **5, 6, 7, 8, 9, 10, 14** |

# Macro Social Work Practice

In honor of and with heartfelt thanks to Team Tice-Captain George,
and of course Miss Jeanne.
CJT

With love to Joan, Noah, Jacob, and Andrew for your
everlasting influence on my life.
DDL

In honor of Aaron and his many fans, including Kyle, Jessica, Mike,
and Emilee. Your spirit, grace, and humility have been and
will continue to be transformative!
LEC

Sara Miller McCune founded SAGE Publishing in 1965 to support the dissemination of usable knowledge and educate a global community. SAGE publishes more than 1000 journals and over 600 new books each year, spanning a wide range of subject areas. Our growing selection of library products includes archives, data, case studies and video. SAGE remains majority owned by our founder and after her lifetime will become owned by a charitable trust that secures the company's continued independence.

Los Angeles | London | New Delhi | Singapore | Washington DC | Melbourne

# Macro Social Work Practice

## Advocacy in Action

Carolyn J. Tice
*University of Maryland, Baltimore County*

Dennis D. Long
*Xavier University*

Lisa E. Cox
*Stockton University*

Los Angeles | London | New Delhi
Singapore | Washington DC | Melbourne

FOR INFORMATION:

SAGE Publications, Inc.
2455 Teller Road
Thousand Oaks, California 91320
E-mail: order@sagepub.com

SAGE Publications Ltd.
1 Oliver's Yard
55 City Road
London EC1Y 1SP
United Kingdom

SAGE Publications India Pvt. Ltd.
B 1/I 1 Mohan Cooperative Industrial Area
Mathura Road, New Delhi 110 044
India

SAGE Publications Asia-Pacific Pte. Ltd.
18 Cross Street
#10-10/11/12
China Square Central
Singapore 048423

Acquisitions Editor: Joshua Perigo
Editorial Assistant: Noelle Cumberbatch
Content Development Editor: Alissa Nance
Production Editor: Tracy Buyan
Copy Editor: Gillian Dickens
Typesetter: C&M Digitals (P) Ltd.
Proofreader: Annette Van Devsen
Indexer: Celia McCoy
Cover Designer: Candice Harman
Marketing Manager: Zina Craft



Printed in the United States of America

*Library of Congress Cataloging-in-Publication Data*

Names: Tice, Carolyn J., author. | Long, Dennis D., author. | Cox, Lisa E., author.

Title: Macro social work practice : advocacy in action / Carolyn J. Tice, Dennis D. Long, Lisa E. Cox.

Description: First Edition. | Thousand Oaks : SAGE Publications, [2019] | Includes bibliographical references and index.

Identifiers: LCCN 2019011937 | ISBN 9781506388410 (pbk. : alk. paper)

Subjects: LCSH: Social service. | Macrosociology.

Classification: LCC HV41 .T543 2019 | DDC 361.3/2—dc23
LC record available at https://lccn.loc.gov/2019011937

This book is printed on acid-free paper.

SFI label applies to text stock

19 20 21 22 23 10 9 8 7 6 5 4 3 2 1

# Detailed Contents

# Preface

Macro social work practice maximizes opportunities for change at the organizational, community, societal, and global levels. Using a "big picture outlook," *Macro Social Work Practice: Advocacy in Action* examines the context of contemporary social issues that often involve the redistribution of power and privilege—a signature aspect of social work education and practice. Readers are challenged throughout chapters to enact advocacy, informed by key orientations and perspectives and grounded in timely and relevant examples and causes (e.g., refugee services and gun violence).

As a primary/core text, this coauthored book's unique contribution involves the contextualization of macro practice. Historical content and current practice examples link personal or individual and community needs to public issues through macro intervention. An emphasis is placed on engaging students in macro practice using the tenets of the advocacy policy and practice model (APPM) that highlight the inclusion of economic and social justice, supportive environment, human needs and rights, and political access.

More specifically, this book was written for social work professionals aspiring to enhance and develop professional abilities and skills in macro-level change. Because the primary focus is on knowledge, values, and skills applicable to generalist social practice, *Macro Social Work Practice: Advocacy in Action* is intended primarily for upper-level practice courses in the undergraduate curriculum and foundation coursework in practice at the graduate (MSW) level.

For the sake of students, materials are presented in an orderly, structured fashion that is both theoretical and applied in nature. At the beginning of each chapter, students can review a list of the topics to be examined. Each chapter concludes with a brief summary, a list of key terms, discussion questions, exercises, and online references.

Instructors will appreciate the time and attention given to the relationship between macro practice and other related perspectives and orientations (e.g., strengths perspective, empowerment theory, problem solving, and the ecological perspective). Professors who traditionally approach macro practice from a community-organizing tradition will be excited about the primacy given to community-based practice and social justice advocacy. Colleagues who embrace macro practice in the form of multiple social work roles and through multilevel activities should also be pleased. For those interested in the pragmatic aspects of social work policy-practice, every effort has been made to provide readers with hands-on, practical suggestions and with skills for embracing basic tenets of a strengths perspective in macro-level intervention.

Finally, the notion of consumerism in relation to social work practice and policy is embraced as a dominant feature throughout the text. The word *consumer* is offered in the spirit of empowerment and is intended as an acknowledgment of the strengths and rights possessed by the people who come to our agencies and organizations for services.

# Acknowledgments

The authors wish to thank the following reviewers for their valuable feedback during the development of this book:

Sheila Dennis, MSW, PhD, Indiana University

Kim Dotson, MSW, LCSW, MSSW, Indiana University MSW Direct

Angela Kaiser, Oakland University

Benjamin Malczyk, MSW, PhD, University of Nebraska at Kearney

Dianna B. Parrish, LPN, LCSW, Mary Baldwin University

Jason Anthony Plummer, California State University, Los Angeles

Kim Releford, Indiana University School of Social Work

C. Shane Robbins, University of Mississippi

Lynda Sowbel, PhD, LCSW-C, BSW Program Director, Hood College

Glenn Stone, Ball State University

Tracy Wharton, PhD, LCSW, University of Central Florida

Additionally, the authors wish to acknowledge and give a very special thanks to Dr. John D. Morison for his intellectual contributions that have facilitated and contributed to the publication of this book. Carolyn Tice would also like to thank Amy Cruz, 2019 UMBC graduate, for her office support. Lisa Cox would also like to thank Allyson Crawford, 2019 Stockton University graduate, for her assistance.

# About the Authors

**Carolyn J. Tice,** DSW, ACSW, Professor and the Associate Dean of the Baccalaureate Social Work Program, School of Social Work, University of Maryland since July 2002. Her prior appointment was chair of the Department of Social Work, Ohio University, a position she held for 9 years. Currently, Dr. Tice teaches a First-Year Seminar and social welfare policy. She received her BSW from West Virginia University, earned an MSW from Temple University, and completed her DSW at the University of Pennsylvania, where she worked with Hmong refugees. The coauthor of numerous books and peer-reviewed articles, Dr. Tice's scholarship focuses primarily on the development of critical thinking skills and social work practice and policy from a strengths perspective. She is on the editorial board of the *Journal of Teaching in Social Work* and serves as a book prospectus reviewer for Wadsworth and John Wiley. In 2008, she was named a Fulbright specialist and traveled to Mongolia to assist in the development of social work programs. Other international social work experiences include program development in Botswana, India, Portugal, Taiwan, Vietnam, and China. Dr. Tice is a member of the Council of Social Work Education, the Association of Baccalaureate Social Work Program Directors, the National Association of Social Workers, and the Friends Committee on National Legislation.

For leisure, Dr. Tice operates *Olde Friends*, a booth in an antique store located on the southern New Jersey coastline. E-mail: tice@umbc.edu.

**Dennis D. Long,** PhD, ACSW, Professor and the Associate Dean of the College of Social Sciences, Health, and Education, Xavier University (Cincinnati, Ohio). Dr. Long previously served as Professor and Chair of the Department of Social Work at Xavier University and, from 2006 to 2012, was a Professor and Chair of the Department of Social Work at the University of North Carolina at Charlotte. He received his BA in sociology and psychology from Ohio Northern University, MSW from The Ohio State University, and PhD in sociology from the University of Cincinnati. The coauthor of numerous other books and articles, Dr. Long's scholarship and teaching have been in the area of macro social work with special interests in community-based and international practice. He serves on the editorial board of the *Journal of Teaching in Social Work* and has been a longstanding member of the National Association of Social Workers and Council on Social Work Education. Over the years, Dr. Long has provided leadership on numerous community and national boards, including the Butler County Mental Health Board, Oesterlen Services for Youth, Charlotte Family Housing, and the National Board of Examiners in Optometry. E-mail: longd3@xavier.edu.

**Lisa E. Cox,** PhD, LCSW, MSW, Professor of Social Work and Gerontology in Stockton University's School of Social & Behavioral Sciences, Social Work Program. Prior to 1999, Dr. Cox held a joint appointment at Virginia

Commonwealth University's (VCU's) School of Medicine and School of Social Work. For 11 years, Dr. Cox served as a pioneering AIDS clinical trial social worker with the National Institute of Allergy and Infectious Disease–funded Terry Beirn Community Programs for Clinical Research on AIDS. Dr. Cox received BA degrees in history/political science and Spanish from Bridgewater College, as well as her Graduate Certificate in Aging Studies and MSW and PhD degrees from VCU. Since 2007, she has served as Research Chair, Fellow, and Research Scholar for The Stockton Center on Successful Aging. Dr. Cox teaches undergraduate- and graduate-level classes in social work practice, gerontology (Aging & Spirituality; Clinical Gerontological Social Work Practice), HIV/AIDS, research, psychopathology, and cultural neuroscience, and she has co-led study tours to Costa Rica. She has been a faculty scholar with the national Geriatric Education Center and is a governor appointee to the New Jersey Board of Social Work Examiners.

Dr. Cox is a longstanding member of the National Association of Social Workers (NASW) and has shared her vast practice experience by holding numerous leadership roles within NASW: National Advisory Board member to the Spectrum HIV/AIDS Project, Chair of the Health Specialty Practice Section, Standards for Social Work Practice in Health Care Settings Task Force expert, Long-Term Care Liaison to The Joint Commission on Health Care, and Unit Chairperson. Dr. Cox has presented her scholarship nationally and internationally. She has authored four other books, several book chapters, and journal articles focused on health social work, gerontology, international social work, social support, and medication adherence. Leisure time is spent playing the piano and enjoying sports, films, and opera. E-mail: lisa.cox@stockton.edu.

# A Historical Perspective of Macro Practice and Advocacy

1

## LIAM DEVELOPS A COMMUNITY-BASED READING PROGRAM

Liam is a community development coordinator in southern West Virginia. In this role, Liam was responsible for collaborating with consumers and community stakeholders to ensure their needs and wants were addressed. This required interpersonal skills, analysis, critical thinking, concise writing, data gathering and analysis, and attention to details. In response to consumers, Liam planned a community-wide effort, and after-school district data revealed that 75% of the county's elementary school students were reading below grade level. Relying on his social work skills, Liam collaborated with public school teachers, child welfare social workers, and parents to organize a community-based reading program for elementary school children.

Throughout the program's development, Liam worked closely with his advisory board to ensure that they were well informed on the project status. He also developed a network of funders associated with local businesses and the faith-based community. Throughout his project interactions, Liam demonstrated an array of skills associated with macro practice: community organizing, community development, planning, administration, financial management, analytical thinking, and grant writing. For example, he organized a breakfast for funders and created a list of possible fundraising activities with people assuming responsibilities for the various activities. He followed up by writing an article for the local newspaper that described the fundraising projects and solicited additional support from the community.

Liam's personal qualities also enhanced his work with others on the reading program. Specifically, Liam's program collaborators described him as energetic, committed, humorous, persistent, and motivated. Liam's activities demonstrated an array of skills that blended interpersonal interactions with his ability to analyze need, gather resources, and articulate goals.

## LEARNING OBJECTIVES

After reading this chapter, you should be able to:

1. Define macro practice and explain its meaning to social work practice
2. Describe the historical context of macro practice
3. Understand the unique contributions of macro practice
4. Define the social work values of macro practice
5. Connect macro practice with advocacy and empowerment

## WHAT IS MACRO PRACTICE?

Although Liam's work on the reading program demonstrates an array of macro-related social work skills, you may still be grappling with the question, "What is macro practice?" Indeed, practitioners and educators often differ when asked to define *macro social work practice.* If you were to ask the instructors in your program for their definition, you might be surprised at the variety of responses. Definitions would most likely vary depending on the era of the social worker's professional education, the program from which he or she graduated, and his or her practice experiences (Hill, Erickson, Donaldson, Fogel, & Ferguson, 2017).

For many social workers educated in the 1950s, 1960s, and 1970s, the term *macro practice* probably still seems somewhat foreign. These social workers are more familiar with the notions of social casework (Perlman, 1957), environmental work (Hollis, 1972), innovation and change with organizations and communities (Rothman, Erlich, & Teresa, 1976), social welfare administration and research (Friedlander, 1976), and group work for social reform (Roberts & Northen, 1976). It would not be unusual for social workers of this era to perceive macro social work in terms of community organization, administration, research, or policy development. Much of this same language continues to be used today, as social workers have a propensity to define macro practice in terms of the roles they enact or the functions they perform (Reisch, 2016).

### Time to Think 1.1

Macro social workers often enact several roles. In nonprofit organizations, like the Red Cross or a social service agency, they are often organization leaders responsible for staff, volunteer, and financial management. They are also community organizers who form movements or groups to challenge social issues like the opioid crisis or the need for adequate community-based mental health services. Advocacy is often the foundation of macro social work. Such advocacy can range from mobilizing groups around concerns, like environmental justice, or a particular policy that will affect a vulnerable population. Embedded in all advocacy action are themes of human rights and social, economic, and environmental justice. How do your academic strengths and professional interests complement the roles of macro practice?

## WHAT DOES MACRO SOCIAL WORK PRACTICE MEAN?

*Macro* means large-scale or big. In social work, it involves the ability to see and intervene in the big picture, specifically with larger systems in the socioeconomic environment. **Macro social work practice** can include collaboration with **consumers** of services to strengthen and maximize opportunities for people at the organizational, community, societal, and global levels. Some social workers would argue that it is the macro level—the attention given by social workers to the big social issues of importance to consumers—that distinguishes social work from other helping professions (Glisson, 1994).

Historically, another term that has been used to describe macro social work practice is *indirect work.* Although this term is becoming less popular, the word *indirect* served for many years as a reference to social work's commitment to environmental modification and the alleviation of social problems. Whereas **direct practice** connoted face-to-face contact with clients aimed at supporting or strengthening them as individuals, **indirect practice** was the catchphrase for change efforts involving the environment and the social welfare system (Pierce, 1989, p. 167). Although schools of social work note that there is a growing trend toward direct practice, the need for indirect or macro practice is persistent, especially in light of policy analysis and development, income distribution, community building, and political organizing.

For many other social workers, the *macro* in *macro practice* is synonymous with community organizing. Rothman (1964, 1974, 1995) provides the social work profession with a pointed conceptualization of large-scale change that emphasizes three basic modes: locality development, social planning, and social action. As summarized by Weil (1996), **locality development** focuses on community capacity building and the role of social workers in engaging citizens in determining and resolving community-based issues. **Social planning** refers to the use of a rational problem-solving strategy aimed at combating community problems. Social workers use their knowledge and skills in research, assessment, and program implementation as they work with clients to identify logical steps and means of addressing community problems. **Social action** references the ability of social workers and consumers of services to confront and change power relationships and the structure and function of important social institutions in communities.

As can be seen, the term *macro* has several connotations, both general and specific. In this text, preference is given to the term *macro social work practice. Indirect practice* is often viewed as a nebulous, uncelebrated term in social work (Johnson, 1999), but conceptualizing macro practice primarily in terms of community organizing is limiting. Macro social work practice is more specific, suggesting the importance of strengthening higher order social systems—organizations, communities, and societies. Thus, macro social work practice changes conditions in environments and addresses community issues through the empowerment of consumers. This action often involves conflict resolution, organizational change, power redistribution where consumers are decision makers, public education, and building on existing strengths in individuals and the communities where they live.

**PHOTO 1.1**
Social justice brings the people of the world together.

## THE HISTORICAL CONTEXT OF MACRO PRACTICE

Throughout the years, social work practice has been concerned with promoting social reform and social justice to advance the well-being of people. Some of the first writings associated with the profession of social work provide insight into the importance of affecting larger structural issues in the lives of consumers. As a student of social work, take some time to acquaint yourself with some of the influential writers in the field—the "ghosts" of social work past. Take time to review the contributions of historic social workers such as Jane Addams, Mary Ellen Richmond, Frances Perkins, Dorothy Height, and George Haynes. There is no substitute for reading the original words and impressions of these great authors and innovators.

Be forewarned that the following historical overview emphasizes social determinism. There is an underlying assumption about the importance of social forces (such as historical occurrences, political climate, and economic circumstances) in affecting people's desire and ability to engage in large-scale social change. Such an outlook is useful for ascertaining the various factors involved in helping to shape and better understanding the methods and forms of macro social work practice over the past century.

### The Progressive Era: Mary Richmond

**Mary Richmond (1861–1928)** is often described as one of the eminent founders of social work. In *Social Diagnosis* (1917), Richmond describes social work as consisting of a common body of knowledge based on collecting and understanding information, especially social evidence. Richmond was one of the first social workers to advocate for a more comprehensive method of inquiry and intervention, including a "wider view of self" (p. 368). Such an approach embraced an analysis of various forms of human relations, consideration of the social situation and surroundings, inquiries concerning social agencies, and an appreciation of economic conditions and neighborhood improvement (pp. 369–370).

While acknowledging that a majority of social workers at the turn of the 20th century engaged in casework, aimed at "the betterment of individuals and families," Richmond clearly recognized the need for "betterment of the mass" (p. 25). But what is meant by *betterment?* The term implies strengthening, improving—making "better off." At a very early stage in the development of our profession, Richmond acknowledges, "Mass betterment and individual betterment are interdependent," with the need for "social reform and social case work of necessity progressing together" (p. 25).

For Richmond, the movement from a focus on the individual to an emphasis on social concerns was directly attributable to the influence of the charity organizations. New methods emphasizing "social" diagnosis or the problems and issues associated with life conditions and living circumstances were born from campaigns by a number of social activists working to improve housing, promote child labor reform, and prevent the spread of diseases like tuberculosis. Richmond notes that in charity organizations, "some of [the] earliest leaders had grasped the idea of the sympathetic study of the individual in his [or her] social environment" (p. 32). Undoubtedly, as social activists worked to strengthen opportunities and economic means for their consumers of services, casework "had at its command more varied resources, adaptable to individual situations." As a consequence, "the diagnosis of those situations assumed [a] fresh [and broader] importance" (p. 32).

Library of Congress Prints and Photographs Division Washington, D.C. 20540 USA http://hdl.loc.gov/loc.pnp/pp.print

**PHOTO 1.2** Recognition is given to Mary Richmond for her contribution to the social work profession.

Mary Richmond is one of the best-known leaders of the **Charity Organization Society (COS)** movement, which was grounded in convictions derived from England. Leaders of the COS often "believed that many poor people were unworthy, so that applicants for aid should be carefully investigated. Records were to be kept about each case, and a central registry was developed to ensure that no person received aid from more than one source" (Suppes & Wells, 2003, p. 87). These written records eventually became important sources of documentation for use in advocating for social change and reform. Many would argue that these early efforts to advocate for reform on the basis of documented human need constituted the beginning of community welfare planning in the United States and eventually gave rise to what we now know as the community-based United Way system.

The relationship between human need, casework, and social reform is an interesting and profound theme when we consider the emergence of macro social work practice. Richmond was astute in advancing the argument that necessity, as evidenced by human struggle, was a driving force for social reform and ultimately responsible for reshaping casework into "social" casework. If Richmond's perceptions are correct, then the movement of social work practice toward a more structural, macro orientation is directly related to consumer plight and not merely a philosophical position fashioned by progressive professionals.

Characterized by intense industrialization and massive immigration, the era from 1900 to 1920 was a decisive period for rethinking and reconstituting social services in the United States. As Mary Richmond was redefining casework, Jane Addams's Hull House became a model for the settlement movement in large urban areas across the nation. In addition to providing a wide array of goods and services in the poorest neighborhoods, settlement houses and the settlement movement "concentrated on the totality of problems in a single geographical area . . . the central focus was on the experiences, thinking, and actions of local populations that could affect broad social and economic reform" (Haynes & Holmes, 1994, p. 65).

**Settlement houses** were neighborhood houses or community centers. In addition to addressing the everyday needs of local residents, they often provided recreational, instructional, and community programs (Federico, 1973, p. 170).

From a macro perspective, settlement houses established a place for people to meet, express ideas, share concerns, and pool their strengths. From this new, informal setting emerged leadership in identifying, specifying, and organizing to meet the issues of the day.

Indeed, the very origins of group work are often traced to the settlement movement. Today, many people simply see group work as synonymous with group therapy. For settlement workers, however, group meetings were not merely a medium to educate and treat people but also a forum for exploring community-based needs. In other social work classes, you will learn more about the multiple functions and purposes of group work. Here, it is important to make a mental note that group work is a valuable method for promoting larger scale change and an important means of promoting collective action.

It is noteworthy that although charity workers and volunteers had been hearing the struggles and misfortunes of individuals for some time, the formation of settlement houses was instrumental in identifying and advancing a united voice from consumers. At settlement houses, social workers could listen and learn directly from the mouths of people living in turmoil. This resulted in new, often group-determined ways of identifying opportunities and contemplating social change.

Given this context, it is not surprising that charity workers began to think of help as something more than face-to-face assistance to the poor for the purpose of addressing basic, everyday needs. What emerged was a penchant to seek ways to improve the neighborhood for the common good of its inhabitants. "This meant, in other words, both strengthening the community's capabilities and improving social conditions, policies, and services" (Perlman & Gurin, 1972, p. 36).

At the settlement house, people—individuals, families, volunteers, workers, community leaders, philanthropists—had a place to congregate, interact, and converse. What developed was a newfound community association—a "coming together." This constituted the birth of community organizing, a term that is used in social work to describe efforts to strengthen community participation and integration. Recognition of community organizing as an area of practice reflects an important conceptual shift in thinking about the delivery of social services. For social work practice, additional credence was given to structural change and to widening the scope of practice beyond treatment of the individual person and family.

## Time to Think 1.2

A university student center can be conceptualized as a dedicated place for students to "come together" to examine and discuss student needs in a university community. Does your university student center serve as a location for students, staff, and faculty members to congregate, interact, meet, and enter dialogue, both formally and informally, about students and university needs? If not, why not?

In summary, within the first 30 years of the 20th century, the origins of social casework, group work, community organizing, and planning were established in the United States. Many social workers continue to perceive themselves as caseworkers, group workers, or community organizers. Caseworkers adhere to a more individual, case-by-case focus, whereas group workers and community organizers are more closely aligned with themes of social reform.

## The Expansion of Social Work in the 1920s to 1940s

The social and environmental conditions of consumers have historically helped to shape social work practice. Indeed, the stock market crash of 1929 and the subsequent Great Depression constituted significant social events that altered how most Americans, including social workers, viewed human need. As Garvin and Tropman (1992) suggest, "The Great Depression was a cataclysmic event in U.S. society and ushered in the era of public development" (p. 21). For those still harboring negativism toward the underprivileged and doubts about public responsibility for social conditions, the Great Depression represented a time for reconceptualization. Economic crisis and massive unemployment signaled the start of a new era for social work. Suddenly, without much warning, most citizens of the United States realized that the very fabric of our society required strengthening and enrichment to preserve both individual and common good.

Simply stated, work was not available during the Depression, regardless of an individual's motivation or will. Banks had failed; finding one's next meal was a challenge—and not just for the "other Americans." In cities, the homeless built small settlements of cardboard and tar paper shacks. In rural areas, farmers, many of whom had gone into debt to purchase land and machinery, could not make a living selling their crops. The United States was in trouble, and widespread unemployment necessitated immediate and decisive societal action.

Eventually, a federal response to this economic catastrophe came in the form of President Franklin Delano Roosevelt's New Deal. A myriad of public works and relief programs, the New Deal had as its backbone the passage of the Social Security Act of 1935. Social workers such as Harry L. Hopkins, who became a top adviser and New Deal administrator for Roosevelt, played an active role in the creation and implementation of New Deal legislation, policies, and social programming. To this day, the Social Security Act continues to fund many of the public assistance and entitlement programs that exist to help children and families.

The 1930s and 1940s were characterized by an ideological shift. Stimulated by the conditions of the Depression, "The [lingering] emphasis of the twenties upon the individual's responsibility for his or her own destiny could not hold up under the circumstances of the thirties" (Garvin & Cox, 1995, p. 86). People in the United States, now more than ever, came to realize the value of government intervention in strengthening the country's faltering socioeconomic system. Extensive and readily observable deprivation prompted citizens to view poverty as a **public issue** rather than a **private trouble** and resulted in the establishment of forms of social insurance, public assistance, and a variety of health and welfare services. This was a crucial period in the history of the United States, as intensive social planning and programming signified society as a legitimate unit of analysis for change.

The advent of World War II and deployment of troops to two battlefronts instilled solidarity in the minds of the American people and promoted a strong federal government and national leadership. First and foremost, national threat demanded a societal response. Individuals were called upon to sacrifice for the common good in many ways—via military service, work in factories, and public service, as well as through the rationing of goods. Patriotism evoked an "all for one and one for all" mentality that accentuated the goal of winning a world war and served to downplay societal divisions.

Once again, the concept of social welfare and the perception of control over human need (public vs. private) were being shaped by social events and occurrences as depression and war provided the broader societal context. The New Deal and World War II years opened the gates for a flood of social legislation and federal initiatives.

It is important to note that societal need and crisis often give rise to creativity and ingenuity among people. Human strengths flourish, individually and collectively, when necessary for the greater good. Times of distress can bring out the best in people. Need is often the precursor to invention, with people finding new and ingenious ways to rally when called upon. "A severely adverse event can serve as a 'wake-up call' . . . signaling that it is time to make significant changes" (McMillen, 1999, p. 459). People often benefit from adversity because they are forced to reevaluate their beliefs about the world and human potential.

During the 1930s and 1940s, social work became a national enterprise. As a result of the proliferation of domestic programs, social workers became heavily engaged in what would now be called social planning and social research. Social workers, like other Americans, had acquired a newfound appreciation for strengthening a high-order social system—our society. Although *macro practice* was not yet a term in social work vocabulary, the idea of macro social work practice was certainly taking shape and being formed.

## The 1950s and Early 1960s

Some social historians point to the 1950s as the dormancy stage of social activism in the United States. Preceding decades had seen the federal government as an active participant in social-economic intervention. Now, with the war over, a "back-to-work" mentality held sway. It was once again seen as the responsibility of individuals and families to provide for the necessities of life.

Women played a major role in winning World War II. They were introduced to the labor force in great numbers during the 1930s and 1940s for employment in the military-industrial complex and as replacements for men serving in the military. It was during this period that many women demonstrated a newfound versatility and resourcefulness in balancing the demands of employment outside of the home with those of child rearing. But in the 1950s, with the war still a recent memory, it was time for families to reunite and redefine the nature of family—particularly in relationship to work.

From a macro perspective, "the period between the Great Depression and the 1950's was not a good one for the women's movement. The conservative swing after the war discouraged militancy among women. Even the League of Women Voters, hardly a radical organization, showed a decline in membership during this time" (Garvin & Cox, 1995, p. 88). Men had returned from overseas and reasserted their social and occupational dominance in a postwar economic system.

Meanwhile, on the political front, fueled by Senator Eugene McCarthy's attack on those he deemed to be communists or "soft on communism," the virtues of social programs were coming under heavy scrutiny. Consequently, "the 1950s saw an increasingly virulent series of attacks on public welfare and health insurance, both viewed as overtures to an un-American welfare state" (Axinn & Levin, 1975, p. 235). Despite lingering unemployment, public sentiment grew in the 1950s for curtailment and reduction of the welfare rolls.

Although few would depict the 1950s as a progressive era with respect to large-scale social change, one of the most powerful court rulings in the history of the United States occurred in 1954 in the form of *Brown v. Board of Education of Topeka.* Amid a postwar sense of overall self-satisfaction, economic laissez-faire, and political conservatism emerged a decisive civil rights action from the U.S. Supreme Court. In a unanimous decision, the Court ruled that segregation of children in public schools on the basis of race, even when physical facilities and other "tangible factors" were equal, deprives the children of the minority group of equal educational opportunities (Rothenberg, 1998, p. 430). Hence, segregation in schools was struck down as a deprivation of equal protection under the Constitution as provided in the Fourteenth Amendment.

Although the 1950s and early 1960s hardly represented a radical age in American development, there was an emerging recognition of the need to create employment opportunities for the poor and upgrade the employment skills of the impoverished. At first, poverty was seen as "spotty" and regional in nature. In response, the Regional Redevelopment Act of 1961 targeted the development of new industry in areas suffering from a depletion of natural resources or a decline in the demand for traditional products (Axinn & Levin, 1975, p. 238). By the mid-1960s, however, research was demonstrating that poverty was not limited to any one geographic locale but could be readily linked to economic and racial discrimination. "**The Civil Rights Act of 1964** included a section prohibiting racial, sexual, or ethnic discrimination in employment and established an enforcement mechanism, the Equal Employment Opportunity Commission" (Axinn & Levin, 1975, p. 239).

Many historians consider the election in 1960 of John F. Kennedy as president of the United States over Richard Nixon particularly noteworthy. Although Kennedy served as president for only 3 years, his election signified a refocusing on the role of the national government in improving the lives of all citizens. Many of you may be familiar with the challenge President Kennedy issued in his inaugural address: "Ask not what your country can do for you; ask what you can do for your country."

The 1960s also experienced an enormous increase in the number of people receiving public assistance, largely in the form of Aid to Families with Dependent

Children (AFDC). The expansion of welfare rolls—the growing numbers of people applying for and receiving public assistance—revealed the magnitude of poverty in America and provided a gauge for measuring it. In an attempt to understand more fully the impact of social forces on joblessness, social scientists turned to the examination of racial discrimination and structural unemployment as dominant poverty-producing factors.

As the civil rights movement gained momentum and worked to strengthen the position and status of racial minorities, Michael Harrington (1962) and others educated citizens about "the other America." Harrington's portrayal of the economic misfortunes of the downtrodden helped to dispel the myth that those experiencing poverty somehow deserved their suffering.

The 1960s was a time of change in the nation. The movement for women's rights, civil rights for people of color, an increase in tolerance and understanding for differences and diversity, and technological breakthroughs were significant trends that marked the decade. Although affluence for most Americans increased, there was also a growing sense of social conscience. The outcome of this was the need for social and structural change that would address the disadvantaged groups being left behind.

## Time to Think 1.3

Congressman John Lewis, representing the Fifth District of Georgia, is a prominent civil rights leader. He was a Freedom Rider in 1960 and one of the Big Six civil rights leaders as chairman of the Student Nonviolent Coordinating Committee (SNCC) from 1963 to 1966. Read about the March 7, 1965, Bloody Sunday events to learn how Lewis made history in Selma, Alabama, along with 600 marchers. What are the overarching themes of Lewis's long-lasting activism? Consider how they related to macro skills and strategies related to macro practice.

### The Mid-1960s to Late 1970s

During the mid-1960s, the profession of social work, in a not-so-subtle way, shifted its outlook toward helping. Remember, this was a period of appreciable social change and upheaval in the United States. Citizens of all ages were questioning the role of the United States in the Vietnam War. Riots were occurring in urban ghettos, civil rights demonstrations abounded, and women were seeking liberation in new ways. Other Americans struggled with the presence of social-economic inequality, particularly amid an observable material abundance in the United States.

Indeed, the mid- to late 1960s was a time when the very ideological tenets of capitalism came under scrutiny, as many people found that simply making money for its own sake was neither sufficient for happiness nor a noble endeavor in its own right. In this climate, social welfare, too, found itself in the midst of a shift—a reconceptualization from charity to social justice (Romanyshyn, 1971). Once again, many people began to see and believe that large-scale social change was necessary to truly improve and strengthen the well-being of the underprivileged.

President Lyndon Johnson's 1964 declaration of a War on Poverty ultimately led to the creation of important societal and community efforts to bolster the nation and improve the general welfare of all its people. These initiatives included Volunteers in Service to America (VISTA), a domestic version of the Peace Corps; the Job Corps, an employment training program for school dropouts; and Head Start, a preschool educational program.

Massive expenditures on social programs inevitably prompted public and political scrutiny concerning the effectiveness of these programs and services. By the early 1970s, under President Richard M. Nixon, a more conservative, traditional approach began to reemerge, questioning community-building efforts and giving preference to a philosophy of self-help, individual responsibility, and private initiatives (Trattner, 1989, p. 305).

Although few would view the Nixon years (1968–1974) as a time of appreciable social advancement in the United States, President Nixon did in fact support—and even initiated—some interesting social policies with broad, wide-ranging implications. For example, it was during the Nixon administration that Daniel Patrick Moynihan proposed a guaranteed income for families via the Family Assistance Plan (FAP). Although never passed into law and widely criticized for the meagerness of its income allowances for the poor, the FAP represented the beginnings of a movement toward economic redistribution and a form of negative income tax. More important, the FAP signified that the role of the federal government in improving the lives of Americans had not been totally set aside, even by conservatives.

Life in the United States in the mid- to late 1970s was characterized by high inflation, rising unemployment, an aging population, and a mounting concern about overtaxation. Although many politicians (including President Jimmy Carter and Massachusetts Senator Edward Kennedy) and various labor organizations (such as the AFL-CIO) sought a workable national health care plan for Americans, little large-scale social change took place. Instead, by the late 1970s, the optimism of the mid- to late 1960s had given way to a sense of skepticism and doubt (Trattner, 1989, pp. 323–324).

## The 1980s and Reaganomics

The election of Ronald Reagan as president in 1980 can best be summarized as an attack on the welfare state in the United States. The mood of politics and public opinion had clearly moved toward a belief "that taxes and government programs are to blame for the deep-rooted problems in the economy" (Piven & Cloward, 1982, p. 13). Instead of advancing policies aimed at improving and strengthening social conditions as a way of eliminating poverty and injustice, human services and programs were now perceived simply as a "safety net." Government was seen as a costly intrusion into the lives of Americans that ideally would be minimized or eliminated. If social programs were to exist at all, they should be tailored to helping only those in the direst circumstances. Social services were a last resort. In this view, it was time for Americans to "pull themselves up by their own bootstraps" and not look to the government for assistance. Most of the spending cuts fell on public service employment, public welfare programs, low-income housing, and food stamp programs.

The crux of Reagan's argument during the 1980s hinged on a belief that tax cuts and benefits for wealthy Americans would create an upward flow of income and monies that in turn would eventually "trickle down" to all Americans via a robust, healthy economy. In other words, followers of "Reaganomics" believed that as people became richer, economic opportunities (new business) and jobs would abound, even for disenfranchised citizens.

Unfortunately, Reagan's attack on the welfare state in America was particularly harsh and punitive for women and children. Abramovitz (1989) notes, "The administration's decision to restrict AFDC eligibility, weaken work incentives, intensify work requirements, and otherwise shrink the program represented the beginning of the latest shift in the strategy for 'encouraging' AFDC mothers to work" (p. 362). Mandating that single mothers work, while ignoring the lack of affordable child day-care services and family health benefits, was both ill-conceived and often punitive to children and parents alike. The irony was that while Reagan sought ways to strengthen the economic system, poor people were asked to do more with less. The decrease in health care and sustenance made for challenging life conditions and called social work into action.

During the Reagan years, efforts involving macro social work practice turned to challenging the premises and misconceptions of conservative ideology and thinking. With special-interest groups, labor unions, various think tanks, and political action committees gaining power and exercising growing political and legislative influence in the United States, social workers acquired a new respect for the value of participation in the political sphere. As a result of Reagan's attack on public welfare, social workers became keenly aware of the importance of political activism. Legislative lobbying and support for the participation of consumers of social services in the political process became a focal point—one born largely of necessity.

Once again, social workers and social work educators were at the forefront of this movement as they initiated voter registration and political awareness campaigns with a focus on consumers of services as a source of power. There was a beginning appreciation for the idea that political action could be driven by and owned by consumers.

By the very nature of our practice, social workers often have firsthand knowledge of the stories of people in need. Disillusioned by a seemingly uncaring and underfunded system, consumers of social services often feel powerless and alienated. Consumers, questioning whether their voice or vote really counts, struggle to see the relevance of becoming politically involved. Social workers gave credence to the premise that when organized and informed, consumers can capture the attention and appreciation of politicians and policymakers.

## The 1990s

In 1994, conservative Republicans achieved a major political victory as their party gained control of the U.S. House of Representatives. Built on the ideological foundation created in the 1980s by Ronald Reagan, and expressed in the newly written conservative rhetoric of House Speaker Newt Gingrich's "Contract for America," the mood of the country had seemingly become crystallized. Dominant beliefs included a continued emphasis on fiscal responsibility through the curtailment of government spending, a punitive outlook suggesting that only the very neediest should receive public assistance, an emphasis on traditional family structure and values, a reaffirmation of the primacy of work, and a desire for local or private control over human services (Long, 2000, pp. 64–66).

Although elected on a platform emphasizing social reform, improvement of social conditions for the poor, and the need for nationalized health care insurance, President Bill Clinton went on to sign into law one of the most restrictive pieces of social legislation in U.S. history—the Personal Responsibility and Work Opportunity Reconciliation Act of 1996. Labeled as "new federalism," this piece of legislation exacerbated the plight of the poor by reducing federal spending for low-income people by a projected $55 million over 6 years and further shifting social responsibility for the needy from the federal government to state, local, and private entities.

Although the 1990s were economically prosperous for many, with an unusually low unemployment rate, prosperity fell far short of reaching all Americans. The growth in the labor market involved the proliferation of low-wage service positions characterized by limited access to medical coverage, quality child care, or other family-friendly benefits.

During the 1990s, time restrictions, such as 5-year restrictions on receiving benefits, were instituted that systematically drove consumers of public assistance from governmental rolls. Many Americans supported this move as fiscally responsible and as necessary to foster economic self-sufficiency by prying the poor away from dependency on the government. Unfortunately, the human consequences—both positive and negative—of forcing people in need off welfare remain largely unknown. How the poor fared through welfare reform, the real-life experiences and consequences of the legislation, clearly took a back seat to welfare reform's cost-saving benefits for the federal budget.

Many people would assert that social welfare programs and services are less needed during times of economic well-being. At face value, this argument would seem credible, but social workers know that certain segments of society (those who are only marginally employable, children, persons restricted by disabilities or by health conditions, and older adults) struggle to meet everyday needs even during prosperous times. Thus, although a strong economy provides employment to those capable of making the transition to work, "advocacy on behalf of those who cannot work is essential" (Cancian, 2001, p. 312). In addition, "poor access to education and training, racism and other forms of discrimination, and local job market conditions are among the factors that limit employment opportunities" (Cancian, 2001, p. 312).

## Time to Think 1.4

The **Society for Social Work Research (SSWR)** was founded in 1994 to support the research conducted by social workers, social work students, and social welfare professionals (www.sswr.org). Review SSWR's mission statement and consider at least three ways in which the association supports the research agendas of social workers.

### The 2000s

The tragedies of September 11, 2001, have most likely changed forever the American way of life and the manner in which Americans view human vulnerability and populations-at-risk. The deadly use of commercial aircraft by terrorists to destroy the World Trade Center and attack the Pentagon awakened a sleepy nation to the need for modernized security measures at airports and to the realities of 21st-century warfare. In addition, the subsequent use of anthrax as a biochemical weapon confirmed that Americans could be attacked in a variety of ways.

Out of these atrocities emerged a unique and unprecedented spirit of patriotism, unity, and rekindled spirit toward giving to others in the United States. In the first 2 months alone following the attacks on September 11, over $1 billion was donated to the American Red Cross and other associations for use in disaster relief. From catastrophe emerged an impulse toward charitable giving, born of the belief that terrorism could strike any of us at any given moment. The attacks on the United States during 2001 exposed the fragile nature of human existence in a graphic and televised manner.

In this way, at the dawn of the new millennium, the United States was abruptly drawn into the international scene. With little warning, Americans were introduced to a relatively new enemy: international terrorists. Economic resources, technological capabilities, and military might be quickly called upon to protect our homeland and preserve the American way of life. President George W. Bush acted promptly to reenergize the military-industrial complex in the United States to mount an unprecedented War on Terrorism.

On both a national and a global scale, the September 11 attacks demonstrate how, particularly in dire circumstances, Republicans and Democrats, allies and unlikely friends, even total strangers can be quickly called upon to bring their powers and capabilities to bear in combating a crisis. Unfortunately, when Americans began providing support and resources to the War on Terrorism or to aid victims of September 11, giving to other charitable efforts predictably suffered. Mobilizing and directing the assets and **strengths** of Americans, for whatever cause, serves to push other issues aside. The buildup of military forces and homeland defense diverts funding from social issues and causes. From a structural viewpoint, it is a matter of priorities and of selectively tapping into a community or society's energy and synergy.

## From 2008 Onward

Barack Hussein Obama, a Democrat, was elected the 44th president of the United States in November 2008 and was inaugurated to office January 20, 2009. As a former community organizer, Obama holds a unique position in American history as the first multiracial president born in Hawaii. In his first term of office, President Obama addressed a financial crisis by introducing a stimulus package and a partial extension of the Bush tax cuts. He also reformed health care by passing the Patient Protection and Affordable Care Act, commonly known as Obamacare. In terms of judicial appointments, President Obama named Elena Kagan and Sonia Sotomayor to the Supreme Court, the latter of whom was the first Hispanic American to serve on the nation's highest court.

When reelected in 2012, Obama was active on domestic and international issues. As a longstanding advocate for lesbian, gay, bisexual, and transgender (LGBT) people, his administration stopped defending the Defense of Marriage Act, which denied federal recognition to same-sex couples. This action helped to clear the way for the Supreme Court's decision in the 2015 *Obergefell v. Hodges* case that ruled the fundamental right to marry is guaranteed to same-sex couples. Internationally, President Obama signed the Paris Agreement, along with 55 other countries, to curb global emissions.

Much of what President Obama accomplished over his 8 years in office was upended by the November 2016 election of Donald Trump, a Republican, an American businessman, and a reality television personality. Upon taking office, President Trump worked with congressional republicans to repeal the Affordable Care Act as he withdrew from the Paris Agreement and rolled back the Cuba Thaw policy of easing restrictions with Cuba.

Infusing his campaign slogan, "Make America Great Again," throughout his administration, President Trump ushered the Tax Cuts and Job Acts. Major elements of this tax reform reduce taxes for business and individuals, introduce a personal tax simplification by increasing standard deduction and family credit, eliminate personal exemptions, and limit mortgage interest deductions. Although many average Americans experienced only a modest tax break, businesses owners were afforded substantial tax reductions.

When considering both the Obama and Trump presidencies, the influence of interest groups becomes obvious. Health-care advocacy groups and other organizations that supported extended health-care coverage advocated for reform by spending millions of dollars on advertising, conducting town hall meetings, and educating and organizing people in their communities. In opposition were pharmaceuticals, insurers, and health-care companies. Thus, the last administration and the current interest groups, in line with

Pool / Pool/ Getty Images

**PHOTO 1.3** The nation's policies influence social work practice.

political parties, established battlegrounds for political control of legislation and elected officials.

## THE UNIQUE CONTRIBUTIONS OF MACRO PRACTICE

Several interesting observations emerge when examining the past century plus in relation to large-scale social change and social welfare. Foremost, the impetus and support for macro-level social work have weathered a somewhat nonlinear, to-and-fro course in U.S. history. There have been bursts of progress, when social workers and consumers of services have successfully moved forward to advance laws, policies, and programs promoting structural change for the needy. Conversely, there have been periods of stagnation, when society and social work practice have been consumed with promoting personal responsibility and individual achievement. And, although many would point to shifts in ideological winds (conservative vs. liberal) as a primary influence on such fluctuations, in fact, the destiny of macro social work practice and social reform seems particularly sensitive to specific, less rational, social-economic conditions.

As examples, it is clear that war, catastrophe, economic crisis (depression, unemployment, stock market failure), demographic changes (population shifts, family composition, immigration), and international threat (war and terrorism) have the potential to affect public and professional sentiment concerning the importance of systemic, structural change in developing community and societal assets. If this assertion is accurate, then aspiring social workers would be wise to prepare for stormy seas. Yes, there will be times of smooth sailing for macro-level change. Conversely, social workers will have to endure steadfast waters dedicated to helping consumers cope and survive. Regardless of the social-historical era, it is important to remember that promoting consumer strengths and resolution of problems cannot be fully addressed "by small-scale solutions no matter how well intentioned our motivations ... [instead] we must abandon those assumptions that constrict our policy responses so we can think and act boldly" (Reisch & Gorin, 2001, p. 16).

As an example of the impact of technological innovation, many social workers are turning to the Internet as a mechanism for promoting social change. Communication via the Internet can be an effective means of educating others about social concerns, promoting people's strengths, and coordinating social advocacy. The Internet can be a timely source of information about various social issues and causes. It can also facilitate ongoing dialogue between colleagues and constituent groups. Information and communication are two important sources of power in relation to macro-level social change (Williams, 2016).

While social workers conscientiously strive each day to include macro activities in their practice, the profession as a whole is dedicated to finding ways to promote human dignity and improve social conditions. The **National Association of Social Workers (NASW)** and the Council on Social Work Education (CSWE) are two important professional organizations putting forward a macro view, both within the profession and in society as a whole. And, although social work has historically demonstrated a dedication to large-scale change, social-historical context often helps shape the forms this commitment takes. Hence, the doctrines, policies, and publications of the NASW and the CSWE serve as compasses in guiding us and keeping us focused on our professional identity.

One of the most profound documents for describing the mission of and rationale for social work is the NASW ***Code of Ethics*** (2017). Here, you can read the first paragraph of the preamble of the *Code of Ethics,* with key words underscored. These terms highlight the "macro" elements of practice and serve as a reminder that social work is more encompassing than our "do-good" image "of helping individuals and families to persevere."

> The primary mission of the social work profession is to enhance human well-being and help meet the basic human needs of all people, with particular attention to the needs and empowerment of people who are vulnerable, oppressed, and living in poverty. A historic and defining feature of social work is the profession's focus on individual well-being in a social context and the well-being of society. Fundamental to social work is attention to the environmental forces that create, contribute to, and address problems in living. (p. 1)



First and foremost, social workers are called upon "to enhance human well-being." This is not limited to the welfare of individuals and single families; it also involves "a social context" and "the well-being of society" in general. Social workers differ from other helping professionals in their focus on environmental forces and their ability to "address problems [and strengths] in living" overall. The "social" in "social work" connotes change for and with larger systems, including groups of people, organizations, communities, and society.

## THE SOCIAL WORK VALUES OF MACRO PRACTICE

The mission of social work is based on a foundation of **core values** (see Figure 1.1). Throughout the history of the social work profession, the following values have guided the purpose of **social work values**, including macro practice:

**Service:** Social workers are often engaged in both working with individuals, micro practice, while helping address social problems on a larger scale. This integration of micro and macro practice necessitates that social workers bring person-in-environment to all interventions with consumers.

**Social Justice:** The value of social justice embodies the notion of equality, fairness, and the distribution of power and privilege. With this in mind, social workers often focus macro practice on the conditions confronting vulnerable, underresourced, marginalized populations and their communities with a focus on redistribution.

**FIGURE 1.1**
Social Work Values and Macro Practice

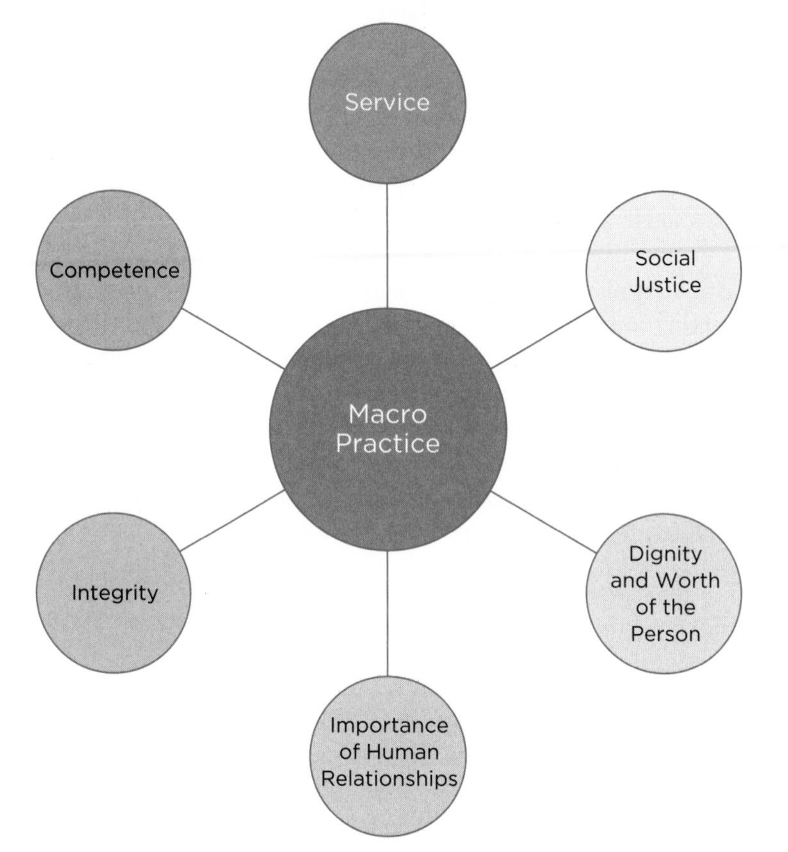


**Dignity and Worth of the Person:** Social workers recognize, respect, honor, and defend the right of people to make decisions that affect their lives. Often referred to as "self-determination," social workers are called upon to reflect on their values and beliefs to better understand conflict, the integrity of others, and freedom to choose.

**Importance of Human Relationships:** Social workers place human relationships at the core of their practice. Building on evidence-based interventions, macro practice engages in strategies across multiple consumer systems that ensure collaborations and partnerships.

**Integrity:** Reflecting the character of individual social workers and the social work profession in general, integrity embraces a constant sense of trustworthiness in all interactions. Centering on consumers and their communities, integrity highlights the reliability of social workers to view social issues in a multidivisional fashion.

**Competence:** Through critical and analytical thinking, social workers as macro practitioners contemplate and intervene based on decisions

> supported by information, data, and resources that coincide with the wants and needs of consumers in their communities. With a focus on both process and accountability, macro interventions are based on a comprehensive understanding of systems and anticipated change results.

The value base of social work emphasizes the intersectionality of social work skill competency, micro and macro practice, knowledge of self, and professional commitment to human rights and social, economic, and environmental justice. Seen in totality, macro practice challenges complex realities by working from a strong core of professional values to facilitate the decision making with consumers in their communities (Azzopardi & McNeill, 2016).

## ADVOCACY AND EMPOWERMENT

Special attention should be given to language in the NASW *Code of Ethics* (2017) pointing to "the empowerment of people." Empowerment is a key term for understanding and directing our efforts in terms of consumer-based "macro" change. In a general way, empowerment refers to the central and direct involvement of consumers in defining, determining, and advocating on behalf of their own struggles, strengths, and future to influence and effect change. Social workers facilitate the empowerment of others by finding ways in which consumers of services can design and implement advocacy activities that accentuate their own unique assets in addressing needs (Mellinger, 2017). Integral to this process is the redistribution of power from those with privilege and resources to those without.

Empowerment involves planned action and liberation. When consumers exercise the ability to plan, advocate, and create social change, they gain control over their life circumstances. Frequently, politicians and policymakers make decisions "for the sake of clients." As well intentioned as this may seem, the net effect of such a paternalistic approach runs counter to self-determination and prevents consumers from using their own capabilities to gain access to power in the social environment.

The **empowerment approach** emphasizes promoting social and economic justice. A major goal of social work practice involves helping consumers to explore and find ways to secure resources and enrich their lives. Social-economic justice also involves empowering consumers to become stakeholders in decision-making processes. Social-economic justice is an ideal condition, connoting a sense of evenhandedness or fairness in which "every person regardless of position in society has fundamental human rights such as freedom, safety, privacy, an adequate standard of living, health care, and education" (Council on Social Work Education, 2015). Practitioners know that when consumers take charge of advocacy actions and the change process, creativity and zeal for finding solutions soon follow. Over time, the entire helping relationship becomes more collaborative:

> As a strategy for social work practice, empowerment necessitates collaboration with informal groups, such as family and neighbors, and formal networks, such as agencies and organizations. The result is collective power that maximizes existing strengths and resources while tapping potential sources of renewal and change. (Cox, Tice, & Long, 2019, p. 45)

Using an empowerment approach, which is also examined in Chapter 2, consumers advocate for rights, services, and resources with assistance from social workers, rather than social workers acting on behalf of consumers. Emerging from this process is a sense of self-determination underpinned by power.

You have probably noticed a preference in this book for the term *consumer* over *client.* Although this distinction may seem minor, it embraces the spirit of empowerment and a commitment to finding and supporting advocacy strategies to advance the status of people and their communities being served. By definition, consumers are acknowledged as possessing certain rights, privileges, and power. As consumers, people expect quality service and feel free to advocate for rights. By contrast, *clients* are seen as people who are being treated by professionals and are in need of professional expertise. The term *consumer* suggests that by virtue of being users of services, people are entitled to exert influence, power, and control over their situation.

Using the term *consumer* in relation to human services has negative connotations, too. Many people, including helping professionals, associate the term *consumer* with a business orientation. In an attempt to sell goods and products, for example, marketing and advertising professionals would like us to believe that "the consumer is always right." This philosophy is put forward in order to maximize financial gain. Yet, we know that consumers are not always right. In addition, consumers often struggle to gain control over product delivery and quality. For many people, accentuating consumer rights in the business world is seen as a strategy for boosting sales, not an earnest effort toward empowerment.

Given these limitations, the term *consumer* is given preference in this book. The quest for people to take control over their own lives, individually and collectively, lies at the heart of social work practice. The term *consumer,* at least in part, captures this spirit. It is important in human services to promote and legitimize the consumer-driven nature of social work practice whenever possible. Toward this end, *consumer* seems more desirable and more positive than *client* or *patient.*

As a social worker, you will probably be surprised to learn how commonly people in power design and implement programs and policies without even the most basic sort of consultation with the consumer. It is a condescending practice—a "we know what is best for you" approach. Control is the salient factor whenever people in positions of power make decisions for others.

You will discover that social workers are particularly skillful in assessing peril for individuals, groups of people, and communities. In macro practice, there is a special sensitivity to **populations-at-risk**, groups of people who are vulnerable to (at risk of) oppression, discrimination, and/or exploitation. Traditionally, populations-at-risk have been defined in the United States in terms of gender, race, ethnicity, disability, sexual orientation, employability, and age. However, this is far from an exhaustive list. Many factors beyond the typical social-economic and demographic considerations can place people in various forms of jeopardy.

As just one example, are college students a potential "population-at-risk"? By virtue of your status as a college student, are you confronted with obstacles and unique forms of exploitation? Take a moment to see if you can identify a few of these hazards. Have you ever attempted to rent an apartment? Is being a college student a disadvantage or advantage? How? What about those irritating phone calls from credit card companies? Do you think that college students are targeted as inexperienced buyers prone to accumulating large debts at high interest rates?

Social work's commitment to enhance well-being and promote social-economic justice reaches far beyond problem-solving strategies focusing on change with individuals and families. In subsequent chapters, a heavy emphasis is placed on the ability of social workers to encourage and advance collective action with a special eye focused on strengths—the abilities of people to grow, learn, and change—and **asset building**—the enrichment of resources and capabilities in organizations, communities, and society.

---

SAGE edge™ Visit **www.edge.sagepub.com/ticemacro** to help you accomplish your coursework goals in an easy-to-use learning environment

---

## SUMMARY

In this first chapter, a host of concepts and terms (macro practice, advocacy, consumer, strengths, empowerment, and social-economic-environmental justice, among others) have been introduced for your consideration. In subsequent chapters, these notions will be further defined, elaborated upon, and applied to practice.

You have also been given a social-historical overview of macro-level change in the United States. We have made the case that opportunities for larger scale social change are often contingent on the social-economic-environmental conditions of any given time period. This is a reality that confronts all social workers in the macro aspects of their practice.

Finally, the concepts of advocacy and empowerment were briefly introduced. Subsequent chapters are dedicated to a more detailed examination of the many realities associated with implementing various orientations and perspectives (e.g., problem solving, strengths orientation, empowerment, and ecological theory) in everyday social work activities.

## TOP 10 KEY CONCEPTS

*Code of Ethics* 17
consumers 2
empowerment approach 19
macro social work practice 2
National Association of Social Workers (NASW) 16
populations-at-risk 20
social action 3
social planning 3
social work values 17
strengths 14

## DISCUSSION QUESTIONS

1. Please reread Liam's work as a community development coordinator in southern West Virginia. How would you define the macro social work practice Liam is doing? What key concepts and skills did you employ to define his macro practice with a community and population-at-risk?
2. This chapter provides you with a historical overview of macro social. What historical time is of most interest to you and why?
3. Describe an advocacy activity taking place in the United States today. Define who is engaged in the advocacy action and why. What types of actions are being taken and what do you perceive to be the goal of the advocacy?
4. Describe a time when you felt empowered at home with your family, in your employment situation, or while a college student. What feelings emerged from your sense of control in a particular situation? What did you learn from the overall experience?
5. Review the values of the social work profession. Which value is easiest for you to embrace and which one is more difficult for you to understand in the context of your life? Take time to reflect upon your responses to better understand yourself in the context of social work practice.

## EXERCISES

1. Ask a social work practitioner for a definition of *macro social work practice.* Encourage this person to give you some examples of activities they perform that involve macro practice. Finally, ask what percentage of the social worker's work week is devoted to macro practice activities. Discuss your results with classmates and contemplate how many hours per week you hope to be engaged in macro social work practice. How does macro social work practice fit into your idea of a professional social worker?
2. On your next visit to a social service agency, take special notice of the terminology surrounding the delivery of services. Are the people participating in services called consumers, clients, patients, or some other name? If the term *consumer* is not being used, consider introducing it as a part of everyday practice. What is the reaction of others? Does the notion of consumerism have any relevance at the agency? If so, how? Do staff and administrators have any sense of what consumers really want to be called?
3. Attend an agency-based group meeting and focus your attention on consumer participation. How much, if any, of the group's dialogue is directed toward efforts for larger scale (social) change in organizations, in the community, or at the societal level? Who seems to be in control of the group's agenda, and for what reasons? How could the group be more consumer driven?
4. As a student, you are also a consumer. What kinds of counseling and intervention programs are provided at your university? Investigate how many social workers are employed in these programs. What opportunities exist for student representation on boards, councils, and other governing bodies of university entities, including those at your counseling center(s)? Identify the ways in which your university encourages

a student (consumer) voice and empowers students in the life of your school.

5. Watch one of the following films with your family and friends. What is the theme of the film you selected and how does it relate to key concepts introduced in this chapter? Possible films: *Gandhi, John Q, Boys Don't Cry, Do the Right Thing, Philadelphia, Erin Brockovich,* and *Best Boy*.

6. Several recent advocacy movements have been led by students. Malala Yousafzai began a movement for the right of all children to education. Patrisse Cullors, Alicia Garza, and Opal Tometi formed the Black Lives Matter movement, which campaigns against violence and systemic racism toward black people. After the February 14, 2018, mass shooting at Marjory Stoneman Douglas High School in Parkland, Florida, students began campaigning for gun control legislation and founded the advocacy group Never Again MSD. Read additional information on these advocacy movements led by students. Then, search for other movements orchestrated by young people that resulted in societal change. Are there any common themes in these movements? How do those themes correspond to social work values and macro practice?

## ONLINE RESOURCES

- The Association for Community Organization and Social Administration (www.acosa.org): A membership organization for community organizers, activists, and nonprofit administrators; community builders; and policy practitioners.
- The Council on Social Work Education (www.cswe.org): The national accrediting body of social work programs. Includes the Education Policy and Academic Standards (EPAS) for undergraduate and graduate programs.
- *Encyclopedia of Social Work* (www.socialwork.oxfordre.com): Defines social work practice and the other key concepts described in this chapter.
- Influential Women in the History (https://www.naswfoundation.org/Our-Work/NASW-Social-Work-Pioneers/NASW-Social-Workers-Pioneers-Bio-Index): Provides a list and description of the most influential women in the history of social work.
- National Association of Social Workers (www.socialworkers.org): The professional organization of social worker in the United States. Approves the profession's *Code of Ethics.*

# 2 Contemporary Macro Practice Perspectives

## LEARNING OBJECTIVES

After reading this chapter, you should be able to

1. Identify and understand contemporary perspectives and orientations for use in macro-level practice
2. Examine how contemporary perspectives and approaches can be integrated and useful in both problem-oriented and strengths-based macro change
3. Identify and consider ethical issues and dilemmas in relationship to macro social work practice

## JUAN ADVOCATES FOR GUN CONTROL LEGISLATION

Juan is a social worker at a community behavioral intervention agency serving school-aged children. During the past year, an emotionally distraught student entered a middle school in Juan's district with an assault rifle and seriously wounded two students. Thankfully, the two students survived. However, many students, teachers, staff members, and family members have suffered emotionally as a result of the traumatic event. In Juan's therapeutic role, he is working with the survivors of this ordeal. In addition, in the wake of this and other school-based shootings, an appreciable number of students, teachers, and parents have initiated efforts to advance state and federal legislation to regulate the possession of assault rifles. Although primarily a therapist, Juan is revisioning his role and practice as a social worker at his agency. He has begun examining research about gun control, preventative best practices, and school shootings. Juan also has identified emerging strengths from his clients and various affected community members as they share their experience, thoughts, emotions, and perspectives. With his colleagues and supervisors at the behavioral intervention center, Juan is exploring and has initiated active dialogue about appropriate, professional ways to advocate with clients and community members to influence gun control policies and legislation in a meaningful manner.

## PLANNED CHANGE PROCESS AND CONTEMPORARY PERSPECTIVES AND ORIENTATIONS

In present-day language, the planned changed process provides social workers with a framework (e.g., engagement, assessment, planning, implementation, and evaluation) to assist consumers of services to address needs (Cox, Tice, & Long, 2019). Such frameworks and processes are predicated on client self-determination and provide steps and an outline to guide social work relationships and practice with consumers of services. Although planned change frameworks can vary in the number and amount of detail included in steps, they are typically suited for use with client systems of all sizes (e.g., individuals, families, groups, organizations, and communities). These frameworks are also amenable for applying various theories, approaches, and orientations in practice for prompting critical thought and providing insight.

In the course of using frameworks in planned change, social workers may struggle with conflicting perspectives, theoretical approaches, paradigms, and models. For example, the strengths perspective recognizes that people do better when someone helps them identify, recognize, and use their unique characteristics, capabilities, and strengths to create solutions to life conditions even when none seem possible (Saleebey, 1992, 1996; Weick, Sullivan, & Kisthardt, 1989). In contrast with the strengths perspective is the history of social work problem solving that is rooted in understanding the complexities and problems associated with the bio-psycho-social environment (Cowger, 1994; Franklin & Jordan, 1992; Graybeal, 2001; Gutheil, 1992; Rodwell, 1987). Another well-established perspective in social work is the advocacy orientation, which is especially suited for macro practice. An advocacy approach promotes change benefiting specific consumers of services as well as efforts to eradicate the root causes of oppressive and unjust issues. Each such perspective or approach can create tension for the social worker, especially when they elicit competing or conflicting thoughts and ideas about decisions and action in the planned change process.

Following the examination of advocacy and macro practice in Chapter 1, this is a good place to consider a variety of relevant and important theories, perspectives, and orientations when entertaining large-scale change in social work practice. Before launching into this topic, it is important to consider the influence of a longstanding problem orientation on the social work profession. For many social workers, multisystem-level (e.g., individual, family, group, organization, community, and society) problem-centered intervention is the cornerstone of macro practice. The **problem-centered focus** involves thinking and activities intended to address an entanglement of social problems or conditions. More specifically, this orientation focuses on the problem or what underpins the problem, examining the cause of the problem by collecting evidence, assessing the data, reformulating the problem (e.g., via a specific problem definition, label, or diagnosis), setting goals, developing an intervention that addresses the problem(s), and evaluating outcomes.

©iStockphoto.com/Maica

**PHOTO 2.1**
Social work builds on the strengths of people and their communities.

This chapter examines the problem-centered approach, the strengths perspective, an advocacy model, ecological theory, empowerment, the person-in-environment orientation, the person-in-environment approach, and interprofessional practice for use in macro social work practice. Shifting from a problem-centered approach toward other orientations provides the social worker with a multitude of lenses for viewing larger scale change. An **eclectic approach** allows social workers to draw upon various applicable outlooks and perspectives when assessing and promoting social change.

## THE PROBLEM-CENTERED APPROACH

Macro practice is often developed in response to social rather than personal problems. For example, a community recognizes a growing problem with truancy in its middle and high schools. A school social worker facilitates a collaborative partnership between concerned parents, students having been truant, concerned classmates, elected officials, area clergy members, and teachers. The result is a multidimensional response. The group's collaboration results in extending morning free play in the gymnasium, providing program alternatives (e.g., work experiences, after-school offerings, and community service), developing an antibullying initiative, and offering peer advising.

Unfortunately, the relationship between social problems and macro practice interventions is often complex, and not all social problems generate macro practice interventions. Sometimes social workers label a condition or situation as insurmountable or a phenomenon to be dealt with later in the context of future problems. A social problem, in this sense, is a condition that affects the quality of life for large groups of people and/or is of concern to economically or socially powerful people but can't be readily addressed or resolved.

### Time to Think 2.1

Unfortunately, large-scale change (e.g., through policy and legislative initiatives) often occurs in the wake of tragedy and loss. The voice of victims and survivors can be very powerful in planned change efforts involving macro-level change. Gun control is a very controversial issue in the United States, as illustrated in the opening case. As a social worker, could you support consumers to advocate for gun control legislation if you personally opposed such laws?

It is important to keep in mind that problem definition is often shaped by a set of societal and personal values that reflect the preference of those in power and holding a decision-making capacity. Thus, a condition is labeled as a problem partially on the basis of analysis and often times based on the beliefs and values of people in powerful positions. For example, the high cost of prescribed drugs may be a significant problem for people with chronic health conditions and limited access to health insurance. Conversely, high drug costs may be of little concern to drug companies and officials, as these industries and their executives stand to profit from the overpriced drugs.

To further illustrate the problem-centered approach, read the following situation, noting the information that appears most important or significant. Even though you may desire additional information, think of what immediately comes to mind in terms of how you might start working on this situation.

> A board member from a rural AIDS task force expresses her anxiety about writing a grant for a community education program. Although the agency's board of directors has approved the grant submission, she fears that the rural community, with its geographic isolation, high poverty rates, conservative political officials, and fundamentalist religious views, is not prepared for AIDS education in the local high school. Nevertheless, the board member also knows that the number of people affected by HIV/AIDS is increasing dramatically in the tri-county region.

The information in this situation is very limited, but often it takes only a few data points to stimulate thinking about what is wrong, what are the community issues, and what may be the area's failings. A list of problems or deficits and beginning assumptions soon emerges. For the most part, the picture is one of problems and program barriers. Problems are emphasized as being most relevant and significant, rather than the positive attributes and areas of strength of the rural community. Indeed, in many ways, social workers are often prompted to document or translate the story told to us by consumers of services and community members into professional language, jargon largely consisting of problems and deficits to which some form of intervention can be applied (Blundo, 2001).

The preoccupation with problems and human deficits, for example, what is broken or has failed in organizations and communities, has traditionally dominated the attention of social work assessment and practice. For micro and macro change, the problem-centered orientation is often associated with a medical/pathology/scientific paradigm that underlies the traditional social work theories, practice models, and educational materials found in many social work curricula. In practice, many factors need to be considered in the social worker's problem assessment. Although the format changes from one agency or work setting to another, the problem assessment process follows a similar procedure across a variety of settings. Problem-based planned change typically involves an analytical framework with some version of the following steps:

1. **Identification and Statement of the Problem.** The majority of social problems can be constructed as the interlocking relationship between three parts: (1) existence of a social condition or situation, (2) people's evaluation of the situation or condition as problematic, and (3) the reasons advanced to support the evaluation (Pincus & Minahon, 1973, pp. 103–104).

Consider a young, single mother who has three children under 8 years of age and a high absentee rate at the chemical factory where she works. The factory manager is concerned with the pattern of missed work. The mother needs reliable child care, especially when school is closed or dismissed early. The children long to be with their mother and enjoy playing with one another. A social worker, employed in the Employee Assistance Program at the factory, is contacted regarding the mother's work absences. The social worker at the elementary school notices that the children are often tardy in arriving at school. The challenge is to examine the three components of the problem and identify the *presenting problem*—the reason that brings the consumer to the social worker (Pincus & Minahon, 1973, p. 106).

The presenting problem should be considered from a dual perspective: as a private situation and as a public issue. A *private problem* is one that has a direct impact on an individual's quality of life or life opportunities— for example, failing health or limited work skills. The social worker must be aware that private situations are often created or exacerbated by a *public problem* or issue. For example, a person's failing health (a private situation) may be directly related to limited access to health care (a public problem). Thus, problem definition often links micro social work practice with the need for macro interventions. Austin, Anthony, Knee, and Mathias (2016) suggest that practitioners experience micro-informed macro practice as well as macro-informed micro practice and develop crossover skills involving communication, relationship building, advocacy, and leadership.

2. **Analysis of the Dynamics of the Social Situation.** At this stage, the social worker expands the problem statement to include the relevant social systems that define the situation. For example, in the presenting problem involving a female single parent, which systems are relevant to the problem? Considerations might include the absence of social support—the father, family members, the school, community resources for daycare, and a lack of state and federal support for daycare.

This broad picture attempts to capture all of the individuals and systems affected by the defined presenting problem. Analyzing or mapping the problem in this way assesses the dynamics of a problematic social situation. To accomplish this, the social worker applies current theories, perspectives, and social work concepts to explain and explore individual behavior, system responses, and societal responsibility. The problem assessment and analysis phase provides the foundation and direction for the remainder of the planned change, sometimes referred to as the problem-solving process.

3. **Establishing Goals and Targets.** The social worker continues to build a relationship and work with the consumer(s) of services to establish goals for the defined problem situation. The goals, short term and long term, must be relevant to the consumer and centered on values, choice, and the self-determination of the consumer as well as feasibility given the available resources and the systems involved.
4. **Determining Tasks and Strategies.** The reason for the problem assessment is to design strategies that affect a course of action toward change. The costs and benefits of various strategies and the anticipated outcomes are weighed in order for the social worker and the consumer to determine action steps, ascertain the sequence for such actions, and establish reasonable goals for desired change. The social worker provides relevant information and perspectives allowing the consumer of services

to exercise informed judgment in making decisions. The social worker and client work collaboratively to address and achieve desired goals.

5. **Stabilizing the Change Effort.** Systems theory suggests that changing one aspect of a person's life or situation will have both anticipated and unanticipated consequences for other elements of the situation. Evaluation of the impact of change strategies is essential and directs the next steps in the problem-solving process as well as when intervention strategies need to be modified, can be ended, or require follow-up.

Problem assessment serves as the traditional blueprint for planned change with consumer systems of all sizes. In the problem assessment process, the social worker is frequently reassessing the nature of the problem to ensure the appropriateness of interventions. Thus, it becomes the problem(s) driving the majority of social work interventions across various consumer systems.

The premise of this problem-centered practice is derived from a medical/pathology framework. It is the incapacity of the consumer(s) that is being addressed, not only in terms of the underlying cause of the problem but also in the ability of people to create change. As described in Chapter 1, organizations such as the Charity Organization Society (COS) and workers like Mary Richmond directed friendly visitors away from seeing poverty and human difficulties as mere moral failings in need of principled uplift. Instead, Richmond advanced the view of human suffering as a phenomenon for rational understanding. Richmond, who was greatly influenced by the community medical practice efforts at Johns Hopkins University Hospital in Baltimore, Maryland, specifically formulated the start of much of our present-day social work language and thinking. The "study, diagnosis, and treatment" model used in the emerging science of medicine was adapted to the practice of social work and included efforts to document and describe need to promote large-scale change.

Over the next decades, these concepts became the basis of practice and the benchmark of good practice within the developing schools of social work. Thus began the diligent practice of lengthy process recordings and intake summaries focused on obtaining a broad spectrum of information, believed to be necessary in constructing a diagnosis of social problems similar to that of an underlying medical condition.

These developments established a course for the social work profession. Specifically, social work embraced the medical/scientific method of data collection, analysis, and diagnosis. This prescribed a focus on the problem or underlying causes to be discovered by means of "objective" observation and inquiry. It demanded the incorporation of and reliance on theories of behavior and emotions to provide a means of understanding the consumer's problem.

As illustrated in Table 2.1, a consequence of these problem-oriented assumptions involves the enormous amount of information, particularly focused at individual and families, that social workers were encouraged to gather. Indeed, in contemporary social work education, many departments and schools of social work continue to assign practice texts and diagnostic assignments containing various assessment forms, inventories, and grids. These analytical tools, often referred to as bio-psycho-social assessments, are created to assist social workers in gathering an appreciable amount of relevant information concerning presenting problems and conditions. Arguably, the remnants of Mary Richmond's translation of the medical pathology model into a form of social diagnosis remain a fundamental underpinning in contemporary social work education and practice.

It is important to note that during social work's early developmental period, social work practitioners and scholars began to embrace psychiatry and the

**TABLE 2.1**
Traditional Assessment Format

| Typical Content Areas | Traditional Information |
|---|---|
| Presenting problem | Detailed description of problem(s)<br>List of symptoms<br>Mental status<br>Coping strategies |
| Problem history | Onset of duration<br>Course of development<br>Interactional sequences<br>Previous treatment history |
| Personal history | Developmental milestones<br>Medical history<br>Physical, emotional, sexual abuse<br>Diet, exercise |
| Substance abuse history | Patterns of use: onset, frequency, quantity<br>Drugs/habits of choice: alcohol, drugs, caffeine, nicotine, gambling<br>Consequences: physical, social, psychological |
| Family history | Age and health of parents, siblings<br>Description of relationships<br>Cultural and ethnic influences<br>History of illness, mental illness |
| Employment and education | Educational history<br>Employment history<br>Achievements, patterns, and problems |
| Summary and treatment recommendations | Summary and prioritization of concerns<br>Diagnosis: DSM-IV, PIE<br>Recommended treatment strategies |

*Source:* "Strengths-Based Social Work Assessment: Transforming the Dominant Paradigm," by C. Graybeal, *Families in Society: The Journal of Contemporary Human Services, 82*(2001), 235. Reprinted with permission from Families in Society (www.familiesinsociety.org), published by the Alliance for Children and Families.

emerging scientific inquiry into personality development, particularly psychoanalytic thinking and practices, along with the methods and practice procedures of medicine. The emerging knowledge base for future generations of social workers would be focused on the internal mental constructs of their clients. The internal, mental status of consumers of social work service and a therapeutic approach was at the heart of social casework. Social work was developing as a profession with a specific common mode or practice, named *social casework,* and a corresponding body of knowledge and practice principles to support that work. To date, some states continue to reserve terms such as *social psychotherapy* in scope of practice sections of licensure laws regulating social work practice.

Interestingly, although research is limited, some social workers argue that given the clinical, therapeutic, and micro practice orientation of state licensure laws, a macro emphasis in social work practice could be a disadvantage for employment (e.g., Rothman, 2012). Other social workers (e.g., Ezell, Chernesky, & Healy, 2004) suggest that macro-level social workers compete for employment with graduate-level prepared professionals from other fields of study (e.g., public policy, management, nonprofit administration, public health). Donaldson, Hill, Ferguson, Fogel, and Erickson (2014) provide a comprehensive examination of the implications of social work licensure for contemporary macro practice and education, indicating that only a few state licensure laws acknowledge advanced macro requirements for licensure.

As noted earlier, this model prescribed a focus on discovering the underlying causes of the problem by means of "objective" observation and inquiry—using theories of behavior and emotions to understand the client's problem. In addition, emphasis was placed on biological, psychological, and social factors contributing to problems, often actualized through bio-psycho-social assessments. It was the scientific knowledge possessed by the social work expert that was seen as necessary to decipher what had gone wrong or had failed, especially the social aspects (e.g., significant others, family, groups impact, and important organizational influences), in order to address problems.

## Time to Think 2.2

Take a moment to consider a condition that has a negative impact on a group of people. Perhaps it is the situation faced by older people who do not yet qualify for Medicare but can't afford conventional health-care insurance. Or, you know Deferred Action for Childhood Arrival (DACA) individuals, having been brought from another country to the United States by their parents, who faced deportation or restrictions concerning educational, recreational, and employment opportunities. Consider what needs to happen in these situations to gain the attention of law and decision makers. What could be some possible macro interventions to address these situations? Why would such situations be ignored by the people in power, especially elected officials?

## THE STRENGTHS PERSPECTIVE

Traditionally, social work practice has focused on the identification definition of a problem(s) as a precursor for assessing the appropriateness of social work interventions. And, although social work has possessed a bias toward approaches and orientations that define and label problems, the profession has not ignored the importance of individual and environmental strengths. Bertha Reynolds (1951) suggested that even before asking a client, "What problem brings you here today?" the social worker should first ask, "You have lived thus far, how have you done it?" (p. 125).

What are *strengths?* To begin this discussion, let's do an exercise to see how it feels to be described by your deficits and your strengths. This exercise can be done with a friend or alone.

> First, using pathology or problem-based descriptive terms or words, describe yourself in 75 words or less—for example: *I suffer from long periods of feeling blue or down. Some call me depressed, When I am down, I don't clean up the house and I don't take good care of my hair or clothing. I often miss appointments on purpose and make up excuses. My eating habits become extreme. I either binge or go for long periods of time without food. Sometimes I drink an excessive amount of beer.*
>
> Now, using strengths-based descriptive terms or words, describe yourself in 75 words or less—for example: *I am a loyal friend who is kind and thoughtful. I really take good care of my family, especially my mother, who lives alone. I am independent, logical, and even enjoy a wonderful career. Even when busy with work, I manage to go to the gym three or four times a week. I am active in a neighborhood association and several social service organizations. My two Scotties give me much joy.* (Adapted from Van Berg & Grealish, 1997)

How did each style of introduction feel to you? If you were a consumer of services, which would you prefer as a starting point in a relationship designed to make major changes in your life? The exercise helps us to consider what it feels like to be defined by our deficits, and it also sheds light on some common aspects of strengths.

As one of the originators of the strengths perspective in social work, Saleebey (1997, pp. 51– 52) indicates strengths can take various forms:

- People learn about their strengths in their world as they cope with the chaos and challenges of daily living.
- Strengths are the unique characteristics, traits, and virtues of people and communities. These attributes can become resources and a source of motivation.
- People's talents—for example, playing an instrument, writing, or home repair—can be tools to assist individuals and groups in attaining their goals.
- Cultural traditions and personal stories can provide inspiration, pride, and motivation to individuals in their communities.

The language of strengths gives us a vocabulary of hope and appreciation concerning common human needs rather than one of disdain for the people with whom we work. Towle's (1965) *Common Human Needs* is a logical companion piece to the strengths perspective because it, too, recasts problems into a positive framework of common human needs. According to Towle,

> We fail to comprehend the interrelatedness of man's [human] needs and the fact that frequently basic dependency needs must be met first in order that he may utilize opportunities for independence. Accordingly, funds are appropriated for school lunches and school clinics less willingly than for schoolbooks. (p. 5)

In the tradition of Towle, social work intervention is a tool for helping people meet their basic needs, including food, shelter, clothing, education, and community participation (Tice & Perkins, 2002). Given this point, "people with similar needs differ widely in the barriers they face in getting their needs met" (Chapin, 1995, p. 509). Placing the emphasis on human needs presents social workers with practice considerations:

- When common needs are highlighted as the basic criteria, people do not have to be described as deficient to justify receiving benefits and having their needs met.
- The social work values of self-determination and respect for worth and dignity are operationalized by focusing on human needs.
- Recognizing common human needs supports the conceptual core of the strengths perspective, whereby social workers collaborate with people as opposed to exerting the power of expert knowledge or of institutions.
- Human needs involve communities as a resource that offers opportunities for growth and development. (Chapin, 1995; Saleebey, 1992; Tice & Perkins, 1996, 2002; Towle, 1965)

Social work scholars, including Shulman (1979), Germain and Gitterman (1980), and Hepworth and Larsen (1990), have stressed the importance of expanding assessments to include a focus on strengths and including the consumer as an active participant in the change process. Saleebey (1992) advanced the assessment of strengths by articulating a strengths perspective for social work practice. According to Saleebey, the strengths perspective is represented by a collection of ideas and techniques rather than a theory or a paradigm. It seeks to develop abilities and capabilities in consumers and "assumes that consumers already have a number of competencies and resources that may improve their situations" (Saleebey, 1992, p. 15).

Table 2.2 defines the principles of the strengths perspective, as compared to problem solving, and provides a lens for examining social work practice. A theme emerges from the principles. Specifically, the strengths perspective demands a

**TABLE 2.2**
Principles of the Strengths Perspective Compared to Problem Solving

| Principle | Relationship to Social Work Practice | Problem-Solving Corollary |
|---|---|---|
| 1. Every individual, group, family, and community have strengths. | • Encourages respect for the stories of consumers and communities. | • The situation and the person in the environment are assessed. |
| 2. Challenges may be threatening, but they may also be sources of opportunity. | • Consumers are viewed as resilient and resourceful.<br>• Meeting life's challenges helps one discover capabilities and self-esteem. | • Problems are identified and prioritized. |
| 3. The aspirations of individuals, groups, and communities must be taken seriously. | • A diagnosis, an assessment, or a program plan does not define the parameters of possibilities for clients.<br>• Individuals and communities have the capacity for restoration. | • Realistic goals and an intervention plan are developed. |
| 4. Consumers are served best through collaboration. | • The role of "expert" or "professional" may not provide the best vantage point from which to appreciate client strengths. | • Professionals facilitate a problem-solving process. |
| 5. Every environment is full of resources. | • Communities are oases of opportunities.<br>• Informal systems of individuals, families, and groups amplify community resilience. | • Available resources are used. |

*Source:* Adapted from Saleebey, Dennis (Ed.), *Strengths perspective in social work practice*, 3/e. Published by Allyn & Bacon, Boston, MA. Copyright © 1998 by Pearson Education.

different way of seeing consumers, their environment, and their current situations. Social workers who approach consumers through a strengths perspective in practice can expect changes in the character of their work and in the nature of their relationship with consumers.

## CASE EXAMPLE: THE STRENGTHS OF CONSUMERS IN PROGRAM DEVELOPMENT

Consider a social worker in a rural social agency in the foothills of the Appalachian region. Consumers of services and other colleagues have identified a significant number of people with persistent mental health challenges. There is a consensus that people would benefit from a drop-in center that provides socialization and recreational opportunities, as well as education and support on legal issues, parenting, housing discrimination, and employment. Consumers have become excited about the prospect of such a center and have initiated a set of planning meetings.

In the past few days, several relatively influential people learned about the plan to petition for the center and responded with outrage. They claimed the center would have a negative impact on real estate prices and would drain an already limited funding stream for social services. The administration at your agency has become concerned about the consequences of the proposed center for fundraising efforts.

What does a strengths perspective offer to this type of situation? What kinds of opportunities exist for consumers, especially those who are vulnerable and disadvantaged? Regardless of what decision is made about proceeding with the center, why is it important that the strengths of consumers be considered and allowed to emerge?

### Thinking Critically About the Case Example

1. What might current research indicate concerning the effectiveness of drop-in centers in providing services and programs for people with persistent mental health challenges?

2. Many people believe that the presence of human service centers "runs down" real estate values. Is this based on information, opinion, social facts, or bias?

3. Watch for newspaper or magazine articles depicting persons with mental health challenges. Do these articles describe the strengths of consumers of services? Strive to recognize and identify any deceptive practices in the reporting of human service delivery in the mass media.

## ECOLOGICAL THEORY

Tice and Perkins (1996) contributed to theoretical understanding and development by specifying the contributions and relevance of ecological theory to the strengths perspective. Carel Germain's **ecological perspective** was first introduced in 1979 and further elaborated upon (Germain, 1991) in an attempt to advance social work theory with an analogy from biological ecology. Germain drew some ideas directly from ecology—most notably the concepts of environment, adaptation, and adaptedness—and used others as suggested analogies. The concept of "environment" includes physical aspects, such as air, geography, water, plants, and material items. However, the environmental components Germain cites as central to the ecological perspective appear to come mainly from the social sciences. The twin notions of *stress* and *coping* come principally from psychology, as do the concepts of *life course, human relatedness, competence, self-direction,* and *self-esteem* (Germain, 1991).

There are several reasons for selecting the ecological theory as a cornerstone of the strengths model. As illustrated in Table 2.3, the social environment component of the ecological theory involves the conditions (social and physical) and interpersonal interactions that permit people to survive and thrive in hostile circumstances. The concept of **social environments** includes people's homes, communities, and financial resources, as well as the laws and expectations that govern social behaviors. The ecological theory encourages active participation of people in their communities that reflects the "individuality of people and presents opportunities for personnel growth, mutual support, and an array of relationships" (Tice & Perkins, 1996, p. 16). Finally, ecological theory supports the value of **transactions** between people and aspects of their physical and social environment as a forum to build on the strengths of informal and formal support systems.

Integral to ecological theory and the strengths model is a commitment to providing services in collaboration with consumers, confronting ineffective service systems, and strengthening existing social structures (e.g., organizations and communities). The notion that services and assessments are collaborative ventures supports the social work value of self-determination and nurtures the relationship between the social worker and the consumer. According to Tice and Perkins (1996), collaborative assessment occurs when (1) engagement is viewed as a distinct activity that constitutes the initial step in developing a relationship, (2) the relationship between the social worker and the consumer is recognized as essential to the helping process, (3) dialogue focuses on the consumer's accomplishments and potential, (4) consumers' directives and desires are addressed and not judged,

**TABLE 2.3**

Relating the Strengths Model to Ecological Concepts

| Term | Ecological Concept | Strengths Model |
|---|---|---|
| Social environment | Conditions, circumstances, and interactions of people | Involves the community and interpersonal relationships as resources that are supportive of growth and development |
| Person-in-environment | People's dynamic interactions with systems | Provides a sense of continuous membership and connectedness |
| Transactions | Positive and negative communications with others in their environment | Fosters dialogue and collaboration to strengthen formal and informal support systems |
| Energy | The natural power generated by interaction between people and their environments | Results in reciprocity that creates new patterns and resources |
| Interface | Specific points at which an individual interacts with the environment | Recognizes that intervention begins in individualized realities |
| Coping | Adaptation in response to a problematic situation | Highlights the innate ability of people to change and be self-motivated |
| Interdependence | Mutual reliance of people on one another and their environment | Occurs in relationships based on reciprocity, a common purpose, and recognition of the community as a resource |

*Source:* Adapted from Tice and Perkins (1996, p. 17).

and (5) mutual trust is discussed, acted upon, and felt by both the consumer and the social worker (p. 24).

Compare the problem assessment format described in Table 2.1 with the one found in Table 2.4. The additional information gathered in the latter format reflects the realization that consumers are the experts on their own lives. In essence, the social worker transforms the content of the assessment by the way it is written, through the questions asked of consumers, and by the inclusion of responses that come from a place of hope and possibility.

**TABLE 2.4**
A Strengths Assessment

| Typical Content Areas | Traditional Information | Additional Information |
|---|---|---|
| Presenting problem | Detailed description of problem(s)<br>List of symptoms<br>Mental status<br>Coping strategies | Emphasis on client's language<br>Exceptions to problem<br>Exploration of resources<br>Emphasis on client's solution<br>Miracle question |
| Problem history | Onset and duration<br>Course of development<br>Interactional sequences<br>Previous treatment history | Exceptions: When was the problem not happening or happening differently?<br>Include "future history"—vision of when problem is solved. |
| Personal history | Developmental milestones<br>Medical history<br>Physical, emotional, sexual abuse<br>Diet, exercise | Physical, psychological, social, spiritual, environmental assets<br>"How did you do that?"<br>"How have you managed to overcome your adversities?"<br>"What have you learned that you would want others to know?" |
| Substance abuse history | Patterns of use: onset, frequency, quantity<br>Drugs/habits of choice: alcohol, drugs, caffeine, nicotine, gambling<br>Consequences: physical, social, psychological | "How does using help?"<br>Periods of using less (difference)<br>Periods of abstinence (exceptions)<br>Person and family rituals: What has endured despite use/abuse? |
| Family history | Age and health of parents, siblings<br>Description of relationships<br>Cultural and ethnic influences<br>History of illness, mental illness | Family rituals (mealtimes/holidays)<br>Role models—nuclear and extended<br>Strategies for enduring<br>Important family stories |

*(Continued)*

**TABLE 2.4** (Continued)

| Typical Content Areas | Traditional Information | Additional Information |
|---|---|---|
| Employment and education | Educational history<br>Employment history<br>Achievements, patterns, and problems | List of skills and interests<br>Homemaking, parenting skills<br>Community involvement<br>Spiritual and church involvement |
| Summary and treatment recommendations | Summary and prioritization of concerns<br>Diagnosis: DSM-V, PIE<br>Recommended treatment strategies | Expanded narrative— reduce focus on diagnosis and problems<br>Summary of resources, options, possibilities, exceptions, and solutions<br>Recommendations to other professionals for how to use strengths in work with client |

*Source:* "Strengths-Based Social Work Assessment: Transforming the Dominant Paradigm," by C. Graybeal, *Families in Society: The Journal of Contemporary Human Services, 82*(2001), 238. Reprinted with permission from Families in Society (www.familiesinsociety.org), published by the Alliance for Children and Families.

## EMPOWERMENT

The liberating nature of empowerment is also related and integral to the strengths orientation and the assessment of strengths in planned change and action. Empowerment involves the process of assisting people, families, and communities to discover and expend the resources and tools within and around them. Empowerment encourages and prompts human service resources to be tailored to individuals in such a way that those receiving help have the opportunity to affect decision making and experience the personal power that leads to and affects change (Rapport, 1990). A product of the 1980s and 1990s, Solomon's (1976) *Black Empowerment: Social Work in Oppressed Communities,* a classic in the policies and practice of empowerment, concludes that the aims of empowerment are to do the following:

- Support consumers in finding solutions to their own problems.
- Recognize the knowledge and skills that social workers can offer consumers.
- Consider social workers and consumers as partners in solving problems.
- Consider the power structure as complex and open to influence. (Payne, 1997, pp. 277–278)

The basic objective of empowerment is social justice—giving people greater security as well as political and social equality—through mutual support and shared learning that moves incrementally from micro- to macro-level goals (Rees, 1991). Considering the following example:

## CASE EXAMPLE: CONSIDERATIONS FOR EMPOWERMENT IN MACRO PRACTICE

Rosa Gonzales is a social worker with the Family Services Center, a multiservice agency for families. During a session with Chung Li, an immigrant from Vietnam, Rosa learns that the Li family has been denied library membership because the family members are not citizens and cannot produce an acceptable identification card. Mrs. Li is concerned because she is working with her children on language acquisition, and the library is a major resource for books and films as well as an array of literacy programs.

After some investigation, Rosa realizes that the Li family is not the only immigrant family denied library membership. In time, Rosa and Mrs. Li organize a few families through the Family Services Center who agree to invite the county librarian to a meeting to discuss their needs. The librarian takes the concerns of the families to the library's board of directors for discussion. Eventually, the board revises the membership qualifications to include individuals and family members such as the Li family for community membership.

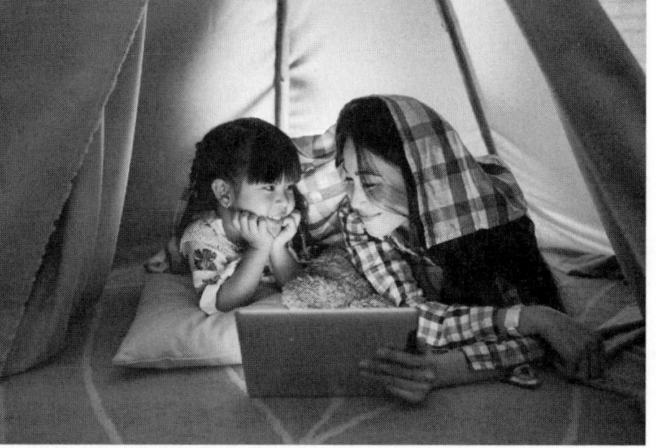

©iStockphoto.com/DragonImages

**PHOTO 2.2** Empowerment leads to problem solving.

How did the individual wants of Mrs. Li incrementally change to a macro focus of the community? What are the political and social issues embedded in the situation? Finally, what are some of the strengths Mrs. Li displayed? As illustrated by Mrs. Li, concepts of empowerment include impact and control over one's life, confidence in the ability to act on one's own behalf, and access to choices and independence from others in making life decisions (Gutierrez, 1995). The following describe other important features of empowering practice:

1. All people and their communities have skills, capabilities, and the ability to change.
2. People have the right to be heard and to control their lives in the communities where they reside.
3. The problems of people and communities always reflect some issues related to oppression and discrimination.
4. Collective action is powerful, and social work practice should build on this.
5. Social workers must facilitate challenges to oppression that lead to empowerment. (Payne, 1997, p. 281)

A strengths assessment nurtures empowerment by supporting the wants and needs of consumers with social work interventions that are designed through collaborative partnerships, based on soliciting and relying on consumer participation, and focused on understanding people within their own frame of reference. In essence, the strengths perspective, including the strengths assessment, recognizes the power of consumers, encourages consumers to use that power, and supports the collaboration of social workers with consumers to organize change across levels of practice.

Consider how the term *empowerment* reflects social values and both professional and consumer responsibility concerning issues. Take some time to write your own definition of empowerment for social work practice. Be prepared to describe how your personal definition of empowerment reflects your values and broader responsibility for social action.

## SYSTEMS THEORY

Systems theory as applied to social work emphasizes the importance of families, groups, organizations, communities, and society in assessing the consumer's social environment as well as when contemplating targets for change in planned change. **Social systems** are ever changing and in a dynamic state of change. Social systems are interrelated and interdependent with each other. As a consequence, a change in one social system can affect both planned and unanticipated changes in other social systems.

Social systems are also important aspects of communities and societies. In macro social work practice, practitioners depend on the strengths of not just individuals but importantly social systems to advance large-scale change. Most systems are defined as one of the following:

- *Formal systems:* Professional agencies, unions, community organizations, and service clubs represent formal systems. Each of these systems provides members with support based on membership criteria and obligations.
- *Informal systems:* These are systems that develop naturally in settings and communities—family members, friends, groups, and neighbors. Informal systems provide people with various types of support, including emotional, spiritual, and financial.
- *Societal systems:* These are national service agencies, hospitals, institutions, and other organizations that provide people and communities with assistance. (Pincus & Minahon, 1973)

To highlight the importance of systems in our lives, take a moment or two to complete the following exercise:

> Consider your informal system of support, and write a paragraph that captures the strength of that system. List an occasion or two when you went to your informal support system for assistance. How do the members of your informal system interact with the community where you live and are there important physical aspects of the environment to be considered?

Ecological theory suggests that we can best understand social systems by doing exactly what you just did in this short exercise on informal systems, focusing on the transactions that occur between different systems. In macro practice from a strengths perspective, social workers address the problems and strengths of interactions between social systems by (1) assessing the strengths of communities; (2) enhancing and building new connections between people, resources, systems, and communities; (3) helping people to use their capabilities and strengths to solve community-based issues; and (4) solidifying change through political tactics, policy initiatives, establishment of an agency, and evaluation of the change effort (Brueggemann, 1996).

## PERSON-IN-ENVIRONMENT

It is important for social workers to conceptualize consumers of services in a dynamic and a continual process of interacting with and adapting to their environment, sometimes intentionally and other times as a result of unanticipated needs. The **person-in-environment** highlights "how people are affected in positive and negative ways by their surroundings" (Cox et al., 2019, p. 43). Adjusting to one's physical and social environment (e.g., conditions and expectations) is an ongoing and natural process, involving both effort and abilities that often require encouragement and strengthening by social workers.

Recognition that consumers of services are confronted by and challenged to adapt to ever-changing needs and conditions is important in social work practice. Such knowledge and understanding are highly aligned with the strengths, social system, and ecological perspectives and orientations by emphasizing the relevance of each person's surrounding environment in everyday life. Consumers of services, be they individuals or groups of people, seek assistance not only because of personal problems, as implied by a problem-solving approach, but also in relationship to changes in various aspects of their social and physical environment.

## ADVOCACY MODEL

Advocacy in social work practice involves activities to "defend, represent, or otherwise advance the cause of one or more clients at the individual, group, organizational, or community level in order to promote social justice" (Hoefer, 2012, p. 3). *Case advocacy* refers to advocating for social justice with one person, family, or entity. *Cause advocacy* encompasses advocating for social justice in a larger fashion to create or develop programs, policies, laws, and practices to advance the rights and abilities of groups of people. Of course, case advocacy can spur cause advocacy as injustice experienced by a specific person, family, or group often prompts an awareness and understanding that a large segment of a population is facing a form of social and/or economic injustice. Cause advocacy is more aligned with macro social work practice, as it involves larger scale change involving larger social systems (e.g., organizations, communities, and society).

Advocating for justice is a complex process, containing a number of key elements for consideration. As can be seen in Figure 2.1, Cox et al. (2019) offer

**FIGURE 2.1**
Dynamic, Interlocking Tenets of Advocacy Practice and Policy Model

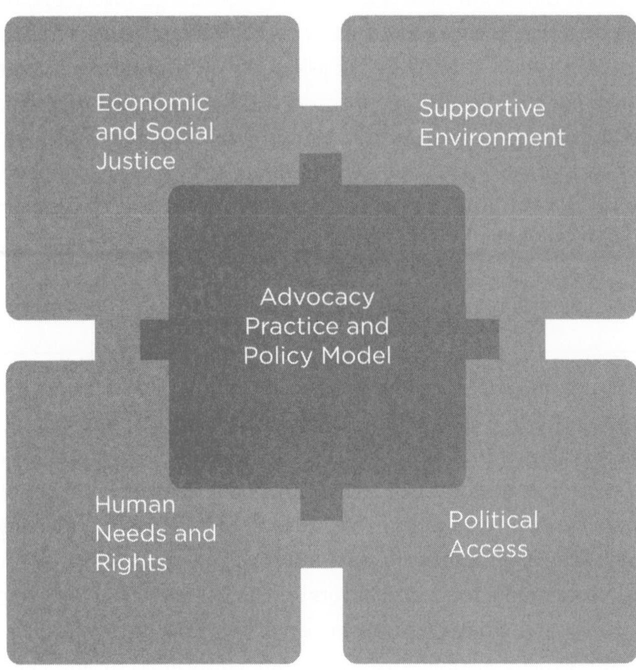


*Source:* Exhibit 4.4 from Cox, Tice, & Long, 2019, p. 70.

and describe a **dynamic advocacy model** that identifies four interlocking tenets (economic and social justice, supportive environment, human needs and rights, and political access) as factors for reflection when advocating for change. It is noted that "in social work practice with real people and situations, these tenets have considerable overlap with and influence on one another" (Cox et al., 2019, p. 69). Although not exhaustive, the advocacy model and its tenets are offered "to prompt critical and multidimensional thought and discussion about advocacy in social work practice" (Cox et al., 2019, p. 69).

A brief and succinct description of the four tenets of the dynamic advocacy model by Cox et al. (2019) is provided in Table 2.5.

## A COMMUNITY-BASED PRACTICE ORIENTATION

At one time, the majority of programs in social work education included courses in community organization, development, and practice. However, over recent years, the profession of social work has often struggled with maintaining community development and community organization as particular areas of practice, education, and inquiry in light of a demand for the employment of clinical social workers. Pritzker and Applewhite (2015) examine and describe this marketplace challenge

**TABLE 2.5**
The Four Tenets of the Dynamic Advocacy Model

| | |
|---|---|
| Economic and social justice | Emphasis is placed on advancing economic and social rights for all people. These efforts are often actualized through the development and establishment of liberties, rights, duties, access, opportunities, and the active voices of people in specific domains (e.g., education, employment, housing, religion, voting, safety, citizenship, and marriage). |
| Supportive environment | Examination of the total social, economic, and physical (natural) environment takes place and is aligned with the aforementioned systems, ecological, and person-in- environment perspectives. A supportive environment for advocacy can be derived from significant others, friends, family members, churches, companies, associations, community entities, and community and national groups and organizations. Natural and tangible aspects of the environment are also important considerations; these could include factors such as buildings, use of land, monetary support, water, food, computer access, technology, and so on. |
| Human needs and rights | Special consideration in advocacy needs to be given to who is defining human needs and why. Implicit in the definition of human needs and rights is power. How should and can consumers of services be involved in defining human needs and rights? The active participation of consumers of services in defining human needs and rights is highly aligned with the notion of empowerment and the ability of consumers to influence and affect decision-making processes. |
| Political access | Who has access to political power and why? Identifying key stakeholders and their influence over policy and legislative development is crucial. Politicians are responsible to the public and their constituency but often beholden to the people and political parties who significantly donated to the campaign fund and assisted with their election. Political access typically involves the building of relationships with politicians, elected officials, and key stakeholders. McBeath (2016, p. 9) identifies "developing external advocacy networks" (e.g., between professional, public, businesses, nonprofit, and private entities) as a top strategy for reenvisioning macro social work practice. |

and the plight of macro practitioners, recognizing that "important benefits accrue to the profession and to its vulnerable clientele when social workers hold [macro-oriented] positions with substantial community or policy influence" (p. 191).

A decision was made to write this book with an emphasis on **community-based practice**, because it is our communities that provide us with a network of care, support, membership, and celebration. The focus is primarily on traditional communities—cities, towns, and villages (Schriver, 1998). Warren (1978) concludes that traditional communities serve a number of vital functions, including socialization, mutual support, and social control, through the enforcement of community norms. Whether urban or rural, traditional communities share similar traits, such as the inclusion of residences, recreation facilities, social service agencies, and businesses. Consequently, social interactions occur through work, play, worship, and other activities.

Take a moment to think about a community with which you are familiar, perhaps the community where you were raised or the one in which your university is located. Now consider the following questions:

1. Is the community located in a rural or urban setting? Describe the buildings of your community. Do you walk, ride public transportation, or use a private car to attend school, see a movie, or visit with a friend or family member?
2. What are some of the recreational opportunities in your community? Do the activities support people across the life cycle? For example, are there activities for young children, such as T-ball or soccer teams? What about organized events or facilities for older people? Describe opportunities for intergenerational activities.
3. Describe some of the social service agencies located in the community. List the churches, synagogues, temples, meeting houses, and mosques where people from your community worship.
4. Who has power in your community? Who is responsible for enforcing the laws and regulations of the community?

The dual professional role of working *in* and *with* the community offers social workers multiple opportunities to initiate macro change (Kirst-Ashman & Hull, 2001). For some, this means working at the polls on election day or supporting a candidate who will further social work goals. Some social workers are active in politically focused organizations such as Amnesty International. Others petition for revisions in laws, policies, or procedures aimed at fundamental social change.

One of the many advantages of social work education is that it develops a knowledge and skill set for working with individuals and groups that is equally appropriate for community-based interventions. For example, communication skills can be used to listen and respond to one person or a mass gathering of people. Writing skills are necessary for preparing social histories and service documentation such as progress notes after an individual counseling session with a consumer; these skills are equally essential for harnessing the media, mounting writing campaigns, and creating educational materials. Advocacy skills, including assertiveness and negotiation, can be used to improve the quality of life for one person or an entire community.

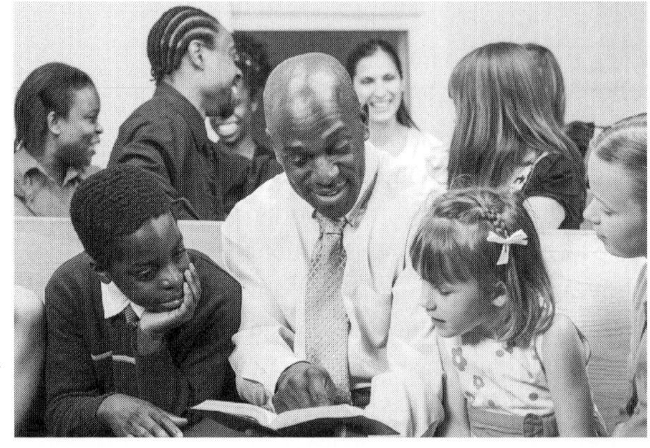



**PHOTO 2.3** Communities often provide socialization opportunities and activities for young children.

In the course of work with individuals, families, groups, and organizations, social workers encounter community problems and opportunities for change. But the idea of intervening in the community or at the societal level may seem overwhelming, especially if you need to go beyond your specific job description. Furthermore, unlike micro and mezzo social work (which involves practice with groups and organizations), macro change involves a variety of people and systems, so you will need extensive support from your colleagues, consumers, and other influential people if your intervention is to succeed. Specht and Courtney

(1994) emphasize the role of macro social work practice in the change process as follows:

> Social work's mission should be to build a meaning, a purpose, and a sense of obligation for the community. It is only by creating a community that we establish a basis for commitment, obligation, and social support. We must build communities that are excited about their child-care systems, that find it exhilarating to care for the mentally ill and the frail aged, and make demands upon people to behave, to contribute, and to care for one another. (p. 27)

## INTEGRATING PERSPECTIVES AND ORIENTATIONS WITH MACRO PRACTICE

How can the various perspectives and orientations examined in this chapter support the planned change process? To answer this question, it will be necessary to examine the foundation of knowledge and the value base of the macro practice. From the outset, you will notice the unifying effect that the strengths perspective has on micro, mezzo, and macro practice (Bronfenbrenner, 1979; Magnusson & Allen, 1983). The strengths perspective recognizes the interactions of each level of practice and the subsequent interconnection process that links strengths with a sense of empowerment (Compton & Galaway, 1994; Tice & Perkins, 1996).

According to Germain (1979), knowledge about people and their environment is a cornerstone of social work practice. Thus, with a person-in-environment focus, the strengths perspective uses ecology theory to conceptualize macro practice. As defined in Table 2.4, macro practice involves addressing environmental problems and human needs where the field of concern is the social and physical environments, including national and international political and economic structures. The power of bureaucratic organizations, their system of status definition, and their socialization of people into unhelpful attitudes can obstruct consumers' adaptation to their communities.

Like micro practice, macro practice from the strengths perspective begins with a strengths assessment. Kretzmann and McKnight (1993) suggest that communities have resources and assets that are often overlooked or underused. They conclude that communities have desperate needs and that:

> In response to this desperate situation well-intended people are seeking solutions by taking one of two divergent paths. The first, which begins by focusing on a community's needs, deficiencies and problems, is still the more traveled, and commands the vast majority of our financial and human resources. By comparison with the second path, which insists on beginning with a clear commitment to discovering a community's capacities and assets, and which is the direction [we] recommend, the first and foremost path is more like an eight-lane superhighway. (p. 1)

This is especially the case in communities in which people have learned to live under difficult situations. Community assets should be accounted for and mapped as a basis for working with and from within a community by compiling an inventory of specific resources in the community, organizing the resources according to partnerships and collaborative relationships, and targeting strong reciprocal relationships to enhance relationships that need support and attention.

Three principles define the macro practice strengths assessment (Saleebey, 1997). Using community as a unit of analysis, the assessment starts with what resources are present in the community, not what is missing. The emphasis on strengths directs attention to community assets, possibilities, and potentials. Second, engagement in the community is necessary for the social worker to conduct internally focused community development. Engagement requires a period of observation and culminates in an understanding of the history, unique experiences, and complexities of the community (Landon, 1999). During this timeframe, social workers use the principle of **professional use of self** to form relationships with others in the community (Kirst-Ashman & Hull, 1999). Finally, the entire process is driven by relationships—relationships between social workers and consumers, consumers and the various systems of support, consumers and the community, and social workers and communities.

A considerable portion of this chapter has been dedicated to an analysis of the relationship between the strengths orientation, traditional problem-solving processes, empowerment theory, and the ecological orientation. Indeed, when compared to traditional approaches, the strengths perspective offers a unique and refreshing outlook for social workers engaged in macro-level change in community-based practice.

It is also important to understand the relationship between the strengths perspective and empowerment theory. Although these orientations have similarities and tend to complement each other, they offer distinct contributions to macro social work practice.

Fundamentally, empowerment theory focuses on the liberating ability of people to gain control and power and have an impact over their lives. As suggested earlier, it involves identifying and building upon both personal and social dimensions of power so that people, organizations, and communities can acquire power in order to effect change. In such, empowerment offers both a conceptual outlook for macro practice and a process to help direct social workers in their work (Miley, O'Melia, & DuBois, 2001, p. 87). An important dimension of acquiring power involves identifying and using strengths and resources. This is true regardless of the system level—individual, family, group, organization, community, or society. Of course, utilization of resources and strengths lies at the core of the strengths orientation.

Similarly, when social workers apply a strengths perspective and move away from a preoccupation with problems, there is a greater appreciation of the resilience, resourcefulness, and strengths found in various social systems. For example, when working with communities, there is a realization that communities have "internal assets and capabilities that can be developed and used in increasing the human and social capital of the community" (Saleebey, 2006, p. 255). The net result of any such awareness involves empowerment, as people recognize their potential in effecting change and taking control over their lives.

In planned change, macro practice that embraces a strengths perspective builds a critical mass of support at the grassroots level. It embraces the environment using concepts, thinking, and principles from ecological theory, the person-in-environment perspective, empowerment, and systems theory. As one community partners with another and then another, the power structure can be challenged to support human well-being and individual and collective efficacy. Toward this end, the dynamic advocacy model by Cox et al. (2019) is provided to promote advocacy, a foundational base of social work, as a vital component in macro practice.

## The Value Base

The knowledge base of macro social work practice, from an eclectic as well as the more focused strengths-oriented perspective, is supported by values or judgments—a **value base**. Values are beliefs about what is good or desirable and what is not. Social workers employ macro interventions in organizations and communities, the environment, laws, and policies; these efforts affect what we can and should do. Table 2.6 applies the core values of social work, as defined by the National Association of Social Workers, to critical elements of macro practice.

Macro social work practice does not mean forcing people and their communities to change. Rather, self-determination, another value of social work, suggests that, when appropriate, social workers and consumers should build on the unique strengths of communities while pursuing three avenues of inquiry:

1. Consider how values may restrict progress toward the objectives desired by the community.
2. Consider possible alternatives and their consequences for achieving the objectives.
3. Consider the rights and needs of others residing in the community. (Compton & Galaway, 1994, p. 111)

Confidentiality, an integral value of social work, requires that social workers and consumers negotiate who will share what information and how the macro intervention will proceed. From a strengths-oriented perspective, confidentiality is a resource that must be offered, but it should not be used as "a justification for failure to act, a justification for shielding consumers from responsibility for their own behavior, or a justification for failure to assist consumers in building support systems and mutual support groups" (Compton & Galaway, 1994, p. 163).

Another value related to those defined in Table 2.6 is social advocacy. Case advocacy refers to activities on behalf of an individual, family, or specific entity that often address the accessibility, availability, and adequacy of services.

**TABLE 2.6**
Social Work Values and the Strengths Perspective

| Value | Relationship to the Strengths Perspective |
|---|---|
| *Service:* Providing service and resources and helping people to reach their potential | Individuals and communities have the capacity to grow and change. Help people change and control the structures affecting them. |
| *Social justice:* Commitment to a society in which all people have the same rights, opportunities, and benefits | Define and respond to human needs on society's behalf, ensuring that resources are effectively used. Socioeconomic structures cause problems. |
| *Dignity and worth of the person:* Belief that each person is to be valued and treated with dignity | Take individual, family, and community visions and hopes seriously. Enable personal change and control. |
| *Importance of human relationships:* Valuing the connection between social work and consumers as essential to creating and maintaining a helping relationship | Share knowledge with consumers, empowering them to act on their own behalf. |
| *Integrity:* Commitment to honesty and trustworthiness | Social work should create structures for client cooperation to advocate for their own needs. |
| *Competence:* Commitment to the necessary knowledge and skill to work effectively with consumers | Social work considers the consumer to be the expert. Social workers engage in lifelong learning. |

By contrast, cause advocacy, more directly related to macro practice, involves addressing issues that affect *groups of* people. In either form, advocacy involves resistance and subsequent efforts to change the status quo (Kirst-Ashman & Hull, 1999). A strengths-oriented perspective toward macro practice embraces advocacy as a method of mediating the inevitable conflict between people and using the strengths and assets of groups of people, social institutions, and community support systems to advance justice.

## Interprofessional Practice

In contemporary practice, social workers are increasingly being educated and trained to work and practice in collaborative and coordinated ways with other professionals in a variety of organizational contexts (e.g., clinics, centers, private practices, schools) with a variety of helping and health-care professionals. When **interprofessional practice** is actualized, each professional brings a unique knowledge and skill base to the practice setting to provide a comprehensive and integrative approach to address the needs and wants of consumers of service in a holistic manner. In interprofessional practice, social workers practice with counselors, psychiatric nurses, psychologists, psychiatrists, physician assistants, physicians, nurses, occupational therapists, health service administrators, and, as appropriate, a variety of specialized health-care providers.

Although social workers are recognized for their clinical and micro-oriented abilities when working with individuals and families, it is the macro practice element that differentiates social work from other professions. Social workers, regardless of their specialization, are committed to larger scale change, promoting social and economic justice, as well as the view that groups, organizations, communities, and societies are important as client systems, areas for assessment, and targets of change in planned change processes. Social workers are known as effective advocates, champions for diversity and inclusion, administrators, and leaders, as well as for their community practice approach.

## ETHICAL CONSIDERATIONS

A major focus of this chapter relates to the knowledge, skill, and value base of social workers engaged in macro, community-based practice. Understanding the perspectives, theories, and orientations underpinning preparation for social work macro practice is essential for social workers. However, social workers often compete with other professionals for macro employment opportunities, especially leadership and administrative positions and other decision-making roles (e.g., supervisors). More specifically, Pritzker and Applewhite (2015) assert that social workers often vie with a variety of graduate-level professionals (e.g., MBAs, MPHs, MPAs, and JDs) for prominent positions in human service organizations.

Ethical practice in social work is guided by the National Association of Social Workers (NASW) *Code of Ethics* (2017) and core values and principles involving ethical versus unethical behavior, client self-determination, accountability, a commitment to social justice, integrity, working with a scope of practice, competency, the dignity and worth of each person, the value of human relationships, and a commitment to service to others above self-interest. Do other professionals hold themselves to these or similar ethical standards when advocating for change, engaging in macro-level change, and/or assuming a leadership or administrative role with a human service organization? Conduct an Internet search to identify and read the NASW *Code of Ethics*. Next, conduct an Internet search for the code of ethics in business, public health, law, or public administration. Do these professions and disciplines possess a similar code of ethics appropriately regulating actions involving large-scale change, advocacy, administration, and/or leadership? Regardless of their educational or professional background, should people engaged in macro-level roles and practice be held to lesser than ethical standards than micro-level clinical practitioners?

SAGE edge™ Visit **www.edge.sagepub.com/ticemacro** to help you accomplish your coursework goals in an easy-to-use learning environment

## SUMMARY

This chapter introduced specific themes that will run throughout the remainder of the book: the value of an eclectic approach when examining macro-level theories and orientation, the limitations associated with a problem-centered approach to planned change, the notion that the strengths perspective holds merits for macro practice, the benefit of a strengths assessment, the value of community-based practice, and the need to empower consumers of services to change systems to address common human needs. The problem-centered approach was examined as the historical base of social work practice and as a model of intervention that defines people and their communities by meticulously assessing pathologies and deficits. Next, the principles and values associated with the strengths perspective, ecological theory, empowerment, person-in-environment, and advocacy were considered. Throughout the chapter, a concerted effort was made to compare and integrate the various perspectives and theories examined. The chapter concluded with an examination of the relevance of macro-level practice for interprofessional practice as well as a consideration of ethical issues associated with macro practice. Examples, exercises, and vignettes were included in an effort to highlight the practical relevance of materials and promote advocacy as an important method to promote large-scale change.

## TOP 10 KEY CONCEPTS

community-based practice 43
eclectic approach 26
ecological perspective 35
interprofessional practice 48
person-in-environment 41
problem-centered focus 25
social environments 35
social systems 40
transactions 36
value base 47

## DISCUSSION QUESTIONS

1. Consider your own personal and professional strengths. How do these strengths support your work with consumers, communities, and other social workers? Do you conceptualize social issues in relationship to social systems and the physical environment? Or, do you see social issues as problems?
2. Discuss the relationship between the strengths of individuals and those of communities. Consider how a particular strength of an individual might influence a community and vice versa.
3. What is the difference between advocating *with* versus *for* consumers of services? Incorporate empowerment and the strengths perspective into your discussion.
4. Have you been exposed to interprofessional education and practice? If so, in what kind of practice setting? And, what are the macro practice advantages of social work participation and engagement? If you have not experienced an example of interprofessional practice, use Long and Rosen's (2017) examination of interprofessional practice between social workers and optometrists for your discussion.
5. Identify and discuss examples of how macro-oriented theories and perspectives prepare social workers for macro practice in planned change.

## EXERCISES

1. Visit a social work agency and speak with a social worker. Ask the social worker whether the agency is oriented toward a problem-centered approach or a strengths perspective. What portion of the social worker's time is oriented to advocacy and large-scale change? What is the professional background of the administrators and leaders at the agency? Are any of the leaders or administrators at the agency social workers?
2. Plan a discussion with a family member or a friend. How does this person view people in need? Is there any respect for the difficulties people go through in life when struggling with changes in the social or physical environment? Is community life an important aspect for your family member or friend? Identify one or two challenges in that person's community affecting the quality of life for residents. Explore how strengths-based advocacy could be implemented to address this challenge(s).
3. Consider visiting a political rally or protest march organized to advocate for social reform, rights, or legislative development. Observe the people at the event. What are the characteristics of those in attendance? Identify observable strengths that contribute to the event. These strengths could include people, resources, technology, and political access. Try to focus on the strengths associated with the event as compared to the problems.

## ONLINE RESOURCES

- NAMI is the abbreviation for the National Alliance on Mental Illness, a national grassroots organization advancing the lives of people struggling with mental health. There are NAMI chapters in communities across the United States. Visit NAMI's website (www.nami.org) and examine how this organization uses the strengths and abilities of consumers of services to advance the rights, opportunities, and quality of life of people experiencing challenges with mental health.
- Visit the GSA Net Work at www.gsanetwork.org—GSA stands for Genders and Sexualities Alliance. It is a student-run club providing a safe space for students, often middle and high school students, to meet and provide support about issues related to sexual orientation and gender identity.
- If your university, like most, is immersed in DACA (Deferred Action for Childhood Arrivals) discussions and issues, visit the United We Dream website at www.unitedwedream.org to obtain up-to-date information concerning DACA and explore ways to support DACA students and legislative initiatives.

# 3 Engage Diversity and Difference

## LEARNING OBJECTIVES

After reading this chapter you ought to be able to:

1. Define and differentiate the terms diversity and difference
2. Describe cultural humility and cultural competence in the context of macro practice
3. Discuss intersectionality and its relationship to human rights and social, economic, and environmental justice
4. Consider the connection of diversity and difference to implicit biases, inclusion, and cultural humility
5. Understand multiple definitions of economic, social, and environmental justice and review related domestic and international examples

## GRANT EMPLOYS CULTURAL HUMILITY

Grant is a child welfare worker who practices in an increasingly diverse and disenfranchised city environment where the homes of consumers are near landfills and toxic waste sites—examples of environmental degradation. In his work, he emphasizes the importance of recognizing diversity and justice issues. Regardless of the environmental issue, Grant uses his social work education as he endeavors to be culturally competent and value diversity. Grant is keenly observant of environmental hazards, like radon and lead paint, in and around the homes of his impoverished consumers, when Grant initiates, negotiates, advocates, plans, brokers, organizes, and mediates. Sometimes Grant observes how his consumers sometime suffer from perfluorochemicals (PFCs; humanmade chemicals found in household products), like radon and gas. PFCs can make water toxic and affect humans' endocrine and immune systems. When Grant completes consumer and community assessments and conducts home visits, he embraces a cultural humility approach by advocating for environmental justice. When conducting assessments, Grant does not assume what cookware is being used but quietly asks if his clients are aware of the toxic effects of PFCs in cookware. Grant thinks about how he, along with his consumers, might improve living conditions through community organizing, training, and advocacy. Grant addresses environmental justice by encouraging community empowerment activities that lead to questions about exposure to health hazards. At town hall meetings, Grant helps his clients prepare brief statements about how environmental issues are adversely affecting them so that legislators and other decision makers can be better informed.

Macro social workers work in tandem with different and diverse consumers, issues, and community/organizational contexts. As illustrated in Figure 3.1, before starting and being aware of the sociopolitical and policy context, they assess affected consumers, discern issues and opportunities, and learn about the community and/or organizational environment. Multiple consumers experience issues that require solutions, and social workers must be aware of contemporary and historical realities related to culture to most effectively collaborate with these diverse and different consumers. As in micro social work practice, macro social workers assess best when they first consider the following: (1) Where is the consumer? (2) How relevant are aspects of intersectionality and oppression? (3) What knowledge exists about the present sociopolitical and economic structures and relationships? (4) What course(s) of action may be implemented to foster opportunities, effectively collaborate, and facilitate change?

©iStockphoto.com/Hxdyl

**PHOTO 3.1** Environmental hazards are a concern for individuals, groups, and nations worldwide.

Engaging consumers "where they are" requires social workers to be culturally competent, listen well, and act with cultural humility. These terms are examined in greater detail, later in this chapter, because effective collaborations require attention to people's attitudes, behaviors, diversity, and differences. Macro social workers do not always hold the same experiences, diversity attributes, knowledge, or values as their consumers, community, or organizations. For example, when a 58-year-old white MSW-prepared male social worker, employed by Jewish Family Services, works with a 16-year-old pregnant African American girl using illicit drugs, they both recognize differences. However, social workers can help consumers who are different from them, and they can work toward reducing substance use in communities, no matter their race/ethnicity, gender, class, or faith perspective.

**FIGURE 3.1**
Macro Social Workers and Diverse Consumers Assess Before and While Collaborating

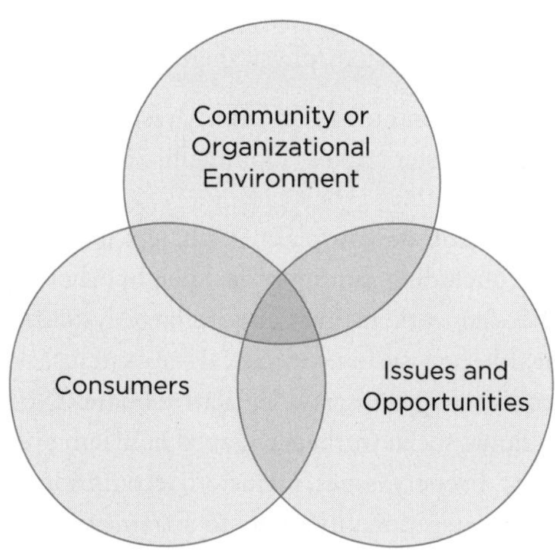

In 1998, educators Tervalon and Murray-Garcia published work concerning components of cultural humility where they reminded readers to also be critically self-aware, address power differentials, and assess mutuality in relationships. The three components of cultural humility identified by Tervalon and Murray-Garcia (1998) are (1) being committed to lifelong self-evaluation and critique, (2) trying to neutralize power imbalances between consumers and social workers, and (3) creating nonpaternalistic collaborations with communities that are mutually beneficial.

Macro social workers work with consumers in situations that require multiple roles and an awareness of complex power dynamics and relationships. As well, social workers, consumers, and large-system decision makers are involved in the mutually beneficial quest to also pursue environmental justice. Such roles include being the following:

- An advocate for people's rights and entitlements
- A coordinator
- A community mobilizer (of people and systems)
- A consultant to government and other agencies
- A cultural interpreter
- An educator, giving out information about how to access relief aid and avoid diseases that can erupt after a disaster
- A facilitator
- An interdisciplinary translator
- A mobilizer of resources
- A negotiator or broker between communities and different levels of government
- A therapist helping people deal with the emotional consequences of disaster
- A protector of the ecosystem/physical environment
- A trainer, especially in how to effectively respond in mobilizing local resources when disaster strikes (Dominelli, 2013)

Macro social work concentrates on planned change intervention for large and often diverse groups, including communities, neighborhoods, populations, and institutions. Macro social workers practice with large systems. Examples of large systems include health-care systems, political subsystems, policy groups, legal systems, national consumer groups, and legislative bodies. No matter the type of large system, professional social workers engaged in macro practice recognize the relevance and value of diversity issues, inclusion, recognition of biases, and intersectionality. In brief, intersectionality refers to a framework designed to explore the dynamic between coexisting identities (e.g., woman, black) and connected systems of oppression (e.g., patriarchy, white supremacy).

## DEFINING DIVERSITY AND DIFFERENCE

The word *diversity* connotes variety rather than homogeneity. In organizational literature, diversity has been used to describe the composition of groups or workforces. In social organizations, **diversity** refers to the range of personnel who represent people from varied backgrounds, cultures, ethnicities, races, viewpoints, and minority populations. Throughout communities, diversity exists in society, cultures, and public policies. Directors of agencies and community leaders strive for diversity when hiring social workers from varied ethnic and racial backgrounds. They also engage consumers of services representing diverse population groups.

**Difference** is the condition or degree of being unlike, dissimilar, or diverse. Typical synonyms for the term *difference* include *dissimilarity, unlikeness, divergence, variation, distinction,* and *discrepancy.* Very often, people who are referred to as "different" from others are perceived as unusual or peculiar. For example, a Muslim woman wearing a hijab may be noticeably different from other members in a typical *Forbes* 500 boardroom. Although this woman wouldn't be unusual or peculiar on her own, she would be different from the individuals who have made up boardrooms in the past.

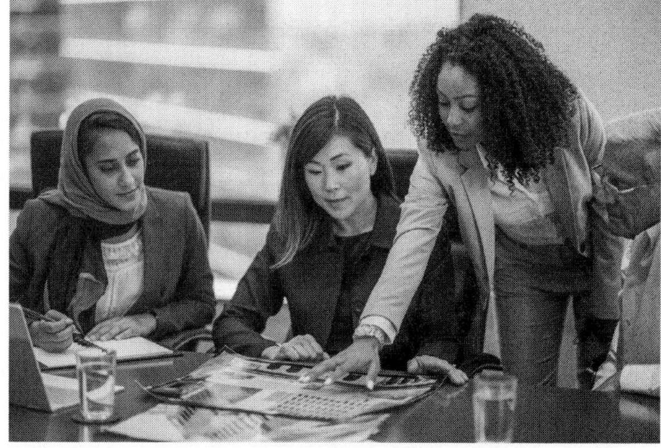

©iStockphoto.com/FatCamera

**PHOTO 3.2** Many businesses now strive for diversity in their hiring practices.

Cultural differences and culture have historically had a major influence on the development of organizations, communities, nations, and groups/families. Social workers like Grant, in the opening case study, as well as you readers will need to continually assess how culture (e.g., diversity and differences) affects how people think and behave. Culture can be a strength in organizations and communities; however, differences in culture foster cultural boundaries that can lead to isolation, discrimination, or limited resources for some people. Cultural differences might also separate social workers from consumers.

### Time to Think 3.1

Identify and reflect upon a time when you were exposed to a culture in a geographical community that made you feel uncomfortable. What were the specific aspects of the culture that created discomfort? Using Grant's situation in the beginning case example, would working with people facing environmental hazards (e.g., pollution) be a challenge? As a social worker, what cultural aspects would you have difficulty accepting? In other words, with what cultural aspects would you have a difficult time reconciling?

Culture is more than distinguishing groups according to differences. Culture prescribes how to act and what to expect in the world. Culture can be a source of inspiration and strength to help people cope with stress, and culture must be interpreted and understood in its social context because "behaviors become meaningful in a community when they are repeated and encoded and eventually take on symbolic value" (Marsiglia & Kulis, 2009, pp. 2–3). Codes get repeated over time and become the backbone of culture. Cultural codes define a set of images that are associated with a particular set of stereotypes in our minds. Cultural codes exist in interpersonal communications among subcultural groups, and they often take the form of idioms, jargon, and gestures.

Ultimately, culture provides filters for people to examine their lives and their social environments. Culturally grounded social work policy-practice combines cultural sensitivity and cultural competency. **Cultural competence** simply means social work professionals possess the attitudes, knowledge, self-awareness, and understanding and practice skills that help them serve diverse consumers. Transformative practice and action are required from culturally grounded social workers who appreciate diversity and differences. Figure 3.2 illustrates five action steps social service agencies, and the professionals employed there, can apply to assess needs and issues and to take action.

As discussed in the opening case, Grant recognized the environmental hazards in the community. When addressing this situation, he also recognized consumers' cultural markers, including language preference, socioeconomic status, resources, and literacy level. When his consumers are poor and unable to speak English, Grant knows he will need to be the visionary change agent to advocate across systems. He may need to advocate for a community cleanup, attend community planning council meetings, or draft a policy. Beyond language, Grant knows that diversity is often associated with arts and crafts, different food, music, dance, folktales, and rituals. Grant also assesses, on the macro level, aspects of "creative diversity" that include societal organization, voting rights, political structure, human rights, kinship structure, rules of inheritance, gender roles, educational systems, labor market, and health services. In this situation, he began where his consumers

**FIGURE 3.2**
Process by Which Macro Social Workers Learn by Doing

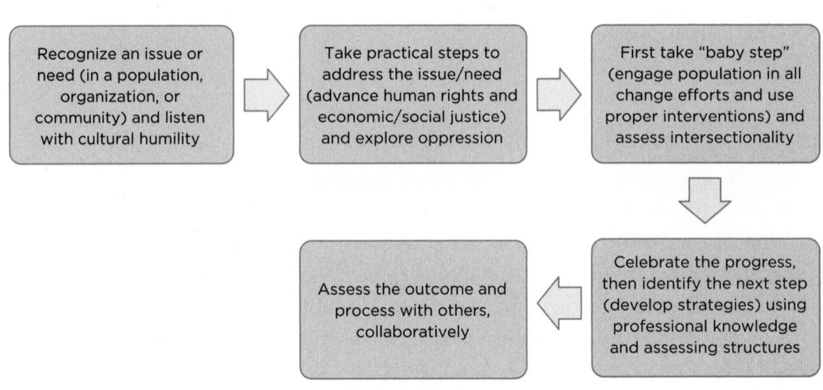

and community were and listened with cultural humility; then, he assessed intersectionality features and explored oppression. Next, Grant examined professional knowledge, assessed social structures and relationships, and strategized and worked with others. Grant focuses on environmental injustices too, which are largely based on disproportionate exposure of poor and minority populations to environmental hazards and harms. Minority population's lack of influence in and access to planning and decision making are often further exacerbated by typical mainstream data collection and mapmaking. The inextricable links between environmental injustices and planning are clearly revealed, for example, when one considers the city of post-Katrina New Orleans or the current city of Flint, Michigan. A city's history of inequality is often revealed in both environmental and planning decision-making processes.

In summary, intersections of diversity require understanding and consideration in large systems—organizations and communities—as they relate to advocacy for environmental justice. In the opening vignette, Grant saw hazards of lead paint, radon, and PFCs and subsequently positioned himself to participate in decision-making processes like the town hall meetings. In some respects, Grant may be conceived as a smart macro social worker who realizes he must work for and between multiple diverse populations of consumers and decision makers. Astute macro social workers understand how community leaders' biases influence their decision making and, ultimately, clients and communities. They also endeavor to be culturally competent and humble.

### Time to Think 3.2

Although "home is where the heart is," sometimes one's living environment is unhealthy. The built environment, in some communities, sometimes contains lead paint, humanmade chemicals, and signs of environmental degradation. Sustainability and economic justice issues are becoming increasingly important to social work. As a social worker, how might you advocate with consumers for a healthier community and environmental justice? In doing so, what would you do to demonstrate cultural humility?

## THE ROLE OF CULTURAL COMPETENCE AND CULTURAL HUMILITY IN MACRO PRACTICE

Cultural competence is "a set of attitudes, skills, behaviors, and policies enabling individuals and organizations to establish effective interpersonal and working relationships that supersede cultural differences" (Fisher-Born, Cain, & Martin, 2015, p. 168). In the late 1980s, Cross, Bazron, Issacs, and Dennis (1989) offered one of the most frequently cited definitions of cultural competence that subsequently included an institutional framework for assessing services for minority populations. Although cultural competence has been included in multiple professional mandates, policies, educational curricula, and social services trainings, several researchers have criticized the assumptions of cultural competency (Duffy, 2001; Furlong & Wight, 2011). Macro social workers must assess aspects of individualism and collectivism, to increase their full understanding of advocacy across micro, mezzo, and macro systems while assuming a culturally competent stance.

Sue et al. (1982) first introduced cultural competency as a core of social work theory and practice and shaped subsequent social work models. Later, Sue (1998) suggested three components for effective culturally competent practice: (1) hypothesis testing, (2) dynamic sizing, and (3) culturally specific expertise. Hypothesis testing uses cultural knowledge about groups tentatively and explores consumers' societal contexts and intersectionality. Dynamic sizing involves the ability to know when certain behaviors and attitudes can be generalized about separate from a person's personality or cultural norms. Culturally specific expertise evolves when one knows how to develop rapport and strong consumer-worker alliances, as when the practitioner is bicultural (Marsiglia & Kulis, 2009). Macro social workers who are equally fluent in English and Spanish and who have assimilated well into American culture may be better adept at forging alliances between consumers and decision makers.

**Cultural humility** is the ability to maintain an interpersonal stance that is other oriented in relationship to aspects about cultural identity that are most important to that person. In other words, if social workers are culturally humble, they will endeavor to put themselves in the shoes of another person and see issues from his or her standpoint. Cultural humility was formed in the physical health-care field and adapted to therapists and social workers to increase the quality of their interactions with consumers. Cultural humility requires an understanding of oneself on a deep level plus a critical examination of power and privilege. Macro social workers must query what structural forces exist when addressing consumer issues and how meaningful engagement can occur around these issues. Figure 3.3 illustrates particular elements that influence cultural humility in institutions and individuals—mainly awareness and accountability.

**FIGURE 3.3**

Recognizing Power and Providing Education Helps Foster Individual and Institutional Accountability

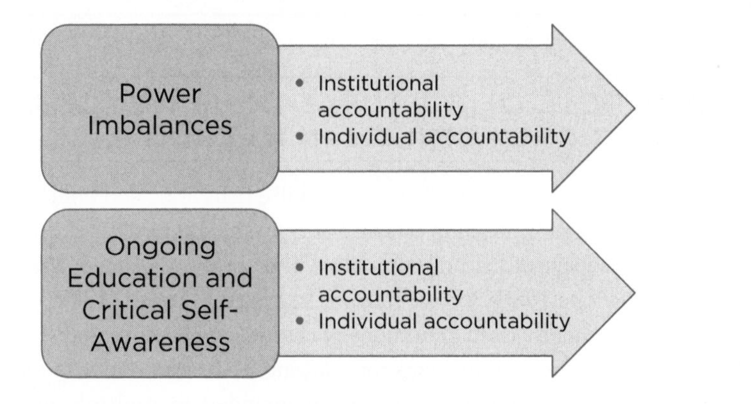

When **power imbalances** occur within organizations, leaders can uphold either institutional or individual accountability. As social workers increase their critical self-awareness and education, their ability to foster individual accountability and institutional accountability grows. For example, corporations wield much more power than an individual consumer, yet social workers can advocate to ensure both individual and institutional accountability. Ongoing education and self-awareness may be increased when organizations and communities create and experience trainings and endeavor to operate with cultural competence and proficiency rather than cultural destructiveness. Culture is so complex that intersections of diversity are required to facilitate a broad understanding of the concept's depth and breadth.

Cultural humility is a promising and important concept for the macro social worker. Those who aspire to be culturally humble go beyond a focus on self-awareness. One who is culturally humble (1) considers the complexity of diversity; (2) remains self-aware and open to learning; (3) endeavors to understand and accept cultural differences; (4) engages in collaborative helping; (5) demonstrates a familiarity with the social, built, and natural environment; and (6) builds organizational support despite visible barriers and obstacles (Fisher-Born et al., 2015, p. 165; Ortega & Faller, 2011, pp. 43–44).

Both cultural competence and cultural humility have similar aims. Culturally humble macro social workers will address service delivery disparities and emphasize individual and institutional accountability. Ortega and Faller (2011) argue that cultural humility is a required trait for child welfare workers, supervisors, and state funders. Organizational district managers can model macro practice skills as they engage in reflection, consider institutional and individual accountability, and mitigate systemic power imbalances (Fisher-Born et al., 2015, p. 173).

## HEALTH-CARE SETTING HONORS DIVERSITY

Philadelphia hospitals, located in one of the largest cities in the United States, are regarded as LGBT friendly. Specifically, nine Philadelphia-area health-care facilities are ranked as national leaders in LGBT consumer care by the 2018 Healthcare Equality Index ("Philly Hospitals," 2018). Philadelphia is home to several civil rights, advocacy, and LGBT youth organizations, including the Bread & Roses community fund, the Gay and Lesbian Latino Education Initiative, and more ("Where Does Philadelphia Rank," 2017), and these memberships helped the city be noticed. A Philadelphia, Pennsylvania, apartment building has also been touted as a national model for low-income LGBT seniors ("A Philadelphia Apartment Building," 2014). Given this ranking and host of community resources for the intergenerational LGBT community, a Philadelphia-based macro social worker practice with a range of LGBT consumers would likely respond differently than a macro social worker employed in Southaven, Mississippi ("The 5 Worst States for LGBT People," 2014). Southaven, Mississippi, widely advertises the services of multiple "Discrimination Lawyers," thereby indicating the amount of bias that naturally occurs in some communities.

As indicated by the case study, integrating micro and macro social work practice is extremely relevant today because of social workers' abilities in helping people and large systems navigate an ever-changing sociopolitical and environmental landscape. Today's practitioners grapple with globalization of industry and human migration, the privatization of services, redistribution of political power and authority to local governments and the nonprofit sector, decreased privacy in social life, and conflicts inherent in the shifting demographics and diversity of the nation's people and cultures (Reisch, 2013).

## WHAT IS INTERSECTIONALITY IN MACRO PRACTICE?

Culture is not monolithic. In the social work literature, the ever-emerging notion of intersectionality challenges the idea that culture is static. Instead, the term **intersectionality** connotes how consumers are whole, complex, and multiracial. By definition, intersectionality is the interconnected nature of social categorizations (e.g., class, gender, race) regarded as creating overlapping and interdependent systems of discrimination or disadvantage. In other words, intersectionality is an orientation based on this premise of conceptualizing a person, group of people, or social problem as affected by multiple disadvantages and forms of discrimination. The term considers people's overlapping identities and experience in an effort to better understand the complexity of prejudices they face. Intersectionality recognizes that identity markers (e.g., "black" and "female") inform the other and create a complex convergence of oppression. For instance, a black man and a white woman may make $0.74 and $0.78 to a white man's dollar, respectively. Yet, black women, faced with multiple forms of oppression, only make $0.64. Understanding intersectionality is crucial to overcoming the interwoven prejudices people face in their daily lives.

Jani, Pierce, Ortiz, and Sowbel's (2011) article provides a critical analysis of the historical development of approaches to teaching diversity content in social work education. These authors note how the Council on Social Work Education (CSWE) Educational Policy 2.1.4 Engage Diversity and Difference in Practice is to be a key focus for today's educators and ironically note how nondiscrimination goes unmentioned. Jani et al. (2011) characterize intersectionality as a multidimensional concept that refers to how intersecting experiences of multiple subordinating identities contribute to one's sense of self, perspectives, and aspirations. Yet, on another level, the term refers to a person's multiple social location where he or she might experience oppression. For example, illiterate, impoverished, and disabled residents of Flint, Michigan, likely had and are having far more challenges accessing clean drinking water than those residents who are educated, wealthy, and fully functional.

Intersectionality in macro social work practice may be observed through the indirect practice of social workers involved in aspects of environmental justice and economic and social justice. In the following pages, examples of indirect practice in relationship to intersectionality are elaborated upon via examples and references to the growing empirical research literature.

## IMPLICIT AND EXPLICIT BIASES

As social workers engage in organizational and community work, they require self-awareness and the ability to assess implicit and explicit biases. **Implicit bias** refers to the stereotypes or attitudes that affect humans' understanding, actions, and decisions in an unconscious manner. Causes of implicit bias include early experiences, cultural biases, cognitive balance principles, affective experiences (anxiety), and "the self." Implicit bias can occur in relationship to groups of people, organizations, programs, communities, geographical regions, and other large systems, not just individuals and families.

These biases may include unfavorable or favorable assessments, and they are activated rather involuntarily—without a person's awareness or intentional control. Implicit biases reside deep within the subconscious, and they are not accessible via introspection (Kirwan Institute for the Study of Race and Ethnicity, http://kirwaninstitute.osu.edu/). The implicit associations people keep in their subconscious affect their attitudes and feelings toward other people based on characteristics such as age, appearance, ethnicity, and race. Particular associations develop over one's life course, starting at a very early age via exposure to indirect and direct messages. In addition, news programming and the media foster implicit associations. Table 3.1 illustrates a few key characteristics of implicit biases as cited on The Ohio State University's website.

Often, the expressions "implicit attitude," "implicit bias," and "stereotype" are taken to be synonyms and are used to refer to the mental states responsible for implicitly biased behavior (Toribo, 2018, p. 42).

**Explicit bias** refers to people's conscious attitudes and beliefs about a group or person. Often these biases and their expression arise because people perceive

**TABLE 3.1**
Characteristics of Implicit Biases

| |
|---|
| Implicit biases are **pervasive.** All people have implicit biases—even judges who vow to be impartial. |
| Implicit and explicit biases are **related but distinct mental constructs.** They are not mutually exclusive and might reinforce each other. |
| Implicit associations people hold **do not necessarily align with declared beliefs** or reflect endorsed stances. |
| People typically hold implicit biases that **favor their own ingroup,** although research reveals people can still hold implicit biases against one's own ingroup. |
| Implicit biases are **malleable.** People's brains are complex and formed implicit associations can be gradually unlearned via multiple debiasing techniques. |

a threat. When people feel threatened, they typically draw group boundaries to distinguish themselves from others. People usually express explicit biases when they feel a threat to their well-being. For example, Caucasians are more apt to express anti-Muslim prejudice when they perceive national security is at risk and express more negative attitudes toward Asian Americans when they perceive an economic threat. When people perceive their biases are valid, they often justify unfair treatment or violence. Such unfair treatment can have long-term negative effects on its victims' physical and mental health. Table 3.2 offers ideas, from the Perception Institute, on how to handle explicit bias (Perception Institute, https://perception.org/research/explicit-bias/).

Implicit bias has been studied less than explicit bias. Although implicit biases have often been assumed to function outside of a person's awareness, this may not preclude them from influencing behavior. Incidents of discrimination due to implicit bias, or an unconscious prejudice in favor or against particular groups, are extremely difficult to challenge in court, because plaintiffs alleging discrimination in violation of the Equal Protection Clause must prove that the discrimination was purposeful. Because our legal system does not always provide relief when implicit bias has caused systemic discrimination, advocates for equity must work toward implementing preventive measures. Implicit and explicit biases create barriers in (1) education, (2) housing, (3) health, and (4) criminal justice.

What can macro social workers do about implicit and explicit biases? Perhaps in assessments of implicit bias, social workers need to recognize how biases based on age, class, race, nationality, religion, and sexual orientation arise when people cannot control their responses. People are involuntarily influenced by biases. Subsequently, people make evaluative decisions when they interact with others in ways that might lead to misunderstanding or discomfort. In essence, to dilute implicit biases, social workers ought to increase their self-awareness, double their efforts to expand policies, and remember the connection between self and cultural milieu. Social workers should also recall how proximity leads to attraction, so

**TABLE 3.2**
Ways to Handle Explicit Bias

| |
|---|
| Expressions of explicit bias (discrimination, hate speech, etc.) occur because of deliberate thought; therefore, **consciously regulate them.** |
| **Reinforce norms in homes, schools, and the media to promote respect** for one's own identity and other groups. People are more motivated to control their biases if social norms exist and dictate that prejudice is not socially acceptable. |
| **Intergroup contact between people of difference races can increase trust and reduce anxiety** that underlies bias. Research reveals how emphasizing a common group identity (e.g., "we're all Americans") can help reduce interracial tensions that might arise between majority and minority U.S. ethnic groups. |

giving people opportunities to become emotionally comfortable with outgroup members may help reduce implicit biases.

Social injustice is disruptive both collectively and personally, and implicit prejudice plays a role in this process. Both explicit and implicit biases (e.g., declarative and procedural) exist and influence social workers and consumers alike. "Implicit biases may be more influenced by early experiences, affective experiences, cultural biases, and cognitive balance principles" (Rudman, 2004, p. 135). Implicit orientations come from past developmental experiences, whereas explicit orientations and biases typically reflect more recent events. Macro social workers might consider posing the following questions in their assessments:

- Do people (organizational culture/communities) realize how they are prejudiced?
- Do people know how explicit and implicit biases are related?
- How do people become biased?
- What are the underlying causes of implicit bias?
- How did happenings in the early 1960s (e.g., 1964 Civil Rights Act), in the 1980s (Reagan years), and during the Obama presidency (2008–2016) affect large organizational and institutional struggles?
- How can organizations and institutions today confront implicit bias so that social progress can be spurred, in socially and economically just ways?

An additional concept useful in guiding macro social workers is inclusion. Inclusion may be viewed as what one actually *does* about diversity.

## INCLUSION

As previously noted, diversity means all the ways we differ or the collective mixture of differences and similarities that include individual and organizational characteristics, beliefs, values, and/or experiences. **Visible diversity traits** include abilities, age, body type, gender, race, and physical abilities. Diversity features of organizations include their assumptions, values, artifacts, culture, leadership style, motivation levels, and resources. Communities also reveal diversity traits; they are open or closed, local, global or international, online (e.g., MoveOn.org, Facebook, Twitter), green (e.g., city councils, urban planners, or environmental activists concerned about healthy living), or gray (e.g., naturally occurring retirement communities or groups of older adult advocates who care about being meaningfully engaged). **Invisible diversity traits** include sexual orientation, religion, socioeconomic status, education, parental status, and so on. People are born with differences, and organizations and communities also come with some differences that can or will not change. For example, a smaller community that is predominantly evangelical may not welcome the lesbian couple who recently moved next door to the church. Therefore, uniqueness is often a part of some definitions of diversity. Thus, diversity describes one aspect of inclusiveness—the extent to which an organization has people from diverse backgrounds or communities involved as board members, staff, and/or volunteers. Perhaps a new rhetoric in the field of diversity is inclusion. However, little attention has been given to the concept of inclusion, however. Meanwhile, typologies of organizational approaches to diversity have included the *discrimination-and-fairness paradigm* and the *newer learning-and-effectiveness paradigm.*

**Inclusion** involves bringing together and harnessing diverse forces and resources in a beneficial way. In a sense, inclusion puts the practice and concept of diversity into action by creating an environment of respect, involvement, and connection—where the richness of backgrounds, ideas, and perspectives is corralled to create organizational or community value. Organizations require both inclusion and diversity to be successful. Metaphorically speaking, diversity can be described as being invited to the party because of who you are, but inclusion is being asked to dance at the party. Being part of an organization or community is one aspect, but inclusiveness is being given a genuine role in the organization through an environment that welcomes and values your input. Diversity can occur during a hiring process, but inclusion involves maintaining a productive and professional atmosphere where all people feel a valued part of the organization (or community or group).

An organization's journey to become inclusive starts with a simple yet critically important inquiry: What actions is this organization taking to foster an inclusive work culture where uniqueness of backgrounds, beliefs, capabilities, talents, and ways of living are welcomed and leveraged for learning and making better decisions? Macro views of diversity consider workforce, philanthropy, and communication and inventory the following:

- Create and work from a well-documented action plan that contains goals, objectives, and small manageable tasks to help realize change.
- Incorporate diversity principles across organizational functions and units.
- Create opportunities for cross-generational work teams and interactions.
- Invest in team building and leadership skills, to instill organizations with competencies that foster successful teams and skills for leading diverse teams.

Some well-intentioned organizations, like many states' large family and child welfare organizations, have prioritized diversity and neglected inclusion, thereby leading to disappointing outcomes that often undermine the totality of diversity and inclusion efforts. People with different lifestyles and different backgrounds challenge each other more, and such challenging can be constructive or destructive. While diversity can create dissent, organizations need that lest they risk becoming too insular and out of touch with individual, group, organizational, or community needs. Underrepresented groups in some organizations are women, people over age 50, people with developmental and physical challenges, and ethnic and religious minorities. Mentorship programs may provide an added benefit of fostering inclusivity by offering organizational members a feeling of belonging and a safe place to discuss sensitive issues. But how frequently do mentorship programs exist for social workers employed in family and child welfare organizations?

Suffice it to say, the linkage of diversity and inclusion is a complex and nuanced topic. Three best practices to help organizations grow are to (1) continually build pipelines of diverse talent, (2) be flexible and lead by example, and (3) emphasize mentoring and coaching. Inclusion is involvement and empowerment, where the inherent worth and dignity of all people are recognized. An inclusive environment promotes and sustains a sense of belonging; it values and practices respect for the backgrounds, beliefs, talents, and ways of living of its members. In macro practice, as previously mentioned, large organizations like child welfare agencies or even community mental health agencies would benefit from hiring staff that are diverse, different, and inclusive. Leaders of these large organizations can build accountability into their hiring and evaluation systems and make directors be responsible for creating a diverse and inclusive work environment. Diverse people must talk about their diversity and difference(s) in order to be effective and understanding. Child welfare and mental health agencies that do not attend to hiring sufficient skilled workers from diverse backgrounds risk being unable to meet consumers' needs because of limited language skills, cultural knowledge, generational differences, and more. In addition, consumers themselves must be part of the change process and advocacy strategies within organizations and communities.

Inclusion differs from equality, but inclusion can be the reason for more inequality. There are different gradations of inclusion via performance roles in organizations that are unequal in terms of accumulated knowledge, influence, power, salary, and status. For example, nurses, plaintiffs, and research assistants are lower status than high-ranking professions, such as physicians, lawyers/judges, and full professors. Licensed Clinical Social Workers (LCSW) in direct practice are perceived, regarded, and paid differently than social workers who engage in indirect macro practice. Yet both LCSWs and macro social workers engage in similar assessment, intervention, and evaluation skills and techniques that require cultural competence and cultural humility. Consumers are more likely to experience inclusion far more when they fall outside systems of oppression, such as ableism, ageism, classism, ethnocentrism, heterosexism/trans oppression, racism, or sexism. Figure 3.4 illustrates said oppression systems. Imagine how much more advocacy efforts will be attended to by city councils when consumers are middle or upper class rather than impoverished.

**FIGURE 3.4**
Examples of Systems Where Oppression Occurs

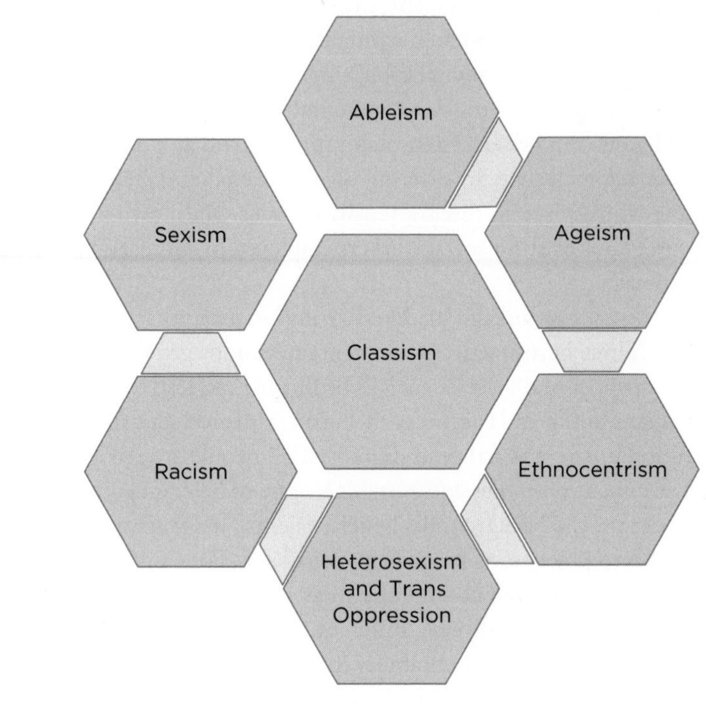


## Time to Think 3.3

Think about an organization or community group with which you have been involved. How do you observe the ingroup members interacting with those who evidence visible or invisible differences? What systems of oppression are at play in this organization or community group? How do you observe the *discrimination-and-fairness paradigm* or the newer *learning-and-effectiveness paradigm* at play in these same organizations or community groups?

Consider the following definitions of each paradigm, as you prepare your response.

- *Discrimination-and-fairness paradigm:* This is perhaps the most dominant diversity theory in the workplace today. It gives leaders an easy way out. Instead of embracing and accepting differences between people, this theory tends to ignore differences in the name of fairness. Instead, people are treated as if they were, metaphorically, Manila folders. (Example: One's name on a submitted resumé. Only assigning mentors to minority employees.)
- *Learning-and-effectiveness paradigm:* This newer theory focuses on integrating deep-level diversity differences like attitudes, beliefs, values, and personality into the actual work of the organization. This approach values people beyond the surface level (e.g., gender, race/ethnicity) for their abilities, experiences, knowledge, and skills.

Organizations employing this paradigm offer diversity training programs—specifically, awareness training (to raise awareness and challenge assumptions) and skill-based training (teaches employees practical skills needed for managing a diverse workforce, such as adaptability, conflict resolution, flexibility, negotiation, and problem solving). Diversity audits are formal assessments to measure employee and management attitudes to investigate fairness in hiring, promotions, and so on.

## ENVIRONMENTAL JUSTICE

The term *environmental justice* is typically placed under the larger umbrella of "social justice." Essentially, social justice is the right to live free of institutionalized oppression and domination. **Environmental justice** refers to people having the right to clean food, soil, air, water, and green space and the right to influence how humankind interacts with each element. Researchers (Dominelli, 2012; McIlvaine-Newsad & Porter, 2013) propose that community gardens represent a "double benefit" in the context of environmental justice because they "remove unhealthy problems like dependence on unsafe, insecure food sources and replace it with an environmentally, socially, and individually health activity and food source."

Environmental racism is an American problem and an issue for present-day macro social workers. Although environmental laws are "on the books," so to speak, they are not often applied or enforced equally. Instead of viewing the "person-in-environment," social workers can instead "view the environment in the person." The ecosystem should be at the core of practice rather than just the person. The American Academy of Social Work and Social Welfare has proposed 12 *Grand Challenges* for the social work profession. This academy has noted how urban development and climate change, for example, threaten health and undermine coping, as well as deepen existing social and environmental inequities. Therefore, a changing global environment requires transformative social responses. These responses could include new partnerships, deep engagement with local communities, and innovations to strengthen collective and individual assets (Dewane, 2017).

Environmental justice is the foundational core of the Green Party, popular in Europe and the United States. The *British Journal of Social Work* (Ramsay & Boddy, 2017) published a content analysis of the environmental justice literature and identified three themes to guide social workers in their exploration of ecosocial work. Creatively apply existing skills to environmental concepts and openness to different values and ways of being or doing: (1) shift practice, theories, and values to incorporate the natural environment; (2) learn from spirituality and indigenous cultures; and (3) appreciate the instrumental and innate value of nonhuman life.

Another piece in a social work helper article captures numerous ways social workers use skills in advocacy, antioppressive practice, community development, empowerment, holistic interventions, management, and team building (Dewane, 2017). Social workers also use adventure-based programs and animal-assisted therapy to reflect the ecosocial work concepts of biosphere and biofilia. Creative social workers may also look to the natural environment for transcendent and restorative experiences for consumers. For example, organizations that help consumers and their families better understand autism might orchestrate summer camps that have educational opportunities as well as fun social events and activities (canoeing, dancing, etc.).

Macro social workers interested in changing society may act as "change agents" to ensure environmental safety, value environmental and ecological justice, and ameliorate environmental injustices through advocacy and legislative initiatives. Social workers may additionally support fair districting and the elimination of gerrymandering that enables marginalized populations to have votes that count.

Macro social workers, in tandem with their consumers, can work across boundaries and multiple spaces. In so doing, they can (1) expand their usual scope of practice and educate, mobilize, and support community activism; (2) develop partnerships and coalitions that show collaboration across boundaries; (3) create dual degree programs such as Masters in Social Work/Masters in Public Health (MSW/MPH); and (4) deliver workshops to illustrate how public health professionals and social workers and consumers can help build resilience for the traumas and toxic stresses of climate change.

When macro social workers work with communities, they, along with consumers, can identify food deserts and organize food cooperatives, community-supported agriculture, and community gardens. Social workers and consumers can share research about how migrant workers have significantly shorter life spans because of pesticide exposure. Along with consumers, social workers can design family interventions, run support groups, manage nonprofit organizations, and educate communities about fracking, mountain-topping, and more (Dewane, 2017).

## Time to Think 3.4

Consider the environmental crisis in Flint, Michigan. Social workers in Flint were involved in going door to door and helped mobilize groups to demand safe drinking water. Consider how rural communities are affected by fracking or mountain-topping—investigate these environmental topics. Consider how, during hurricanes, evacuation orders come yet immigrants identified with Deferred Action for Childhood Arrivals (DACA) still resist going to shelters because they fear being deported. How can social workers engaged in macro practice advocate and provide safety to such vulnerable populations?

Environmental injustice is a vastly growing human rights concern because climate change and environmental degradation appear to be quickly increasing. The social work profession must accelerate its pace in engaging in dialogue at the practice, policy, and research levels (Gray, Coates, & Hetherington, 2013). Social workers must recognize the implicit connections between human rights and the environment, as well as consider aspects of implicit and explicit biases as they endeavor to envision a fair and just worldwide culture of environmental sustainability and inclusion.

Brett Carlsen/Getty Images

**PHOTO 3.3**
Flint Mayor Karen Weaver speaks to residents during a town hall on water, public safety, and job opportunities on March 17, 2016. The water supply of Flint, Michigan, is an example of environmental injustice.

Environmental justice is defined several ways with no single agreed-upon definition. However, two recurring themes focus upon how degradation is equally shared across all communities and demographic groups and how there is equal inclusion in decision-making processes that evolve into environmentally related actions and policies (Nesmith & Smyth, 2015, p. 485). The source of environmental injustice in rich countries is multifaceted, often linked to racism, poverty, lack of power, and lack of mobility. Grosse Pointe Woods and Grosse Pointe Shores, Michigan, represent the finest of neighborhoods near Detroit, Michigan, and nearby Henry Ford Hospital and Wayne State University. Grosse Pointe has had no worries with polluted water. Yet consider how Flint, Michigan, has now been plagued for some time with water problems.

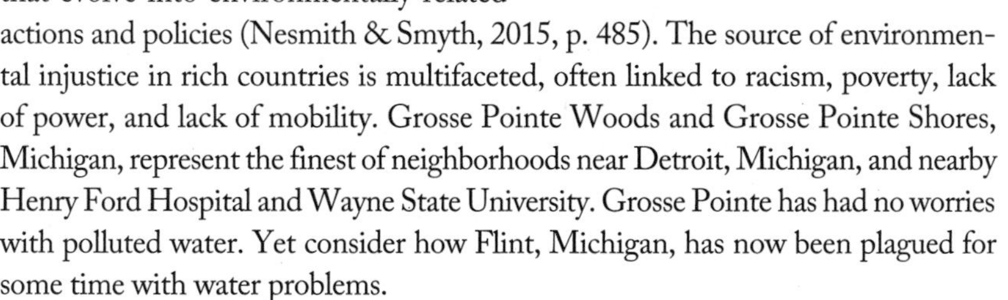

Environmental injustice—the "failure to share the earth's resources equitably, is rooted in environmental degradation caused by the normal processes of industrialization and disasters, whether natural or (hu)man made" (Dominelli, 2013, p. 431). Although everyone has a role to play in maintaining the earth's environment for future generations, social work professionals need to specialize in mobilizing resources and people when environmental degradation is observed and deemed unacceptable.

## Domestic Examples

Environmental hazards are disproportionately experienced among communities of color and low-income people in rich countries. For example, in the United States, environmental hazards (defined as a substance, an event, or a state that can potentially threaten the surrounding natural environment that negatively affects consumer's health, e.g., pollution, natural disasters) most often affect people with the least power and fewest resources, yielding strong correlations with economic class, gender, and race (McKibben, 2010). Macro social workers can easily observe how communities where consumers reside too often experience drought, unsafe drinking water, or uncontrolled flooding. As noted earlier in this section, macro social workers can act as first responders to organize emergency relief when hurricanes or floods hit. In such instances, social workers can act as "change agents" to ensure environmental safety, value environmental and ecological justice, and ameliorate environmental injustices through advocacy and legislative initiatives.

Domestically speaking, common environmental hazards found across the United States are water and air pollution. Pesticides and herbicides used in farming, like Atrazine, can cause heart problems and cancer. Harmful benzenes are used in manufacturing, air pollution affects urban communities in the form of automobile emissions, and "fracking" (hydraulic fracturing) and natural disasters have likely contributed to extreme weather such as hurricanes (Nesmith & Smyth, 2015). The state of Alaska has unique environmental issues related to arctic drilling and the risks of oil spills. In instances such as these, boundless opportunities exist for social workers to engage in macro practice to address the needs of people in communities. Aware of arctic drilling, social workers might act as change agents to challenge the political structure to further progressive environmental causes. They might also engage in antioppressive practice and demand that those who wield political power be challenged and questioned so that they protect people and environments rather than just control them.

## International Examples

Internationally, other developed countries have similar stories of environmental degradation. One U.K. study found that the poor communities were typically found along clustered risk sites next to active waste landfills, industrial sites, and flood zones (Fairburn, Butler, & Smith, 2009). In Canada, poor neighborhoods evidenced heavy concentrations of nitrogen dioxide air pollution, and First Nations reservations had contaminated drinking water (Buzzelli, 2008). Low-income communities in the Netherlands have reported increased noise pollution near waste disposal sites and limited access to green spaces. Meanwhile, similar situations have been documented in Australia, France, Germany, Scotland, and Sweden (Nesmith & Smyth, 2015, p. 486).

Coastal cities are vulnerable to flooding and constantly growing populations as they absorb migrants from rural hinterlands and rising numbers of births, thereby making already vulnerable ecosystems even more fragile. An example of one of these areas is coastal Bangladesh, which has had many initiatives aimed at controlling coastal erosion through the planting of mangrove plantations (Dominelli, 2013, pp. 431–432). In such areas, social workers are called upon to use macro skills such as educating communities and advocating for legislative changes.

Natural disasters may be defined as those that lack human intervention and include earthquakes, tsunamis, volcanic eruptions, floods, and landslides. (Hu)man-made disasters include poverty, armed conflict, industrial pollution, overurbanization in the form of mega-cities lacking adequate public health infrastructures and utilities, and "industrial accidents" such as the one that happened in Bhopal, India (Dominelli, 2013, p. 432). In reality, the lines between these types, in the literature, are becoming blurred all the time. For example, poverty worsens disasters, yet the disaster literature rarely considers a disaster in its own right. Such are indicators of social and economic justice issues for communities.

## Social and Economic Justice

Using existing theories can help macro social workers and their consumers better understand and advocate for social and economic justice. For example, green social work (GSW) is a theory that was defined by Lena Dominelli and outlined in her book published in 2012, *Green Social Work: From Environmental Crisis to Environmental Justice*. Dominelli defines GSW as "a form of holistic professional social work practice that focuses on: the interdependencies among people; the social organization of relationships between people and the flora and fauna in their physical habitats; and the interaction between socio-economic and physical environmental crises and interpersonal behavior that undermine the well-being of human beings on Planet Earth" (Dominelli, 2012, p. 25). Dominelli (2012, p. 194) goes on to describe the key components of her GSW model:

1. Respect all living things alongside their sociocultural and physical environments.
2. Develop empowering and sustainable relationships between people and their environments.
3. Advocate for the importance of embedding the social in all economic activities, including those aimed at eradicating poverty.
4. Question the relevance of an industrial model of development that relies on overurbanization and overconsumption as the basis for social progress.
5. Promote social and environmental justice; GSW is explicitly political and criticizes traditional social work frameworks such as ecological or environmental social work for relegating the definition of environment to include only the social. (Dominelli, 2012, p. 25)

Dominelli (2012) argues that "mainstream ecological writings are implicitly political in that they ignore power relations based on existing geo-political social structures, even though these define identity issues, power relations and resource distribution" (p. 26).

Figure 3.5 reveals how green social workers can be involved in macro social work practice as they care about the following and are knowledgeable of organizations and communities, skills, resources, and issues related to power and privilege:

- Human rights violations
- Environmental degradation
- An economic system that perpetuates inequalities and lacks corporate accountability
- The neglect of cultural diversity and the nonaffirmation of aboriginal and indigenous lifestyles
- The lack of people-friendly localities and supportive community relationships, especially those associated with unsustainable economic developments
- The lack of provision for the health and social services that promote the well-being of people
- The lack of care for the physical environment
- The lack of recognition of the interdependency among people and between people and the geo-ecosystems, as well as a lack of resilient-built infrastructures, resources, and communities (Dominelli, 2012)

**FIGURE 3.5**
Green Social Work Interventions Related to Social Work Knowledge Domains

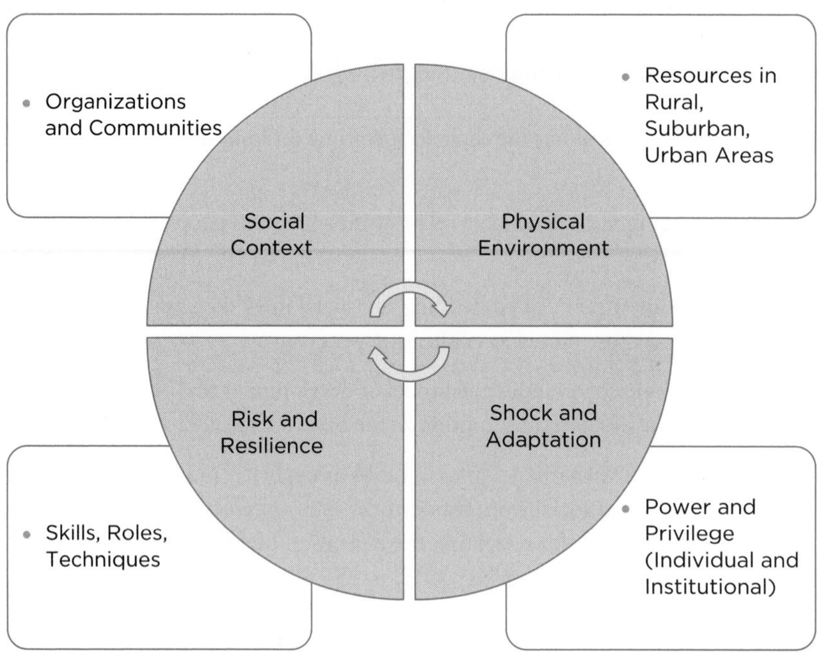


*Source:* Modified from figure in Dominelli (2013, p. 437).

Worldwide, examples of environmental injustice may be found. For example, an international example of environmental justice is found in a master's thesis by John Mailhot (2015) of Norway who focuses on the vital role of community gardens across multiple populations and countries. He cites Dominelli's work/model and introduces readers to what is happening in the community gardens arena through the borrowing of teachings from the First Nations people of Canada.

Nationally and globally, the social work profession has long used the "person-in-environment" (PIE) perspective to understand community- and individual-level problems. Although social workers have typically defined this environmental perspective only through the lens of the social environment, even though knowledge exists as to how the **built and natural environments** are also related to health and well-being, increasingly social workers are using a global social work paradigm to describe and practically infuse environmental justice content into curricula to educate and train social workers. Teixeria and Krings (2015) have recognized the intersectionality of social and environmental inequality and published an original framework that integrates environmental justice principles with global social work standards.

Figure 3.5 illustrates how social workers and gardeners have used green social work interventions, related to social work knowledge domains, and First Nations people's teachings to conceptualize and create better resources for an entire community, while partnering with an array of community and human service-type organizations.

Visit **www.edge.sagepub.com/ticemacro** to help you accomplish your coursework goals in an easy-to-use learning environment

## SUMMARY

This chapter's content illustrates how diversity is multifaceted and involves attributes and characteristics of inclusion and an understanding of intersectionality. Social workers examine diversity deeply and consider how layers of oppression exist and how to advocate to herald the voices of marginalized consumers. Consumers served by social workers may experience biases as a result of their diversity and differentness. Members of groups, organizations, and communities possess biases and vary in their degrees of cultural competence and humility. Therefore, social work educators and practitioners alike must reconceptualize cultural competence to acknowledge power and privilege in consumer-system relationships. The concept of cultural humility can positively influence our institutions, agencies, and organizations. Social work educators must start posing and asking challenging questions about social work's curriculum, pedagogy, and organizational structure. As well, cultural humility must be embraced and social workers must be challenged to ask difficult questions to themselves and others. Macro social workers must avoid the tendency to reduce consumers and their strengths and problems to certain norms learned from trainings or courses about "difference" or "diversity" categories.

## TOP 10 KEY CONCEPTS

built and natural environments 72
cultural competence 56
cultural humility 58
difference 55
diversity 55
environmental justice 67
explicit bias 61
inclusion 64
intersectionality 60
power imbalances 59

## DISCUSSION QUESTIONS

1. Please reread the chapter's opening case study. What macro practice skills would Grant need to address the environmental issues facing the community where he works?
2. How would you define the term *environmental justice?*
3. Why is intersectionality so crucial to macro social workers' understanding of environmental justice and environmental racism?
4. How might explicit and implicit biases affect your social work practice with consumers?

## EXERCISES

1. Contact a child welfare worker and inquire about how much they assess a consumer's built and natural environments as well as their social environment. Report your findings.

2. Interview two social work faculty members or social work community-based practitioners and ask them to differentiate between the concepts of cultural competence and cultural humility. Record their definitions and analyze them to decide which best resonates with your own professional views.
3. Look for newspaper stories about environmental hazards. Evaluate how the environmental degradation was assessed and managed. What was the effect of the hazards on consumers, and how could they be involved in any interventions?
4. Revisit the macro social work roles outlined in the chapter and think of how you might intervene in multiple situations and fields of social work, involving human rights and environmental, economic, and social justice. What social work skills would you use?
5. Researchers in the 1980s and 1990s (Devore & Schlesinger, 1981; Fong & Furuto, 2001; Green, 1995; Lum, 1986) published work concerning the terms *ethnic-sensitive* social work practice, *cultural awareness, cross-cultural social work, ethnic competency,* and *process-stage approach with people of color*. Definitions and approaches to cultural competency widely differ depending upon discipline, practice context, or worldview. Compare and contrast these terms from the perspective of a macro social worker.

## ONLINE RESOURCES

- U.S. Environmental Protection Agency (https://www.epa.gov/environmentaljustice/learn-about-environmental-justice): The EPA website contains information about environmental justice and laws and regulations.
- Office of Legacy Management: An Office of the U.S. Department of Energy (https://www.energy.gov/lm/services/environmental-justice/environmental-justice-history): Environmental justice history information may be found.
- NASW-NJ Environmental Justice Special Interest Group (http://www.naswnj.org/page/envjustice/Environmental-Justice.htm): A group of New Jersey social workers who formed a special interest group offers information.
- Cultural Competence vs. Cultural Humility YouTube (https://www.youtube.com/watch?v=cVmOXVIF8wc): This media source differentiates the terms from a social work perspective. Great and varied visual images are shown.

# An Advocacy Model for Dynamic Practice

# 4

## COMMUNITY-BASED ADVOCACY

Ashley is a medical social worker who coordinates home health care services for older adults. Also, she works as a consultant to an Area on Aging Council, which attempts to coordinate an array of interprofessional services for consumers and their families. On a daily basis, Ashley sees firsthand the needs of consumers and the commitment of family and friends to care for older people in need of medical attention. Such medical needs range from monitoring of vital signs like heart rate and blood pressure to advanced interventions associated with cancer. Most care providers have no or limited medical training and few resources to support an often rigorous routine of medical care.

Over time, Ashley begins to document the everyday and medical needs of consumers and their care providers. She organizes her documentation into three broad categories: *basic,* which involves monitoring and medication distribution; *intermediate,* which comprises more physical care like lifting, positioning, ambulation, and feeding; and *advanced,* which necessities medical apparatus and equipment, injections, and multiple medications. Many forms of service delivery involve a variety of activities and a diversity of skills associated with advocacy. Thus, one of the features of this book is that it describes advocacy as a major feature in all social work practice, including macro practice involving program, policy, and personnel development.

## LEARNING OBJECTIVES

After reading this chapter you should be able to:

1. Define the term *advocacy* in the context of macro practice
2. Discuss ethical principles and standards in relation to advocacy
3. Describe the connection between advocacy and macro practice
4. Define the advocacy practice and policy model (APPM)
5. Understand the theoretical foundations of the APPM
6. Describe how the APPM applies to macro social work practice

## WHAT IS ADVOCACY?

People have the right to control their lives, but sometimes life circumstances (e.g., financial hardship, health-care issues, lack of employment, or social attitudes) minimize their ability to exercise free choice or represent personal interests in a meaningful way. It is often in these circumstances that social workers' advocacy can enhance an individual's right to be heard and create spaces where views, wishes, and needs are respected and acted upon.

©iStockphoto.com/ kate_sept2004

PHOTO 4.1
Social workers create supportive environments through interactions.

Advocacy involves effectively communicating with people possessing power and privilege over a particular condition or situation, so that decisions can empower and strengthen consumers rather than worsening circumstances. Restated, advocacy is taking action to assist people, groups, and communities to effectively promote their wants, secure rights, represent interests, and obtain services. Table 4.1 lists skills and traits that are often used in advocacy action to promote dignity, security, social inclusion, and equality by shifting the balance of power.

The goal of advocacy is not merely to represent the views of another but also to enable people to speak and act for themselves. Advocacy in all of its forms helps ensure that people, particularly those who are most vulnerable in society, are able to

- Have their voice heard on issues that are important to them
- Defend and safeguard their rights
- Have their views and wishes genuinely considered when decisions are being made about their lives

Advocacy is a process of supporting and enabling people to

- Express their views and concerns
- Access information and services
- Defend and promote their rights and responsibilities
- Explore choices and options

**TABLE 4.1**
Important Advocacy Skills and Traits

| | | |
|---|---|---|
| Organization | Concise writing | Timeliness |
| Fact finding | Respectful communication | Patience |
| Problem identification | Perspectives | Tenacity |
| Identifying decision makers | Resourcefulness | Long-term commitment |
| Collaborative | Humble | Knowledge of government |
| Articulate | Creativity | Analytical competencies |

*Source:* Paraphrased from Schneider and Lester (2001).

## Time to Think 4.1

Refer to the opening case. Consider Ashley's professional knowledge and skill base and how she uses both practice and policy to enhance the quality of life for people in their community. When considering the medical nature of her work and interprofessional practice, how might nurses, occupational therapists, physical therapists, and other health-care professionals be embraced and included in Ashley's effort? In your own life, how has the quality and efficacy of a service(s) affected not only your life but also the lives of those around you?

Advocacy involves a number of activities, most of which consist of ways of "getting involved" with developing or changing policies, legislation, practices, personnel, projects, and programs through education, negotiation, and persuasion (Hoefer, 2012). Specific tasks include working with politicians, legislatures, and agencies for policy development; seeking changes through involvement with legal systems (e.g., courts and law officials); educating and influencing major stakeholders (e.g., politicians and public officials); using media to inform and sway public option; and promoting change through demonstrations, boycotts, and protest (Walker, 1991).

It is important to consider several interrelated themes when examining advocacy's essential features. The first is the relationship between advocacy and social justice. **Social justice** is conceptualized by social workers in various ways ranging from a utilitarian perspective, which weighs benefits and harms to determine the greatest good for the largest numbers of people, to the idea of egalitarianism, which advances the notion of avoiding extreme inequalities in order to create a just society (Garcia & Van Sorest, 2006). In this book, we apply a human rights approach to social justice, whereby basic human needs are met, without discrimination, through the equitable sharing of resources (Garcia & Van Sorest, 2006).

Advocacy from a social justice perspective supports a sense of empowerment where relatively powerless individuals or groups, regardless of their race, gender, or class, gain support to influence or challenge the more powerful elements in society. Consequently, advocacy plays a significant role in enhancing consumers' sense of autonomy to advance and make changes in their world, both individually and structurally. The intersections of advocacy, empowerment, and social justice are evident when consumers speak and promote causes and issues for themselves. Thus, the intent and outcome of advocacy is to promote power, instill confidence and dignity, and advance choices in life's conditions.

Social work advocacy also intersects with a sense of empowerment. With empowerment as a theme in advocacy, social workers ensure consumers are as mindful, active, and present in decisions about and for them. Empowerment can be accomplished as social workers

- Promote, model, and deliver self-advocacy tools/examples
- Encourage supportive decision making to ensure that consumers are intrinsically involved in the actions that affect their lives

- Design or select methods of advocacy action in which consumers offer feedback and guidance to ensure they have a say in their own lives and become enabled to access relevant services
- Record, applaud, and celebrate the outcomes achieved by consumers
- Identify ways for consumers to become involved in research, civic, governmental, and political processes influencing decision making

Another theme present in advocacy is the recognition of the existing strengths of consumers. Here the goal of advocacy is not merely to represent the views of another but also to enable consumers to use and develop abilities, skills, and active voices to seek important rights and confront inequalities. In this way, advocacy expands the participation of consumers in the development and implementation of various strategies (e.g., involving policies, programs, projects, politics, and personnel) to best address needs and reshape existing practices and institutions.

## Time to Think 4.2

Take a moment to list your strengths and those of a community familiar to you. What quickly comes to mind and why? Have you used your personal and community strengths to enhance the quality of your life and that of others? If so, how? Identify strengths you like to enhance or build upon as a result of attending college in relationship to large-scale, macro-level change?

## ADVOCACY AND ETHICS

Like many professions, social work follows a *Code of Ethics* that guides professional conduct with consumers of services. The *Code* comprises four sections: The "Preamble" summarizes the profession's mission and values, the "Purpose of the *Code of Ethics*" introduces an overview of the *Code*'s primary functions and provides a guide to deliberate ethical dilemmas, "Ethical Principles" integrates social work's values with **ethical principles**, and "Ethical Standards" states specific ethical standards that guide social work practice (National Association of Social Workers, 2018).

As seen in Table 4.2, ethical principles form the foundation of social work values as seen in practice and policy. The ethical principle of social justice underpins advocacy action by social workers as does the principle on dignity and worth of the person.

Advocacy is very much a part of the ethical standards to the profession of social work. As stated in the *Code of Ethics,* social work activities must demonstrate ethical responsibilities to consumers, colleagues, in practice settings, as professionals, and to the broader society (National Association of Social Workers, 2018).

**TABLE 4.2**
The Ethical Principles of Social Work

| Value | Ethical Principle | Description |
|---|---|---|
| **Service** | *Social workers' primary goal is to help people in need and to address social problems.* | Social workers elevate service to others above self-interest. Social workers draw on their knowledge, values, and skills to help people in need and to address social problems. Social workers are encouraged to volunteer some portion of their professional skills with no expectation of significant financial return (pro bono service). |
| **Social justice** | *Social workers challenge social injustice. Social workers pursue social change, particularly with and on behalf of vulnerable and oppressed individuals and groups of people.* | Social workers' social change efforts are focused primarily on issues of poverty, unemployment, discrimination, and other forms of social injustice. These activities seek to promote sensitivity to and knowledge about oppression and cultural and ethnic diversity. Social workers strive to ensure access to needed information, services, and resources; equality of opportunity; and meaningful participation in decision making for all people. |
| **Dignity and worth of the person** | *Social workers respect the inherent dignity and worth of the person.* | Social workers treat each person in a caring and respectful fashion, mindful of individual differences and cultural and ethnic diversity. Social workers promote clients' socially responsible self-determination. Social workers seek to enhance clients' capacity and opportunity to change and to address their own needs. Social workers are cognizant of their dual responsibility to clients and to the broader society. They seek to resolve conflicts between clients' interests and the broader society's interests in a socially responsible manner consistent with the values, ethical principles, and ethical standards of the profession. |
| **Importance of human relationships** | *Social workers recognize the central importance of human relationships.* | Social workers understand that relationships between and among people are an important vehicle for change. Social workers engage people as partners in the helping process. Social workers seek to strengthen relationships among people in a purposeful effort to promote, restore, maintain, and enhance the well-being of individuals, families, social groups, organizations, and communities. |

*(Continued)*

**TABLE 4.2** (Continued)

| Value | Ethical Principle | Description |
|---|---|---|
| **Integrity** | *Social workers behave in a trustworthy manner. Social workers are continually aware of the profession's mission, values, ethical principles, and ethical standards and practice in a manner consistent with them.* | Social workers act honestly and responsibly and promote ethical practices on the part of the organizations with which they are affiliated. |
| **Competence** | *Social workers practice within their areas of competence and develop and enhance their professional expertise.* | Social workers continually strive to increase their professional knowledge and skills and to apply them in practice. Social workers should aspire to contribute to the knowledge base of the profession. |

Of particular relevance to advocacy action are the following two standards taken from the *Code of Ethics*: Both standards highlight their role and responsibilities of social workers to maintain their ethical positions in practice and policy.

**6. Social Workers' Ethical Responsibilities to the Broader Society**

6.01 Social Welfare Social workers should promote the general welfare of society, from local to global levels, and the development of people, their communities, and their environments. Social workers should advocate for living conditions conducive to the fulfillment of basic human needs and should promote social, economic, political, and cultural values and institutions that are compatible with the realization of social justice.

**6.04 Social and Political Action**

(a) Social workers should engage in social and political action that seeks to ensure that all people have equal access to the resources, employment, services, and opportunities they require to meet their basic human needs and to develop fully. Social workers should be aware of the impact of the political arena on practice and should advocate for changes in policy and legislation to improve social conditions in order to meet basic human needs and promote social justice.

(b) Social workers should act to expand choice and opportunity for all people, with special regard for vulnerable, disadvantaged, oppressed, and exploited people and groups.

(c) Social workers should promote conditions that encourage respect for cultural and social diversity within the United States and globally. Social workers should promote policies and practices that demonstrate respect for difference, support the expansion of cultural knowledge and resources, advocate for programs and institutions that demonstrate cultural competence, and promote policies that safeguard the rights of and confirm equity and social justice for all people.

(d) Social workers should act to prevent and eliminate domination of, exploitation of, and discrimination against any person, group, or class on the basis of race, ethnicity, national origin, color, sex, sexual orientation, gender identity or expression, age, marital status, political belief, religion, immigration status, or mental or physical ability.



What can be gained from reviewing the excerpts from the *Code of Ethics* on advocacy, and its connection to social justice, is the profession's obligation to practice advocacy with consumers, not for, and regardless of an employment setting. Advocacy is identified and supported as a critical professional role for social workers and transcends types of services and programs and population groups served.

## Time to Think 4.3

In the context of social work, an **ethical dilemma** is a situation in which two or more professionally identified values are in conflict. For example, a consumer wants to give a social worker a gift for services received or an agency administrator wants the social worker to discuss what was said in a staff meeting. When faced with an ethical dilemma, social workers turn to the profession's *Code of Ethics*. Please give thought to an ethical dilemma you might confront when advocating with consumers for macro-level change and how you could resolve the situation. What values and principles did you rely on to guide your actions?

Strategies associated with advocacy have expanded over the past decade with the increased use of social media. Specifically, electronic advocacy constitutes an aspect of advocacy action for examination and consideration in relationship to ethical principles and standards. Referred to as **online advocacy** or **cyber activism**, advanced communication tools are used to expand the reach and speed that social workers can connect with consumers (Delany, 2006). Queiro-Tajallil, Campbell, and McNutt (2003, pp. 154–156) identified four elements of electronic advocacy:

1. Issue research: Access to information is significantly enhanced through the Internet. This access is vital to informing consumers and colleagues of educational material, research findings, political issues, and resources.
2. Information dissemination and awareness: Websites, blogs, YouTube, Twitter, and other platforms allow individuals, groups, and communities

to communicate quickly in an ongoing manner. Advocates can use these communication devices to inform, educate, and evaluate.

3. Coordination and organizing: Individuals, groups, communities, and organizations use electronic advocacy to rally and inform their supporters. Such communication is rapid, is cost-effective, and allows for tracking messages.

4. Influence: Electronic advocacy can be used to place pressure on those in power by writing letters of support or opposition, comment on particular issues, and engage in other forms of opinion sharing by weighing in on the decision-making process.

The intersection of advocacy and ethics supports the use of high-speed technology to explore and examine the interrelationship of consumers' needs, the ethical obligations of the profession, and possibility of rallying people for macro-level change. With a keen interest in advocacy and keeping ethics in mind, social work students and professionals can use technology to seek new and innovative ways and practices for being change agents.

## ADVOCACY AND MACRO PRACTICE

By now it should be understood that social work integrates values, ethics, empowerment, and advocacy to promote change across systems small and large. Also integral to all social work practice is the engagement with human processes and relationships to alter conditions for the improved well-being of individuals, families, groups, organizations, and communities. In this way, problems and their solutions are viewed from a holistic rather than a fragmented perspective.

This book does not support the longstanding divide between micro and macro social work practice. Rather, practice is viewed as a unified pattern of interventions that integrates community and societal concerns with human and social development (Netting et al., 2016). This is not to minimize defined roles, career paths, and specializations in social work but is meant to suggest that to understand people and their life conditions in their environment requires a continuum of methods that span the micro and macro skill base. Thus, when speaking of macro practice, the importance of micro practice philosophies and methods is not to be minimized but rather viewed as a component of the preparation needed for effective macro practice (Pritzker & Applewhite, 2015).



**PHOTO 4.2** Advocacy means taking and defending a position.

How does the relationship between micro and macro practice affect advocacy? To answer this question, in professional development, consider the need to develop alternative helping strategies embracing multiple system sizes, collect evidence at multiple level sizes, understand power (e.g., power bases and dynamics), take well-thought-out risks, and be persistent with consumers of services and their causes.

## Develop Alternative Strategies

Macro practice necessitates a comprehensive assessment of the current state of a problem or condition in which assumptions are tested. Reamer (1993, p. 2) identified five reasons in which assumptions may vary: (1) the goals of the government, (2) the rights of citizens in relation to the state, (3) the obligation of the state to its citizens, (4) the nature of political or civil liberty, and (5) the nature of social justice (Netting, 2005). For social workers, assessment of assumptions leads to an analysis of divergent views and the possibilities of alternatives while entertaining the importance of various systems (e.g., individuals, families, groups, organizations, communities, and society). As an example, consider the persistent problem of hunger in the United States. To develop alternatives to national hunger, assumptions about the goals of government and the obligation to citizens must be assessed to better understand the root of the problem. It is through this multilevel, complex assessment of viewpoints that alternatives to hunger can be identified and described along with a sense of the support and opposition to any advocacy change effort.

Through the assessment of a problem and a critical review of alternatives, a vision or a new perspective can emerge. Working with consumers to identify the "what if . . ." enhances a social worker's ability to communicate not only the proposed change but also the advocacy strategies to drive the change.

## Collect Evidence

For a social worker to advocate for change, there needs to be evidence that a problem exists, accompanied by evidence that the proposed change has merit. In both cases, evidence is needed. According to the National Association of Social Workers (2018), **evidence-based practice** is a process where the best evidence available is used to answer a question pertaining to an individual, family, group, community, or organization. In order for evidence-based practice to occur, there must be research findings based on well-researched interventions. Table 4.3 offers a process that evaluates the change effort based on the information collected from consumers. Consumer participation in research endeavors adds the potential for consumer empowerment and the active use of consumer voices in various research questions and decisions.

In terms of advocacy action, social workers must consider the extent to which the evidence-based strategies or interventions are adoptable and adaptable for a particular situation. This requires not only research and critical thinking skills but also a keen sense of anticipated and unanticipated consequences. For example, research findings frequently lack generalizability when considering the population group served and settings.

**TABLE 4.3**
Evidence-Based Macro Practice Process

| | |
|---|---|
| Step 1 | Convert information needs into a relevant question for practice in a community and/or organizational context. |
| Step 2 | Track down with maximum efficiency the best evidence to answer a question. |
| Step 3 | Critically appraise the evidence for its validity and usefulness. |
| Step 4 | Provide clients with appropriate information about the efficacy of different interventions and collaborate with them in making the final decision in selecting the best practice. |
| Step 5 | Apply the results of this appraisal in making policy/practice decisions that affect organizational and/or community change. |
| Step 6 | Assess the fidelity implementation of the macro practice intervention. |
| Step 7 | Evaluate service outcomes from implementing the best practice. |

*Source:* Adapted from Hoefer and Jordan (2008).

## Understand Power

Social workers must recognize that no matter what consumer group they are working with, the influence of power and politics is inevitable. To effectively advocate in any format, workers must understand social and **political power** and develop skills to analyze power sources and dynamics. Attributes of power include self-interest, possession of resources (e.g., money, wealth, and technology), influence, and the ability to impose value orientations on others. It is important to recognize that in many social contexts (e.g., organizations, communities, and societies), power is aligned with factors such as race, ethnicity, gender, sexual orientation, and religion, which serve to privilege or disadvantage various individuals and groups of people. However, with ethical principles and standards in mind and the use of analytical thinking, it is often possible to embrace politics and seek ways to effectively influence power brokers for the greater good of consumers of services.

Adapted from the work of Jansson (1998), the following list reflects the nature of power relationships.

- Distribution of Power Relationships
    - What persons, interests, and factions are likely to participate in certain policy deliberations?
    - What are their power resources?
    - What are their likely positions on a proposal?
    - How strongly do they hold these positions?
- Political Stakes in an Issue
    - What political benefits and risks will I encounter if I participate in certain policy deliberations?
    - Should I be a leader, a follower, or a bystander?

- Political Feasibility
    - What patterns of opposition and support are likely to be associated with specific policy options?
    - Which position, on balance, should I support?
- Political Strategy
    - What power resources do I (or my allies) currently have that are relevant to these deliberations?
    - What power resources might I (or my allies) develop that will be relevant to these deliberations?
    - What strategies will we use as the deliberations proceed?
- Revising Strategy
    - How should I change my strategy in light of evolving political realities, including my opponents' likely moves?
    - As the political realities changes, how should my role change?

What emerges from the model is that political decisions are usually shaped in a give-and-take manner that highlights deliberations, the scope of the conflict, and the influence of affiliations. Conflicts occur in a context or setting and are influenced by the prevailing power structure (key groups of people and individuals). For example, the context of an organization could be its rural location where new ideas and people new to the organization are initially met with suspicion. An affiliation is often represented by membership in a political party, association, or a recognized group.

Whatever the composition of the power base, social workers need to avoid attacking the character, ideology, assumptions, and motivations of the opponents. Rather, successful advocacy is often attributed to personal credibility, persistence, and willingness to compromise. What seems to be clear is that negotiating political power does not always conform to a formulaic strategy or approach. Layers of potential support along with barriers to change intersect and call for adroit advocacy and negotiating strategies if a substantive redistribution of power is to occur.

## Take a Risk

It seems that an appreciable portion of social work involves taking a risk of some sort. For instance, it may be that a social worker advocates for employment opportunities with teenagers knowing that there will be backlash from unemployed adults. It could be that an agency is having administrative problems and people are hesitant to speak out because of possible employment and/or salary repercussions. Nevertheless, the agency social worker assists with the research and compiles a list of concerns for the administration. Such examples of risk taking are certainly chancy but at times unavoidable.

When a risk is taken, social workers are usually able to forecast an anticipated consequence of possible consequences from the selected intervention, but at times the end result can be a surprise to all involved. Given the resources of time and energy, social workers must consider the cost and benefits to any advocacy action taken, especially actions and effort that come with considerable physical, psychological, social, and economic consequences.

There are advantages to some risk taking. New partnerships and coalitions can form, and successful advocacy in one instance can provide evidence for the development of another advocacy action. Throughout the risk-taking assessment, the social worker must keep the consumers closely informed and aligned. Much as with micro-level practice, consumers of services need to exert client self-determination. Risk taking should not enhance the status or cause(s) of the social worker but rather reflect the needs and wants of consumers.

### Persistence

Understanding the dynamics of individuals, groups, communities, and organizations involves maintaining a persistently questioning eye. Appreciating the components of life, including norms, values, attitudes, strengths, and areas to improvement, takes not only time but also reflection and ongoing communication with others (e.g., consumers, colleagues, and supervisors). As might be expected, it is essential to keep recognizing and confronting ill-conceived and shortsighted notions and biases before moving forward on any advocacy action.

Persistence, with a long-term vision of change, is seen as essential to advocacy but is not always a component of all forms of social work practice. Specifically, when working with a consumer in an agency setting, social workers are usually required to follow a timetable associated with delivering billable services. Usually the timetable follows a linear approach, whereby an intake form is completed, a bio-psycho-social history is collected and written, a service plan for treatment is designed, and a number of sessions are scheduled with the social worker, as determined by some sort of insurance or government payment plan.

In comparison to a linear plan of intervention, macro advocacy action can be more fluid and require significant flexibility on the part of social workers, consumers, and agency expectations. These challenges point to the need for more persistence by all involved, especially the social worker and consumers. Undoubtedly when integrating macro advocacy into practice, researching and documenting best practices and effective advocacy actions is necessary when examining persistence and relationship building with stakeholders.

## Time to Think 4.4

List at least three ways in which developing alternative strategies, collecting evidence, understanding power, taking a risk, or persistence can cut across and/or bridge micro and macro social work. Describe a situation in which social workers can be called upon to attend to the immediate needs of a consumer, but they are also involved in organizing and building systems to prevent the needs from occurring again.

## THE ADVOCACY PRACTICE AND POLICY MODEL (APPM)

Advocacy in social work practice involves activities to "defend, represent, or otherwise advance the cause of one or more clients at the individual, group, organizational, or community level in order to promote social justice" (Hoefer, 2012, p. 3). Advocating for social justice is a complex process, containing a number of key elements for consideration. Cox, Tice, and Long (2019), as seen in Figure 4.1, offer and describe a dynamic advocacy model that identifies four interlocking tenets (economic and social justice, supportive environment, human needs and rights, and political access) as factors for reflection when advocating for change. It is noted that "in social work practice with real people and situations, these tenets have considerable overlap with and influence on one another" (Cox et al., 2019, p. 69). Although not exhaustive, the advocacy model and its tenets are offered "to prompt critical and multidimensional thought and discussion about advocacy in social work practice" (Cox et al., 2019, p. 69).

A succinct description of the four tenets of the dynamic advocacy model is provided in Table 4.4.

What is important when reviewing the **advocacy practice and policy model (APPM)** is that the four tenets are not meant to be identified as distinctive or independent from one another. Rather, the tenets overlap and inform, as well as influence one another, when placed in the context of consumers. Thus, the model is designed to encourage critical and intersectional thought, discussion, and action related to practice and policy advocacy.

**FIGURE 4.1**
Theoretical Framework for the Advocacy Practice and Policy Model

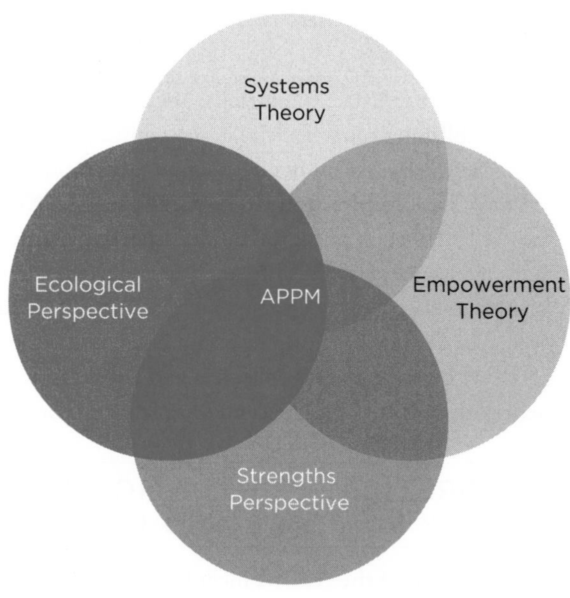


*Source:* Cox, Tice, and Long (2019).

**TABLE 4.4**
The Four Tenets of the Advocacy Practice and Policy Model (APPM)

| | |
|---|---|
| Economic and social justice | Emphasis is placed on advancing economic and social rights for all people. These efforts are often actualized through the development and establishment of liberties, rights, duties, access, opportunities, and the active voices of people in specific domains (e.g., education, employment, housing, religion, voting, safety, citizenship, and marriage). |
| Supportive environment | Examination of the total social, economic, and physical (natural) environment takes place and is aligned with the aforementioned systems and the ecological and person-in-the-environment perspectives. A supportive environment for advocacy can be derived from significant others, friends, family members, churches, companies, associations, community entities, and community and national groups and organizations. Natural and tangible aspects of the environment are also important considerations; these could include factors such as buildings, use of land, monetary support, water, food, computer access, technology, and so on. |
| Human needs and rights | Special consideration in advocacy needs to be given to who is defining human needs and why. Implicit in the definition of human needs and rights is power. How should and can consumers of services be involved in defining human needs and rights? The active participation of consumers of services in defining human needs and rights is highly aligned with the notion of empowerment and the ability of consumers to influence and affect decision-making processes. |
| Political access | Who has access to political power and why? Identifying key stakeholders and their influence over policy and legislative development is crucial. Politicians are responsible to the public and their constituency but often beholden to the people and political parties who significantly donated to the campaign fund and assisted with their election. Political access typically involves the building of relationships with politicians, elected officials, and key stakeholders. McBeath (2016, p. 9) identifies "developing external advocacy networks" (e.g., between professional, public, businesses, nonprofit, and private entities) as a top strategy for reenvisioning macro social work practice. |

The APPM indicates that justice is integral to social work policy and practice by "promoting and establishing equal liberties, rights, duties, and opportunities in the social institutions (economy, policy, family, religion, education, etc.) of a society for all [people]" (Long, Tice, & Morrison, 2006, p. 208; see also Cox et al., 2019, p. 69). Thus, the APPM fosters a "big picture perspective" of people in their environments that enables social workers to analyze issues outside of a box and focus not only on the amelioration of an issue but also, equally as important, its prevention (Reisch, 2016). The idea of purposeful change is a theme that runs throughout the APPM by encouraging collective and collaborative practice and policy development with consumers at the center of planned change.

## THEORETICAL FOUNDATION OF THE ADVOCACY PRACTICE AND POLICY MODEL

The **theoretical foundation of the APPM** includes systems and empowerment theory, the strengths perspective, and the ecological perspective. These theories support the importance of considering both problems and strengths, as well as the encompassing nature of people and systems involved in advocacy—individuals (the micro level) and organizations, communities, and societies (the macro level) (Cox et al., 2019).

- *Systems theory:* In **systems theory**, advocacy takes place in systems of all sizes. Often an issue arises by way of an individual or group of consumers but is rooted in the very structure of a governmental, economic, or political system. An example is homelessness, which affects individuals on a daily basis but reflects the employment status, salary scales, the presence of affordable living, the housing market, and banking in relation to mortgages.
- *Empowerment theory:* It has already been stated in this chapter that social workers build relationships with consumers of various sizes. **Empowerment theory** gives voices to the needs and desires of consumers in such a way that the balance of power shifts and consumers recognize that they can be heard and far-reaching change can occur. Marriage equality reflects the empowerment of the gay community to realize their rights as citizens. The ramifications of marriage equality extend beyond a couple to a family, community, organizations, and local, state, and federal policy.
- *Strengths perspective:* This chapter highlights the importance of the **strengths perspective** when advocating with consumers. The APPM recognizes strengths across consumer systems as resources to support any change effort. An example of this is Wounded Warriors (www.woundedwarriorproject.org), an organization of veterans who have sustained injuries. They advocate from a strengths perspective by educating the public of their injuries while demonstrating their immeasurable ability to succeed in all phases of life, including work, leisure, and family life.
- *Ecological perspective:* The physical and natural environment are significant elements across consumer systems. The community where a person lives, the air, soil, trash, sewage, and parks in their community are but a few examples of the environment. Vulnerable communities, including those in both rural and urban areas, challenge the health and mental well-being of people. Given this, it makes sense that the APPM assumes a holistic perspective when assessing and advocating for change in the environment. Earthjustice (www.earthjustice.org) does just this. As a nonprofit advocacy group, Earthjustice uses an **ecological perspective** to advocate on the federal and international level for policies that protect the environment, including issues related to toxic cleanup, synthetic chemicals in baked goods, and the leaking of methane oil and gases.

## Time to Think 4.5

The advocacy practice and policy model is a way of conceptualizing advocacy and the four tenets—economic and social justice, a supportive environment, human needs and rights, and political access—to ensure ethical and effective practice. An idea behind the model is that the tenets are dynamic and shift constantly; they are also interlocking because it is hard to define boundaries between the tenets. Can you think of an issue facing the nation where advocacy is needed and the APPM could be applied? What role would consumers play when implementing the model?

## HOW THE APPM APPLIES TO MACRO PRACTICE

The dichotomy of micro and macro practice historically imposed on social work knowledge can divide the profession's content and skill application into discrete fragments. In response, the APPM suggests that both micro and macro knowledge and skills are essential to good social work outcomes and supports a bridge between the two. To promote a more unified approach, attention is given to the Association of Community Organization and Social Administration (ACOSA), a research, teaching, and practice organization that has attempted to understand and define the goals and competencies of macro social work through research, best practice identification, and effective teaching/learning strategies (Gamble, 2011). The overriding conclusion is that micro and macro practice reflect a commitment to values of the social work profession and share the profession's respect for diversity in all forms as seen in social justice and human dignity and multisystem-level change.

MARK RALSTON/Staff/Getty Images

**PHOTO 4.3** On November 24, 2010, a group of Long Beach homeowners was faced with eviction over the holiday period. Housing is critical to economic and social justice.

With this in mind, Figure 4.2 illustrates the bridge between micro and macro practice used to advocate for consumers across systems.

The listed activities highlight that any change advocated by social workers is purposeful and planned and supported by knowledge and skills based on research and practice experience (Reisch, 2016). Understanding the dynamic nature of the tenets of the APPM is seen as an essential component of practice with every population and problem with which social work is involved. What the model implies is that participation of consumers in the identification of needs and desired advocacy outcomes is essential, as is the development and implementation of advocacy strategies and the ongoing evaluation of such strategies.

An example of an advocacy action that requires micro and macro skills and follows the tenets of the APPM is depicted in Table 4.5. The significance of

**FIGURE 4.2**
Advocacy Activities Related to the Advocacy Practice and Policy Model

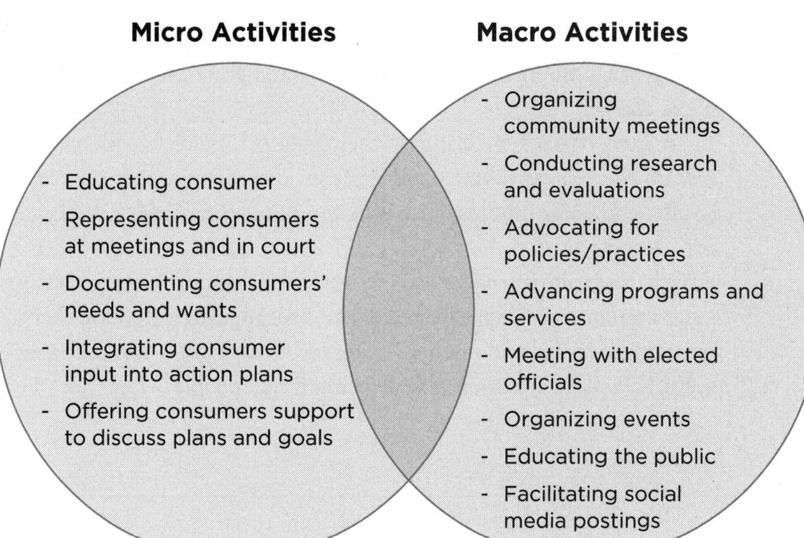


*Source:* Adapted from Reisch (2016).

**TABLE 4.5**
Visiting Legislators

| | |
|---|---|
| • Develop and maintain a good working relationship directly with the legislators in a district.<br>• Always call ahead for an appointment and briefly explain the purpose of the meeting.<br>• Be on time and professionally dressed.<br>• Keep all comments to the point and limit any presentation/discussion to the time scheduled, unless the legislator extends the meeting.<br>• Use bill numbers and titles when possible.<br>• Tell the legislator why the issue is important to consumers in their district. | • When possible and appropriate, bring consumers of services to talk with the legislators.<br>• Ask the legislator for his or her position on the issue and how he or she will vote. If supportive, thank him or her for the support. If undecided or for removing funds for services, offer additional information on the issue.<br>• Always be courteous, even if the legislator disagrees with a particular position on the issue.<br>• Leave information for the legislator to review after the meeting.<br>• Thank the legislator for his or her time.<br>• Send a short letter thanking the legislator for the meeting. |

*Source:* Adapted from National Association of Social Workers (2018).

this table is that it highlights the need for micro, relational skills to engage a legislator and the macro aspects of practice to connect and convey the needs and wants of consumers with a broad vision of change. Macro roles and functions for social workers have traditionally been conceptualized as the use of organizing, planning, administering, and evaluating knowledge and skills for producing social change (Meenghan, Washington, & Ryan, 1982). The combination of micro and macro practice is seen in the presentation of a social issue; the communication of an initiative that aims to organize, plan, and assist people in their communities; the advocacy for and with a population; and the education of a power base for social change.

A face-to-face meeting with legislators is an excellent opportunity to discuss the relevant issues and policies and their impact on consumers, their family, and communities. The following guidelines may be helpful when visiting a legislator.

The overriding goal of the APPM is to support effective efforts that promote human rights, empowerment, and social justice; develop inclusiveness that respects diversity; and open an array of opportunities for the economic, social, political, and environmental well-being for all people.

---



---

## SUMMARY

The social work profession faces many national and international changes in an ever-changing world. Social workers are called upon to address these issues through advocacy action that bridges micro and macro practice across systems.

In this chapter, the advocacy model for practice and policy (APPM) is introduced as a model to guide social workers in a manner that combines micro and macro practice to bring about planned change. Throughout the chapter, social justice, empowerment, values, and ethics are discussed to highlight the foundation of social work. Special attention is given to organizations and asks workers to make the transition from thinking about interventions on the micro level to conceptualizing methods of enriching the life of organizations, communities, and society through macro interventions. One bridge between these practice areas is empowerment. In the larger context, the advocacy related to the empowerment process ensures that program design, policies, and organizational development promote consumer input, self-determination, power, and dignity.

---

## TOP 10 KEY CONCEPTS

advocacy practice and policy model (APPM) 87
empowerment theory 89
ethical dilemma 81
ethical principles 78
evidence-based practice 83
online advocacy 81
political power 84
social justice 77
systems theory 89
theoretical foundation of the APPM 88

## DISCUSSION QUESTIONS

1. Consider the advocacy action that occurs on your university or college campus. What issues are students, faculty, and staff addressing through advocacy action and why?
2. What does social justice mean to you based on your life experiences? What factors have influenced your definition of social justice and why?
3. Describe the importance of the concept of empowerment as it relates to your life as a university or college student. What does empowerment have to do with our sense of confidence?
4. Examine the tenets of the advocacy practice and policy model. Which tenet is easier for you to understand and which one is more abstract? Consider the reasons behind your answer.
5. Does online advocacy have appeal to you in terms of a strategy to initiate planned change? What ethical dilemmas are associated with this form of advocacy?

## EXERCISES

1. As a social work student, what are your thoughts about the bridge between micro and macro practice? Ask at least two of your instructors, along with your field instructor, their opinion on the topic. What were your main takeaway points from the discussions? Were there any surprises?
2. Go online and review the website of a nonprofit advocacy group. What did you learn from the posted information that was of particular interest to you? Did the website offer you opportunities to join advocacy efforts? If so, consider why the efforts did or did not appeal to you.
3. In the chapter, attention is given to political action with regard to visiting a legislator. Who are your state and federal legislators and what political parties do they represent? Visit your legislators' websites and read about their policy positions on various issues. Given what you learned, would you endorse their reelection? How does your answer reflect your values?
4. The Association of Community Organization and Social Administration (ACOSA) (http://www.acosa.org/) is mentioned in this chapter. Visit the organization's website to learn of its mission and goals. Is ACOSA an organization you would join? Please explain your response.
5. Table 4.1 is related to social workers engaged in macro practice. Review the list in the context of your developing skill base and personal traits. What are your particular strengths and what areas would you like to improve as a social work student?
6. Everytown For Gun Safety (everytown.org) is an advocacy group in support of gun control and is composed of citizens and community-based organizations. Everytown advocates primarily through text messages and website updates. Visit the Everytown site. Consider what strategies Everytown uses to connect personal issues to public concerns. What ethical principles does Everytown embrace?

## ONLINE RESOURCES

- You might be surprised by the sheer number of advocacy groups recruiting volunteers and donations. Visit https://www.opensecrets.org/527s/types.php to view a list of such organizations and learn of their focus and goals.
- The National Association of Social Workers (NASW) was mentioned throughout the chapter. Visit the NASW website at https://www.socialworkers.org/ to view the complete *Code of Ethics* and its relationship to all facets of social work practice.
- Go to https://www.socialworkers.org/Advocacy/Social-Justice and learn how social work defines and advocates for social justice. Also, this site provides information on Social Work Talks, a podcast on social justice.
- Lobbyists are paid advocates for a specific cause or issue. Visit https://lobbyingdisclosure.house.gov/register.html to learn how to register as a lobbyist and what the role of the lobbyist is in the political process.
- The Carter Center, in partnership with Emory University, is committed to human rights, the alleviation of human suffering, the prevention and resolution of conflicts, and the enhancement of freedom and democracy. Visit the Carter Center's website at https://www.cartercenter.org/about/index.html to see how advocacy strategies are put into action.

# Understanding and Enriching Organizational Life

## NINA ADVANCES DIVERSITY AND INCLUSION AT THE BEHAVIORAL HEALTH CENTER

Nina is a social worker at a small behavioral health center. As a result of a retirement, her agency is seeking to hire a new social worker to provide counseling for an average of 25 sessions with consumers per week, primarily African American and Hispanic/Latino adults. Nina is very aware that the six current social workers on the counseling staff at her center are Caucasian. Routinely, consumers of services ask about the availability of either an African American or a Hispanic/Latino social worker as their counseling provider. Nina volunteered to be a member of the search committee and has begun advocating for ways (e.g., advertisement, networking, signing bonus, startup packaging, etc.) to encourage, identify, and secure a racially and ethnically diverse candidate pool. The center is making a concerted effort to pursue and recruit African American and Hispanic/Latino social workers for this position. Indeed, the organization's leadership has decided that the search process will not move to the phone interview state until a minimum of two viable African American and/or Hispanic/Latino social workers can be interviewed.

## LEARNING OBJECTIVES

After reading this chapter, you should be able to

1. Understand and describe the relevance of organizations to social work practice
2. Identify and understand key organizational aspects for use in macro-level practice
3. Examine the subsystems that make up an organization and describe how they interact
4. Describe the importance of organizational culture and values, and apply contemporary orientations to organizational change
5. Examine ethical issues that may occur within organizations

## THE RELEVANCE OF ORGANIZATIONS IN SOCIAL WORK

Organizations, such as private and public social service agencies, must be well informed and flexible if they are to flourish and thrive in an ever-changing environment. Organizations must be adaptable to assess current and future needs, envision possible service strategies, and engage in often far-reaching change. Such change might involve promoting a diverse labor force, introducing training programs for staff, designing new programs or services, developing new community-based collaborations, serving new consumers, and securing new funding streams.

Organizations are typically required to establish their own policies, rules, and procedures based on guidelines that specify where, how, when, and to whom services are to be provided. Such policies affect the behavior of social workers and consumers of services. The impact of organizational policies and procedures for professionals and consumers of services are wide ranging. As one example, Evans (2013) examines the relationship between the proliferation of organizational rules and policies on the professional discretion and freedom of social workers, suggesting that social workers can retain professional autonomy and choice, even when practicing in rule-saturated agencies.

It is also essential that social workers examine and engage in organizational life because of the environment within which contemporary social problems exist. For example, consider the complexities of poverty, substance use, mental health, violence, and health care. With all these issues, a maze of organizations and subsequent services has been designed and operates to address the needs of people in their communities. Indeed, organizations have far-reaching influences on people's lives. Think about the impact that organizations have had in your own life. More than likely you were born in a hospital, were educated through a system of schools, belonged to various clubs or associations, attended a faith-based gathering, and were employed in various settings. Organizations are at the core of all of these services, memberships, and activities, so it should come as no surprise to you that macro social work practice involves studying these important social systems. This point is expressed by Etzioni (1964) in his classic book on organizations:

> We are born in organizations, educated by organizations, and most of us spend much of our lives working for organizations. We spend much of our leisure time paying, playing, and praying in organizations. Most of us will die in an organization, and when the time comes for burial, the largest organization of all—the state—must grant official permission. (p. 1)

This chapter will acquaint you with the basic concepts and attributes of organizations, which includes the relevance and influence of human diversity

## Time to Think 5.1

Each organization is characterized by unique values, norms, culture, and composition. Take a moment and identify the racial, ethnic, and gender makeup of an organization playing an important role in your life. Is or would the organization be open to promoting human diversity? If so, how might organizational life be enriched through a concerted effort to advance inclusion and diversity? Given the mission of this organization, what other forms of diversity (e.g., cognitive or physical challenge, age, sexual orientation, and social-economic class) might also be important to consider? What about the presence of intersectionality in diversity?

(e.g., as highlighted by Nina's experience in this chapter's opening vignette). The idea of organizations as open systems is examined and emphasized. Sections on organization development and the role of organization developers present a number of techniques by which macro practitioners can assess and help organizational systems improve their functioning. Empowerment, leading to consumer participation and a healthy organizational culture, is a central theme throughout the chapter.

## THE CONCEPT OF ORGANIZATION

Many social workers likely reference and/or define organization on the basis of their agency experiences. As with other complex terms, everyday definitions can vary, especially when considering the context in which a term is conceptualized and used. However, basically, an organization is a group of people intentionally and formally organized to accomplish a common goal or set of goals. Traditionally, **organizations** have been identified in terms of the following kinds of attributes: a formal membership, self-identification, geographical and/or physical presence, and shared cultural values and norms (Olsen, 1978).

Organizations are important because of their pervasiveness and power. Historically, the influence of human assistance organizations in the United States can be traced to the Great Depression, when large-scale public organizations were first introduced for the provision of human services. The programs of the New Deal created an infrastructure of organizations at the federal level that became both the foundation of the welfare state and the first large government human service bureaucracies (Netting, Kettner, & McMurtry, 1998). Large public bureaucracies and nationwide networks of affiliated agencies in the private sector greatly changed the size and complexity of human service organizations. As stated by Perrow (1979),

> Because of the superiority as a social tool over other forms of organization, bureaucracy generates an enormous degree of unregulated and often unperceived social power; and this power is placed in the hands of very few leaders. (p. 7)

As the size, complexity, and sophistication of organizations changed, so did the role of macro practitioners within these organizations. Trends such as the size of human service organizations, their complexity, the diversity of services, advancements in technology, and changes in standard budgetary policies all forced administrators to seek new skills. Implicit in these changes was a shift in the orientation of macro practice from external considerations to internal considerations, including operational efficiency and program effectiveness. At this juncture, the practice of social work supported a high degree of specialization based on professional training. Individuals were given specific job assignments and organized in levels based on both education and expertise. Finally, social workers became accountable for achieving certain goals related to consumers and the organization as a whole.

The auspice of human service organizations can generally be classified as either public or private. **Public agencies** are typically funded and supported as a "result of a mandate, policy initiative, or law, from a public (e.g., federal, state, county, or municipal) decision-making body" (Long, 2004, p. 6). Public human service agencies are often designed to implement a wide range of programs serving a large number of consumers, often via a bureaucratic organizational structure and division of labor. Conversely, **private agencies** are predominantly supported by private (e.g., donated and contributed) monies targeting smaller, specified population groups and administered in a manner deemed necessary by the funding source(s) (Long, 2004).

The goals of an organization, public or private, include some that are explicit (deliberate and recognized) and others that are implicit (operating unrecognized). Organizational goals embrace (1) **vision**, an image of how the organization should be working; (2) **mission**, an overall purpose; (3) *values,* priorities in the organization's activities; and (4) *strategies,* several overall general approaches to reaching goals.

The importance of goals in human service organizations relates to the need for a standard by which to measure the success of social workers and of the organization. That is, effective performance, on whatever level one operates, must be related to some standard of evaluation. This goal model of evaluating an organization's effectiveness is built on Weber's (1924/1947) studies of bureaucracy and assumes that organizations are designed to achieve specific ends and that decision makers purposively act in accordance with goals (Maynard-Moody, 1987, p. 172). Goals are the organizing principles around which procedures, staff responsibilities, and structures are built.

## TYPES OF ORGANIZATIONS

Macro social workers may find themselves employed in an array of organizations. Predominant types of organizations differentiated in the literature include the following: public, nonprofit, for-profit, and self-help groups.

Key differences exist in public- versus private-sector organizations, in that goals and motives vary as do funding sources, governance principles, the relevance of professional autonomy, and the oversight of procedures and actions. Organizations in the private sector often experience greater freedom to operate and make decisions, which are guided by mission statements developed from values (e.g., from religious or humanistic traditions) overseen by a board of trustees or directors. Professionals in private organizations can experience greater autonomy and professional authority as afforded and delegated by the leadership. Employees are often recruited for their alignment to the goals and mission of the sponsoring organization and evaluated on the basis of effectiveness.

Public organizations are governed by laws and public officials emphasizing rules, bureaucratic checks and balances, and efficiencies associated with serving a large number of consumers. Public organizations are accountable to elected and government-appointed officials as well as voters and taxpayers. Agency officials set and enact the organizational goals and desired outcomes in accordance with public policy and law. Social workers and consumers of services often become frustrated with cumbersome procurement, operational, and hiring processes as well as mandated documentation (paperwork) requirements.

## Public and Nonprofit Organizations

Examples of **public organizations** are those government agencies created to serve a large number of people with various needs. The federal agency called the Centers for Medicare & Medicaid Services (CMS) is part of the Department of Health and Human Services (DHHS), formerly known as the Health Care Financing Administration (HCFA). The CMS employs thousands of people, and the head administrator is appointed by the president and confirmed by the Senate. Public organizations include county, state, or federal agencies that are government controlled and resourced through public monies (e.g., taxation). County and state departments of human services are mainstay public organizations servicing children and families across the nation. Police and fire services are other examples of public organizations. Public organizations are unique with regard to transparency, susceptibility to public and political inspection, and vulnerability to criticism. Their goals and outcomes are often publicly scrutinized to ensure productivity and promote high standards. Public organizations are not profit oriented, as they provide a variety of means-tested and qualified services and programs to a multitude of consumers through support from taxpayer dollars. However, public organizations can at times be business oriented in policies and practices, as leaders and managers can bring and implement standards and rules from experience in the private sector.

**Nonprofit organizations** are private organizations that are granted special tax status and designation, often receiving and spending funds to address the organization's mission-driven identified needs with fewer public restrictions, mandates, and oversight. Nonprofit organizations are created to address the needs of specified population groups and do not involve generating profit for owners or investors. Nonprofits can take a variety of forms through sponsorship from entities such as churches/faith-based organizations, neighborhood associations, and charities; labor unions, philanthropic groups, and community hospitals; and universities. If nonprofits generate excess revenues, such funds are used to support the mission and operation of the organization.

The legal forms of nonprofits can be divided into two types: (1) the 501(c)(3) public benefit organizations and (2) 501(c)(4) social welfare organizations. The 501(c)(3) public benefit organizations are eligible for tax deduction donations from individuals or corporations. Advocacy organizations and civic leagues exemplify 501(c)(4) social welfare organizations. The nonprofit Planned Parenthood has both types of 501(c) organizations incorporated. Nonprofits are based on field of interest, which are typically broken up into groupings (e.g., arts, culture, and humanities; education; environment and animals; health; human services; international; foreign affairs; public-societal benefit; religion related; mutual/membership benefit; or unknown/unclassified). Nonprofit organizations make up the nonprofit or philanthropic sector in the United States.

The nonprofit sector fulfills vital functions for modern societies. According to Payton and Moody (2008), there are five roles of the philanthropic sector. These roles are illustrated in Table 5.1.

**TABLE 5.1**
Five Roles Found in Nonprofit Organizations

| Role | Function |
|---|---|
| Service role | Providing services, especially when other sectors do not provide them |
| Advocacy role | Representing and advocating for the interests of diverse consumers, for differing views of the public good and for reform |
| Cultural role | Expressing and preserving values, traditions, and other aspects of culture |
| Civic role | Building community, fostering civic engagement |
| Vanguard role | Providing opportunities for innovation, experimentation |

### For-Profit Organizations

**For-profit organizations** are companies and businesses that charge people or government agencies for their services and products to profit—accumulate resources and wealth. For-profits aim to collect and retain earnings through their operations with a primary concern for their own financial interests. These organizations usually operate in the private sector and are referenced as businesses or companies (e.g., retail stores, restaurants, insurance companies, and real estate companies).

### Self-Help Groups

**Self-help groups** or mutual aid societies are founded by a group of people with common or similar problems (e.g., alcoholism, divorce, health challenges, interpersonal violence) to provide help and support to members of the group. Most self-help groups are either nonprofit organizations or informal organizations.

### Formal and Informal Organizations

Organizations, especially self-help groups, can be formal or informal. **Formal organizations** have a definitive structure and an established decision-making process. It is easy to identify membership and the chain of command and authority in a formal organization. **Informal organizations** can simply be a fluid group of people with similar needs or interests who come together to solve a problem (a block club, neighbors who exchange childcare, volunteers who maintain a food pantry, etc.). It may be difficult to discern who is or who is not a member in an informal organization. There may be no definite leader or process to facilitate decision making.

## Time to Think 5.2

Select a role from Table 5.1 present in a human service organization in your community. Write a paragraph or two about how this organization is essential to civil society and creating services that neither the market nor public sectors are willing to provide.

## UNDERSTANDING ORGANIZATIONS USING THEORIES AND PERSPECTIVES

Enhanced understanding and critical thinking about organizations can be facilitated by the consideration of applicable and relevant theories and perspectives. Although not limited to the examples below, a number of theories and perspectives are provided, which can be helpful when contemplating how and why nonprofit organizations form, function, and exist.

- **Market Failure Theory:** The bottom line is that business companies are designed to make money. They sell goods and services but do not want to provide "public goods" to those in need, especially without a profit, so nonprofits address this void.
- **Contract Failure Theory:** It has been proposed that in select markets, some companies fail to provide consumers with sufficient information to judge the quality of a product or service. In these instances, companies may be reducing the quality of their product or service to maximize profits. When this process occurs, nonprofit alternatives appear to respond to consumer needs with quality products and services.
- **Government Failure Theory:** The government acts to satisfy the wants of the majority of voters or desires of lawmakers in power. Consequently, some needs are unmet by both the business sector and the government, resulting in a failure to provide goods and services required by certain segments of society. High demanders then turn to nonprofits to provide products and services to meet their needs.
- **Voluntary Failure Theory:** Nonprofits also fail, which can be replaced by other nonprofit organizations.
- **Political Theories of Nonprofit Organizations:** Offer concepts and principles used to describe, explain, and evaluate political events and institutions.
    - **Decision-Making Theory** (March & Olsen, 1976; Simon, 1957): Limited rationality exists when constraints reduce decision making in organizations (e.g., loyalties toward a certain group; ability to know all variables that influence decisions; and the abilities, habits, personal characteristics people use to decide something) (cited in Netting, Kettner, McMurty, & Thomas, 2017, pp. 212–213).
    - **Resource Dependency and Political-Economy Theories** (Pfeffer, 1981): The bureaucratic model, rational-choice model, and political model assume that decision making is oriented toward a clear organizational goal rather than a range of goals and motivations (cited in Netting et al., 2017, pp. 212–213).

- **Critical and Feminist Theories** (Giddens, 1979; Habermas, 1971): These theories question everything about the status quo in organizations and espouse the need for critical thinking to fend off potential ethical conflicts or unintended consequences that may be overlooked in organizational work (Netting et al., 2017).

- **Community Theories of Nonprofit Organizations (Netting et al., 2017)**
- **Symbolic Theories and Perspectives:** Mainly focus on artifacts, values, underlying assumptions, and organizational culture and identity. These recognize the political nature of organizational life—inside and outside.
  - **Organizational Culture Theory** (Schein, 2010): Three levels of culture exist: (1) artifacts (reflect the organization's climate, such as behaviors, processes, and structures; (2) espoused beliefs and values—what members say is important, as in a mission statement; and (3) basic underlying assumptions—often taken for granted (cited in Netting et al., 2017, pp. 217–218).
  - **Sensemaking Theory** (Weick, 1995): An analytical approach grounded in communications theory that notes how people process and make sense of what they see and sense around them—conclusions from what they have heard and observed from internal conversations in a given environment. Culture is used as a metaphor to describe how organizations work (Morgan, 1986, as cited in Netting et al., 2017, pp. 221–222).

It can be argued that at times, social workers have had an ambivalent relationship with theory. Some professionals are uncertain of the relevance of theories; therefore, they often lack an adequate theoretical and conceptual base for purposeful practice. Often, frontline social workers are unable to articulate the skills and knowledge that guide their practice or the specific forms of intervention or practice theory they are applying to their work, and they leave such conceptualizing to academics.

Theory knowledge involves the broader context of using abstract theory and perspectives for engagement in deductive, critical thinking in professional practice. The use of contemporary theory, knowledge, and research professionalism can be considered as both a professional obligation as well as the excursion of power and control by social workers. However, in a nutshell, social workers must be able to (1) analyze and evaluate their own and others' personal experience, (2) analyze and clarify concepts and issues, (3) apply knowledge and understanding to practice, and (4) use research findings in practice—all of which can frequently be assisted by the use of appropriate theories and perspectives. Unfortunately, many traditional approaches to human service organizations take little or no account of issues of discrimination and oppression. However, a number of models and orientations have been used to help social workers understand the workings and functions of organizations and human service agencies. These include the decision-making model, human relations model, mechanical model, social systems model, total quality management, and Parson's paradigm. Some of these theories are discussed in Table 5.2.

**TABLE 5.2**

Selected Organizational Theories by Frame

| Theory (Theorist) | Frame | Concepts | Context Conception |
|---|---|---|---|
| Bureaucracy (Weber, 1947) | Structural | Hierarchy, structure | Closed |
| Scientific and universalistic management (Taylor, 1911) | Structural | Efficiency, measurement | Closed |
| Organizational goals (1915) | Structural | Goal displacement, natural systems | Closed |
| Management by objectives (Drucker, 1954) | Structural | Setting goals and objectives | Closed |
| Open systems (Katz & Kahn, 1966) | Structural | Systems theory, inputs, throughputs, outputs | Open |
| Contingency theory (Burns & Stalker, 1961; Morse & Lorsch, 1970) | Structural | Environmental constraints, task environment | Varies |
| Human relations | Human resources | Social rewards, informal structure | Closed |
| Theory X, Theory Y (McGregor, 1960) | Human resources | Higher order rewards | Closed |
| Quality-oriented management (Deming, 1982) | Human resources | Consumer/quality, process focus | Open |
| Decision making (Simon, 1957) | Political | Bound rationality, satisficing | Closed |
| Resource dependency and political-economy theories (Pfeffer, 1981; Walmsley & Zald, 1973) | Political | Power, politics | Open |
| Critical and feminist theories (1960) (Acker, 1990; Habermas, 1971) | Political | Inequity, feminism, social construction | Open |
| Organizational culture | Symbolic | Assumptions, beliefs, diversity, values metaphor, and sensemaking | Open |
| Organizational learning (1990) (Argyris & Schon, 1996; Senge, 1990) | Symbolic | Learning organization, systemic understanding | Open |

*Source:* Framework model adapted from Bolman and Deal (2013).

## HOW ORGANIZATIONS FUNCTION

Foremost, human service organizations primarily function to serve people in need and through the procurement and use of resources. To operate, organizations typically raise funds and obtain resources from multiple sources (e.g., individual donors, government grants or contracts, foundations and businesses, or charge fees for their services). Next, the organization makes mission and goal-directed decisions for the use of finances, as described in an annual budget.

Essentially, organizations require consumers, economic support, effective personnel (e.g., leaders and workers), a positive reputation, and sufficient resources and methods to deliver quality services and products. Professional organizations are required to be attentive to licensing or accrediting bodies that set standards for effective delivery of programs and services and hold a responsibility to the general public in relationship to fair and just delivery of service and treatment of consumers. Organizations do not operate in a vacuum but interact with other organizations in various societal institutions (e.g., economic, politics, education, religious, and social welfare) and organizations to acquire information and participate in networking and collaborative efforts.

Social workers are employed by a wide array of organizations: public, nonprofit, for-profit, and hybrid. Acting as change agents, they in part derive their authority and sanction from "the organization." An organization's philosophy and environmental setting or context may influence how they practice and what barriers may exist (Furman & Gibelman, 2013). According to Jaskyte (2010), there is a correlation between a social service agency's organizational culture and its client outcomes. The culture of an organization drives the innovative practices that can help an organization thrive. Also, the culture (values, norms, practices, and beliefs) of an organization affects the daily experiences and satisfaction, positive and negative, of consumers and agency professionals. Multiple dimensions of an organizational culture affect "respect for people, team orientation, stability, aggressiveness, and attention to detail" (Jaskyte, 2010, p. 125).

Organizations, organizational culture, and organizational effectiveness are central concepts in macro social work. Organizations are the primary setting for social work practice and the social structure for delivery of services and social change. Yet too often, organizations can pose barriers to ensuring social justice and meeting the routine and complex needs of people, particularly those challenged or unable to afford goods and services.

### Time to Think 5.3

How might the culture of an organization drive the creation of effective and impactful practices that can help an organization thrive and help address social problems experienced by consumers? What are some cultural attributes that you believe are important for a successful organization?

## HUMAN DIVERSITY AND HUMAN SERVICE ORGANIZATIONS

At the beginning of this chapter, Nina sought ways to advocate for a more diverse labor force in her behavioral health agency. In everyday social work practice, appreciation for and understanding of the impact of diversity in human service organizations can take many forms, often revealed and exemplified through the wishes and well-being of consumers. Social workers must strive to be conscious and aware of the organizational environments to which they belong and practice as well as competing interests of consumers and organizations. Once again, a focus and dedication to advocacy and promoting change with larger systems, which can often include advocating for change in one's own agency, is key. Consider the struggles of Ansuya in the following case study.

### Respect for Ansuya and Diversity

Ansuya Solanky was admitted to a nursing home when her family no longer felt they could care for her. Initially, she appeared to settle well, but she soon became very depressed and withdrawn. Her relatives were impressed with the quality of nursing care in the home; therefore, they made no connection between the nursing care provided and Ansuya's deteriorating condition. However, on one specific visit, Asha, Ansuya's daughter, noticed an uneaten meal on a nearby tray. Asha was disappointed and surprised to see that the meal consisted of traditional Western fare, totally unlike the food her mom was used to eating. Further investigation revealed that no allowance had been made for her mother's cultural preferences, with regard to food and other aspects of daily living. A picture then began to form—a distressing picture in which Ansuya felt marginalized, alienated, and devalued. When the issue was raised with the nursing home supervisor, her response was direct and simple. She believed that everyone was to be treated the same, so as not to draw attention to people's differences. Despite the good intentions underlying the "color-blind approach," the actual outcome was discriminatory and negative. Despite nursing and social services standards being high in other respects, this lack of sensitivity to ethnic needs had produced a racist outcome. Ansuya's predicament illustrates how social organizations, such as long-term care settings, affect consumers' lives and a macro social worker's advocacy role.

©iStockphoto.com/PeopleImages

**PHOTO 5.1** Diversity adds to the richness of organizations.

### NASW Code of Ethics

The 2018 National Association of Social Workers (NASW) *Code of Ethics* obligates social workers to balance tensions between conflicting commitments to both the consumer and the practice setting (NASW, 2008, 2017). Social workers must manage the tension of valuing consumers involving issues related to cultural respect, human dignity, wellness, and financial burdens with respect to one's practice setting, which often involves the agency, colleagues, and supervisors.

In the 2018 *Code of Ethics* and the Council on Social Work Education's (CSWE) 2015 Educational Policy and Accreditation Standards (EPAS), obligations and considerations of the importance of communities and organizations in relationship to human relationships and service delivery are noteworthy. Although organizations and communities are connected in textbooks and foundational documents, in reality, organizational systems and the community systems are two distinctive, intersecting units for analysis and consideration. In the organizational system, social workers engage in micro and mezzo aspects differently than in a community context. For example, in a community context, social workers commonly engage with business constituents, the local community, and government. In contrast, in the organizational environment, social workers interact with these constituents as well as employees, funders, regulatory agencies, and so on. While organizations serve communities, the organizational context is a separate and distinctive area for assessment and intervention.

### Time to Think 5.4

Consider Ansuya and Asha's experience. In addition to the problem of racism, sexism is a significant aspect of human services organizations. A common problem in older age is the tendency to be treated as a "nonperson." Unfortunately, dehumanization and ageism can occur and organizations may fail to respond optimally or creatively. If you were the director of social services in Ansuya's nursing home setting, how would you proactively respond and advocate for policies and practices to eradicate discrimination and change the organization's culture and policies? Would you anticipate resistance from the long-term care organization for cultural accommodations for food and other aspects of daily living? If so, why?

## ORGANIZATION AS A SYSTEM

Sometimes social workers and other professionals have difficulty understanding the concept of organizational goals because they work primarily on a one-to-one basis and do not visualize or think about the organization as a unit. Although professionals can readily understand that individuals have purposes and objectives, they have difficulty comprehending that organizations can also have specific objectives (Neugeboren, 1991). Their orientation to direct service gives them a perspective that inhibits thinking on a "systems" level.

### Social Systems

Indeed, much of social work practice with individuals and families is based on systems theory to support the holistic assessment of people in their communities.

It also helps to think of organizations as systems (Katz & Kahn, 1978). Simply put, a system is an organized collection of parts that are highly integrated in order to accomplish an overall goal. As illustrated in Figure 5.1, systems have inputs, processes, outputs, and feedback. **Inputs** to the system include resources such as money and people. These inputs come through *processes* in a coordinated fashion to achieve the goals established for the organization. **Outputs** are tangible results produced by the processes in the system such as services for consumers. Finally, feedback is a special form of input whereby a system receives information about its performance. Feedback can be either positive or negative. Positive feedback is input about a system's positive functioning, whereas negative feedback suggests an organization's malfunctioning (Kirst-Ashman & Hull, 2001). It is important to note that if one part of the system is changed, the nature of the entire system changes. Thus, there is an interconnected relationship between the overall system and its parts.

This approach is based on the work of biologist Ludwig von Bertalanffy (1950), who believed that lessons from fields such as ecology, which concerns organisms' interdependence with their surroundings, provide a basis for conceptualizing other phenomena as systems engaged in environmental interactions (Netting et al., 1998). In this model, "consumers" or organizations are viewed not as isolated entities driven primarily by internal psychological needs. Instead, they are seen as social beings whose personalities and behaviors can be analyzed in terms of their constant interaction with the world around them. As **open systems**,

**FIGURE 5.1**
The Open System Model

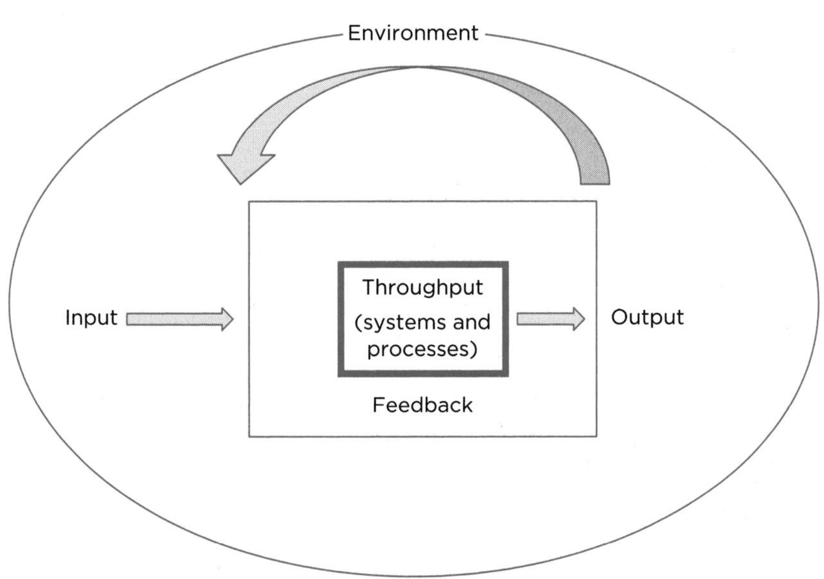


*Source:* Image extracted from http://preventiontraining.samhsa.gov/cti02/17H-ode1.htm Track: Organizational Development, from the CSAP Institute for Partnership Development from the United States Department of Health and Human Services.

©iStockphoto.com/Drazen_

**PHOTO 5.2** Organizations function as a system of shared activities.

organizations both give to and draw from elements external to themselves. The key to understanding organizations lies in this ongoing process of exchange with critical elements (e.g., culture, community, family) that constitute the personal environments of consumers.

## Human Service Organizations

Several features distinguish human service organizations from others. Most important, they work directly with people whose characteristics or concerns they address. The "raw material" for these organizations is the people themselves. The interactions between service providers and consumers of services are the core production process. The output and justification of existence of such organizations is the protection, promotion, and enhancement of the well-being of the people they serve.

The effect of systems theory is that macro social workers can examine human service organizations from a broader perspective. Specifically, systems theory provides an interpretation of patterns of interaction and events in organizations. Social workers can identify the interrelations of the organizational parts, the need for coordination, the presence of conflict, and the benefits of collaboration. More attention is given to feedback, assessment, and evaluation in order to focus on structures and strategies that promote behaviors that determine events rather than simply reacting to occurrences.

### Time to Think 5.5

Complete the following exercise as a means of integrating the information on organizations with systems theory. During the exercise, consider your professional responsibility as a social worker to continuously assess the effectiveness of organizations as a means of improving services (Kirst-Ashman & Hull, 2001).

Select at least two dissimilar human service agencies and browse the websites for each organization. For each agency, try to identify the following information: (1) the organizational goals; (2) methods to achieve the goals; (3) various processes such as services and treatment modalities, outputs, or ways that effectiveness is determined; and (4) ways that feedback is solicited and used concerning effectiveness of services.

With information about the agencies in hand, can you identify distinct differences regarding the goals and functions of the agencies? If not, what are your thoughts as to why this type of organizational information is not being shared on the agency's website? Do these organizations appear to be open systems or closed systems and why?

A major strength of the systems model is the encouragement it gives to social workers to think of themselves as part of a network that, as a totality, can serve consumers in a coordinated and meaningful fashion. Ideally, by using the systems model, social workers will develop structures that nurture relationships between the human service organizations and other systems. Methods of coordination with community groups, funding sources, government agencies, other helping agencies, educational institutions, professional organizations, and a variety of other systems are identified and nurtured (Lewis, Lewis, Packard, & Souflee, 2001).

## Organizational Culture

The totality of the subsystems that make up an organization develops shared experiences—what Schein (1985) refers to as **organizational culture**. In this sense, *culture* involves a sense of group identity that permeates decision making and communication within the organization. It is such an important factor in organizational life that it merits special attention. More specifically, organizational culture is

> a pattern of basic assumptions—invented, discovered, or developed by a given group as it learns to cope with its problems of external adaptation and internal integration—that has worked well enough to be considered valid and, therefore, to be taught to new members as the correct way to perceive, think, and feel in relation to those problems. (Schein, 1985, p. 9)

Why should macro social workers be concerned with organizational culture? As with viewing organizations using a systems model, culture provides insight into an organization's successes and values. It has a strong influence on the behavior of an organization over time. Furthermore, the influence of culture is predictable. The information gathered from culture is crucial for social workers because it spells out the informal rules of behavior and expectations while providing a value system within which to operate. In addition, organizational culture can set an important tone for promoting the dignity and rights of consumers of services, while managing and resisting negative stigmatization of consumers (Savio, 2017).

### An Illustration Promoting the Dignity of Consumers: The Virtues of Karen's Korner

Karen's Korner is a cluster of four two-bedroom apartments owned by The First Church of the Resurrection. The buildings were donated to the church by the heir of Karen Conners, a local philanthropist. Upon receiving the gift, the social outreach division of the church earmarked the dwellings for transitional living for single mothers through a cooperative agreement with Target Services, a local agency serving homeless mothers with small children.

Target Services provides case management services for residents at Karen's Korner. Congregation members at The First Church of the Resurrection have formed a Karen's Korner group to maintain the apartments and to function as a landlord. Residents pay a modest rent, $200 a month, and are provided with utilities.

Residents of Karen's Korner do not view themselves as consumers of services at their temporary residence. Special effort has been taken to avoid stigmatization by church members and professionals at Target Services. Apartments have a "home feel," and residents are empowered with a sense of ownership over their lives. They can paint and decorate apartments to their tastes. Residents are expected to follow a few basic rules and maintain a professional working relationship with social workers from Target Services.

In this case example, Target Services and The First Church of the Resurrection have formed a cooperative arrangement. They share important elements in their organizational cultures that have facilitated a successful partnership.

Both organizations demonstrate commitment to empowerment and destigmatization. Their organizational culture and goals emphasize short-term (transitional) services, interagency collaboration, flexibility, minimal exertion of authority and control over the lives of consumers, and responsiveness to feedback from consumers and partner organizations.

This brief example constitutes a clear illustration of the virtues of an open-system approach to organizational development. The ability of leaders, professionals, consumers, and citizens to be open and proactive in forming interorganizational alliances is a noteworthy attribute. It suggests a level of maturity, as organizations are ready and willing to change, adapt, and enter relationships when called upon.

Values are the foundation of organizational culture. Organizations that stand for something, such as social justice or self-determination, have an explicit philosophy that drives the service delivery system. Macro social workers who pay attention to values ensure that the organization is consumer centered and based on the principles of the social work profession. For effectiveness, organizational values are known, shared, and promoted by all workers and consumers of organization services.

Organizational culture is complex and can be difficult to understand. Yet, improving a human services organizational culture can lead to improvement of practice outcomes (Stanley & Lincoln, 2016). How does organizational culture develop and how does it continue even as individual organization members come and go? According to Ott (1989, p. 75), organizational culture has three sources or determinants:

1. The broader societal culture in which the organization resides
2. The nature of the organization's business
3. The beliefs, values, and basic assumptions held by the organization's leaders

The three sources are not necessarily independent of each other. Rather, an organization's culture is the sum of the composite of the three general sources. Consequently, each organizational culture is unique.

How does a social worker begin to read or assess a culture in order to understand the unique features of an organization? Somewhat as a clinical social worker does with a client, a macro social worker conducts a holistic assessment of an organization through a process. Other than values, of particular interest are the role models for employees and consumers to follow. Such models might be leaders within the organization. However, any person can demonstrate what it takes to be a successful participant in the organization. The organization's rituals, as displayed in celebrations and honors, also show how employees and consumers are expected to behave.

Finally, the cultural network or the manner of communication (e.g., face-to-face, e-mail, texting, and/or through social media) within the organization provides insight into the ways that values are transmitted and the expected patterns of interaction. Ott (1989) provides a broad range of cultural elements (e.g., attitudes, art, beliefs, expressions, feelings, material objects, norms, symbols, and views) worthy of consideration in conjunction with organizational assessment. A beginning point in the assessment process is often study of the physical setting. Are the organization's buildings well maintained, accessible, and appropriate for the services offered? What are the decorations like? For example, what hangs on the walls? Who are the organization's neighbors? Are they a possible source for collaborative relationships? Is the organization located in close proximity to its consumers?

The organization's statements about itself and its services reveal much about its values and resultant culture. Spend time reading annual reports, press releases, policy and procedures manuals, educational material designed for consumers, and brochures. Is the message the same in print and nonprint material? Follow up the review of information with an examination of how consumers are treated when they enter the organization. Is there a comfortable reception area? Does the organization appear informal or formal, and why? Are people called by their first names or their titles? Does the culture embrace human diversity and inclusion? How are consumers referred to and how are they addressed?

The diagnostic profile of an organization should include interviews with staff. It is important to ask people questions about their history in the organization and their perception of the organization's history. What are described as the organization's successes and failures? How does the organization celebrate events or accomplishments? On the basis of the interview process, begin to consider the type of people who work at the organization and why. Consider lengths of employment with the agency, recruitment procedures, and reward systems.

Finally, observe how people spend their time. How much effort is spent on paper or computer work? What are interpersonal interactions like in terms of frequency and spontaneity? Is the organization's language formal or casual? Does humor seem to be appreciated and, if so, in what way? Pay particular attention to anecdotes and stories that seem to pass through the organization.

The cultural assessment requires the use of multiple methodologies, especially qualitative and ethnographic strategies. It gives social workers a fix on the organization's culture, particularly whether it is weak or strong, focused or fragmented (Deal & Kennedy, 1982). Organizational culture serves as a source of energy and focus, providing meaning and direction for organization members. Organizational

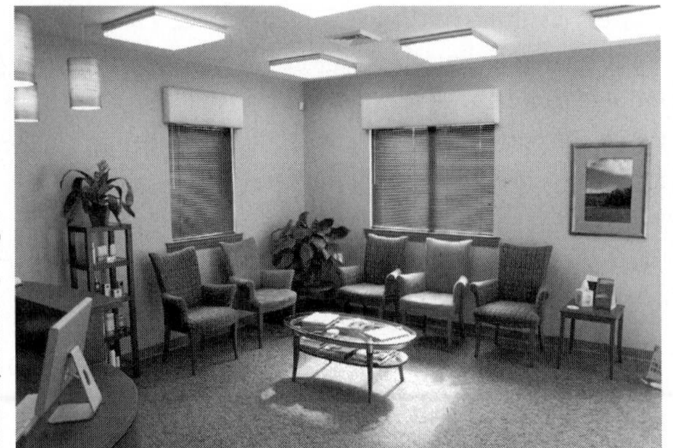

©iStockphoto.com/rdegrie

**PHOTO 5.3** The environment of organizations reflects values.

culture not only gives an organization its unique identity—it *is* the unique character or personality of an organization. People in organizations need culture for identity, purpose, feelings of belongingness, communication, stability, and cognitive efficiency.

Many of the elements of organizational culture are present in the following case example. Read the case and analyze the cultural elements of the agency.

### A Contemporary Illustration of Aspects of Organizational Culture

Located by a church and across from the street from a family-owned restaurant, the family health and counseling center is a primary service agency for the rural county area. With a staff of 15, the agency has been in operation for over 20 years. It serves as a placement site for undergraduate and graduate social work students from a nearby state university.

The building is old but well maintained. As Amy Wieland, a consumer, enters the agency, she is greeted by first name by a receptionist. Amy replies in kind. Her appointment is scheduled in 10 minutes; while waiting, she has a cup of coffee provided in a reception area. The reception area is comfortably furnished. There are recent health and family life magazines and the local paper for reading. On the walls are photos of local scenes and a plaque honoring outstanding agency employers and volunteers, recognized for their community service contributions.

The social worker also greets Amy by first name and with a handshake at the designated appointment time. They walk back to the worker's office together. In the hallway, they pass the agency's director, who speaks to Amy about a community culture fair that the agency will host next month.

What do the cultural elements tell you about the values and philosophy of the agency? How would you describe the relationships illustrated in the case? Is this an agency where you think you would like to work or receive services? Why or why not?

## ORGANIZATIONAL DEVELOPERS

As you begin to examine the structure, functioning, and culture of organizations, try to consider the organization as a potential consumer and/or target system for change. Macro social workers who work with dysfunctional organizational systems are called **organizational developers.** According to Rieman (1992), organizational developers enhance knowledge, improve skills, modify attitudes, and change behaviors in order to provide better services to consumers. They use organization development to initiate organizational change, improving the effectiveness of the organization and its members (Brueggemann, 2002).

## Organizational Development

**Organizational development** (OD), historically one of the most commonly used consultative methods in business and industry, is also used in human service organizations. In OD, the consultant or organization developer and the client organization jointly assess an organization's change needs and develop an action plan for addressing them. To change the way an organization solves its problems, the organization developer may use any one of a vast number of possible interventions, including these common ones:

- Group process interventions such as team building
- Intergroup process interventions, including conflict resolution strategies, intergroup confrontation meetings, and joint problem-solving sessions
- Training programs designed to enhance organizational skills and using innovative educational strategies such as simulation and gaming
- Survey feedback or the gathering and sharing of diagnostic data about the organization and its current norms and processes
- Action research, which involves broad participation in the development of change strategies based on structural research and behavioral science technologies
- Change in organizational structure based on group agreement about suggested alterations (Lewis et al., 2001, p. 285)

The basic assumptions on which organizational development is premised are as follows:

1. The answers to OD assessment and intervention strategies will vary depending on the perspective of different constituent groups.
2. Clear and widespread consensus on organizational issues is rare within organizations.
3. The broader information sources (horizontal and vertical), the nearer the conclusions will be to reality.
4. The data-gathering process itself offers a unique opportunity to build trust and clarity. (Feinstein, 1987)

On the basis of these premises, the role of the organization developer is to establish a wide communication loop, receiving information from key constituent groups throughout the process.

### The Role of the Organizational Developer

Of primary importance are two objectives: The organization developer encourages the organization to regard the conclusions and recommendations as its own, and the developer facilitates the broadest possible participation in the change effort. In this way, the organization developer is preparing subsystems of the organization to accept and understand recommendations for change. Thus, the key to defining an intervention through OD is not the specific strategy used but the democratic involvement of organization members (especially consumers) who might be affected by the change. All organizational development is done under the assumption that the organization must be able to deal effectively with future needs. This assumes that the organization and its members must gain purposeful control over the change process.

According to Brueggemann (2002), there are two types of organization developers. The first is a developer internal to the organization. This is an individual or an employee of the organization (e.g., a mental health center) who works exclusively for and with consumers, employees, and administrators of the agency. Internal organization developers must be cautious and thoughtful in their recommendations because they will have to live with the changes they recommend (Robbins, 1992). Furthermore, they come under constant scrutiny of consumers and their colleagues.

In contrast, external organization developers work either as private consultants or as members of an organizational development firm; they provide management consultations, training, and problem solving to many different organizations and agencies. Although external consultants can offer objective perspectives because they are from outside the organization, they often do not have an intimate understanding of the organization's history, goals, and procedures. As a result, external consultants may have a tendency to institute drastic changes because they do not have to live with the results.

Whether working as an internal or external organization developer, the process is a collaborative venture involving various stakeholders, especially consumers. Harrison (1987) describes the steps in organization development as follows:

- *Scouting:* The organization developer seeks to determine how ready and able the members of the organization are to follow through on a project and to change their behavior and their organization.
- *Entry:* The organization developer and stakeholders of the organization negotiate about their expectations for the project and formalize them in a contract specifying the timing and nature of the developer's activities.
- *Diagnosis:* The organization developer gathers information about the nature and sources of the organization's problems and its unique strengths, then analyzes this information, examines possible solutions, considers ways to improve effectiveness, and provides feedback to the organization through presentations, reports, and interviews.
- *Planning:* Organization developers and stakeholders of the organization jointly establish objectives for the project's action phase and plan any steps (interventions) to be taken to solve problems and improve effectiveness.

- *Action:* The organization implements these plans with the help of the developer.
- *Evaluation:* The organization and stakeholders assess the impacts of the action phase and consider further actions. Under ideal conditions, an independent researcher evaluates project outcomes.
- *Termination:* If no further action is planned, the project terminates. The project may break off earlier if clients or developers become dissatisfied with it (Brueggemann, 2002).

## Organizational Politics and Change

A distinguishing feature of both internal and external organization developers is **organizational politics.** According to Gummer and Edwards (1985, p. 14), the concept of an organization as a political system offers a particularly useful scheme for understanding organizations and for developing ideas that lead to effective practice with them. A central feature of political decision making is its explicit recognition of power and some degree of conflict as normal functions in organizational life and the provisions they make for transforming potentially disruptive conflicts into negotiated settlements.

How does this relate to the role of organization developers? An essential skill for the organization developer is the ability to identify sources of organizational power that can be used to produce support for desired policies and programs. In other words, power is viewed as the ability to make things happen or get things done in an effective manner. Consequently, the ability to assess the structure and operation of power is a central attribute of the organization developer.

Building on the idea of organizational power and the personal power of social workers, Kirst-Ashman and Hull (2001) introduced a way of assessing **organizational change potential**, which they call "PREPARE: An Assessment of Organizational Change Potential." It is designed for organization developers and other macro practitioners to use in considering organizational problems and possible change in a general way (pp. 108–109). The elements of PREPARE are summarized in Figure 5.2. The steps associated with the process follow:

STEP 1. PREPARE: *Identify Problems to Be Addressed.* Most organizations have problems that have a negative impact on the work environment. The first step for the organization developer is to identify and prioritize problems in the context of the organization's culture. Consider if and how the problems have an impact on consumers. Are the problems significant enough to warrant a change effort? Will the staff and consumers support the proposed change?

STEP 2. PREPARE: *Review Your Macro and Personal Reality.* Evaluate the chances of introducing a successful macro change. To do this, consider the organization's environment, including its subsystems, resources, funding sources, culture, and staff composition. What are the constraints to change, such as the political climate, regulations, or cultural components? Consider your own skills, qualities, and relationships. How will your assets affect the change effort?

STEP 3. PREPARE: *Establish Primary Goals.* What goals do you think you can accomplish? Establish a sense of direction for your proposed interventions that supports the strengths of the organization's culture. A concrete course of action defines a system of accountability.

STEP 4. PREPARE: *Identify Relevant People of Influence.* Who will help in the change effort? Consider both consumers and employees of the organization in terms of their commitment to and energy for change. Identify possible opponents to change. How will you address their resistance?

STEP 5. PREPARE: *Assess Potential Financial Costs and Potential Benefits to Consumers and the Organization.* Think about the costs associated with the macro change. Is the cost reasonable given the financial situation of the organization and the anticipated benefit of making the change?

STEP 6. PREPARE: *Review Professional and Personal Risks.* Does the proposed change effort place you in jeopardy of losing your job or contract? How will it affect your chances for career mobility? How will you be perceived by consumers? Will any of your relationships become strained as a result of the macro change?

STEP 7. PREPARE: *Evaluate the Potential Success of the Macro Change Process.* After reviewing the PREPARE process, decide whether the change effort deserves your commitment and the organization's time and resources. Should the effort be initiated, delayed, or canceled?

**FIGURE 5.2**

PREPARE: An Assessment of Organizational Change Potential

**Step**

1. **P** Identify **PROBLEMS** to address.
2. **R** Review your macro and personal **REALITY**.
3. **E** **ESTABLISH** your macro reality and primary goals.
4. **P** Identify relevant **PEOPLE** of influence.
5. **A** **ASSESS** potential financial costs and potential benefits to consumers and the organization.
6. **R** Review professional and personal **RISKS**.
7. **E** **EVALUATE** the potential success of the macro change process.

*Source:* Republished with permission of South-Western College Publishing, a division of Cengage Learning from *Macro Skills Workbook: A Generalist Approach*, 2nd edition, by Kirst-Ashman/Hull Jr., © 2001; permission conveyed through Copyright Clearance Center, Inc.

## Time to Think 5.6

You have been employed by an urban child welfare agency for approximately 3 years. During that time, you established yourself as a productive organization developer by assessing the need for staff training, formalizing the Program Advisory Committee, introducing consumer focus groups to evaluate services for adolescents, and initiating a community service recognition program.

The administrator is concerned about a decrease in consumer contact hours and asks you to review the admissions packet to ensure that the material is relevant. Your review indicates that the forms are over 10 pages long and take well over an hour to complete. The font used on many of the forms is small, the text is complicated, and personal questions related to marital status, finances, and resources are asked without a clear reason for doing so. Furthermore, the admissions packet is available only in English and is written at a 10th-grade level of reading difficulty. The admissions packets are printed, processed, and filed by three workers who have been employed by the agency for a number of years.

The center's area of service has a high portion of people over the age of 65. An increasing number of residents are Hispanic, with strong Roman Catholic affiliations.

1. What are some possible problems with the admissions packet? What are some of its strengths?
2. What are some constraints on any proposed change effort? Are resources available to assist with the change? Are there reasonable technological solutions?
3. What are some possible goals related to the admissions packet?
4. Who are the people relevant to the change effort? What is the possible relationship between the admissions packet and the decrease in consumer contact? How will you test this relationship?
5. Are any professional or personal risks associated with the proposed change?

*Source:* Adapted from Kirst-Ashman and Hull (2001, p. 124).

## EMPOWERMENT

The concept of empowerment, when applied to an organizational setting, brings together the material presented in previous chapters with the information on organizations and the role of the organization developer. Saul Alinsky, the social activist who wrote *Reveille for Radicals* (1969), laid the foundation for the empowerment process by stating that an organization functions to achieve power to realize the people's program—a set of principles, purposes, and practices commonly agreed upon by the people. Building on the work of Alinsky, Solomon (1976) concluded that the term *empowerment* described the process of assisting "clients who manifest powerlessness to develop their latent powers and to exert these powers to obtain needed resources" (Hepworth & Larsen, 1993, p. 495). Her more comprehensive definition of empowerment is as follows:

> a process whereby the social worker engages in a set of activities with the client . . . that aim to reduce the powerlessness that has been created by negative valuations based on membership in a stigmatized group. It involves identification of the power blocks that contribute to the problem as well as the development and implementing of specific strategies aimed at either the reduction of the effects from indirect power blocks or the reduction of the operations of direct power blocks. (Solomon, 1976, p. 19)

When applied to an organization, the empowerment process pulls together diverse elements or subsystems and builds on their strengths to improve the social and economic conditions of consumers. This is accomplished through the three interlocking dimensions of empowerment (Lee, 1994, p. 13). The first is the development of a more positive and potent sense of self. In the context of an organization, this dimension refers to a coherent philosophy supported by goals that build on the strengths of the organization. The positive image of the organization is conveyed to consumers through such avenues as print and nonprint material, interpersonal communication, and formal as well as informal celebrations. The second interlocking dimension is the fund of knowledge an organization accumulates in order to understand the realities of its environment. Consumers are a major source of such knowledge, as are employees, other agencies, and funding sources. Finally, Lee (1994) concludes that organizations must cultivate resources and strategies for the attainment of personal and collective goals. This dimension clearly speaks to the relationship between empowerment, collaboration, and the formation of a community with a broad-based constituency.

Organizational development themes included in the empowerment process involve democratic procedures, voluntary cooperation, self-help, development of indigenous leadership, and educational objectives to foster empowerment (Rothman & Tropman, 1987). Organization developers emphasize organizational building based on the assumption that there is common good that people working together can realize (Brager & Specht, 1973).

When empowerment is an organizational aim, social workers will find themselves questioning both public policy issues and their role in relation to dependent people. Specifically, social workers committed to the empowerment of their organizations will challenge policies or programs designed *to use on* consumers rather than actively designed *in conjunction with* consumers. Furthermore, social workers will confront the "paradox that even people most incompetent, in need, and apparently unable to function require more than less control over their own lives; and that fostering more control does not necessarily mean ignoring them" (Rappaport, 1985, p. 18). In this way, empowerment presses a different set of metaphors upon the social work profession than the traditional helping model.

The empowerment ideology contains at least two requirements (Lee, 1994). It demands that macro social work practitioners examine many diverse settings in which people are already handling their own problems, in order to learn more about how they do it. Simultaneously, it demands that social workers find ways to apply what they learn from people handling life problems to organizational settings through policies and programs. In light of both of these requirements, the organization is viewed as a resource to help people gain control over their lives.

Raeymaeckers and Dierckx (2013) view empowerment of consumers in human service organizations as a matter of activating consumers of services. They identify and examine three key organizational characteristics for consideration in support of consumer activation—participation in decision making, leadership, and collegial support (Raeymaeckers & Dierckx, 2013).

Including empowerment in organizations requires many intervention tools such as those included in this chapter: examining subsystems, assessing culture, activating consumers of services, and evaluating the potential for organizational change. These tools enhance organizational functioning and, in turn, consumer empowerment, through social investigation, humane policies, and program development (Simon, 1994). As described in Table 5.3, another intervention tool is an organizational strengths-based assessment. Designed to assess the strengths and obstacles within an organization, the strengths-based assessment helps macro social workers and consumers to focus on present organizational conditions in order to direct future change efforts.

As with building on the strengths of people, developing organizational strengths shifts from the search for a monolithic way of doing things and providing services. By contrast, the strengths assessment offers a bottom-up process that starts with people telling administrators what social policies and programs are necessary. This means that the outcome of empowerment will not only look different depending on the issues being confronted but may even look different by organizational unit and setting. The strengths assessment suggests that diversity of person, thought, and perspective rather than homogeneity in organizations should dominate if the operating process is one of empowerment.

**TABLE 5.3**

The Organizational Empowerment Assessment

| Subsystem | Obstacles | Strengths | Effect on Problem Situation |
|---|---|---|---|
| Internal policies and procedures | | | |
| External policies and procedures | | | |
| Professional staff pattern | | | |
| Support staff pattern | | | |
| Workload | | | |
| Organizational support | | | |
| Professional autonomy | | | |
| Degree of trust among administrators, professional staff, and support staff | | | |

*Source:* Republished with permission of Cengage from *Collaborative Social Work: Strengths-Based Generalist Practice*, 1st edition, by Poulin. © 2000; permission conveyed through Copyright Clearance Center.

In conclusion, there are two vital components of success with organizational empowerment. The first involves absolute commitment to an empowerment ideology as displayed in language and action. The other is an ongoing collaboration with the professional community and service consumers, who are viewed as invaluable resources. This interactive venture is empowering in itself. The end result is a new and vibrant organizational culture, based not on dependence, professional expertise, and passive acceptance but, rather, on the power and dignity of people.

### Organizational Change From Within the Organization

Organizational change *is* possible, particularly when leadership and professionals are committed to consumers and their needs. However, changing an organization from within can be a challenging endeavor as some employees are endeared to the status quo and can be resistant. For social workers, Mosley (2013) advances the notion of professional, collaborative policy advocacy as an important function in everyday practice. Social workers intentionally seek democratic forms of representation, which include consumers, to advocate for organizational policies representing consumer concerns.

As a means to prompt organizational change "from within," consider the merits of creating an **improvement team** (Brueggemann, 2002, p. 338), sometimes also known as a working group. Forming a team or group of consumers and professionals to discuss improvement ideas at a social service agency can be a valuable mechanism for discussing a number of topics (e.g., quality assurance, policy development, innovative programming, new practices, enhanced procedures, and climate issues).

The establishment of an improvement team recognizes that organizational change is inevitable, is necessary, and can be positive. The primary goal of the improvement team is to discuss important issues and timely topics—"to ask people to talk about what matters to them, not to ask people to support what matters to you or the leaders. . . . Dialogue is key" (Brueggemann, 2002, p. 338).

## ETHICAL ISSUES THAT OCCUR WITHIN ORGANIZATIONS

Within organizations, albeit public, for-profit, nonprofit, or hybrid, social workers may bemoan poor communication, micromanagement, and passive-aggressive supervision. Social workers and consumers alike may feel frustrated with agency policy, and practitioners may feel mistreated by supervisors. This is why relationship building, rapport, active listening skills, and careful assessment are so important. Executive directors of organizations and agencies must often engage in micro work with employees in their organization, as well as consumers that their organization is designed to serve. To navigate these issues effectively, executive directors of organizations require organizational skills (Busch & Hostetter, 2009).

The organization's directors or leaders must create a cohesive group environment where everyone feels comfortable voicing concerns and problem solving how to best help consumers. A focus must be on achieving organizational excellence rather than personality or role. Without happy employees, you won't find many happy consumers. It is saddening when student interns or paid social workers observe the devaluing of employees via passive-aggressive behavior, inconsistent rules and expectations, salary inconsistencies, favoritism, or a lack of communication. Supervisors require strong boundaries and must respect consumers their organization serves.

SAGE edge™ Visit **www.edge.sagepub.com/ticemacro** to help you accomplish your coursework goals in an easy-to-use learning environment

## SUMMARY

Social work students often enter educational and field experiences thinking that a primary function in social work is that of a clinician working with individuals and families. Students can struggle with the impact of larger systems in their lives and the experiences of consumers.

This chapter calls attention to organizations and asks readers to engage in a transition from thinking about interventions on the micro level to conceptualizing methods of enriching the life of organizations through macro interventions. One bridge between these practice areas is empowerment. In the larger context, the empowerment process ensures that program design, policies, and organizational development promote consumer input, self-determination, power, and dignity.

## TOP 10 KEY CONCEPTS

improvement team 120
nonprofit organization 99
open systems 107
organization 97
organizational change potential 115
organizational culture 109
organizational developer 112
organizational development 113
organizational politics 115
self-help groups 100

## DISCUSSION QUESTIONS

1. Examine and discuss organizational life at your university. Who are the consumers of services? How are students empowered and able to affect policies, programs, and practices at your university?
2. Presumably, human service agencies develop organizational cultures based on a group of core values. Identify and discuss several such core values that would commonly shape organizational cultures in social work agencies.
3. Discuss and debate the pros and cons associated with using an external organizational developer versus an internal organizational developer.
4. Examine how social workers can facilitate organizational cultures that manage and resist negative stigmas (Savio, 2017) for consumers of services.
5. How might technological solutions and the use of social media be helpful or a barrier for empowering consumers of services in human service organizations?
6. How can social organizations and/or human service organizations

help their workplace environments be culturally competent and culturally humble?

7. Identify for-profit and nonprofit organizations in your county and discuss to what extent they are "diversity friendly."

## EXERCISES

1. As a student in social work, you will participate in and complete field education. Ask your field instructor about visiting social workers at human service organizations that closely collaborate with your field placement agency. Identify important aspects of organizational culture at the agency(s) that you visit. Is there a sense of empowerment at the agency(s) you visit? When thinking about employment as a social worker, what are important elements of organizational culture to you, professionally and personally?
2. Many college students need to participate in part-time employment during their academic studies. Discuss with other students their job experiences, focusing on the goals, functions, strengths, and challenges associated with employment with each company. If students were organizational developers, what kinds of changes could be offered to improve working conditions, morale, and the overall organizational culture?
3. As a consumer of services at your university, how does your university, school, and/or program solicit feedback from students concerning your program's ability to obtain educational goals and objectives? Do students in your program participate in student advisory boards, working groups, or improvement teams designed to enhance and improve organizational life? If not, consider discussing with your faculty members and program leadership how to create mechanisms to activate the voices of students for quality improvement.
4. How can social organizations and/or human service organizations help their workplace environments be culturally competent and culturally humble? Search the Internet for cultural competency workshops offered to human service organizations or companies and businesses.
5. Identify for-profit and nonprofit organizations in your county and discuss to what extent they are "diversity friendly." How do these organizations recruit and retain diverse population groups?

## ONLINE RESOURCES

- Interested in which companies have been identified as having a valued organizational culture? Visit https://www.entrepreneur.com/article/249174 to view a top 10 list of companies cited with fantastic cultures.
- The professional organization for social workers is the National Association of Social Workers (NASW). Visit the NASW website at https://www.socialworkers.org/ to view and explore the mission and goals of the NASW as well as membership benefits.
- To view an example of empowerment in action, visit https://www.thebalancecareers.com/empowerment-in-action-how-to-empower-your-employees-1918102 to see how one organization worked to empower its employees.

# Exploring the Concept of Communities and Community Practice

## SOCIAL WORK WITH LOCAL GOVERNMENT

Jeanne is a social worker in a community center in a 2-square-mile borough of southern New Jersey. In this position, she is responsible for organizing events and activities for all ages while making referrals to area social service agencies when needed. She also interfaces with the borough council to ensure appropriate funds are allocated to the center and collaborates with borough officials in all phases of grant writing to secure much-needed county and state funding.

The borough where Jeanne works holds much significance to her. Her grandparents were Polish immigrants who settled in the area while using public transportation to work in a nearby city. They gave Jeanne's parents a plot of land adjacent to their property on which the house she grew up in was built. As a lifelong resident of the borough, Jeanne knows the current residents of the community and has a sense of family histories. Particular places in the borough, like the lake, veterans memorial, and firehouse, hold special memories for Jeanne as does the school system and various civic organizations. In brief, Jeanne feels a strong allegiance to the borough, its history, citizens, and recreational and park spaces. Jeanne's social work practice builds on this strong sense of community and subsequent commitment to the borough's residents.

## LEARNING OBJECTIVES

After reading this chapter you should be able to:

1. Define aspects of various geographic and shared or nonplace communities
2. Explain the function of communities and their role in consumers' lives
3. Conceptualize community practice, community development, and associated contemporary trends
4. Review the history of community organizing
5. Describe and apply various theoretical orientations and roles of social work in the context of community practice
6. Consider ethical issues associated with community practice

## HOW ARE COMMUNITIES DEFINED?

Although *community* is a word that is frequently used in everyday conversation, it is a slippery concept to define. The term *community* often elicits a particular image or images—a small town with its main street, the neighborhood in which you grew up, or the apartment complex where you reside. Obviously, *community* is a commonly used expression in our vocabulary, but it is also a term that can have multiple meanings.

Even people working professionally with community experience difficulty in settling on a definition. Generally speaking, **community** can be conceptualized in two different but related ways: (1) that which is shared and (2) an area with a common geography. In all likelihood, the richest connotation for social work practice involves the connotation of sharing.

### Community as Nonplace, Sharing, or Collective Affiliation

Increasingly, you hear discussions of the importance of nongeographic communities—"communities of interest." These include professional communities (e.g., the social work community), ethnic communities (e.g., the African American community), and religious communities (e.g., the St. Rita Parish community). In using the term *community* in relation to nongeographic entities, an assumption is made that people in a community possess common, shared experiences and identity. In these instances, the extent to which a community exists can be described by the amount of sharing that transpires in any given situation. It also is understood that community involves close communication, common bonds, and face-to-face relationships or "Gemeinschaft" (Lyon, 1987, pp. 7–8). In this sense, members of a community are viewed holistically (together) as a single entity.

A community is distinguishable from a society in several important ways. A society is not typically characterized by face-to-face relationships. Societal membership is at a distance and impersonal. Furthermore, societies (countries) operate by means of rules, intended to treat members alike—in similar or prescribed ways. This is functional but not personal. Communities, both localities or communities of interest, usually engage people in more personal ways and can thus serve as **mediating structures** between individuals or families and the more impersonal society.

## Time to Think 6.1

After reading how communities are defined, how would you define Jeanne's community? Consider at least three reasons why Jeanne is attached to the community and its residents. Do you have a strong sense of community? Explain why or why not. What type of community has appeal to you and how does that appeal reflect what you value?

### Self-Help/Mutual-Aid Groups as Community

Most of us are familiar with self-help groups, also called **mutual-aid groups**. In our society, these groups seemingly exist for every conceivable human issue. Examples include alcoholism (Alcoholics Anonymous) and mental illness (National Alliance on Mental Illness).

Self-help groups typically function as nongeographic communities, in that their members share a particular condition and life experiences associated with it. In a sense, self-help groups and other nongeographic communities take on some of the more important activities and responsibilities that traditionally were assumed by geographic communities and neighborhoods. Mutual-aid groups can be very important to consumers, as these groups often recast problems either as normal or as opportunities, facilitate the mobilization of collective resources, and empower individuals to help themselves through helping others.

## Geographic Communities

The most traditional way of conceptualizing a community involves geographic location. Each of us lives in some kind of a community. Your community could be a densely populated urban neighborhood, a sprawling suburb, or a small town in rural America. People in large metropolitan areas often identify a small section of the city as their community. For college students, their university campus often represents a physical community.

In **geographic communities**, people have neighbors. As a consequence of the availability of transportation and various means of communication (e.g., social media and computers), many people in communities enjoy the ability to control and place limits on face-to-face interaction with their geographic neighbors. In the past, direct contact with neighbors, local businesspeople, and residents of the neighborhood was difficult to avoid. Indeed, the ability to regulate one's engagement and social interaction with neighbors suggests the existence of individualism, privacy, and independence.

However, it is important to note that Americans do not enjoy equal access to technological advancements in our society. Furthermore, the local geographic community (neighborhood) is often considerably more important to certain demographic and social-economic groups than to others. For people with limited access to transportation (e.g., the economically disadvantaged, older adults, children, and persons with disabilities), neighbors living within walking distance constitute a very real and viable resource. In impoverished communities, neighbors learn to rely on one another for many things, including child care, food, supplies, tools, knowledge, skill, and ingenuity.

In social work practice, a crucial consideration with regard to any geographic community involves its potential for human sharing and exchange. Unfortunately, limited resources and a collective sense of pessimism characterize many impoverished geographic communities. Under these circumstances, community members become immobilized and fail to recognize the many assets and strengths that surround them. In many instances, this is not intentional. Instead, the physical design and construction of space in neighborhoods (e.g., the positioning of dwellings, public buildings, businesses, and recreation areas) has a limiting effect on social interaction. The appropriate design and use of physical space in a geographic community is a key factor in promoting human exchange and sharing.

## Nonplace Communities

Hardcastle, Powers, and Wenocur (2015) added to the concept of communities by highlighting the idea of nonplace communities that occur beyond the spatial and structural geographic communities. **Nonplace communities** are influential

**FIGURE 6.1**

Similarities and Differences Between Geographic and Nonplace Communities

DIFFERENCES

| Geographic Community | Nonplace Community |
|---|---|
| Bounded location | Bounded interest |
| Collective territorial identity | Relationship identity |
| Intertwined process | Specialized processes |
| Empathic connection | Mixed allegiances |

SIMILARITIES

History
Traditions
Mutual constraints
Lack of absolute boundaries

*Source:* Adapted from Hardcastle, David A., Powers, Patricia R., Wenocur, Stanley. *Community Practice: Theories and Skills for Social Workers.* Reproduced with permission of the Licensor through PLSclear.

groupings based on "identity, professional religion, ideology, interests and other social bounds that represent a more amorphous type of community" (Hardcastle et al., 2015, p. 97). Social workers must be mindful of such communities because both geographic and nonplace communities often figure into an individual or group's life conditions and value system. Figure 6.1 compares the differences and similarities between geographic and nonplace communities.

## Time to Think 6.2

Taylor proudly serves as the supervising social worker in her community's Women Helping Women (WHW) agency, an organization committed to advocacy for the rights and protection of women. A primary emphasis of WHW involves providing services and promoting opportunities and rights for women experiencing or surviving interpersonal and sexual violence. Much of Taylor's practice is devoted to working with women to develop healthy significant other (e.g., spouse, boyfriend, and girlfriend) relationships and boundaries. Common topics include separation, divorce, physical relocation, and reunification. Taylor and her social work colleagues also actively seek various forms of collective and community awareness, acknowledgment, leadership, and support for anti–sexual assault and the empowerment of women.

The **#MeToo movement** has been in existence in Taylor's community for several years but gained significant momentum after allegations of sexual assault and harassment were levied against Hollywood film producer and mogul Harvey Weinstein. Importantly, the #MeToo movement has drawn attention to and focused on the healing and survivorship of women having been assaulted and harassed. The #MeToo movement has been a catalyst in Taylor's geographical area for advancing and building community awareness, input, and action to obtain needed community resources (e.g., funding, volunteers, programming, and political support). In addition, many of

WHW's consumers of services now view themselves as members of a community of survivors. Through both in-person meetings and social media, WHW employees and consumers have been able to more actively speak out as a community of survivors about sexual violence and harassment to develop an active voice about common needs, hopes, and goals.

## FUNCTIONS OF COMMUNITIES

The significance of community in U.S. society is complicated, multifaceted, and changing. For some people, one's community represents a bastion of goods, services, amenities, and opportunities for relationship building. For others, a community can serve as a source of personal identity. How many times have you heard, "I came from such-and-such side of town"?

Warren and Warren (1997) identify a number of specific functions of geographic communities. These include the following:

- *Sociability arena:* A neighborhood can be a place to establish and sustain friendships.
- *Interpersonal influence center:* Thinking and perception are influenced by those around us, including neighbors.
- *Mutual aid:* This can be as basic as "borrowing a cup of sugar" or as complicated as providing daycare for a neighbor's child.
- *Status arena:* Neighborhoods often reflect the social status of their residents. Certain neighborhoods, such as the Upper East Side of Manhattan, can easily be recognized as a community inhabited by people of high social-economic means.
- *Identity and meaning:* When neighbors share values and common perspectives, a community can be a powerful referent for personal identity and meaning.
- *Site for human services:* Communities support and provide a working context for a variety of social services. From the earliest developments in social work (the Charity Organization Societies and settlement houses), social service delivery has been shaped by and grounded in neighborhood settings.

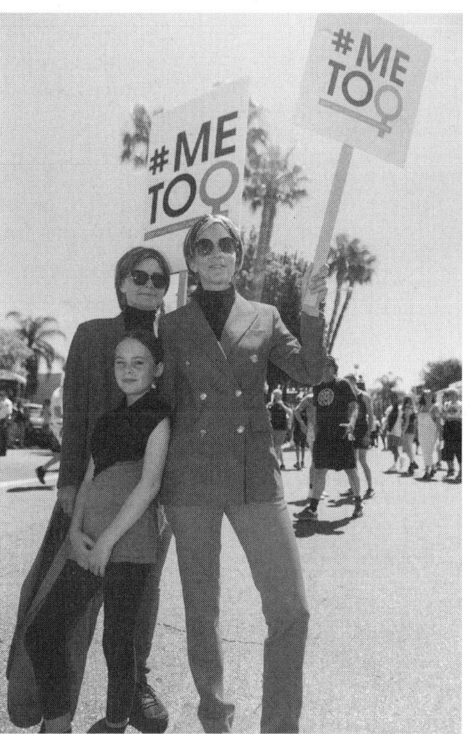




**PHOTO 6.1** Groups form movements and communities for change.

The concern related to improving community functions is not new to social work. As stated in previous chapters, macro social work emphasizes empowering community members to ensure their individual well-being and that of groups, communities, and organizations (Gamble, 2011). Conceptualizing a well-being community is defined in Table 6.1.

By understanding and assessing **community well-being**, social workers have a foundation to begin working with consumers to improve their environment through advocacy actions. Such actions can be evaluated based on desired benchmarks or outcomes to ascertain how action efforts are moving toward stated needs and progress.

**TABLE 6.1**

Conceptualizing Community Well-Being

| | |
|---|---|
| Social well-being | • All people need access to the supports and opportunities provided by social institutions and relationships in the context of families, neighborhoods, and communities.<br>• Everyone should have the opportunity to engage in education, recreation, cultural organizations, spiritual and religious institutions, and political organizations.<br>• Families, neighborhoods, and communities must have supportive health, welfare, educational, security (i.e., basic human needs), and political organizations to help them invest in their children and future generations. |
| Economic well-being | • Economic systems should include opportunities for paid and unpaid work and asset development.<br>• Wages should be sufficient to meet a family's needs for shelter, food, health care, transportation, and continuing or higher education.<br>• All human strivings, both paid and volunteer, are valuable to civilizations. Therefore, economic measures like gross domestic product and gross national income that exclude such things as parenting or volunteering to help neighbors or community members should be considered deficient for measuring well-being. |
| Political well-being | • All people should have freedom to associate, speak, vote, and participate in the governments that make policy for them.<br>• Social workers should empower the consumers using their services in all aspects of decisions and actions affecting their lives. |
| Environmental well-being | • Everyone should have access to clean water and air, as well as access to natural resources, ecosystem services, and the beauty of nature.<br>• Present generations must not live beyond the resources in the biosphere and must restore, to the extent possible, damage to air, water, soil, fisheries, forests, and other species.<br>• Social workers should help consumers in their communities strive to restore social institutions and economic development that enable the environment to serve all people. |

*Sources:* Adapted from Gamble (2011) and Gamble and Weil (2010).

## SOCIAL WORK AND COMMUNITY PRACTICE

**Community practice** has traditionally been acknowledged as a specific mode of practice in social work based on a variety of activities aimed at helping communities challenge injustices (Brady & O'Connor, 2014). However, it is also a type of practice that has continued to evolve and now carries a variety of connotations. Interestingly, *community organization* is a phrase that has traditionally been used to describe social work intervention at the community level. However, *community practice, community-based practice, community-based service delivery,* and *community building* are all terms used to describe social work at the community level.

Two terms capture the range of activities within community practice: *community building* and *community-based service delivery.* **Community building** suggests that the community's own abilities to confront and take care of issues are being mobilized and used. In this vein, terms such as *community empowerment* and *competent communities* are also relevant. Community building assumes that community members are engaged in strategies and techniques that can be used to intentionally enhance a community. This entails creating opportunities for people in the community to become more involved in making decisions concerning important issues and the general quality of life in the community.

Community building can take many forms and use many methods. Examples include the development of issue-specific focus groups, a neighborhood crime-watch group, a block club that sponsors block parties to enhance social interaction among residents, a cultural group that brings amateur musicians together, and a child-care cooperative.

Collectively, neighbors can positively affect the social image of a given area, both internally and externally. Neighborhood groups often publish local newspapers, host house tours, sponsor cultural events (e.g., parades, flower shows, and concerts), and create symbolic items (e.g., tote bags, T-shirts, hats, and signs) in an effort to promote their neighborhood. For current residents, these activities tend to accentuate the benefits of community life. Meanwhile, prospective residents are introduced to the virtues of becoming a member of a community.

Nongeographic communities can use similar techniques to increase member involvement and to facilitate positive changes in the perception of a particular condition. In doing so, they too are building community. In particular, Naparstek (1999) suggests that community building is comprehensive and integrative, facilitates new forms of collaboration and partnerships, strengthens existing social networks, uses and builds on a variety of neighborhood assets, and makes a concerted effort to target specific neighborhoods and groups of people to enhance participation.

The term **community-based service delivery** acknowledges that agencies often provide valuable and much-needed services in a neighborhood or community setting. Geographic communities vary considerably with regard to the availability of community-based services within their bounds. Similarly, communities of sharing rely on and vie for convenient service delivery based on their interests.

Community building and community-based service delivery are not mutually exclusive. Community practice involves both notions. Effective social work practice with communities promotes effective service delivery systems in and for communities and also involves working with community members to build collective capacities.

In community practice, interorganizational collaboration in promoting social change is both expected and encouraged—particularly by funding sources. When community-based organizations communicate and collaborate with one another, assets and resources can be more effectively used (e.g., through the elimination of duplicative services and programs). In addition, collaborative efforts between organizations can serve to bring together, organize, and structure the interests of consumers to garner political influence and establish prominence in decision-making processes. When members of social service agencies, voluntary associations, and planning groups act collaboratively, a unique synergy can be formed.

## Time to Think 6.3

Understanding the influence of communities involves self-reflection on the communities that have made a difference in your own life. For example, what geographic community have you lived in the longest and how did that community influence you in terms of attitudes and opportunities? Now consider what type of geographic community you hope to live in after college. What did you expect from that community and why?

Now pause and consider a nonplace community that you feel membership in. Why do you feel membership in that community, and how is your membership maintained over time? How do relationships figure into both your geographic and nonplace communities?

### Trends in Community Practice

Community practice has traditionally been acknowledged as a specific mode of practice in social work. However, it is also a type of practice that has continued to evolve and now carries a variety of connotations. Increasingly, *community practice, community-based practice, community-based service delivery,* and *community building* are all terms used to describe social work at the community level. In recent years, *community practice* has evolved as a more inclusive expression than *community organization.* In many instances, *community organization* has been narrowly used in social work circles to specify one of a number of community intervention options. Meanwhile, *community practice* has taken on a much broader meaning.

In response to macro social work practice as seen in the community practice, the **Association for Community and Social Administration (ACOSA)** was formed in 1987 and is recognized for advancing macro practice. ACOSA's primary mission is to strengthen community organization and social administration. As stated on its website (https://www.acosa.org/joomla/about-acosa/acosapurpose), the purposes of ACOSA are the following:

- To facilitate and support an annual national symposium
- To provide a forum for sharing information on teaching materials, literature, models/theory, research, and practice issues
- To facilitate networking activities among educators and practitioners
- To promote the development of teaching material, research, and literature about community organization and social administration
- To network with other professional associations in promoting development of community organization and social administration

ACOSA members receive e-blasts with news, announcements, newsletters, and other forms of valuable information as well as online access to the *Journal of Community Practice*.

## OVERVIEW AND HISTORY OF COMMUNITY PRACTICE AND ORGANIZING

The Charity Organization Society (COS), described in Chapter 1, was an attempt to develop a mechanism to coordinate the work of the many small charities that had emerged in many cities in the United States. A national office, which was under the leadership of Mary Richmond for many years, served as a way of providing the local COS with helpful information and support. Several features characterized the work of the local COS. Foremost, the COS offered a systematic means of coordinating social service delivery and operations, focusing both on individual capabilities and on the impact of social conditions. Indeed, the aforementioned *Social Diagnosis* (1917/1955) was written by Mary Richmond to assist in the training of charity workers.

To minimize duplication of cash assistance from more than one charity, recipients of charity assistance were registered with their local COS office. A worker from the COS, sometimes called a "friendly visitor," was assigned to provide service to families in a specific geographic district of the municipality. The workers, predominantly women, then set out to determine the need for assistance and any underlying causes that precipitated the request for help. The work of the COS became more refined over the years, and increasingly, workers relied on the use of modern counseling techniques. Much of the macro work of the COS focused on organizing the efforts of separate charities and developing a rational system for service delivery. The COS described its method as "scientific charity." By contemporary standards, however, it was probably more of a systematic approach than a truly scientific endeavor.

During the 1930s, the COS was unable to meet the extraordinary need for cash assistance created by the Great Depression. As a consequence, the government assumed the burden of providing financial assistance, as seen in the passage of the Social Security Act, with the bulk of the funding provided by the federal government. With less responsibility for monetary relief, the mission of the COS evolved toward an increasing emphasis on family counseling. Local affiliates soon changed their names to incorporate the term *family service,* and a national association formed, called Family Service America (FSA). In recent years, partially as a result of merger, FSA has become known as the Alliance for Children and Families. Family service agencies are among the oldest and best-established agencies in communities throughout the United States.

As a result of this history, family service agencies have continued to emphasize community-based approaches in providing services and advocating for policy formation and development. In addition, many social workers would argue that the community orientation and approach offered by the COS constituted the very origin of social planning in the United States.

## The Settlement House Movement

Community practice and **community organizing** go back to the settlement house movement, an early attempt to ameliorate problems associated with rapid urbanization and massive immigration (Brady & O'Connor, 2014). Between the 1880s and 1920s, hundreds of settlement houses were established in neighborhood centers that provided a variety of programs. Staff, often young (traditional college-age) women, moved into a neighborhood and lived in settlement houses. Volunteers with middle- and upper-class backgrounds hoped to experience firsthand conditions in poorer communities and thus to become better informed.

The specific services provided in a neighborhood were determined by each settlement house but typically included preschool education as well as programs for school-age children, adolescents, and adults. These services were commonly offered using some form of group format. Clubs, classes, and mass activities (e.g., open gym sessions) were the staple of most settlements. Emphasis was placed on promoting healthy development, prevention, and group intervention. Classes included music, arts, crafts, cooking, and activities accentuating ethnic heritage, as well as literacy programs. As suggested in earlier chapters, the group orientation and outlook associated with the settlement house movement served as an important backdrop for the development of group work as a distinct method in social work practice. Similarly, the recreation and adult education movements often trace their historical roots to this same settlement house movement.

It is important to note that while the vast majority of settlement houses were concerned about local neighborhood conditions, settlement houses also were free to approach issues in more individualized ways. As an example, many settlement houses established a system of neighborhood associations as a mechanism to encourage local residents to organize into smaller social units. Each neighborhood association would prioritize concerns and then identify its unique strengths and abilities for addressing and resolving issues. Settlement houses were also involved in broader social issues. For example, staff at Chicago's Hull House, headed by Jane Addams, were associated with major reforms such as the development of juvenile courts and provided national leadership in government and for major nonprofit associations. As you will recall, the settlement house movement was strongly associated with the "progressive movement," which championed reforms in labor, health, housing, and food production. Settlement houses continue to do important work, although they are now more likely to be known as community or neighborhood centers. The settlement houses clearly fit into both the community development and the social advocacy models.

### Community Chest and the United Way

Larger communities in the United States typically establish a United Way. Originally known as "community chests," these organizations provide an organized system of community-based fundraising for nonprofit agencies. United Ways solicit contributions from local residents and employees to develop a funding pool ("chest") to help underwrite nonprofit, voluntary agencies. On an annual basis, employers often ask for contributions from their workers, usually through payroll deduction plans.

United Way is also highly involved in making determinations concerning local community needs and decisions about how funds should be allocated to various agencies. Traditionally, United Ways have worked via a committee structure (e.g., committees dedicated to allocations and appropriations and to evaluation and planning) composed of volunteers from the community. Top donors, both companies and individuals, frequently vie to make sure that their representatives secure positions of authority on the more powerful committees of the United Way.

This is an interesting—and potentially self-serving—practice for making committee appointments. Using an empowerment orientation, it would seem imperative that consumers have adequate representation with regard to decisions involving the prioritizing and funding of local services. From a strengths perspective, the recruitment of able and well-suited stakeholders (consumers and others) for committee membership also seems prudent and wise when developing community capacities.

### International Community Development

Following the end of World War II, there was a surge of interest in the notion of community development. Some of this interest came from the British Colonial Office, which was interested in improving local conditions in British colonies. This was particularly true in East Africa, an area soon to become independent (Midgely, 1995).

A central theme of community development in this context was that local (village) residents could be mobilized to identify problems and to develop imaginative, tailor-made solutions. A major emphasis of **community development** involved building on the strengths of community members and teaching the skills needed for successful engagement in the community development process. Priority was given to "low" or "appropriate" technologies requiring little expertise that could be more easily implemented at the grassroots level. The community development approach was broadly accepted by many developing countries and continues to enjoy widespread support among major foundations and organizations in the Americas (e.g., the U.S. Agency for International Development). This approach has also been used as a mechanism for community engagement within poorer, disenfranchised areas in the United States.

## The Civil Rights Movement and the War on Poverty

Two movements in the 1960s helped to shape macro practice and are particularly relevant when considering community practice. The civil rights movement attempted to address historic patterns of exclusion, segregation, and discrimination. It was instituted by African American minorities and their allies and involved the use of a variety of innovative strategies for change (e.g., lawsuits, legislative initiatives, sit-ins, passive noncompliance, and demonstrations). Social workers and consumers united with community leaders across the United States to employ new techniques—often times labeled "radical"—to advance the cause of racial minorities. A newfound sense of strength, opportunity, and unbridled passion emerged, as minorities united and rallied behind more progressive forms of community leadership.

The so-called War on Poverty was an attempt by government to deal with both civil rights issues and the rediscovery of poverty (Harrington, 1974). The most visible federal agency was the Office of Economic Opportunity (OEO), which sponsored a number of community-oriented programs, including the Head Start preschool program, Job Corps (a training program for unemployed young adults), and the Community Action Program (CAP).

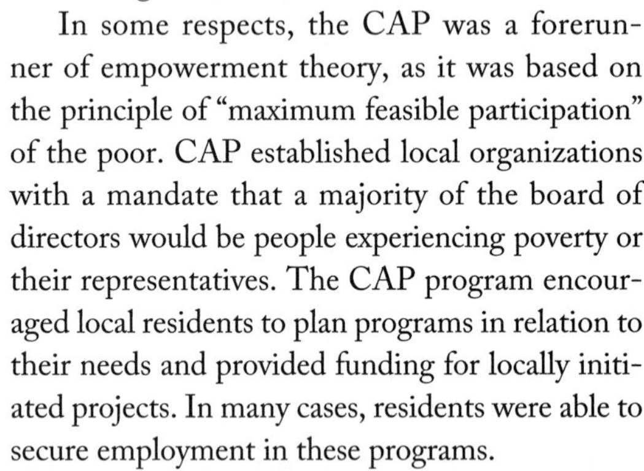

In some respects, the CAP was a forerunner of empowerment theory, as it was based on the principle of "maximum feasible participation" of the poor. CAP established local organizations with a mandate that a majority of the board of directors would be people experiencing poverty or their representatives. The CAP program encouraged local residents to plan programs in relation to their needs and provided funding for locally initiated projects. In many cases, residents were able to secure employment in these programs.

BARRIERS
1920s–1950s
From its earliest days, Birmingham was a city of two worlds: Black and White. People lived and worked side by side, however, double standards and segregation of all the races were facts of life. Here and throughout the South, unequal opportunity was a barrier to the hopes and dreams of nearly half the population.
WHITE
COLORED




**PHOTO 6.2** Separate water fountains were a key form of segregation between white Americans and African Americans.

Ultimately, a wide range of programs were funded through CAP, many of which included a strong emphasis on social advocacy and on organizing poor residents. Some of these programs were controversial, and clashes with established institutions and political structures were not uncommon. The CAP and similar programs encouraged people to become engaged in the social-political life of their communities. This meant that people had to overcome the apathy and sense of hopelessness that often accompany poverty.

As an encouraging by-product of this process, many local leaders emerged during the 1960s and 1970s, some of whom sought and won political office. Equally important, many traditional social agencies and organizations achieved a beginning-level awareness of the importance of involving users of services in identifying needs and designing programs.

Though not part of the antipoverty program, a key figure during the War on Poverty years was Saul Alinsky, who worked with several Chicago neighborhoods, particularly Woodlawn and Back of the Yards. Alinsky typically used dramatic, confrontational approaches designed to draw attention to causes. His approach to community organizing was to identify issues involving marginalized people and to confront established institutions and leadership concerning their role in perpetuating these problems. His tactics had the potential to embarrass powerful people; they were designed to persuade the local power structure to negotiate in good faith with representatives of consumer groups.

For a brief description of Alinsky's overall approach, see the work of Lyon (1987, pp. 121–125). The Industrial Areas Foundation in Chicago, founded by Alinsky, continues to serve as a national training center for community organizers and is recognized as one of the nation's largest networks of local faith and community-based organizations. Alinsky's approach is an aggressive and confrontational form of social advocacy. It is empowering in that it uses the strengths of consumers and their allies to challenge local powerbrokers over decision-making processes.

## USEFUL THEORETICAL PERSPECTIVES IN COMMUNITY PRACTICE STRATEGIES

For decades, Rothman's (1979) three modes or strategies of community practice (locality development, social planning, and social action) have served as a basis for examining community-level change. (As a point of clarification, the term *community development* may be preferable to *locality development,* as it includes the possibility of using such approaches with nongeographic as well as geographic communities.) In addition, Rothman's three strategies are similar to those identified by James Christenson (cited in Lyon, 1987, pp. 115, 126): (1) self-help (community development), (2) technical assistance (social planning), and (3) conflict (social action).

Since his original publication, Rothman has continued to develop his thoughts concerning community organizing. In particular, he suggested the need for a more elaborate range of strategies than his original three modes. As a result, several writers have worked to identify and describe additional types of community work.

For example, Taylor and Roberts (1985) put forward five models of community work. These include Rothman's original models with the addition of community liaison and program development. Taylor and Roberts also suggest that models of community practice should be analyzed and evaluated in relation to the amount of energy and action that is agency driven versus consumer determined.

Marie Weil (1996) has identified eight models of community practice. To Rothman's original modes, she has added organizing functional communities, community social and economic development, program development and community liaison, coalitions, and social movements. In each mode, the theme of building on the strengths of consumers through collective reflection and critical analysis (among consumers and with professionals) is an important element. Although not always the case, the decision as to which strategies to use in community practice should be a primary function of the will of consumers.

## Collaboration, Campaign, and Contest Strategies

Three useful strategies have been identified for bringing about change at the community level and within organizations. These are collaboration, campaign, and contest (Netting, Kettner, & McMurtry, 2001).

The least confrontational and least conflict-oriented technique involves **collaboration**, where the intent is to minimize power differentials between actors and to seek agreement among the various players. Collaborative efforts are particularly appropriate and effective when relevant parties exhibit relatively few differences, are open to change, and espouse compatible goals. As seen in Table 6.2, collaboration closely aligns with Rothman's "locality development," as both emphasize the "pulling together" of sentiment and the establishment of workable alliances between groups of people (i.e., capacity building). Collaborative efforts often assist and empower people in acquiring or gaining political influence.

A **campaign strategy** is more confrontational, as it involves convincing individuals or groups of the rightness of a particular plan, proposal, or direction. This is often an important tactic in Rothman's "social planning," as it assumes that one actor, often a paid professional, has expertise and special knowledge concerning the issues at hand, as well as viable resolutions. Examples of campaign tactics would include educational efforts (e.g., community forums, distribution of information, media presentations) aimed at convincing organizations and public officials of the merits of a plan or policy.

Unfortunately, campaign approaches can be structured in ways that minimize the ability and knowledge of consumers and ordinary citizens to determine appropriate courses of action, in favor of professional expertise and consultation.

**TABLE 6.2**
Strategies/Models of Community Practice

| Model | Auspice | Change Accomplished by | Typical Worker Roles |
|---|---|---|---|
| Program development | Fully sponsor-determined | Campaign | Administrator, implementer |
| **Social planning**[a] | 7/8 sponsor-determined | Campaign | Analyst, planner |
| Community liaison/networks | 1/2 sponsor-, 1/2 client-determined | Collaboration[b] | Broker, mediator |
| **Community development** | 7/8 client-determined | Collaboration | Teacher, coach |
| **Social action/political empowerment** | Fully client-determined | Contest[b] | Advocate, agitator, negotiator |

*Sources:* Derived from the work of Rothman (1979), Taylor and Roberts (1985), and Netting, Kettner, and McMurtry (2001).

[a]Bold type indicates Rothman's original strategies.

[b]Collaboration and contest are approaches aimed at attitudinal change. "Contest strategy" involves power and confrontation.

Special attention must be given to the strengths of consumers (e.g., experiences, public speaking, media presentations) when attempting to sway public sentiment.

Collaborations and campaigns both involve "attitude change," as each seeks to alter or sway people's attitudes. In both approaches, pressure is brought to bear to convince others of the merits of a particular goal or plan. However, neither strategy endorses coercion or strong-arm, confrontational tactics as means of gaining acceptance.

A **contest strategy**, by contrast, condones and is dedicated to a much more open use of conflict and confrontation as a means of promoting change. Tactics used include legal challenges, protest, bargaining and negotiation, civil disobedience, boycotts, marches, and demonstration. The contest approach fits nicely with Rothman's social action model, as contest tactics aim to promote and advance the equalizing of power between unequal actors through collective (planned) action.

Although they are presented separately here, it is not uncommon for consumers and community practitioners to implement these approaches in concerted, often stepwise, ways. For example, larger community-based public agencies often can wield greater power over decision makers than voluntary associations of consumers. A group of consumers advocating for needed change in organizational policy might first approach the agency with their request using collaboration and then resort to a campaign strategy. If both strategies were to fail, then the consumer group would likely entertain a contest strategy as a means of achieving their goals.

Conversely, consumers might conclude that the best first step is to mount a pointed, high-profile protest concerning the unreasonableness and insensitivity of the agency's policy. Functionally, the use of contest strategies in community-based change often serves to grab the attention of authorities, so that good-faith discussions using collaboration or campaigns can then take place. The aforementioned #MeToo movement employed contest strategies by conducting marches and confronting people in positions of power concerning accusations and claims of sexual abuse against women.

Of course, strategy choices are calculated decisions, not to be taken lightly. The ramifications of employing any of these strategies, but especially a contest tactic, need to be fully explored. Most important, determinations of this kind need to be made and fully endorsed by consumers. The role of the social worker is to encourage and assist consumers in defining their strengths and in making informed decisions. Some consumer groups are well organized and equipped to confront power differences and public opposition. Other consumer groups need assistance in nurturing and developing their capabilities. Regardless, an overall self-assessment of the strengths of consumers is a necessary step before implementing any community change tactic.

## Current Community Action Groups

Across the nation, people are organizing to address geographic and nonplace community needs. An example is the community-based need and subsequent action to address the increase in suicide. Involved in these groups are people who agree about the need for suicide prevention and have the skills to develop an action plan. Thus, membership in the action group should reflect the following:

- The organizations, services, and people who will carry out the planned strategies and activities
- The organizations, services, and people who will be the focus of those strategies and activities
- Community leaders who will help spread the message and encourage people to join in (e.g., religious leaders and doctors) as a way of getting in touch with isolated older people
- All relevant local groups, voluntary organizations, and government agencies working toward suicide prevention in a specific area (Community Matters, 2018)

At first, the goals of such groups might be short term and include distribution of available information or running a forum on community well-being, resilience, and social connectedness. Once the group is established, it may become involved with the wider community in discussing and deciding what needs to be done in the medium to long term, such as ways to reduce the isolation of older people who live on their own (Community Matters, 2018).

The Community Outreach and Resident Education program (CORE) is geographic community response to the Flint, Michigan, water supply that was found to have dangerously high iron and copper content. Supported by the federal, state, and local governments, CORE advocates for water quality improvements, pipe replacement, health care, food resources, educational resources, job training and creation, and more, going door to door so every resident has information on how to properly install and maintain their water filter (Community Outreach and Resident Education, 2018).

CORE members provide information on resources to help with water recovery, nutrition, and medical support. Furthermore, CORE encourages Flint residents to get their water tested on a regular basis through public education and the distribution of testing kits. CORE helps ensure the kits are available free of charge at the water resource sites within Flint fire stations and at the city hall (Community Outreach and Resident Education, 2018).

## Time to Think 6.4

As you read through the content on community practice and organizing, you gain a sense that action and advocacy come from a sense of need, values, and opportunities. Also embedded in the content is the idea that community practice and organizing shifts the balance of power and privilege to citizens and the consumers of services. After considering your values and needs, what type of advocacy action could you envision yourself participating in and for what desired outcome? Is there a group on your campus or hometown that seems to be aligned with your concepts of social justice? What will you and others gain by being a part of a community organizing effort?

## Roles for Social Work in Community Practice

When engaged in community practice, it is useful to consider some of the specific roles that are appropriate for social workers in macro social work practice. When considering the community, as either a consumer or a system for change, several **roles for social workers in community practice** have particular relevance. For example, the role of *mediator* is important, particularly in collaborative strategies. Social workers often seek ways to reconcile differences between groups of people. This involves accentuating group commonalities and shared strengths, while learning to minimize or accept differences.

As a mediator, social workers are involved in resolving arguments or conflicts within individual, group, community, and organizational systems. What is important to remember about a mediator is that a mediator remains neutral and does not side with a particular party or position. Rather, a social worker in this role helps opposing parties come to a mutually beneficial resolution.

A social work **facilitator** serves as a leader in a group. The group may be a consumer group, a task group, an educational group, a self-help group, or a group with some other community-based focus. In this role, a social worker will bring together people and open lines and patterns of communication, channeling activities and resources toward the resolution of a shared goal.

Similarly, in collaborative strategies, social workers often serve as **brokers**. Expertise and knowledge concerning community-based agencies, services, associations, and organizations allow social workers to become active agents in negotiating agreements and associations between various actors and social entities. Once again, this "brokering" is performed in response and as a complement to consumer participation and determination.

A social worker as a **lobbyist** involves political activity and actions that voices the concerns of groups and communities with the goal of influencing and shaping local, state, and national policy. In this role, a social worker will speak on behalf of the groups that they represent with politicians at the local, state, and national levels.

With respect to contest tactics, social workers can be seen as active participants in rousing the interests and ire of consumers. Social workers as *advocates* often work with consumers to bring important issues to the forefront. Envision a social worker with a bullhorn in hand making announcements at a rally or a social worker helping consumers to create and distribute pamphlets. To the extent that social workers enter the fray of raising public consciousness and awareness concerning community issues, they can be rightfully viewed as advocates for change.

The role of a social worker in community practice and organizing may change over time given the circumstances and needs of the community and its members. However, certain skills are needed in all the described roles, including the following:

- Active Listening—Giving full attention to what other people are saying, taking time to understand the points being made, asking questions as appropriate, and not interrupting at inappropriate times
- Social Perceptiveness—Being aware of others' reactions and understanding why they react as they do

- Speaking—Talking to others to convey information effectively
- Critical Thinking—Using logic and reasoning to identify the strengths and weaknesses of alternative solutions, conclusions, or approaches to problems
- Coordination—Adjusting actions in relation to others' actions
- Reading Comprehension—Understanding written sentences and paragraphs in work-related documents
- Service Orientation—Actively looking for ways to help people
- Writing—Communicating effectively in writing as appropriate for the needs of the audience
- Complex Problem Solving—Identifying complex problems and reviewing related information to develop and evaluate options and implement solutions
- Judgment and Decision Making—Considering the relative costs and benefits of potential actions to choose the most appropriate one

(Fanning, 2018)

### Time to Think 6.5

Consider the following: Students in your neighborhood school score poorly on standardized testing (proficiency exams). You have been asked to meet with a group of parents from the local school district. Identify some roles you might assume in your initial steps with the parents. If parents have arranged a meeting with the school administrators, consider how your role might change when preparing for such a meeting. How can you help ensure that consumers, not professionals, are directing the community practice and organizing process?

## APPLYING THE ADVOCACY PRACTICE AND POLICY MODEL TO COMMUNITY PRACTICE

Reflective examination of helping processes has been an ongoing theme throughout the history of social work. As you will recall from earlier chapters, the advocacy practice and policy model (APPM) uses as a dynamic framework comprising interlocking tenets, economic and social justice, a supportive environment, human needs and rights, and political access. Seen in totality, the APPM is designed for engaging consumers in planned change.

In this book, social work intervention has been viewed through two lenses: that of the advocacy and the strengths perspective. It is helpful to understand that community change, like other forms of social work practice, can be conceptualized and structured in terms of phases or steps. Phases of intervention keep consumers and professionals focused on the issues at hand and present considerations for each step in the process.

Many social workers would argue that the strength of our profession lies in two areas. First, social workers are particularly adept in facilitating *analytical assessment* (with consumers) and examining a community, or any other social system, from a multitude of perspectives, including the strengths orientation. Second, by virtue of their education and professional development, social workers have excellent *interpersonal and organizational skills*. This is particularly true when working with individuals, families, and consumer groups in communities.

Many social workers would agree that interpersonal skills and the ability to view phenomena from multiple viewpoints are two crucial elements when considering social advocacy. Professionals and consumers must work together in communities to assess both strengths and barriers, so that they can successfully identify relevant issues and actors and calculate meaningful change. Knowledge, information, theoretical wisdom, analytical abilities, relational skills, and practical experiences are some of the cornerstones of successful community intervention.

## Economic and Social Justice

Economic and social justice embodies the principles of equity and justice for all people, while highlighting those individuals, groups, and communities who are underrepresented or underserved. It includes a focus on citizen participation and challenges inequalities when they are perceived and where they arise. It includes efforts to exercise the right of freedom of speech, freedom of assembly, and freedom to organize (Checkoway, 2013).

The APPM recognizes the differences found in community membership, attempts to bridge boundaries that separate people by the sharing of perspectives and ideas, and maintains the values of equity and justice at its core. Beginning with people sharing ideas, needs and wants, and desired goals, the economic and social justice tenet of the APPM offers social workers a reason and spirit for people joining together to strengthen community. Ideally, over a period time, relationships and team formation community practice will help to facilitate opportunities to organize and advocate for diverse actions that have a core base—justice as seen by the redistribution of power and privilege. Thus, economic and social justice is about involving people in the decisions that affect their lives.

Within the tenet of economic and social justice, social workers must engage in reflective practice and ask the following questions:

- Am I supporting consumers to think and act independently?
- Am I treating consumers in their communities in a just and fair manner?

**PHOTO 6.3**
Focusing on economic well-being enhances reflection on self and others.

- Am I encouraging consumers to participate in the decision-making process?
- Am I assisting consumers to uncover and seize opportunities that enhance economic and social justice?
- Am I ensuring that all parties and voices are being heard?

(Cox, Tice, & Long, 2019)

### Supportive Environment

Person-in-environment is a critical concept for social work. The term is used to consider an individual and individual behavior within the environmental context in which that person lives and acts. The APPM expands person-in-environment to include all the people and social systems, along with natural resources, that surround a person. Within this framework, the APPM considers elements within the environment that add quality to life and those that detract from optimal living circumstances.

Relationships are intrinsic to a supportive environment. In community practice, relationships span the gamut from community members and service consumers to elected officials at the local, state, and federal levels. In all instances, social workers must be mindful of communication pathways and strategies. The goals are always to empower consumers to have a voice in all decisions at all systems levels.

In the APPM, environment also involves the natural or tangible environment. Therefore, air, land, and water pollution; climate control; and resource allocation interface with issues of social and economic justice. Examples of the environment components are housing, food, and health care availability and affordability. The question becomes one of environmental quality and sustainability at what cost to whom. Table 6.3 suggest skills that are needed for community-based environmental engagement. As indicated, an understanding of human rights is a key element to effectiveness.

### Human Needs and Rights

Social work has a longstanding commitment in addressing human needs. Social workers engage in community practice that assesses needs along with consumer systems. They advocate for the needs with consumers, as well as empowering consumers and communities to address their needs (Dover, 2017). They also advocate for social welfare benefits and services and overall social policies that take human needs into account.

**TABLE 6.3**

Skill Sets for Effective Environmental Education and Engagement

| Communications Skills | Building Relationships | Developing an Understanding of the Environmental Context | Building a Network and Community | Educating the Educators |
|---|---|---|---|---|
| • Writing letters to the media<br>• Using the Internet<br>• Issuing press releases<br>• Talking with the media<br>• Identifying and using language and worldview of audience to build common dialogic space<br>• Empowering distinctions in language to build engagement<br>• Facilitating conversations | • Developing alliances with opinion leaders and decision makers in a variety of sectors, such as politics, business, professional groups, and political leaders<br>• Identifying strategic opportunities, such as government budgets<br>• Facilitation skills of meetings, groups, workshops, conferences | • Basics of climate science and ecological decline: scale, time, and urgency<br>• Climate change and ecological decline as moral issues<br>• Justice and international development issues<br>• Food frame<br>• Environmental legacy frame<br>• Health frame<br>• Economy frame<br>• Justice and human rights frame<br>• Adaption possibilities for faith communities in partnership with other communities | • Identifying and building relationships with allies<br>• Relationship building<br>• Thinking and planning strategically<br>• Using resources from other movements as models | • Implementing processes of effective education in communities<br>• Identifying personal teaching style and existing skill sets |

*Sources:* Adapted from Lysack (2012).

The preamble of the *Code of Ethics* of the National Association of Social Workers (2018) states that

> the primary mission of the social work profession is to enhance human well-being and help meet the basic human needs of all people, with particular attention to the needs and empowerment of people who are vulnerable, oppressed, and living in poverty. A historic and defining feature of social work is the profession's focus on individual wellbeing in a social context and the well-being of society. Fundamental to social work is attention to the environmental forces that create, contribute to, and address problems in living.



The social work profession shares a close relationship with human rights, because it adheres to values such as respect, dignity, and self-determination—values that are strongly embedded in all fields of practice. The unique and candid relationship between a social worker and consumer has long been celebrated. The profession is steadfast in challenging the inhumane treatment of vulnerable people, its confrontation of oppressive practice, and ensuring that vulnerable people are empowered to voice their opinions and participate in the decision-making process. A persistent question that social workers ask is, Who is defining the need and for whose benefit?

## Political Access

Social workers provide vital services to support the well-being of people. Advocacy for political access becomes more essential as economic, health, and housing disparities increase; as the population ages; and as the middle class struggles to maintain stability. The social work professional recognizes that local, state, and federal policymakers play critical roles in promoting policies that help individuals, families, and communities to fulfill their potential and to lead healthy, productive lives.

**Political Action for Candidate Election (PACE)** is the political action arm of the National Association for Social Workers (NASW). As a political action committee, PACE endorses and financially contributes to candidates from any party who support NASW's policy agenda (NASW, 2017). The national PACE Board of Trustees endorses and contributes to federal candidates running for U.S. House and Senate seats. State chapter PACE units decide on local and state races.

In the context of community practice, social workers should consider the following questions:

- Am I working with consumers to understand the "bigger picture" issues and how such issues relate to daily life situations in homes and communities?
- Am I facilitating collaborations and partnerships, including with political entities, that empower consumers to develop and advocate for political strategies that enhance their well-being?

- Am I supporting consumers as they make their voices heard through actions and verbal and written words?
- Am I encouraging and seeking support for politicians to assess structural changes needed to help ensure the better distribution of power and privilege?

(Cox et al., 2019)

## PRINCIPLES ON USING A STRENGTHS PERSPECTIVE

In light of the APPM and as indicated earlier in this chapter, many social workers would argue that the strength of our profession lies in these two areas. First, social workers are particularly adept in facilitating analytical assessment (with consumers) and examining a community, or any other social system, from a multitude of perspectives, including the strengths perspective. Second, by virtue of their education and professional development, social workers have excellent interpersonal and organizational skills. This is particularly true when working with individuals, families, and consumer groups in communities.

Many social workers would agree that interpersonal skills and the ability to view phenomena from multiple viewpoints are two crucial elements when considering advocacy action. Professionals and consumers must work together in communities to assess both strengths and barriers, so that they can successfully identify relevant issues and actors and calculate meaningful change. Knowledge, information, theoretical wisdom, analytical abilities, relational skills, and practical experiences are some of the cornerstones of successful community intervention.

The following are a few helpful suggestions for everyday **community-based practice** using the strengths perspective:

***Social worker role:***

- Be clear about your roles in community organizing. Are you an advocate, group leader, evaluator, facilitator, administrator, or what? Strive to ensure that your role definitions allow for the strengths of consumers to emerge, develop, and take primacy.
- Listen! Practice active listening skills. People need to tell their story, often in detail. The thoughts, perceptions, feelings, and decisions of consumers constitute the foundation, the bricks and mortar, of macro social work practice and community-level change.
- Avoid the temptation to tell the group what you believe are their problems and their strengths. This should be a process of discovery, aimed at consumer ownership and empowerment.
- One of your most important tasks involves process. Help the group to reach a sense of consensus on the topics to be addressed and on

consumer strengths in pursuing community change. Often the social worker plays a useful role in clarifying issues and tactics and in keeping the consumer group on task. Helpful undertakings can include finding a meeting place and times, formalizing agendas, making clear what needs to be done before the next meeting, reiterating the agreed-on division of labor, assisting leadership efforts, summarizing agreements reached during meetings, and spelling out the next steps in the process.

- Allow people to do for themselves and to assume their own form of leadership in community change. The social worker should perform roles endorsed by consumers. The temptation for some people is to ask the social worker to resolve problems. The goal of social work is to empower people to address their own issues and to build capacities for use in the future. If the worker takes on an issue for a community group, people will miss opportunities, collectively and individually, to enhance their abilities.
- Be honest about your abilities, your professional limitations, and the resources available at your agency. For community change to be successful, there must be an appreciable investment (of time, energies, and funds) from many parties. Early in the process, consumers need to be aware of these types of obligations.
- Be clear with the group that you and your agency may not be able to support some goals or tactics.

***Process considerations:***

- Think about community-level change as beginning in smaller ways, through individual contacts and small-group meetings (e.g., in homes or at community centers). This will allow consumers to build momentum, assess their strengths, and develop a proper pace for subsequent actions. To begin community change efforts with a large forum is often premature, grandiose, and ineffective.
- Assist consumers in establishing a climate that promotes successful action. The group should be conceptualized as achievement oriented, not simply a "talking group." Identify and clarify the purposes of the consumer group or association.
- Involve people in the change process, and nurture respect for even the most basic form of participation.
- Don't forget that community-level change can be fulfilling. People get involved in community groups for a variety of reasons, including social ones, and these motives should be recognized. Some people are better than others at addressing the social-emotional needs of members. For example, basic efforts, like serving refreshments, may increase participation and make work more enjoyable.
- Strike a good balance between process (how goals are achieved) and product (actual goal achievement). Consumers need to experience some

degree of success in order to sustain interest, but the process of achieving goals is also important in its own right. Be attentive to both process and product in relation to human capacity building. Becoming skillful and able actors in the community is valuable, regardless of goal attainment.

- Encourage group members to avoid the tendency to plan so many activities that people become overwhelmed and bow out of planned change. In community work, as with other forms of intervention, activities need to be prioritized on the basis of overall group goals and probability of success.
- Identify the major stakeholders with respect to your consumer group. These individuals will most likely constitute the leadership and will play a major role in decision making. Take measures to ensure that consumer leadership is receptive and responsive to the strengths and concerns of other consumers.
- Timely follow-up and feedback are important ingredients in sustaining consumer interest in community change. Some form of regular contact with each member should take place between meetings. Phone calls, fliers, and e-mails help ensure a flow of information and can facilitate active engagement.

***Organizational considerations:***

- The organizational structure of a community group should reflect the functions and tasks that are needed. Organizational structure should provide support and consultation for decision making but need not be any more complicated than is required to get the job done. Social workers working with community groups should advise them to avoid creating more offices or committees than needed.
- Similarly, procedures need not be more complicated than is needed to achieve group goals. At times, *Robert's Rules of Order* can be too complex. Encourage consumers to adopt inclusive processes, where people are encouraged to voice opinions, use their talents and abilities, and participate freely in decision making.
- Assume that consumer participation will vary over time. Some people will come and go, particularly in the early phases. Nurture and develop individuals for leadership roles, and consider multiperson (co-leadership) models. Organizations often exhibit greater endurance when they are less reliant on a single person for leadership.
- Allow for multiple levels and kinds of participation by consumers. Some people may desire only occasional or intermittent involvement. People who choose not to talk may like to engage in tangible actions (e.g., creating a website or distributing fliers). Consumers with political connections may prefer contacting community leaders. As with the settlement house movement, consumers benefit when organizational climate is open, warm, inclusive, and receptive.

## Time to Think 6.6

After reading about the advocacy practice and policy model and the strengths perspective, discuss how you think they interface to encourage consumer participation in community-based needs assessment, establishment of goals, and outcomes measurement. What roles might the social worker assume in this process?

## USING COMMUNITY ORGANIZATION THEORY TO IMPROVE PRACTICE

Knowledge and theory in an applied field such as social work are intended to improve the effectiveness of practice. The following points, stimulated by the scholarly works and perspectives examined in this chapter, are offered as means of sharpening your community practice.

1. *Determine the focus of community organizing.* Clarify whether the target for change is the community, the consumer (client) system, or both. In other words, who are you working for, and with, as a social worker? As much as possible, have consumers define the issues at hand and the scope of your work within the community context. Is *community* defined geographically or as a community of sharing? With consumers, determine the assets of your employing agency as well as the usefulness of relevant individuals, organizations, resources, and other entities in the community.
2. *Decide which community practice strategies are most appropriate.* Rothman (1979), Taylor and Roberts (1985), and others provide social workers with conceptual models for engaging in community practice. Contemplate the overall direction being called for in your practice. Once again, this is a participatory process that beckons for direct involvement and ownership by consumers. Everyone benefits when a clear sense of direction is defined and determined in community practice.
3. *Agree on which roles you are assuming as a social worker.* Which role or roles do you plan to perform? What expectations and behaviors are associated with these roles? The will of consumers concerning role assumption and definition is crucial. It is important to remember that a primary obligation is for the social worker to act as a coinvestigator, working in tandem with consumers. Whatever your role (e.g., advocate, mediator, organizer, facilitator, policy analyst), consumer endorsement legitimizes, directs, and places limitations on your status and actions. As suggested earlier, it will be helpful to discuss role enactment in the context of the particular types of strategies being employed—collaboration, campaign, and/or contest.

4. *Identify the type of neighborhood/community involved.* Warren and Warren (1977) suggest that neighborhoods can be differentiated by type—classified according to identity, interaction patterns, diversity, and ability to access external resources. Given these dimensions, work with consumers to identify community strengths and assets.

5. *Outline with consumers a process or steps for proceeding with planned change, and estimate a reasonable timeline.* What do previous research, local experience, up-to-date information, and contemporary theory suggest with respect to consumer plans? Nurture and develop relationships, channels of communication, and dialogue with consumers and relevant actors to maximize the probability of success (Perlman & Gurin, 1972). Consider and promote diversity and inclusion in relationship to participation in planned change. Agree on a reasonable timeline for pursuing change. Consider embedding critical junctures or turning points as identifiable elements in the process.

6. *Establish mechanisms for ongoing evaluation.* Consumers and professionals should be engaged in ongoing review of efforts directed at community change, using both formal and informal means. Mechanisms could include the use of consumer meetings, organization and special interest group feedback, group discussions, surveys, commissioned focus groups, and review by external professional research bodies. Information derived from multiple indicators using a variety of sources often yields some of the best, most thought-provoking feedback.

## CONSIDER ETHICAL ISSUES ASSOCIATED WITH COMMUNITY PRACTICE

Social workers have always been concerned with service coordination, interagency networks, and partnerships. They realize that no single agency has the resources to address the many needs of consumers of services. A variety of mechanisms have potential for enhancing coordination, including collaboration, coalitions, partnerships, and community involvement teams.

Community partnering can help agencies achieve more effective and efficient service for consumers and can be a vehicle for securing additional support or sharing resources for programming. When contemplating potential partners, consumer participation and an understanding of ethics are vital. For example, consumers are keenly aware of the cluster of services they commonly use. For families with children, schools, preschool programs like Head Start, the local child and family services agency, the family guidance clinic, and after-school programs may be logical. For older adults, a partnership between senior centers, nutritional programs, and health agencies would make more sense. Another set of partnerships could be clustered with respect to physical disability. When examining the potential of partnerships, the hopes and desires of consumer groups are a primary consideration, as are the ethical issues associated with confidentiality and informed consent.

Confidentiality involves maintaining consumer identity, overt comments, opinions about and by consumers, consumer images (e.g., photos), and all consumer information private; such information cannot be disclosed without the consumer's written consent. For example, community schools are one mechanism for enhancing coordination of services at a neighborhood level (Morrison et al., 1998). Because public schools are conveniently located in neighborhoods, serve most children, and have good facilities, they are natural sites for coordinated services that have detailed consumer information. However, such information cannot be shared in the network of agencies without the written consent of a consumer.

Trust is a key element in the ethics of confidentiality. According to the NASW's (2017) *Code of Ethics,* the duty of social workers is to inform consumers of their right to privacy. As a corollary, the social worker needs to explain informed consent whereby the consumer grants permission to share information to specific agencies or service providers. It is important to note that consumers must fully understand their rights before the consent to share information is granted.

Throughout social work practice, including practice in communities, social workers encounter ethical dilemmas. Ethical dilemmas emerge in situations when ethical principles are in conflict. For example, in a community where funds allocated for a recreation center have been drastically reduced, consumers have organized and are advocating for lower center membership fees. The social worker could advocate for the needs of community members to have access to recreational space while recognizing the financial straits of the local government.

In this situation, a social worker should gather information regarding the community's fiscal circumstances, its allocations to the recreation center, and the cost of operating the center. Simultaneously, along with consumers, consideration could be given to other sources of funding for the center, including volunteer time, and sponsorship of the center through private donations. In essence, once the situation is evaluated based on ethical principles—in this case, the right and access to recreational space—the next step is creative identification of possible alternatives to pursue. Thus, professional ethics address questions about what actions are ethically correct and how social workers should proceed. The NASW's (2017) *Code of Ethics* is invaluable in documenting social workers' responsibilities to consumer systems.

---

SAGE edge™ Visit **www.edge.sagepub.com/ticemacro** to help you accomplish your coursework goals in an easy-to-use learning environment

---

## SUMMARY

This chapter examines community practice and the importance of the community in supporting people and achieving mutually defined goals. Community was defined as either a geographic or a nonplace community. Many considerations and practical suggestions were provided for social workers engaged in helping people to build community capacities while enhancing consumer empowerment. In addition, the advocacy practice and policy model was examined for use in community practice.

A recurring theme in this chapter involved using the strengths of consumers in community practice. The role of the social worker in community practice was viewed as being defined by the hopes and desires of consumers. In the tradition of the COS and settlement house movements, a primary responsibility of the social worker is to seek ways to promote community consciousness and empower consumers of services.

Finally, ethical issues were examined with an emphasis on consumer participation and ownership in creating social change. When there is an ethical dilemma, social workers are called upon to assess professional obligations in light of consumers' interest.

## TOP 10 KEY CONCEPTS

collaboration 136
community 123
community-based service delivery 129
community building 129
community organizing 132
community-based practice 145
community well-being 128
geographic communities 125
mediating structures 124
mutual-aid groups 124
nonplace community 125

## DISCUSSION QUESTIONS

1. Consider a nonplace community that you have an affinity for or hold membership in. What are the traditions that keep you engaged in the community? How do the traditions reflect your values?
2. Review the roles for social workers in community practice and consider what roles interest you and why. What skills are needed for the roles you selected?
3. Your college or university campus could be considered a community. Discuss with the students in your class what the strengths of the community are and what areas or elements you think need improvement. How would you go about organizing for change for the campus?
4. After reviewing the advocacy practice and policy model, give thought to the tenet of economic and social justice. Make a list of the social justice issues that could affect a geographic community and the strategies that consumers could take to address such conditions.
5. Community schools are funded through property taxes. This means the higher the home prices in a neighborhood, the greater the tax base and revenue, resulting in better resources for schools. In your mind, is there an ethical issue in this taxation process? Why or why not?

## EXERCISES

1. Go to the U.S. Census website (www.census.gov) and use the tools provided there to develop a profile for your community. Include both demographic and housing information. Determine the census tract for your area. Compare census tract and ZIP code information. How might this type of information be useful to consumer groups in

the community? Can you envision consumer leadership using this type of data from the Internet?

2. You are employed at a community health center. In a cost-cutting move, city council members are questioning program utilization and effectiveness at your agency. Politicians are looking to reduce spending and eliminate programs. Consumers and agency professionals have already heard about the intentions of council members. Professional staff members at the health center are highly invested in several programs. The sentiment of consumers concerning program implementation and efficacy is far less clear. Several consumers have asked you to assist them in efforts to maintain current programming. Outline how you would proceed to work with and empower consumers.
3. You have been working with a community group that has expressed a concern about trash pickup in the neighborhood. The group does not want to be confrontational but would like to entertain various ways to remedy the situation. What are some initial thoughts concerning data gathering, potential alliances, and the value of collaboration?
4. You have been asked to collaborate with an Area on Aging Agency to design a public transportation system for older people who reside in a rural community. As you consider this process of community practice, think about the following points and your responses: (1) Which individuals would you ask to help you with this organizing effort, (2) what would be your process in achieving your goal of a transportation system, and (3) how will you evaluate the timeline and progress you make?
5. When thinking about consumer participation in a community-based project, develop a plan that reflects how you could develop leadership with consumers. How will the community's history and tradition influence both consumer participation and leadership development?

## ONLINE RESOURCES

- The Association for Community Organization and Social Administration (www.acosa.org): A membership organization for community organizers, activists, nonprofit administrators, community builders, and policy practitioners.
- The National Council of Nonprofits (www.councilofnonprofits): A national group that shares best community practice ideas through peer-to-peer interactions.
- Resources for Community Organizers (www.politicalsocialworker.org): Provides written material and consulting services for social workers involved in community practice.
- *Dissent Magazine* (www.dissentmagazine.org): Based on Saul Alinsky community organizing, the magazine provides articles on community-based programs and organizing strategies and events.
- Association of Community Organizations for Reform Now (www.acron.org): Was once the largest national organization for community-based social justice initiatives. Provides articles and policy updates.

# Social Planning

## ANGELA EMBRACES SOCIAL PLANNING

Angela is a social worker employed at a neighborhood community center. Her time is almost evenly split between family preservation services and activities aimed at community planning and organizing. Angela enjoys both the micro and macro elements of her practice. She finds working for planned change at multiple levels interesting and a source of professional motivation.

Over the past 5 years, the city's Latino population has grown, enriching the urban area with new ideas and customs. In general, people have welcomed the changing composition of the population. In fact, public officials often tout the fact that the city is becoming more diverse and now has an appreciable Latino population.

Nearly half of the recent immigrants originated from Mexico and the remainder from Guatemala, Puerto Rico, and Nicaragua. Most of the people are economically challenged and do not speak English. In addition, people are segregated in their living and social interaction by country of origin and social-economic status. Consumers from each group frequent the community center and receive a wide variety of services. Unfortunately, there is currently little sense of homogeneity among these groups. To the contrary, at times, there has been friction and conflict as traditions have clashed.

To her credit, Angela has built excellent working relationships with individuals from each of the Latino groups. As a result, she has been successful in working with consumers to facilitate a beginning level of awareness and appreciation of the commonalities and strengths that the various Latino groups share. Angela and representatives from each of the local Latino groups formed a social planning group that includes consumers, agency administrators, professionals, and community leaders. Everyone senses a readiness for the various Latino population groups to come together and plan for change. A concerted effort was made to embrace inclusion, the desire to ensure that a wide variety of people participate and are included in planning processes. Angela and others intentionally participated in "inreach" and found people able and willing to participate in social planning.

## LEARNING OBJECTIVES

After reading this chapter, you should be able to:

1. Define and describe social planning in the context of social work practice
2. Identify the relevance and importance of consumer participation and engagement in social planning
3. Examine and contemplate models, approaches, and ways of implementing social planning in social work practice
4. Embrace an advocacy model in relationship to social planning
5. Identify key factors and consider strategic and social planning from an organizational standpoint in social work practice

Interestingly, the first point of contention in the planning process involved language. Many people did not speak English, but not everyone spoke Spanish, and those who did speak Spanish often struggled with dialect. Although Angela speaks Spanish, she is not fluent. Ultimately, the consensus of the social planning group was to speak in English but to hire a translator.

The second decision of the social planning group was to establish itself as a formal unit. They chose the name Uno Latino as a gesture of solidarity. Rather than becoming an issue- or agency-specific planning group, Uno Latino was to be the community's collaborative entity for the Latino population. Uno Latino has developed a vision statement. It articulates the desire to promote education, safety, health, and employment for all Latinos in the city. Although Uno Latino is currently only at the "persuading people to take responsibility" phase of social planning, most agree that the organization has already been highly successful in raising consciousness about shared concerns, creating a spirit of shared leadership, and rallying people to use their strengths to contemplate planned change.

## WHAT IS SOCIAL PLANNING?

Social planning is an activity typically associated with community practice, community organizing, and leadership in human services. Indeed, it is an important function in any community or society. Social planning involves processes that allow people to collectively explore assets and areas for improvement, develop plans of action, and evaluate the effectiveness of policies and programs in creating large-scale social change.

Planning involves mapping out or making arrangements for doing and accomplishing something. Students engage in personal planning when they develop a strategy to complete a class assignment or study for an examination. Although this type of planning is an individual endeavor, the benefits of collective thought and contemplation are many. The veteran learner knows that conversations with other students yield valuable information and insight for approaching projects, exams, and papers.

Social planning is a cooperative process, associated with the strengthening of organizations, communities, and societies through the development and successful implementation of social policies and programs. In its most general form, social planning is an ongoing course of action, both formal and informal, in which consumers, citizens, leaders, and professionals work together to brainstorm and develop strategies to improve human functioning and the social environment.

### Time to Think 7.1

Angela and agency officials are approaching social planning with sensitivity to social diversity, including specific groups of people (e.g., differentiated by country of origin). Angela speaks some Spanish, but she is not fluent in Spanish. Clearly, language is a barrier. Contemplate professional and organizational responsibilities with respect to cultural competencies in social work practice. Is providing a translator for social planning meetings a reasonable and effective solution? What would be the optimum situation? How could members of Uno Latino offer insight and suggestions concerning ways to enhance communication?

Uno Latino has successfully formed a vision statement. This is an important first step in social planning. Consider possible subsequent steps. For example, is a more formal mission statement needed? At what point should the members of Uno Latino establish concrete short- and long-term goals? These are typical questions and considerations in social planning.

As one might imagine, social planning is related to and often performed in conjunction with a variety of social work roles and functions. For example, it is imperative that social planners keep abreast of policy initiatives and developments as well as current research depicting "best practices" and effective interventions in promoting social change. Being an effective communicator and mediator concerning disputes and facilitator of meetings, events, and activities are also important roles and functions. Table 7.1 provides a brief overview of the relationship between important elements of social work and engagement in social planning.

Social planning is closely related to community practice and administration and a number of helping and health-related professions. Community-based leaders and practitioners are typically engaged in some type of social or strategic planning, whether it is building a new community center, forming a task force, promoting a fund drive, or lobbying for a legislative initiative to provide opportunities for consumers. Therefore, it is important to view social planning as being encompassing, contextual, and a primary function in the professional life of social workers.

As with most forms of social work practice, a multitude of approaches can be used to conceptualize and engage in social planning. This book is dedicated to examining advocacy in action and in Chapter 2 provided a variety of orientations and models applicable to social planning. However, it is noteworthy that social planning has traditionally been grounded in a problem-solving (deficit) orientation. For many people, social planning has been and continues to be a mechanism to address, correct, and resolve social problems and injustices.

©iStockphoto.com/fstop123

**PHOTO 7.1** Empowerment enhances patterns of communication.

Although the problem-solving orientation toward social planning is a social work mainstay, it is only one possible approach. As suggested in previous chapters, seasoned social workers know the virtues of using an eclectic approach—considering a multitude of theories, approaches, and models for use in psychosocial intervention. As a rule, it is helpful to analyze social processes and phenomena in a variety of ways, being

**TABLE 7.1**
Social Planning and Social Work

Dudley (1978) examines the relationship between social planning and social work using the five elements in this table, which are relevant in contemporary social work practice.

| Social Work Element | Relevance to Social Planning |
| --- | --- |
| **Values**—a base for professional practice and ethical behavior | Leadership and participation of social workers in social planning is guided by professional values and code of ethics that inform and guide their actions and the primacy of consumer self-determination and respect for diversity and self-worth. |
| **Knowledge**—knowledge about people and practice, guided by values | Social workers acquire knowledge in the areas such as macro practice, human behavior, communication, diversity, research, policy, and the social environment, which contributes to an understanding of and ability to critically analyze social planning. |
| **Purpose**—the quest for desirable outcomes as a result of defining goals | Social planning is often prompted by issues and causes requiring the definition of goals and specific, measurable outcomes. The value orientation and knowledge of social workers is important for consumer participation and empowerment in social planning. |
| **Sanction**—the basis by which social workers are charged and legitimized to practice | Social workers received professional degrees sanctioned by the Council on Social Work Education and seek state licenses that sanction and legitimize their knowledge, skills, and adherence to values as expressed by the NASW *Code of Ethics.* |
| **Method**—the way values, knowledge, purpose, and sanction are actualized and placed into action | Social workers are required to complete field education experiences under the supervision of social workers, which contributes to their ability to use knowledge, skills, and values in various forms of macro practice, including social planning. |

careful to cue into the voices, passion, and will of consumers. Social planning, by definition, involves numerous actors and vested interest groups. As a result, it is important from the outset of the social planning process to be attentive to the tone or approach being advocated by various stakeholders.

## CONSUMER PARTICIPATION IN SOCIAL PLANNING

Historically, the profession of social work has demonstrated a rich commitment to identifying and fostering modes of consumer and citizen participation in grassroots (community-based) social planning. Some of the most basic tenets of grassroots planning include "rituals of engagement; the sharing of power; a culture of participation characterized by safety, respect, and high expectations; and skilful, yet humble, facilitation to create solidarity and equality within the group" (Zachary, 2000, p. 71).

Typically approaching social planning in a nonauthoritarian manner, the tradition of social work practice has often relied on the ability of professionals to mobilize consumers and citizens to rally behind causes, win battles, and build a sense of "we-ness" among people. Kahn (1991) and Staples (1984) highlight the benefits of broad-based participation over personal power in leadership and planning processes. These advantages include the ability to influence decision makers and power structures, enhanced fundraising, advancement of the views of consumers, and grounding causes in real-life experiences and human strife.

Consumers bring to the planning table firsthand knowledge about and involvement with social phenomena involving human struggles and strengths. Consumer voices are often filled with information, emotion, and a unique sense of urgency. Social workers are key professionals for identifying and encouraging participation by consumers of services who are able, willing, and passionate about promoting social change, which frequently involves challenging the status quo and people in positions of influence and power.

## WAYS OF APPROACHING SOCIAL PLANNING

When working with people, it becomes obvious fairly quickly that consumers, professionals, citizens, business leaders, politicians, government leaders, community organizers, social planners, and administrators conceptualize social planning from varied perspectives and often differ in the approaches they offer to create social change. For example, politicians typically view social planning as a question of political clout and alignment: What are the best ways for people to position themselves in a manner to effect change?

Meanwhile, business leaders tend to see social planning in terms of cost-effectiveness and judicious investment of resources: Can we afford to do this? Would such plans make economic sense? And, although no single approach can capture the magnitude and complexity of social planning, each of the following approaches has merit and constitutes a unique source of insight concerning planned change.

### Rational Model

The first inclination of many people is to think of social planning as a rational process. When a community or societal issue arises, they think: Let's bring a group of people together (e.g., commission, committee, task force) and, in an analytical and objective manner, assess the situation, define the problems, establish short-term and long-term goals, plan a course of action to reach the specified goals, and evaluate the effectiveness of the plan. Does this sound familiar?

The basic premise surrounding a rational approach in social planning involves the ability of people to sort out, understand, weigh, and agree on social problems and ways to address and resolve identified problems. A rational approach requires a careful examination of the values of society and relevant social groupings and the impact of these value orientations in acquiring information, considering policy alternatives, and anticipating outcomes. DiNitto (2000) states, "Rationality requires the intelligence to calculate correctly the ratio of costs to benefits for each policy alternative. This means calculating all present and future benefits and costs to both the target groups [the segment of the population intended to be affected] and nontarget groups in society" (p. 5).

Ideally, the rational approach to social planning allows participants to identify and study the roles and relevance of various actors, groups, social forces, and value orientations (social, political, and economic) in developing policy and program options. Because social problems and issues are typically complex and value laden, multiple views of causation, solution, and outcome can be anticipated. Although consumers and social workers can strive for rationality in social planning, it is reasonable to assert that social planning is never completely rational, often gives way to subjectivity, seldom results in complete agreement among actors concerning the causes of social problems and the desired outcomes, and is vulnerable to political views and ideological beliefs.

### Political Model

Many people, professionals and nonprofessionals alike, would argue that social change and social planning are inherently political. In this view, individuals and special interest groups participate in a process of vying and positioning themselves to secure a greater share of limited resources (e.g., employment, prestige, money, goods and services). This is based in the somewhat hedonistic view that political persuasion and influence are rooted in an ongoing quest to acquire or sustain assets, resources, and power.

Given this premise, social planning constitutes a process by which actors work to garner support to acquire what they want, whenever it is desired. For example, influential individuals and groups of people portray needs, issues, and assets in terms that support and reinforce their preferred status in the social-economic ladder. In contrast, consumer groups and professionals often define social issues and policies in ways that address their needs and hopes.

Political action committees, special interest groups, unions, voluntary associations, agencies, and political parties are examples of organizations that compete with one another to shape public policy and social programming. Each group

## Time to Think 7.2

Social workers have a political action committee. It is called PACE—Political Action for Candidate Election. This organization makes contributions to political candidates that further the views and perspectives of social workers and their consumers via legislative initiatives. Consider jumping to the PACE website at https://www.socialworkers.org/Advocacy/Political-Action-for-Candidate-Election-PACE to examine how social workers can get involved in and influence the important candidate elections. Advocacy tips for social workers include making phone calls, promoting campaign events, and supporting campaign offices.

presents its case through impassioned oratory, debate, lobbying, promulgation of information, campaigning, contributions, and public declaration of ideals and values. The intent of each political faction is that leaders and social planners will examine and address social change from their own vested point of view. Ideally, in a democratic society, the role of government and leadership is to develop a system and sets of rules that allow for and encourage free expression and appreciation of different opinions. Open discourse allows for the balancing of interests in public policy formation and development and in social programming (DiNitto, 2000).

Unfortunately, it is frequently a challenge to promote the voices and perspectives of consumers in the process of social planning. Influential people and groups often have ready access to information supporting their positions, develop an inside track to decision makers and powerbrokers, and approach planning in a sophisticated and savvy manner. People in power are adept at using behind-the-scenes means of persuading others to adopt their point of view.

To complicate matters, time and again, it is the political dimension that presents consumers and social workers with barriers to active participation in social planning processes. The social worker's employing agency may prohibit her or him from engaging in political activities during work hours. Subtle pressure can be exerted to avoid "rocking the boat" of powerbrokers. Contacting influential people may be frowned on or even prohibited by the agency in fear of losing financial support. It is easy to see how the careful analysis of various actors and groups and their political stances, ties, and clout is a prudent step in the social planning process.

### Empowerment Model

So far, social planning has been described as a social, participatory process. Typically, social planning is conceptualized in terms of planning groups and coalitions. Stakeholders and representatives in a society, community, or organization are brought together to engage in planning. For social workers, there is a special interest is the inclusion of consumers of services in each and every planning process.

How professionals and others think about consumers often shapes how people interact with consumers. When consumers are viewed as equals, full members, and coparticipants in planning processes, their role is validated and their perspective valued. Social workers bring to the planning group a degree of expertise and knowledge. Consumers possess talents and skills, and they are also experiential experts. Consumers have firsthand knowledge of conditions and factors that others cannot fully understand.

It is important to note that social planners can be influential in producing change in a community or at the national level. They have the capability of exerting influence by putting forward strategies, plans, and recommendations. "The promise—or the threat—of empowerment lies in its socio-political dimension, its potential to generate collective thought, action, and research" (Ramon, 1999, p. 43). Hence, empowerment in social planning can be judged by the extent to which consumers become active players in designing policies and programs

**PHOTO 7.2** Understanding the strengths and assets of others is necessary when planning change.

affecting their lives. In empowerment theory, this is furthered by assisting consumers to advocate for themselves (directly) and helping consumers "to build alliances with others for affirmation, support, consciousness raising, and social activism" to affect decision making (O'Melia, 2002, p. 9).

To the extent that empowerment involves issues of power and the redistribution of power in the planning process, empowerment-based social planning certainly can be seen as political. **Consumer participation** in social planning represents a sense of inclusion—the idea that consumers, like other people, belong at the decision-making table. This often requires a reorientation of leaders, professionals, and others to acknowledge consumers as worthy stakeholders and rightful members of the social planning group.

In order for consumers to be major stakeholders in the planning process, a sense of trust needs to be nurtured and developed. Members of planning groups form working relationships based on mutual respect and trust. The successful establishment of working relationships is a key ingredient in the planning processes.

If you have the occasion to attend and observe a social planning meeting, attempt to assess who is actually hearing comments offered by others. Try to distinguish between passive listening and actually hearing (processing) the points being raised. Many times, hearing (cognitively processing) information at a planning meeting is based on relationships, current or past. If social planners know and respect someone, they are more likely to ponder the information or positions he or she is presenting.

Whitmore and Wilson (1997) offer distinct principles that, when applied to planning groups, encourage consumer participation in empowerment-based social planning. These include creating the possibility of nonintrusive collaboration, establishing mutual trust and respect, encouraging common analysis of problems and strengths, promoting a commitment to solidarity, emphasizing equality in relationships, focusing explicitly on process (participatory and inclusive), and recognizing the importance of language in promoting collegiality and permitting the strengths of members to emerge.

## Strengths Model

As previously noted, the ability to shift from identifying problems in organizations, communities, and society to examining and building strengths, assets, opportunities, and capabilities of people and larger social systems can be a formidable task. In social planning, embracing a strengths perspective involves adopting a mind-set of looking at the physical and social environment as "rich with resources: people, institutions, associations, families who are willing to and can provide instruction, succor, relief, resources, time, and mirroring" (Saleebey, 2002, p. 91).

Strengths-based social planning seeks ways to use existing strengths in organizations, communities, and society to enrich the environment and create opportunities for people. Unfortunately, consumers, professionals, and community leaders frequently lose sight of the resources and competencies that surround them. This is often accompanied by a sense of entrapment, where people lack confidence, feel inadequate, experience stifled ambition, and possess a limited view of the potential for change in the environment (Rapp, 1998, p. 102). Of particular concern is the ability to reach out to consumers and tap their strengths in the planning process. This is especially true when consumers have a history of alienation from planning processes and feel disenfranchised and unmotivated to share their thoughts concerning planned change.

©iStockphoto.com/laflor

**PHOTO 7.3** Strategic planning necessitates a shared vision.

Nonetheless, the strengths of consumers are real and vital elements for consideration and inclusion in the planning process. The key in macro-level social work practice is identifying ways to allow for the strengths of consumers and environmental assets to emerge and be used.

## ADVOCACY MODEL

As demonstrated in previous chapters, the advocacy practice and policy model (APPM) is designed to be thought provoking, offering a dynamic framework comprising interlocking tenets—economic and social justice, a supportive environment, human needs and rights, and political access. The APPM is useful for identifying key elements for deliberation and reflection and is applicable for use in macro-oriented practice involving social planning processes and groups.

### Economic and Social Justice

In social planning, careful consideration needs to be given to who is present and participating and who is missing and silenced. Promoting economic and social justice involves advocating with disadvantaged individuals and groups of people to promote important causes as well as advancing the fair and just voices of consumers in social planning processes and decision making. As an example, it is not unusual for social planning groups to be unwelcoming and passively dismissive of participation of consumer group members. Or, some planning groups will simply permit token representation, allowing only one consumer to be a group member. Conversely, stakeholders with economic and social privilege are frequently afforded a privileged number of seats and leadership positions at the social planning table. Token representation of consumers in social planning places such individuals in a difficult position. For example, how can the consumer's voice compete with more voices and powerful voices?

In social planning, even well-intended people inadvertently contribute to the further social-economic demise of consumers, when consumer voices are weakened. Indeed, one important role of the social worker in social planning is to protect, empower, and enrich the voices of people in social and economic need and despair.

## Time to Think 7.3

Does your school's social work program have an advisory board that assists the department or school's leadership with planning and suggestions regarding key decisions? Do current students hold membership positions on such a board, often composed of agency leaders, alumni, faculty members, and field placement supervisors? When considering issues of social and economic justice, how might the composition of this board be improved?

### Supportive Environment

A careful examination and assessment of the social and physical environment for social planning can help facilitate advocacy efforts for consumers of services. For example, is the meeting location reasonably accessible and conducive for consumer participation? Consumers may have to rely on public transportation or experience difficulties with parking. Although affluent social planning members may graciously offer beautiful, high-tech conference rooms for meetings, would consumers feel uncomfortable or intimidated by plush, corporate surroundings? And, does providing one's own office space for meetings provide such individuals and their sponsoring organizations "homecourt" advantages for power and control in social planning? As an alternative, at times, consumers and their causes can be better understood when social planning takes place in locations and venues exposing planning members to conditions experienced by consumers.

Envision a social planning group tasked and dedicated to examining a particularly high violent crime rate in a struggling section of the city, facing urban blight. Consumers of services include people living in this urban area, living with daily violence, threat, and safety concerns. What are the merits to having planning meetings take place at buildings in the heart of this community? For social workers, how might the physical and social presence of consumers and their causes enhance advocacy efforts and the influence of consumers on decision making? If social planners were to hold meetings in such an urban environment, there can be an enhanced appreciation for the expertise, insight, and knowledge of consumers for navigating everyday life circumstances and events.

## Human Needs and Rights

With advocacy efforts, a common issue and point of contention involves who defines human needs and rights. All too often, people in positions of authority and power seek to determine and specify what others need or are able to exercise as rights. Although research is needed to assess and document human needs and violations of rights, the qualitative descriptions, perspectives, and voices of consumers can yield meaningful and powerful depictions when advocating for social change.

Many times, social planning groups are called into and motivated for action by specific instances and evidence of human suffering and oppression. At the time of such occurrences, there is an energy and an impetus for examining change. However, even in times of dire need and the severe oppression of rights, it should not be assumed that social planners will gravitate to the experiences and outlook of people having been directly hurt or wronged. Although consumers may feel helpless and overwhelmed as a result of immediate needs and circumstances, their perspective and voice are vital and can be embraced when appropriate for consumers, in accordance with consumer self-determination.

In social planning, it is important to point out that members and constituent groups come to the planning process with vested interests—values, concerns, predispositions, commitments, alliances, and obligations grounded in the self-benefit, prosperity, and well-being of their employing organizations. Consciously or unknowingly, members of social planning groups may vie before, during, or after meetings to advance personal or organizational interests. Meanwhile, the focus of social workers should center on objectivity and identifying ways to advocate for human needs and rights by empowering consumer involvement prior to and throughout the social planning process.

## Political Access

Consumers of services often experience limited access to politicians and political groups. Furthermore, acquiring meaningful contact and building relationships with political figures and entities can be difficult. Politicians are often beholden to their supporters and donors. Hence, appointments and recommendations for appointments by politicians to sought-after social planning groups and commissions are frequently influenced by favoritism. The old adage "It is not what you know, it's who you know" seems particularly relevant with planning group appointments.

However, the influence of politicians does not end with the appointment of members. The designation of leadership for the group is a key issue. And, as social planning groups go about work, politicians and key stakeholders often contact members to directly or indirectly sway the planning group's direction, key votes, and recommendations concerning resource allocations. Professionals experienced with social planning groups recognize that numerous informal meetings and conversations often occur prior to formal social planning meetings. These are often termed "the meeting before the meeting" and serve as an acknowledgment that social planning members are often contacted before as well as after formal meetings to be influenced.

Working together, social workers and consumers assess and identify opportunities to bring forward the voices and perspectives of consumers. It is important to remember that politicians are human beings serving in specific roles. Although political figures often have a chief of staff and other gatekeepers to screen and buffer their contact with others, politicians lead lives and, through their own personal and family experience, may have an affinity for or against specific consumer groups and causes. Identifying how best to reach out and connect to politicians involves the type of communication (e.g., e-mail, phone message, letter), sound messaging, and a determination about which individual(s) or groups are best suited to initiate contact.

Given one's affiliation and status, consider how outlooks about the purpose, goals, and intended outcomes of social planning can vary in social planning. Table 7.2 summarizes several visions of social planning, which might or might not be shared among social planning participants.

**TABLE 7.2**

Visions of Social Planning

Bromley (2003, pp. 821–823) offers five visions of social planning priorities for consideration in social work practice.

| Vision | Explanation for Social Planning |
|---|---|
| Societal transformation | Involves major societal change to enrich and improve the conditions and functioning of a country (e.g., through legislative change, constitutional development, and policy initiatives). |
| Redistribution | Reforms are sought to combat social and economic inequalities and injustice through the redistribution of resources and power. |
| Participation | Seeks ways to include the general public and consumers of services in decision-making processes by challenging social elites, leaders, technocratic planners, and entrenched professionals. |
| Social sectors | Acknowledges and differentiates planning models and methods for economic and social sectors. With social sector planning, emphasis is placed on planning in governmental sectoral agencies (e.g., education, health, and human services) and nonprofits. |
| Social services | Recognizes that social workers will play an important role in social planning involving disadvantaged groups (e.g., people economically challenged, having been victimized, struggling with substance use, dealing with developmental challenges, having migrated, and/or having mental health problems). Everyday practice in social services involves multiple functions and responsibilities (e.g., community development, direct intervention with individuals and families, casework, and institutional care) that competes for the attention and time of social workers. |

## PRACTICAL CONSIDERATIONS IN MACRO SOCIAL WORK PRACTICE

1. Seek ways to reach into the environment in social planning. **Inreach** refers to a conscious, concerted, and active process of reaching or tapping into consumer groups, organizations, and associations for participation in social planning.

2. Build structures that include consumers and recognize strengths in the environment at each step of the planning process. Communities and organizations that are serious about social planning from a strengths orientation create a visible and identifiable assets-based component, unit, committee, or institute as an integral aspect of their organization or community. This produces a clear pathway and linkage to consumers and partners for collaboration. It also provides a forum where consumers can be viewed as partners in social planning. Does your school or university sponsor a community-building collaborative involving students, faculty members, and staff members?

3. Recognize empowerment and advocacy as functions in social planning. People advocate for positions, perspectives, policies, programs, and practices in self-serving ways as a part of the planning process. This is not necessarily bad, if it is recognized and if consumers have an adequate voice. Encourage people and groups to be upfront about advocating for their interests and to take responsibility for their vested interest in social planning and efforts directed at planned change.

4. Bring social planning to the public. Meetings should be open and accessible to the general public, with solicitation of input. Social planning best uses the strengths of the environment and empowers people when it functions in highly visible and inviting ways. Be skeptical of private, backroom (the meeting before the meeting) gatherings where people gather and secretly devise schemes to affect social planning. Recognize that phoning in and use of videoconferencing to attend meetings may not be the most viable or effective options for consumers' participation.

5. Think of social planning as a collaborative process: Who should be, could be, and/or needs to be included in planning? It is very important to regularly contemplate *who is and is not represented at the planning table*—people, groups, organizations, and constituencies.

6. Educate the general public about the perspective of the consumer. People need to be informed about social issues and causes through the voices and eyes of consumers. Use appropriate means of advancing this perspective (e.g., print and broadcast media, publications, websites, use of social media, and public testimonials).

7. Make building coalitions a strategic priority. Reach out to groups and organizations that share a common interest in attaining consumer goals. This can enhance the consumer power base and maximize the potential for success.
8. Endorse programs and interventions emphasizing prevention and the building of the strengths of people, organizations, communities, and society. Delgado (2000) advocates for a capacity enhancement orientation whereby communities develop plans and projects to accentuate common, core features and values. This includes the formation and strengthening of social programs and services and can extend to the strategic use of physical space (e.g., through murals, gardens, playgrounds, and sculptures).
9. Present human services and social programs as investments rather than costs. Typically, the long-term benefits of social programs and services are not emphasized. The general public and special interest groups need to be able to appreciate the investment value of these programs and to see the concrete dividends they provide for the greater whole, whether at the community or the societal level.

## STRATEGIC PLANNING FROM AN ORGANIZATIONAL STANDPOINT

Social workers typically participate in social planning as part of their organization, agency, or program. **Strategic planning** occurs when organizations take a concerted look at themselves in the context of their environment and in relation to other social structures. Periodically, sometimes as a part of a 5- or 10-year plan, agencies examine how they operate and look at the long-term viability of the agency and its programs.

It is often useful to think of social service agencies as adaptive organisms or entities that seek sustenance (e.g., resources and consumers) and nurturance (e.g., acceptance and support) from their surroundings. Of course, a comprehensive analysis of the practicality of any organization involves sound input from multiple sources and a variety of vantage points. The goal of strategic planning is to obtain an objective and critical view of the organization that describes both its strengths and areas that need strengthening. On the basis of this information, a vision can be formed that looks forward and guides the agency in a fruitful, productive, and rewarding direction.

### The SWOT Analysis

A variety of approaches have been used throughout the years to structure strategic planning. One approach is a systematic analysis of the *S*trengths, *W*eaknesses, *O*pportunities, and *T*hreats of an organization, often known as the **SWOT analysis**. Strengths and weaknesses are internal attributes of an organization, whereas opportunities and threats come from the external environment. Figure 7.1 gives an example format for the SWOT analysis.

**FIGURE 7.1**
SWOT Analysis

| SWOT ANALYSIS | | | |
|---|---|---|---|
| Internal | | External | |
| Strengths | Weaknesses | Opportunities | Threats |
| | | | |

*Source:* SWOT Analysis Table, CC BY-SA 3.0, https://commons.wikimedia.org/wiki/File:SWOT_Analysis_ssw_2.png.

Although the precise methodology varies, organizations typically empower or commission a strategic planning group (e.g., a steering committee) to conduct a SWOT analysis. Employees from the various programs and divisions of the organization complete a SWOT assessment tool, and their comments are summarized. Similarly, external stakeholders are asked for their views.

In strengths-based SWOT analyses, the goal is to effectively tap into the abilities of consumers to identify various organizational strengths, weaknesses, opportunities, and threats. This involves reaching out to consumers in a fashion that is inclusive and representative. Asking whoever is available to participate in a SWOT analysis is the equivalent of gathering a convenience sample.

It is also important to keep in mind that the loudest voice, regardless of the constituency group, is not necessarily the best or most accurate source of data. The organization will benefit the most from information that accurately describes internal and external conditions.

Is there a social planning component, arm, or group associated with the organization and delineated in strategic planning? Is this an area of strength, weakness, opportunity, or threat and why, particularly in relationship to the involvement or lack of involvement of consumers of services?

## Task Environment

An examination of an organization's **task environment**, or ecology, identifies important relationships with funding sources, collaborators, competitors, regulators, consumers, and the general public. The intent is to depict how an organization relates to external entities.

Many social planners formulate charts or maps to illustrate graphically how various social organizations connect and relate to their agency. Coding schemes are devised. For example, solid lines might indicate intense relations, or arrows might connote flow of information. Specific symbols are used to point out coalitions, conflict, collaboration, and competition.

As with each form of strategic planning, social workers and consumers have an obligation to work to broaden the sources of input and information, especially to include the perspective of consumers. Assessing the task environment is often laden with assumptions, perceptions, and conjecture. For the sake of validity, any such assertions need to be questioned and challenged in a direct manner by consumers of services.

Again, to be effective, strategic planning needs to take place in an open (above-board) fashion. Constituency groups and stakeholders need to feel free to debate the accuracy of task environment maps and the assumptions underlining the depictions of interorganizational relationships. This can yield an accurate picture of the current state of the organization and can be a useful tool in planning for the organization's future. Be sure to note how professionals, consumers, and community leaders hold similar or differing views of the nature of interorganizational relationships. For example, people with a business background may be prone to view similar and allied organizations as competitors rather than collaborators, especially in the realms of resources, consumers, and employees.

## Constructing Mission and Vision Statements

For many human service agencies, the mission statement constitutes a summary of the current activities and philosophical premises surrounding the work of the organization. The mission statement describes why the agency is important, who is served, and the reason for the agency's existence. A well-written mission statement reflects the unique identity and distinct attributes (competencies) of the agency and allows the reader to differentiate this agency from other, similar organizations. For example, the mission statement of an Alzheimer's organization might espouse a commitment to improving the health and well-being of persons with Alzheimer's, promoting the dignity of people with Alzheimer's, and supporting caretakers of people with Alzheimer's.

A good mission statement also affirms the strengths, values, and culture of an organization. It describes what the agency stands for and why. The mission statement is a tangible opportunity to confirm the primacy and importance of consumers in the agency.

The mission statement is an important element in strategic planning. It is a document that requires ownership by major stakeholders, especially consumers. The agency mission statement sets the tone and parameters by which an agency works and commits itself to work with consumers. Refinement or development of the mission statement is an important element in strategic planning, as it defines the essence of the enterprise.

An organization's vision statement is a future-oriented document that is aspirational in nature. It identifies where the agency *wants* to be. Much like a compass, the vision statement serves as a guide to direct planning, organizational activities, and decision making. The vision statement can be used to show the way for organizational changes and program development. The vision statement for the previously cited Alzheimer's agency could be to improve the lives and functioning of people with Alzheimer's as well as those supporting people with Alzheimer's through care management, day-care services, program development, research, and the active involvement of people representing the needs of people with Alzheimer's in decision-making processes.

Many people would say that a good leader provides an organization with a vision. This assertion may be valid, but the means by which a leader develops a vision merit consideration. Vision statements, like mission statements, require broad-based ownership. They need to be derived from a process that involves a collectivity of stakeholders. Vision is a product of dialogue, contemplation, and debate, not an individual creation.

In strategic planning, the vision statement becomes the driving force behind organizational behavior and decision making. It constitutes an organizational directive for the future and becomes a source of reference for every planning initiative.

## Marketing

For many social workers, the term **marketing** has historically carried negative connotations. It evokes images of a business tactic to promote product identification for the sake of profit. In a selling sense, marketers encourage people to consider goods and services and foster a sense of desire and need.

In human services, marketing can be viewed as a comprehensive approach of identifying consumer strengths and needs in order to discern the best ways of responding to any such demands. Most important, a marketing outlook can change the planning focus from what an organization or special interest group wants or needs to the hopes and desires of consumers.

Although marketing is of particular interest to profit-making organizations, the general tenets of a marketing perspective can also be applied to nonprofit agencies, particularly in the context of macro social work practice (Kotler, 1982). For example, marketing principles can be especially helpful in identifying the specific needs and wants of consumers. A basic assumption in marketing is that "one size *does not* fit all." In social planning, it is always useful to contemplate who is and is not being served. Marketing efforts help organizations refine their programming niches and attract and retain consumers of services, the lifeblood of human service agencies.

Marketing takes into account lifestyles, demographic information, and the developmental characteristics of consumers in order to use their strengths and respond to their needs in the formation and development of programs. Marketing recognizes that organizations serve distinct groups of people and encourages tailoring services to better address the differential strengths and needs of different groups. This is often referred to as *market segmentation* or *target marketing.* It breaks the "average customer" into "specific somebodies" (Kotler, Ferrell, & Lamb, 1987, p. 164).

Finally, marketing can be used to help secure resources and as a means of educating and providing awareness to the public, providers of services, consumers, and professionals about important news and impending issues (Stoner, 1986). In strategic planning, it is important to keep various parties, especially those capable of giving, interested, informed, and engaged in the planning process.

## Time to Think 7.4

Does your agency have a symbol or insignia that captures the essence of the organization? Around the world, people recognize the golden "M" of McDonald's. Contemplate with other professionals and consumers what your social service agency stands for and how this is portrayed to and engages the public. Furthermore, does it make sense for social service agencies to have a public relations person on staff? How might social media be used to promote interest and connectivity during social planning and for promoting the interests and causes of an agency? Have you heard marketing spots for social service organizations on your local National Public Radio station, and if so, what was your reaction?

## SOCIAL PLANNING PROCESS

Whether at the societal, community, or organizational level, social planning can be viewed as a series of phases. Over the years, a number of models have been proposed to help guide social planning processes. Traditionally, many of these approaches have deemphasized the role of consumers in social planning in favor of professionally or administratively directed and rendered assessment, planning, goal setting, implementing, and evaluation (Dudley, 1978).

The notion of consumer-driven social planning demands a slightly different way of thinking. First, full-fledged participatory social planning requires a sense of readiness on behalf of consumers as well as other members of the planning processes. Prior to initiating consumer-oriented social planning, there needs to be a determination of whether conditions are favorable for the active and meaningful involvement of consumers. In writing about readiness for participatory research, Altpeter, Schopler, Galinsky, and Pennell (1999) offer several interesting considerations for consumer-driven social planning.

1. At the individual level, are there actors ill prepared or unready to engage in participatory, democratically oriented social planning involving consumers? "Long-standing planning members" may be skeptical about bringing new faces to the planning table. Similarly, the planning group may oppose changes in participatory behavior that threaten established ways.
2. Consumer involvement in planning efforts should be viewed as a process of empowerment. The level of commitment provided by consumers will vary over time. The goal is to find ways to enable consumers to build confidence and skills in sharing their knowledge and expertise. Social workers should expect variations in the ability

and willingness of consumers to participate in social planning and advocacy efforts.

3. Over the long run, are you as a social worker ready to promote and sustain consumer involvement in social planning? Meaningful participation from consumers in social planning processes requires encouragement and an appreciable investment of time and energy on the part of social workers to nurture and support consumers.

4. Promoting and establishing a sense of equity in social planning for diverse groups of consumers is an important consideration. Does it make sense to have both primary consumers and secondary consumers (e.g., family members and friends) involved in the planning process? How can the planning process be enriched through sensitivity to diversity on the basis of race, ethnicity, gender, age, class, disability, sexual orientation, and other factors? Optimally, the planning group will function in a democratic fashion with a commitment to free expression and a diversity of ideas and opinions from a variety of perspectives and positions.

## A Three-Phase Model

Once it has been established that consumer participation in social planning is viable, social workers and consumers can move forward with a degree of self-assurance. This is with the realization that many planning initiatives take time—months if not years. Indeed, the actual process of social planning can be described in terms of three distinct phases. According to Jones and Harris (1987), social planning involves (1) being socially aware of the need for planning, (2) taking responsibility for planning, and (3) achieving institutional change. Each phase is important and presents distinct opportunities for consumer involvement and participation.

With respect to *heightening consciousness and awareness,* the tone and direction of social planning are set early. The call for social planning typically comes from a group of people or a set of powerful leaders and is framed around specific areas in need of strengthening and particular agendas. The general public is often unaware of social issues and will have to learn about the subject matter and become convinced that there are good reasons for engaging in social planning, so marketing efforts may be helpful. Consumers of services possess expertise that personalizes appeals for change and grounds them in real-life experience. Hearing about the impetus for social planning from the mouths of consumers makes the plea more real and more human, and it aligns the planning process with the will of consumers.

*Persuading people to take responsibility* can be a delicate ordeal. Assuming responsibility to pursue a cause goes beyond recognition; it entails a degree of commitment of time, resources, and funding. Usually a social organization or group, private or public, believes that an important issue or cause exists, and this group legitimizes and sanctions social planning efforts. Even when issues have a direct impact on the quality of life of citizens, people may be reluctant to invest their energies to pursue resolutions. This can be especially true for consumers who already feel disenfranchised or alienated from decision making or are in the midst of emotional pain and suffering. Indeed, it only makes sense that people are more likely to assume responsibility for social planning when they have a direct interest in an outcome, believe their involvement will make a difference, and feel there is a likelihood of success.

It is clearly a mischaracterization to describe social planning solely in terms of activities and steps associated with the actual planning group and its deliberations. A considerable amount of "advance work" occurs in preparation for planned change. And, once formal planning begins, it often entails **incremental planning**, smaller step-by-step changes that will occur over an extended time period. While many people would prefer to invest in **comprehensive planning**, attempts to bring about large-scale change quickly, this is often less practical and can be unrealistic.

Large-scale **institutional change** encompasses actions and activities in the planning process directed at creating macro-level change (e.g., program development, policy formation, and legislative initiatives). Like community leaders, citizens, and policymakers, consumers of services should be viewed as fully endorsed partners in weighing circumstances, strategizing alternatives, and authorizing courses of action.

## THE NIMBY PHENOMENON

As a response to proposed housing initiatives, the "not in my backyard" **(NIMBY) phenomenon** emerged. It is the name devised decades ago to describe community members' efforts to prevent deinstitutionalized people from living in "my backyard." People resisted the development of group homes and engaged in negative campaigns (e.g., media, petitions, door-to-door canvassing, and public meetings) to thwart housing initiatives close to their homes.

Opposition to community-based group homes was often based on misinformation, a lack of understanding, and an aura of distrust. Piat (2000) suggests that residents believed that "the development of group homes was motivated by financial considerations, either by the government or by the group home developers" (p. 131). In addition, community members often argued that consumers did not want to integrate into a neighborhood lifestyle and, as a result, would feel "self-conscious and uncomfortable participating in routine community activities" (p. 134).

Clearly, in the cases examined by Piat (2000), ordinary citizens and policymakers differed in their beliefs concerning the value of community-based group homes. However, noticeably absent from these analyses was any consideration of consumer participation in social planning. Indeed, most studies of the NIMBY phenomenon "examine only the perceptions of administrators, staff, or group home developers, disregarding the general community's perspective" and the point of view of consumers of services (p. 128).

One can only imagine the power of an aggressive and proactive approach designed to include consumers in the very earliest phases of the social planning process for deinstitutionalized persons. When this takes place, community leaders and citizens hear directly from the mouths of consumers about the importance and meaning of living in and belonging to a community (awareness and consciousness). For many people, this represents new information and works to dispel myths and assumptions associated with people leaving institutionalized settings.

As illustrated by the NIMBY phenomenon, community members could benefit greatly from the views and voices of consumers. Persons having experienced deinstitutionalization represent intersections of diversity (e.g., involving mental health, economic challenge, and race) and can make more affluent people feel uncomfortable. Such uneasiness can be helpful, particularly when it presses citizens to think critically and reflect upon new and differing views of and circumstances in the world. Constructive dialogue and reflection between divergent groups of people as partners in social planning can be the stimulus for creativity and innovation that builds capacities for effecting social change.

In the instance of the NIMBY phenomenon, structured dialogue between residents, consumers, policymakers, professionals, and administrators from the outset of the planning process would likely have yielded a multitude of viewpoints and findings concerning the usefulness of establishing community-based group homes for people experiencing deinstitutionalization. Regardless of the eventual outcome, all parties, including the community as a whole, would have benefited from a thorough and comprehensive discussion of housing for deinstitutionalized people from varying experiences and perspectives.

## RESOURCE CONSIDERATIONS IN SOCIAL PLANNING

Social planning, like almost all activities, requires resources, including time, talent, and money. Resources devoted to social planning can be viewed as an investment in the health and well-being of an organization, community, or society.

In human services, resources of all kinds are notoriously short in supply. This means that agencies and organizations are forced to use their assets in wise and well-thought-out ways. Accounting for investment behavior in social planning is a valid consideration and a functional imperative. Budgeting can be divided into human costs (e.g., time, wages, salaries, and fringe benefits) and nonpersonnel commitments (e.g., meeting space, transportation, communications, and supplies).

Consumers of services need to be included in decision making with respect to the use of resources. Investment in social planning needs to be productive and fruitful, as it could divert resources from other important activities (e.g., counseling, group work, and program implementation). Any mandate to use resources for social planning needs to be shared by consumers.

## SOCIAL PLANNING AS A COOPERATIVE EDUCATIONAL PROCESS

Social planning need not be conceptualized as an authoritarian, top-down process. Instead, planning represents an opportunity for various parties and constituencies to learn from one another about common interests and concerns through structured social interaction. Healthy, evenhanded exchange of ideas is the motor that drives participatory planning. From a strengths orientation, the goal is to promote constructive dialogue and debate between citizens, leaders, and consumers and to foster a spirit of shared governance.

If social planning is to be educational in nature, then people need to respect one another and strive for cooperation. This includes agreeing to disagree. This sounds simple, but it is often difficult for people to acknowledge and validate opposing beliefs, positions, and ideas. Humans are creatures of rational thinking and also of emotion. When passionate about a subject, even the most reasonable people can lose their perspective and temper. Indeed, the ability to learn from others presupposes a certain level of maturity—a discarding of the "I am right" philosophy.

Fruitful dialogue, collaboration, and coalition building involve differences of opinion. Divergent views challenge our frames of mind. Consumers can cause us to see phenomena in unique and thought-provoking ways. The ability to approach assumptions and evidence in social planning from multiple frames of mind allows us to envision change through the eyes of others.

Purposeful selection of consumers to participate in the planning process is crucial. They need to be endorsed by their peers and exhibit the aptitude, enthusiasm, maturity, confidence, and skills necessary to press forward with ideas and proposals for planned change. The ability to hold one's own is a useful barometer. Successful consumer leaders seek the backing and support of their constituency group and are careful not to stray from the will of those they represent.

Forming and establishing coalitions with groups of people is another important consideration in social planning and efforts to create social change. See Table 7.3 for a description of important factors to think through for coalition building in social work practice.

**TABLE 7.3**

Considerations With Coalition Building

Watson-Thompson, Fawcett, and Schultz (2008) suggest factors for consideration in strategic planning and coalition building efforts with community change.

| Factor for Consideration | Explanation | Implication for Practice |
| --- | --- | --- |
| Consistent leadership in social planning | Social planning benefits from consistent and dedicated leadership over a time period and can enhance community coalitions. | Social workers nurture social planning leadership by identifying and supporting the strengths of people to lead and facilitate coalition building. |
| Community coalitions provide resources for social planning | Community coalitions constitute sources of support for obtaining grants, meeting/training space, collateral materials, and technological support and equipment. | Social workers should view community coalitions for their strengths and assets in social planning. |

| Factor for Consideration | Explanation | Implication for Practice |
|---|---|---|
| Community coalitions serve important functions in social planning | Community coalitions can identify and encourage key stakeholders (e.g., consumers, politicians, community leaders, and government officials) for participation in social planning. | Social workers work to build community coalitions and prompt coalition membership to identify and involve key stakeholders. |
| Use memorandum of understandings (MOUs) | MOUs establish a formal recognition of conditions for shared work and the dedication and use of resources in social planning. | Social workers facilitate the creation, understanding, and formalization of working relationships between organizations and groups of people dedicated to and participating in social planning. |

## PLANNING FOR SUSTAINABLE DEVELOPMENT

All too often, social planning is nearsighted. It involves short-term thinking designed to address immediate needs and concerns, with little consideration given to the sustainability of proposed programs and projects.

In macro-level social work practice, the prospect of creating enduring, long-term social change should always be a consideration. As an example, in Nicaragua, social workers in association with the Center for Development in Central America (CDCA) have worked hand in hand with consumers to plan for and create several successful employment cooperatives (e.g., sewing, concrete construction materials, clay water filter, coffee, and security).

Confronted with dire poverty, natural catastrophes, and harsh (subsistence-level) living conditions, the people of Nicaragua have overcome disease, economic barriers, and political obstacles to build business cooperatives that use their interests, talents, and natural resources. The goal is **sustainable development**. The CDCA's longstanding focus has centered on community development and sustainability, especially in the areas of agriculture, economic development, healthcare, and education (visit https://jhc-cdca.org/ for additional information).

Visit **www.edge.sagepub.com/ticemacro** to help you accomplish your coursework goals in an easy-to-use learning environment

## SUMMARY

In this chapter, social planning is depicted as a participatory, collaborative process between consumers of services and others. In reality, this is not always the case. The impetus for social planning can come from multiple sources (e.g., elected officials, administrators, and funding sources) and may be imposed. Indeed, actors with specific vested interests often move to undermine and discredit the active participation of consumers in social planning.

Even under undesirable circumstances, however, it is the professional responsibility of social workers to work with consumers in collaborative ways to promote and advocate for social planning as an open, inclusive, and didactic process.

The term *inreach* is offered with great enthusiasm. View consumers as a pool of stakeholders and encourage inreach so that their talents and expertise can be fully used and appreciated as a cherished resource.

In the last (third) part of this book, the similarities between social planning and participatory research will become even more evident. Both processes seek to empower consumers as full-fledged members at all stages; both conceptualize consumers as co-learners and co-experts. In each instance, a major role of the social worker involves helping consumers identify their strengths and abilities to effect change.

## TOP 10 KEY CONCEPTS

comprehensive planning 172
consumer participation 160
inreach 165
institutional change 172
marketing 169
NIMBY phenomenon 172
strategic planning 166
sustainable development 175
SWOT analysis 166
task environment 167

## DISCUSSION QUESTIONS

1. Is your field placement agency actively involved in social planning? Identify the current phase of social planning, ascertain consumer involvement, and estimate the degree to which the views of consumers are valued. Discuss with your supervisor or coworkers how and when consumer participation in social planning could have been enhanced.
2. If you have direct contact with consumers, individually or in a group context, consider discussing their vision for the agency's future. Contemplate how these dreams could be formalized and included in social planning.
3. How could professionals and consumers better market the essence (the "biological DNA") of an agency or program? Allow yourself to be creative and "corny." The U.S. Marines asks people to "be all that you can be." Is there a slogan, phrase, symbol, or image that captures the purpose of your agency and would educate people concerning organizational goals?

## EXERCISES

1. If you have been placed in or are entering field placement, identify your agency's mission statement. Is the mission statement clear and reflective of the purpose of your agency or what it benefits from updating? Do you believe consumers of services at your agency would agree and be in alignment with the mission statement? Why or why not?
2. Identify a social or strategic planning group in your community or organization. Closely examine the membership and reasoning associated with their appointment to this group. If this is a public planning group, the membership roster should be a matter of public knowledge. Consider the possibility or presence of political agendas given the membership and composition of the group. Are consumers of services an ample or simply a tokenistic presence in the group?

## ONLINE RESOURCES

1. Visit https://www.planetizen.com/news/2018/01/96557-rise-nimby-movement-and-how-homeowners-came-own-whole-neighborhood to examine the origin and history surrounding the NIMBY movement. In relationship to social planning and community change, contemplate the advantages NIMBY groups have when seeking to influence and affect social planning, especially in the areas of residential programs supporting mental health and people struggling with substance use.
2. The Whistler Centre for Sustainability (WCS) is a nonprofit organization dedicated to assisting communities and organizations sharing the vision of working toward a "healthy, prosperous and sustainable world." Visit http://www.whistlercentre.ca/about-us/ to examine examples of how the WCS has contributed to social and strategic planning in communities.
3. Visit the American Planning Association at https://www.planning.org/ to examine how you can access materials, develop advocacy skills, connect with others, and attend conferences and meetings to refine and develop your abilities in social and strategic planning.

# Administration and Leadership

## BUILDING ON ADVOCACY AND STRENGTHS

### LEARNING OBJECTIVES

After reading this chapter you should be able to:

1. Define the term *administration*
2. Define the various roles and tasks of an administrator
3. Consider how the strengths perspective applies to administration
4. Apply the advocacy practice and policy model to social work administration
5. Describe ethical issues associated with administration

### ADMINISTRATION IN A RURAL COMMUNITY

George William, a social worker, is the administrator of a rural mental health agency, McDowell Outreach Program. Much like agencies across the state, McDowell Outreach Program is undergoing severe budget constraints and a consequent hiring freeze. Simultaneously, the region is experiencing the effects of the opioid epidemic. George must explain the fiscal situation and the impact of the opioid crisis to the agency's advisory board, service consumers, and staff. Furthermore, as a member of the county's Social Service Council, George plans to discuss the mounting consumer needs for service along with the budget issues at the next council meeting.

To address the budget crisis, George is considering volunteer recruitment, staff furloughs, and program retrenchment. Such decisions are significant to the immediate and long-term operation of McDowell Outreach Program. During an interdisciplinary meeting, program supervisors present their concerns to George, who notes increased consumer demands coupled with competitiveness and anxiety among the supervisors.

As seen in George's situation, administration is a crucial aspect of macro social work practice. Consider for a moment just how much every issue George is confronted with depends on the quality of his administrative leadership and commitment to consumers. To perform administrative responsibilities effectively, George, like other social work social administrators, must have an extensive set of skills to meet the challenges presented in social welfare organizations at the local, state, and national levels. Implied in this statement is the need for schools of social work to design curricula that develop administrative skills and strategies that are both consumer centered and viable in complicated political arenas (Hoefer & Sliva, 2014; Patti, 1977). Simultaneously, social work students must explore their professional interests and career options in light of the complexities of social administration.

In support of these efforts, this chapter broadly defines the term *administration* and several concepts associated with social workers as administrators. It also describes **ethical issues** that are common in organizational systems. If administrators do not deal with these dilemmas, then direct-line social workers must be prepared to initiate individual action or develop collective strategies to resolve them.

The advocacy practice and policy model and the strengths perspective are described as a guide for social workers leading human service organizations. As in previous chapters, the focus is on consumers as the principal element associated with administration. The unique strengths and wants of consumers are the driving force in administrative decisions related to organizational goals, budget allocations, personnel issues, and program design.

## WHAT IS ADMINISTRATION?

The word *administrator* comes from the Latin *administrare,* meaning "to minister to" or "to serve." The word **administration** refers to the processes by which social worker administrators address social and personal needs, confront social problems, and create the conditions in which people's welfare can be improved by the efforts of a social service agency (Brueggemann, 1996; Shera & Bejan, 2017). Administration, then, is a process that has to do with running an agency and that involves goals, policies, staff, management, services, and evaluation (Shera & Bejan, 2017; Skidmore, 1990).

Throughout the discussion of administration, think about administrators you've worked with in your jobs, volunteer activities, or field placement. Based on your experiences, consider the following:

- Was the administrator a professional social worker?
- From your perspective, what were the responsibilities and duties of the administrator?
- How available was the administrator to you, staff members, and consumers?
- What four adjectives would you use to describe the administrator?

Ideally, your experiences with an administrator support the notion that administrators assume several responsibilities and hold many job titles, including line supervisors, department managers, and executive directors. Whatever the title given to the administrator, assume the following:

- The social work administrator works with people based on a philosophy of practice, including an explicit value and belief system and a theoretical framework.
- Administrative practice occurs in organizations, policies, programs, and direct services.

- The social work administrator is responsible for the resources, both material and symbolic, necessary for the organization to achieve its purpose.
- The organization's structure and processes largely reflect the character of the social work administrator.
- The social work administrator influences the technical base of the organization—that is, the knowledge and skills required to maintain the program and service system.
- The method of supervision, leadership, and management mirrors the social work administrator's practice model.

An administrator's performance is intricately linked to the overall performance and public image of the organization where the administrator is employed. As seen in Figure 8.1, administrators are deemed responsible for the functions of the entity they manage, whether it is an interdisciplinary team, a social service office,

**FIGURE 8.1**
Administrative Duties and Responsibilities

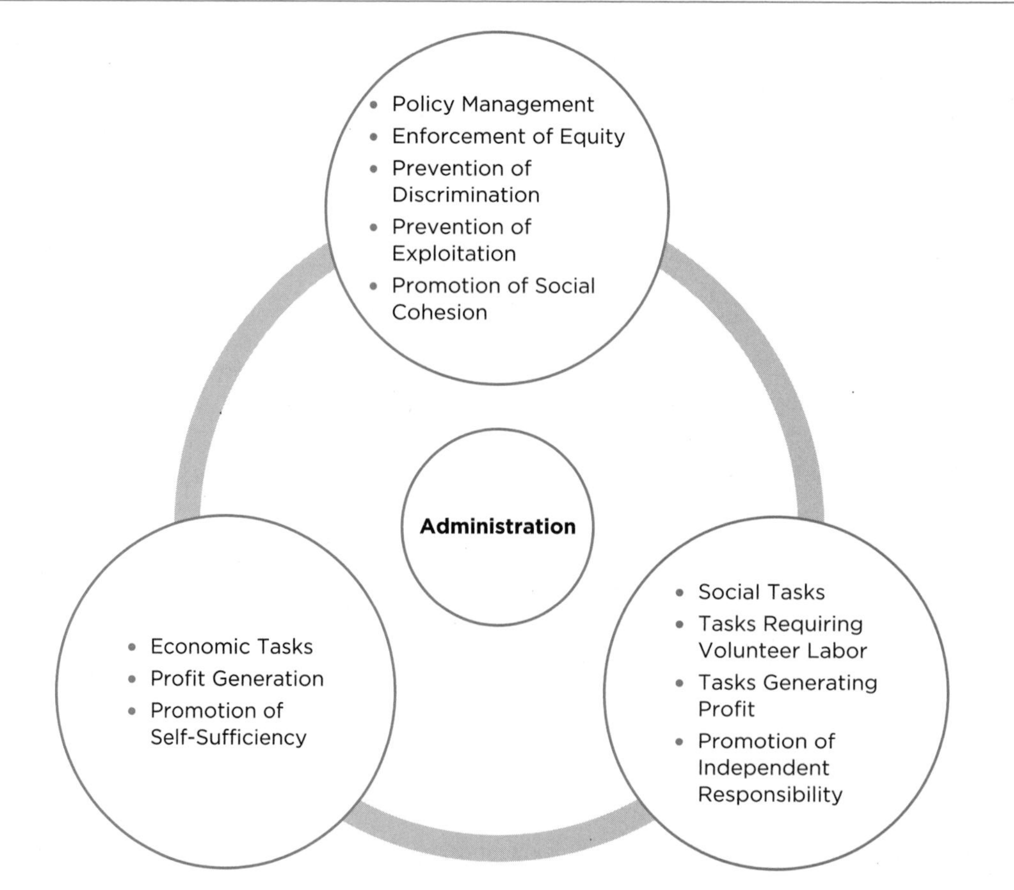

a particular program, or a complex agency. It is highly uncommon to find an outstanding administrator responsible for a dysfunctional program or an effective team being supervised by an ineffectual administrator.

The centerpiece of agency and administrative performance are the benefits accrued by consumers. A successful administrator focuses on the outcomes that reflect improvement of the consumer's life situation or thwart the further deterioration of that situation. Consumer outcomes act as the bottom line in human services in much the same way that profits serve business (Rapp & Poertner, 1992; Watson & Hegar, 2013). Consequently, administrators perform in a variety of areas, but adequate performance in these areas is neither sufficient nor a proxy for consumer outcomes.

### Time to Think 8.1

Why can it be argued that social work administrators, no matter what their agency setting, are in the position to influence issues on human rights and social, economic, and environmental justice? In considering your response, please refer to the position George is faced with at McDowell Outreach Program and Figure 8.1. Provide examples of the justice issues you think an administrator might address in the course of daily duties and responsibilities.

## ADMINISTRATIVE ROLES

Any social service organization is an integral component of the entire community where it is located. As such, it is a social tool for improving the quality of life for the residents in its proximity. The organization's administrator is ultimately responsible for ensuring that this occurs through a variety of roles, including the following.

### Leader

The hallmark of administration is dynamic leadership. The administrator as leader helps communities of individuals to take calculated risks and imagine improvements in life. Furthermore, the administrator encourages commitment to change from staff and consumers alike and facilitates the movement of people along a path to meet their needs and wants.

The administrator as leader sometimes assumes several incongruent roles. For example, the administrator must understand the complexities of the community where the social service organization resides. Simultaneously, the administrator as leader must relate the organization's mission, goals, and value system to the community at large. Thus, the administrator is called upon to be skilled as a ceremonial figure capable of symbolizing and articulating the social service organization while also living in the community and serving its ideals. In this way, the administrator represents a bridge between the community and the

**FIGURE 8.2**
Principled Leadership

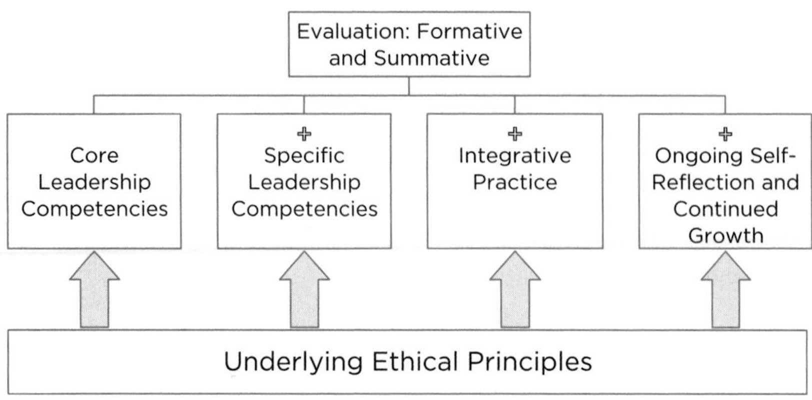


*Source:* Adapted from Bliss, Pecukonis, and Snyder-Vogel (2014).

organization—a leader in the public eye demonstrating how both entities can learn and grow from one another.

As illustrated in Figure 8.2, principled leadership, based on collective social work practice, addresses contextual and situational variables. Although competencies, integrative practice, and ongoing self-reflection are core to leadership, it is the ethical principles that provide the foundation for administrative leadership. For social work administrators, such ethics are provided by the *Code of Ethics* (National Association of Social Workers, 2017).

## Time to Think 8.2

Read through the *Code of Ethics* (https://www.socialworkers.org/About/Ethics/Code-ofEthics/Code-of-Ethics) and list at least four ethical principles that apply directly to social work administrative leadership. Then review the ethical standards and consider when they are relevant to the professional activities of all social workers.

### Decision Maker

**Decision making** is a crucial aspect of administration. Administrators as decision makers affect organizational goals, relationships with the community and consumers, internal harmony, organizational change, and fiscal stability (Hasenfeld & English, 1974; Raney, 2014). At all levels of the organization, administrators are required to make decisions on personnel selection, labor relations, service delivery, community relations, and budget allocations.

Although "decision making" appears at first glance to be individualistic, most administrators attempt to use a rational approach to decision making (Katz & Kahn, 1978; Neugeboren, 1991; Raney, 2014). Such an approach includes four sequential stages:

1. *Respond to immediate pressures.* Pressures that the administrator must consider may be internal or external to the social service organization. Internal pressures include opinions from upper-level administration, staff assignments and training, consumers' service needs, fiscal limitations, and space allocations. External pressures often derive from interagency relationships, public and media relations, and funding requirements.
2. *Define the problem.* Basic to decision making is problem definition. The more information the administrator has about the problem, the greater the likelihood that a successful decision will be made. It is essential that administrators assess problems holistically. This is accomplished by reviewing all available information and consulting with a variety of people—most important, consumers. Furthermore, the history, scope, and duration of the problem must be examined.
3. *Search for solutions.* More often than not, administrators will attempt to use existing policies and procedures to solve presenting problems. However, administrators must be prepared to initiate more innovative solutions if necessary.
4. *Evaluate alternatives.* The final stage of the approach requires that the administrator assess the cost and benefits of the decision. Although the evaluation may differ depending on perspective and organizational position, the administrator must be able to connect any proposed alternative solution to the organization's existing goals and objectives.

Although rational decision making is part of the administrator's repertoire of skills, it is always necessary to consider how nonrational features such as emotions and intuition impinge on the decision-making process. On occasion, administrators will settle for a satisfactory decision rather than an optimal one.

## Mediator

It is the responsibility of the organization's administrator to mediate diverse interests, both internal and external to the organization. Mediation helps to reduce irrationality and promote rationality among the parties, provides opportunities for development, facilitates communication, explores resources, reveals alternative solutions to problems, and expands professional and personal opportunities (Gilliam, Chandler, Al-Hajjaj, Mooney, & Vakalahl, 2016; Hardcastle, Wenocur, & Powers, 1997). As a **mediator**, the administrator is

**PHOTO 8.1** Consensus building is part of leadership.

the link between administrative actions and direct services, between policy formulation and policy implementation.

An essential aspect of the role of administrator as mediator involves the interdependence between the administrator and other levels and units of the organization. Specifically, it is not unusual for the administrator to serve as the mediator between supervisees and the organization's environment, including consumers and other service providers. This role requires considerable skills in decision making and conflict management, as well as sensitivity to the needs of consumers, staff, and the organization as a whole.

Administrators comment that the role of mediator sometimes places them in a no-win situation, a feeling of being caught in the middle. To avoid such a predicament, administrators must try to establish a sufficiently harmonious relationship with all parties involved in the mediation process. Administrators are successful in mediation when participants feel they have received what they wanted and when the mediation process is considered efficient and effective. Indeed, the dynamics of mediation are similar to those that social work counselors employ with couples and families. Administrators require the same authority and credibility that counselors need to conduct clinical sessions. The analogy with counseling can be taken a step further in that administrators often seek to show contending parties how to negotiate successfully with each other. For organizations with little experience in negotiation or conflict management, the development of effective mediating skills is a major accomplishment in itself that can have benefits beyond the immediate situation (Bliss, Pecukonis, & Snyder-Vogel, 2014; Gummer, 1991).

## Collaborator

Collaboration implies the notion of a joint venture. Administrative collaborations involve agreements in which two or more organizations within the community agree to establish common goals, such as a new program or service. When an administrator assumes the role of collaborator, a partnership emerges. Partnerships may expand resources or generate new ideas. However, the collaboration necessary to foster partnerships requires administrators to relinquish a degree of power, expertise, and control to others. In this way, collaboration often alters the balance of power and authority of the administrator (Frahm & Martin, 2009; Poulin, 2000). According to Johnson, McLaughlin, and Christenson (1982), administrative collaboration does the following:

- It encourages and facilitates an open and honest exchange of ideas, plans, approaches, and resources across disciplines, programs, and agencies.

- It enables all participants to jointly define their separate interest by mutually identifying changes that may be needed to best achieve common purposes.
- It uses formal procedures to help clarify issues, define problems, and make decisions about them.

At the outset of collaboration, individual personalities, style, and readiness to collaborate certainly affect the interactions. The major issues on the collaborative agenda reflect the agencies' individual interests, resources, and ideas about the potential outcome around which collaborations will occur (Garner & Orelove, 1994; MorBarak, 2000). Additionally, information about policies and procedures, eligibility requirements, target populations, geographic boundaries, legislative initiatives, confidentiality policies, and funding streams need to be shared and related to the other agencies.

At any level and on any issue, administrative collaboration takes time to develop. Just as individual professionals become increasingly responsive to collaboration on consumer service plans, administrators representing agencies also experience a parallel growth process before collaboration is achieved.

## Politician

Over half a century ago, Bertha Reynolds (1951/1987) offered comments on the role of political activity in social work practice:

> The philosophy of social work cannot be separated from the philosophy of a nation, as to how it values people, and what importance it sets upon their welfare. . . . [We are] faced with a choice between contradictory forces in our society: those which are moving toward the welfare of people . . . and those which destroy human life in preventable misery and war, and relieve poverty only grudgingly to keep the privileged position they hold. (p. 45)

These words prove a guidepost for social work administrators. More specifically, administrators cannot divorce their practice from the political debates that surround social welfare organizations (Reisch & Gambrill, 1997; Williams-Gray, 2014). In fact, in many cases, administrators are in the midst of policy debates, as exemplified in public discussions on immigration, health care, and prison reform.

Organizational politics provide the administrator with an arena for making critical decisions about issues, including the establishment of agency goals and objectives, procedures for pursuing them, and distribution of resources. When there are apparently irreconcilable conflicts among organizational members over these issues, it becomes necessary for the administrator to engage in political decision making. An essential feature of decision making from a political perspective is the explicit recognition of conflict as a normal part of organizational life and the provisions it makes for transforming potentially disruptive conflicts into negotiated settlements.

It has been suggested that it is incumbent on administrators to work at acquiring and using power in their organizations (DiTomaso, Post, & Parks-Yancy, 2007; Gummer & Edwards, 1985). They should do so not merely to gain power but from the conviction that the acquisition and appropriate use of power ensures that social work principles and values are infused throughout social welfare organizations.

The administrator-as-politician assumes that consideration will be given to important elements before reaching premature conclusions about the political landscape. For example, once the relevant groups and individuals, or organizational stakeholders, have been identified, it is imperative that the administrator assess their strengths (Pfeffer, 1981). In this context, an important step for the administrator to take is to distinguish between the power and foresight of stakeholders. Some individuals are adept at forecasting what is likely to happen in an organization and then aligning themselves with the winning side. Administrators must come to understand this power, especially in terms of organizational change efforts. In many ways, administrators can be perceived as powerful because of their association with the powerful. Thus, administrators must be mindful that the skill of foresight is a good one to develop, but it is also important to be able to recognize and develop it in others.

### Time to Think 8.3

Presidential administrations often change the organizational climate and funding stream of human services and agencies. Consider how the administrative roles of mediator, collaborator, and politician would likely be affected by President Donald Trump's administration. What critical issues do you think social work administrators would be called upon to address?

## ADMINISTRATIVE TASKS

Most human service administrators are employed in public organizations, such as departments of social services, hospitals, and schools, or in nonprofit agencies that have been created to meet specific community needs, including community mental health centers. Whether social service organizations provide direct or indirect services and whether they are housed in public or private agencies, they tend to require similar administrative functions, as described in this section.

### Planning

Social agencies are always in a state of change. Policies introduce new services, new problems demand attention, new contingencies emerge, the agency's environment changes, and new political and economic agendas develop. Consequently, an administrator devotes considerable time and effort to day-to-day and long-term planning. Planning is one of the major tasks of administration.

Planning is the development, expansion, and coordination of social services and social policies "utilizing rational problem solving at the local and societal level" (Frahm & Martin, 2009; Lauffer, 1981, p. 583; Wimpfheimer, 2004). Planning is an administrative task that provides for the welfare of society—to ensure that social programs, policies, and services meet the people's needs to the greatest extent possible. Therefore, administrators must ensure that individuals with few resources, little power, and minimal influence be given the opportunity to engage in program planning. Only through integration into the planning process can people gain the sense of empowerment and control over their lives that is a prerequisite for achieving social and economic justice.

Planning involves activities and structures that are used as tools to construct future events in organizations. Plans are usually presented in written form to guide employees and consumers in specified directions. Goals and objectives are crucial elements of planning. They provide a roadmap for accomplishing tasks within an organization and offer a system of accountability for program evaluation. Planning is also tied to the development of internal policies, procedures, programs, and budgets.

An administrator initiates the planning process with a comprehensive assessment of community and consumer needs. The administrator employs a variety of methods to determine what problems and opportunities exist within a given population and, just as important, what consumers and community members see as their most pressing priorities. Current services are also analyzed, providing the administrator with an understanding of gaps in the service system. The recognition of needs and service gaps gives the administrator a vision of a desired future state for the organization, which is eventually reflected in the agency's mission statement.

The assessment of needs and the identification of community strengths or assets provide the basis for selecting the potential goals of the agency or program (DiTomaso et al., 2007; Kretzmann & McKnight, 1996). It is essential that community members, consumers, and service providers all be involved in designing service goals. These goals lead to the development of actual programs. Thus, the administrator designs programs through an integrative process that involves consumers from the outset.

## Human Resource Development

Social welfare organizations are labor intensive: An organization's plans and design are put into operation by people. Although human resource development has received considerable attention, the area still creates problems for social work administrators. Therefore, the success of services is highly dependent on the administrator's ability to make effective use of valuable human resources so as to address the immediate and long-term needs of the organization and its consumers.

To ensure desired consumer outcomes, the administrator must remain focused on staff behavior, competencies, and morale. From this perspective, staff and consumers are the anchors of the organization. Furthermore, the development of human resources is seen as a crucial administrative task that recognizes the unique contributions staff members offer to the human service enterprise. This is especially true of the knowledge and skills that women and people of color bring to the organization (Asamoah, 1995; Bailey, 1995; Healy, Havens, & Pine, 1995; Jani, Osteen, & Shipe, 2016).

Administrators must be as concerned about the needs, growth, and development of their staff members as they are about consumers if consumers are to receive services in an effective manner. Considering the ever-changing environment and program activities of social welfare organizations, administrators understand that ongoing staff development is essential. In other words, if consumers are to receive needed services, the professional needs of staff must be a priority to an administrator. It is difficult to imagine an instance in which a depressed and cynical social worker would be as effective in producing positive consumer outcomes as an energized social worker whose work needs are satisfied (Lewis, Lewis, Packard, & Souflée, 2001; Raney, 2014).

It should be obvious by now that securing personnel is a critical responsibility for administrators. Recruitment efforts involve not only the number of people needed but also their characteristics, qualifications, and talents. An administrator may want to recruit and hire minority staff to better match personnel with consumers being served. Or perhaps staff must have certain educational credentials to be reimbursed for services.

Volunteers are an important human resource of social welfare organizations, and they require the attention of administrators (Netting, Nelson, Borders, & Huber, 2004). Administrators need to ensure that the recruitment and assignment of volunteers are planned as carefully as the hiring of professional employees. Volunteers with creative ideas and strong ties to the community can add significant energy to a program. The community participation that comes with volunteers increases the agency's service delivery capacity when volunteer contributions are respected as highly as those of paid personnel.

## Supervision

The administrator engages in supervision to help a staff member maximize his or her effectiveness in service delivery. **Supervision** has several aspects, including the following:

- *Providing support and encouragement:* Staff members need to know that administrators are both accessible and available. Such support comes by way of regular feedback and ongoing open communication.
- *Building skills and competencies:* As organizations change, the demands on staff change as well. Therefore, ongoing staff development, membership in professional organizations, attendance at conferences, and interagency collaboration are essential to maintain staff competencies. This also includes identification and nurturing of consumers as leaders and active participants in leadership roles.
- *Performance feedback:* Stated performance goals and objectives, specified methods of evaluation, and appropriate compensation all send the message that staff members are needed and respected for the contributions

they offer the organization. Performance feedback should be both vertical and horizontal. In other words, administrators should expect to receive feedback on their performance from staff in much the same way that staff is evaluated by administrators. Establishing mechanisms for feedback from consumers is crucial.

When considering the elements of supervision, it is obvious that the nature of the supervisory relationship depends on the administrator's leadership style, the worker's motivation, and the organization's needs.

The supervisory role requires that the administrator perform a number of interrelated tasks (Unguru & Sandu, 2017). Leadership is central to all the tasks associated with the position of the supervisor, which uses formal authority to guide others in achieving organizational goals.

As a supervisor, the administrator is accorded certain powers of reward and coercion by the organization (Lewis et al., 2001). Consequently, he or she must possess knowledge and skills relevant to the day-to-day direction and control of unit operations—for example, assigning, delegating, and coordinating work. Furthermore, the supervisory tasks of the administrator often involve mediating relationships between members of the organization and the environment (Kadushin, 1985; Shulman, 1993).

## Resource Acquisition

To function, a social welfare organization needs funds, personnel, technology, consumers, and public support and influence. Understanding the operating budget and streams of funding allows an administrator to understand an organization. The administrative process of designing and monitoring the budget is closely related to organizational planning and evaluation. In fact, many would argue that a budget is fundamentally an organization in fiscal terms. The more closely related the budget is to the goals of people who hold a stake in the agency's success, the more effectively it is likely to work (Lewis et al., 2001).

A budget must be seen as the concrete documentation of the planning process, bringing ideals, not reality. According to Flynn (1985), the budget process has four stages:

1. Define the problem and target groups to be addressed, set actual goals and objectives, and determine the program models or interventions.
2. Estimate revenues (based on available funds) and expenditures.
3. Monitor expenditures and revenues.
4. Make necessary revisions.

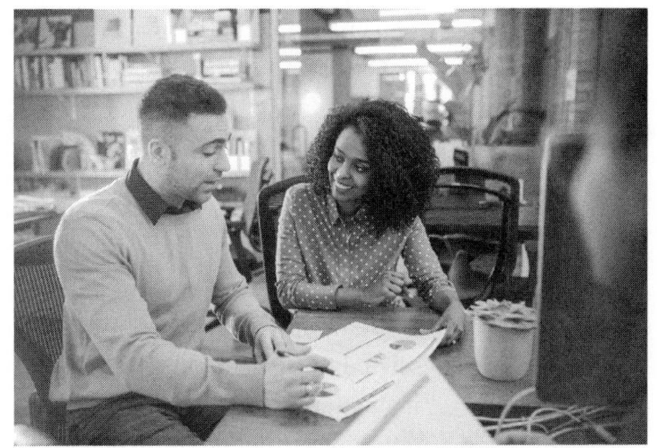



**PHOTO 8.2** Using feedback is critical to professional growth and development.

An annual budget can be based on recognition of program goals and the costs of activities expected to attain those goals. More specifically, a goal of program budgeting is to develop a system of accountability for programs whereby the allocation of resources is tied to the achievement of stated objectives rather than to "line items" such as supplies or personnel costs.

Budget making is definitely an exercise in decision making through which funds are allocated to one program or service rather than another. In the budget process, it is important to solicit input from key staff and consumers. At the very least, they need to be aware of how the planning process has been translated into financial terms. This will help people understand the decisions an administrator makes throughout the fiscal year and will link people to the costs of programs. Although such understanding is crucial at any time, it is essential during times of fiscal difficulty or program retrenchment (Packard, Patti, Daly, Tucker-Tatlow, & Farrell, 2008).

There can be little doubt that social welfare administrators devote a vast amount of time and energy to resource acquisition activities. For example, grant writing, legislative testimony, private fundraising, and program advocacy within a larger organization are all administrative tasks associated with the budget.

Over the past two decades, the ability of an administrator to acquire funds from varying funding sources has come to be viewed as a major criterion for performance. Public agencies are highly dependent on legislative appropriations as sources of revenue. Private, nonprofit agencies tend to depend on grants, contracts, contributions, and fees paid for services, either by consumers or third parties, as sources of financial support. As one might imagine, the brand of funding has a major impact on an agency's programs because (1) the length and stipulations of funding vary, (2) some services encourage more funding support than others, (3) some populations of consumers are more likely to receive funding support than others, and (4) the community may support certain services more than others. However, administrators must maintain a balance between program goals and funding sources. In other words, funding should not dictate services or jeopardize the integrity of agency goals. At all times, administrators must remember that budgeting and funding tasks should remain subsidiary to planning (Packard et al., 2008).

## Evaluation

Tasks associated with program evaluation are used by administrators to assess whether programs and services have met stated goals and the related needs of consumers. The information generated by evaluations gives administrators a basis for making decisions about current or projected programs. For example, data related to particular services can help in decisions about resource allocation, staffing patterns, and provision of services (Briggs & McBeath, 2009). Simultaneously, data concerning program outcomes can support more rational decisions about the continuation, expansion, or elimination of programs. Equally important, decisions concerning the development of new programs can also be made.

Social research procedures are used in **program evaluation**. Administrators build on their liberal arts foundation to construct evaluation processes that include the following:

- *Systematic processes:* The process is well thought out and developed to measure stated goals and objectives.
- *Reviews of interventions:* Policies and programs are examined in light of meeting consumers' needs and wants, with consideration given to the efficient and effective use of resources.
- *Questions related to adequacy:* The evaluation process should reveal the extent to which identified and anticipated needs are addressed by programs and services.
- *Scanning the political environment:* The organization's stakeholders, such as community members, advisory board, politicians, and other agencies, need to be included in the evaluation to ensure their continued support and regular input into program design and implementation.
- *Scanning the internal environment:* The organization must be an integral part of the evaluation. In particular, staff morale and satisfaction should be considered. (Lewis et al., 2001, p. 236)

## SOCIAL WORK ADMINISTRATION FROM A STRENGTHS PERSPECTIVE

It should be clear at this point that administration demands a set of skills and tasks, as well as attitudes, that administrators can employ in situations with communities, organizations, consumers, and staff alike. Administrators communicate the values of a program to those who use it and to the community in which it operates. Additionally, consciously or unconsciously, social work administrators must also display in their daily actions how people should be treated in keeping with the values and principles of the social work profession.

Conceptualizing administration from a strengths perspective is crucial. Central to seeing consumers as individuals and agencies as a tool for social action is the view of strengths, growth, and change. From such a perspective, administrators value and respect an agency's ability to survive and adapt, as well as to complement the development of community life. How can administrators incorporate a strengths perspective into their practice? The following principles should be considered as a way for administrators to nurture the strengths, needs, and interests of people and communities involved in their agencies.

### Stay Consumer Centered

The raison d'être of the social work administrator is the well-being of consumers and the quality of their life in communities. Administrators accomplish this by knowing who their consumers are, not just in terms of problems but as whole individuals who have lives beyond their needs and the services they receive. From this perspective, "individuals are valued and respected for their ability to survive and adapt, and there is a sense of hope regarding each person's capability to continue to learn and develop over time in relationship with others" (Rapp & Poertner, 1992, p. 17; Bliss et al., 2014).

All planning and goal setting are guided by consumers' perceptions of their own needs and desires. The role of the administrator is to assist and facilitate consumers and agency staff in making program and personal goals specific, to explore alternatives, and to identify resources (Saleebey, 1997, 2013). In this way, consumers experience the following:

- They are engaged in ongoing communication with agency staff.
- They are not judged by their life conditions but are congratulated for their resiliency and ability to cope with difficult situations.
- They are recognized as the experts on their lives.
- They are members of a larger community.
- They are often supported by informal systems that can be incorporated into the program plans and intervention.

As indicated, administrators are called on to focus on the strengths of people and of communities, to convey the belief that people want to be the directors of their lives, to view the entire community as a place of possibilities, and to advocate for resources to promote social justice. The administrator has a firm commitment to people as active and creative agents who form social meaning for themselves.

### Conduct Holistic Assessment

Central to the strengths component is the role and place of assessment. **Holistic assessments** allow an administrator to analyze what is occurring within the agency's service area. The strengths perspective assumes that an agency has the competence, in partnership with the community, to articulate the nature of social issues, identify a course of action, explore alternatives for achieving goals, and achieve those goals. Assessment for administrative practice requires (1) focused and precise data collection, (2) analysis of historical trends, and (3) a thorough understanding of qualitative elements that reflect human experiences, interactions, and relationships (Netting, Kettner, & McMurtry, 1998).

For administrators, such assessment ensures the integration of the community and its resources into the fiber of service delivery. Thus, the community in which the agency is located and which it serves has a lot to do with not only the social problems faced by an administrator but also the strengths and the resources available to consumers. Comprehensively assessing the community leads to conceptualizing it as an arena in which consumers experience hope and draw strength, as well as face oppression and frustration. Administration from a strengths perspective quickly highlights whether or not an agency's mission and goals are feasible in the context of community influences.

### Know the Agency's Story

The administrator who takes the time to understand the history and development of an agency will uncover its unique characteristics, virtues, and past and current status in the service delivery system. With this information as a backdrop, the administrator has a better grasp of the agency's values, development, and traditions and the significance of these elements in either maintaining the status quo or allowing for agency change. Therefore, administration from a strengths perspective means believing that an agency has the ability to resolve difficult situations, learn from experiences, and change.

Inherent in administration from a strengths perspective is the recognition that to focus on agency possibilities is to practice with an explicit power consciousness (Cowger, 1994; Wimpfheimer, 2004). Whatever else administration is, it is always political, because it encompasses power and power relationships. Indeed, exploring the agency's history with specific obstacles to empowerment and power relationships provides the administrator with guidelines to identify, secure, and sustain external and internal resources to ensure that consumers gain as much support as they need to maintain as much control over their lives as possible.

### Maintain the Focus

In administration from a strengths perspective, monitoring is a continuous process that begins when agency goals are established. According to Rapp and Poertner (1992), this can be accomplished by doing the following:

1. Selecting and establishing an agency focus
2. Defining the focus in terms of consumer outcomes
3. Eliminating potentially worthwhile goals and activities that do not support the focus
4. Committing, through a preoccupation or obsession, to achieving that focus (p. 19)

To maintain a focus, the administrator frequently contacts and collaborates with not only staff and other agencies but also consumers, their family members, and informal systems of support. Ongoing contacts with the network of service providers enable the administrator to influence agency strategies and cost-effectiveness by increasing, decreasing, or terminating programs or services expeditiously.

Rapid responsiveness to consumers and community changes can have a dramatic impact on service costs. Reductions in costs can be expected in administration from a strengths perspective because services are reduced and shifted to consumers on the basis of their needs and regained levels of self-sufficiency.

## THE ADVOCACY PRACTICE AND POLICY MODEL AND SOCIAL WORK ADMINISTRATION

As described in Chapter 4, the advocacy practice and policy model (APPM) comprises four dynamic tenets: economic and social justice, human rights and needs, supportive environment, and political access. As social work administrators transform or translate social policy into services with consumers, goal setting and the distribution of resources come to the forefront of all actions (Tsui & Cheung, 2009). As seen in Table 8.1, the APPM can be used to highlight the social work values and standards associated with **administrative roles** and **administrative tasks**.

When reviewing Table 8.1, the special place advocacy holds in social work administration becomes obvious. Also, as mentioned previously, the four interlocking tenets of the APPM are dynamic and shift according to issues and consumer needs or perspectives of their life situations. When considered separately or in totality, the tenets motivate and guide critical and multidimensional thought about advocacy actions in administration (Cox, Tice, & Long, 2019).

The APPM tenet of *economic and social justice* reflects the influence of the National Association of Social Workers and its emphasis on social justice. Vital to social justice is the participatory governance, whereby people see themselves in interdependent relationships with society and government. This idea of

**TABLE 8.1**
The Advocacy Practice and Policy Model and Social Work Administration

| Tenets | Values/Standards | Administrative Roles | Administrative Tasks |
|---|---|---|---|
| Economic and social justice | • Equality<br>• Participatory governance<br>• Empowerment<br>• Social responsibility | • Leader<br>• Decision maker<br>• Collaborator<br>• Mediator<br>• Politician<br>• Advocate | • Planning<br>• Resources acquisition<br>• Evaluation |
| Supportive environment | • Human relationships<br>• Dignity and worth of the person<br>• Cultural diversity<br>• Competence | • Mediator<br>• Advocate<br>• Collaborator<br>• Politician | • Human resource development<br>• Resources acquisition<br>• Evaluation |
| Human rights and needs | • Self-determination<br>• Equality<br>• Empowerment<br>• Dignity and worth of individuals<br>• Relationships | • Advocate<br>• Mediator<br>• Collaborator<br>• Politician | • Planning<br>• Human resource development<br>• Supervision<br>• Evaluation |
| Political access | • Competence<br>• Service<br>• Social justice<br>• Human relationships<br>• Integrity | • Advocate<br>• Mediator<br>• Collaborator<br>• Politician | • Planning<br>• Evaluation |

interdependence gives rise to the empowerment of self and others as seen in the administrative roles of collaboration and mediator. Ideally, by increasing the empowerment of consumers and by providing information and support to them, administrators and staff will enable consumers to form a strong contingent, capable of exercising their own rights (Tsui & Cheung, 2009).

A **supportive environment**, another tenet in the APPM, relies on a focus on human relationships and the dignity and worth of individuals. This requires competence in cultural humanity, a lifelong process of self-reflection and discovery to build honest and trustworthy relationships. For administrators, supportive environments often require mediating with other social service organizations coupled with advocacy for the needs of consumers in the context of their communities and the agency. Resources are needed to establish and sustain a supportive environment as is ongoing assessment of evaluation. Said another way, administrators must ensure that the environment supports the changing demands of consumers in a responsible and timely manner.

Corresponding in many ways to a supportive environment is the tenet of *human rights and needs*. In this context, administrators are called upon to advocate, collaborate, and mediate the reality of human needs from the standpoint of consumers (Cox et al., 2019). Often this process requires that the administrator participate in the political arena in order to gain the endorsement of elected officials and subsequent local, state, or federal funding. Needless to say, the energy, time, and planning needed to move forward in the area of human rights and needs are considerable with gains often achieved over a long period of time. The assessment and evaluation, from a consumer's perspective, is essential to marking and celebrating success in goal achievement.

In terms of *political access*, an administrator might experience firsthand what consumers often know all too well: With privilege comes power—power to form policies, allocate funds, and define rights. By serving as an advocate, mediator, or politician, an administrator can sometimes shift the power base to include desired consumer goals. This has been done in the area of HIV/AIDS awareness, education, and services and in the gay rights movement for marriage equality. In both of these examples, it is noteworthy that service consumers were active participants in the political process—demonstrating the goal of social work—to help people help themselves (Tsui & Cheung, 2009).

Seen in the totality of a model, the APPM highlights the role of advocacy in all dimensions of social work practice, including administrative roles and tasks. When reflecting the model, it is essential to keep in mind consumers and their critical participation in relation to programs, services, and policy. Regardless of the issue or concern, the APPM is consumer centered with participation, empowerment, and interdependence underpinning administrative action.

©iStockphoto.com/Vasyl Dolmatov

**PHOTO 8.3**
Teams reflect roles, tasks, and ethical decision making.

## Administration in a Community Agency

Maria is the executive director at The Women's Center, a service organization dedicated to providing services for women and promoting women's rights. Maria's original appointment at The Women's Center was as a social advocate, and she worked her way up through the administrative chain of command to become director. During her time as a frontline worker, Maria developed a profound appreciation for keeping her practice activities consumer centered and directed. This philosophy has extended into her administrative approach.

Within weeks of assuming her position as director, Maria organized what is called "the group of 20" (GO20). Each program and constituent group at The Women's Center was asked to put forward the name of a consumer representative for appointment to the GO20. Members serve 1-year terms, with a term limit of 3 years.

The GO20 meets with Maria on a monthly basis. Its charge is to give Maria information and feedback with respect to organizational performance (goals, policies, programming, staff, management, services, budget, and evaluation). In addition, the GO20 completes an annual evaluation of Maria's ability to supervise, manage resources, and provide organizational leadership.

Maria uses the GO20 as a sounding board with respect to decision making. This has allowed for various perspectives, including the consumer viewpoint, to gain prominence. On several occasions, the GO20 has made recommendations concerning policy and program initiatives. The group is politically astute. Because of their influence and close working relationship with Maria, membership in the GO20 is sought after and seen as prestigious at The Women's Center.

The GO20 is a reflection of Maria's and the organization's commitment to reaching out and tapping into the strengths of consumers in administration. Employees and consumers at the agency believe that The Women's Center is a stronger, more effective organization as a result of the value placed on consumer involvement and participation in leadership. For Maria, the GO20 is an exceptional asset in her attempts to balance competing interests and demands for resources.

**Questions**

1. While members of "the group of 20" (GO20) represent programs and constituency groups, how are people selected for membership? Potentially, people in the GO20 could be hand-picked by Maria. Devise a system for selecting members of the GO20 that reflects tenets of the APPM and a strengths perspective, as well as promotes active, impartial voices.
2. Maria worked her way from being a frontline social worker to a position as the top administrator of the agency. Although she exemplifies many of the virtues of the organization (e.g., hard work, advocacy, and consumer centeredness), identify some of the pitfalls associated with promoting people from within an organization.
3. The GO20 is described as a "sounding board" for decision making at the agency. How could the role of the GO20 be strengthened? Is the sounding board approach sufficient from the empowerment or strengths perspective?

## ETHICAL CONSIDERATIONS

The values and principles of social work provide an administrator with the road map necessary to guide an organization on a course in the pursuit of organizational effectiveness. Professional values help administrators focus their technical, efficiency-oriented decisions and actions on consumers' needs rather than on production quotas or political exigencies. It is not that productivity and politics are without import, but their importance is as means of achieving the goal of quality service delivery (Homan, 2016). The values of the social work profession in turn serve to define the profession's code of ethics, which are essentially behavioral guidelines for practice.

Ethical dilemmas can sometimes be avoided or made easier to deal with if an organization has clearly articulated values that are used regularly to guide decision making. Dolgoff, Harrington, and Loewenberg (2011) propose a hierarchy based on defined ethical principles to evaluate one's possible actions when confronted with ethical dilemmas:

1. Life
2. Equality
3. Autonomy
4. Least harm
5. Quality of life
6. Privacy
7. Truthfulness

The hierarchy, which shows how each principle takes precedence over the ones below it, gives an administrator a clear guide for thinking through perplexing situations.

Some additional helpful principles for administrators to consider are the following:

- *Review State and Federal Laws*
  Be sure administrative decisions are sound, not only ethically but also legally. An administrator must remember assistance cannot be offered to consumers if such assistance places the administrator or agency in a precarious position.
- *Seek Supervision*
  It does not matter how long one has an administrator position if he or she has doubts and questions, just needs a sounding board, or seeks supervision. Everyone needs a second opinion once in a while. Supervisors can be particularly helpful in guiding toward the best decision possible in a difficult situation.

- *Consult the National Association of Social Workers*

  A vital benefit to being a member of the NASW is having the support of a national organization associated with decision making. Most states have a hotline that social workers can call when they experience ethical dilemmas. A social worker can discuss a situation confidentially, without using identifying consumer details, and get professional advice on how to handle things. Sometimes a neutral party is the best resource to help when considering things from a new perspective.

- *Take Time to Process What You've Learned*

  After completing a research project and consulting with the experts, it is often necessary to take some time to process everything before making a decision. Often, when faced with an ethical dilemma, it is important to note that you cannot undo a decision once it has been made. At the end of the day, the decision maker needs to be able to live with the final decision and to feel confident the action taken is in the best interest of the agency and its staff and consumers (National Association of Social Workers, 2017).

Like all social workers, administrators must consider the need to document actions and interventions. Such documentation is a way for administrators to defend decisions and protect against ethics complaints or lawsuits (Madden, 2003). Thus, linked to documentation is the concept of risk management. Social work administrators should document significant discussions, consultations, and meetings that address ethical and legal issues (Reamer, 2005). For example, they should record the steps taken to determine whether to disclose confidential information without a consumer's consent to protect a third party from harm, address an employee's impairment or unethical conduct, or develop conflict-of-interest guidelines for agency personnel (Reamer, 2005).

## Time to Think 8.4

You attended a conference for regional social agency administrators. During the conference, you directly hear a colleague present misinformation to sway the vote on resource allocation to favor her agency. You are appalled by this behavior and wonder what is the appropriate response. Consider what action you would take in light of the National Association of Social Workers' (2017) *Code of Ethics*.

SAGE edge™ Visit **www.edge.sagepub.com/ticemacro** to help you accomplish your coursework goals in an easy-to-use learning environment

## SUMMARY

In light of recent trends at the national and state levels, it appears likely that administrators will be given greater discretion regarding the organization, funding, and delivery of services to consumers. Consequently, it becomes imperative for administrators to develop consumer-centered practices that ensure efficient responses to needs.

This chapter's description and examples demonstrate how administrators can affect social programs through a process of interactions with consumers, staff, and the community. A strengths perspective and the APPM offer administration support for advocacy, self-determination, and consumer participation, choice, and empowerment. It is hoped that administrators will better discover their own strengths as they implement advocacy actions based on a consumer and strengths approach to leadership.

## TOP 10 KEY CONCEPTS

administration 179
administrative roles 194
administrative tasks 194
decision making 182
ethical issues 179
holistic assessment 192
mediator 183
program evaluation 190
supervision 188
supportive environment 195

## DISCUSSION QUESTIONS

1. On a daily basis, administrators are called upon to address an array of issues and associated tasks. Provide an example of a situation where you had to prioritize tasks. What was the outcome? How do you deal with a large variety of tasks all requiring simultaneous completion? Discuss the skills that were most helpful to you.
2. Social work administration requires performing well under stress. Discuss an example of how you performed well under pressure at school or in a job. What strengths did you use to work through the stressful situation?
3. Administrators work with a variety of staff members like social workers, psychologists, receptionists, and janitors while simultaneously interacting with consumers and community members. Consider your interrelationship skills and how you would establish communication patterns across the agency. How would your communication pattern help to diffuse conflict?
4. Strong organization skills are a must for administrators. Be specific and describe how you keep on top of your time and workspace. What messaging system and calendar programs do you use?
5. How would you define confidential information in an agency setting? As an administrator, how would you handle a staff member who disclosed consumer-related confidential information with consent? How does the advocacy practice and policy model apply to this situation?
6. Imagine there is an administrator of a large metropolitan child welfare delivery system.

Answer the following questions: (1) How could this administrator design a delivery system that responds to the growing needs of a diverse and bilingual population? (2) How can the administrator convey the agency's mission and goals? (3) How can the administrator involve the community with the agency? (4) What can the administrator do to support the agency's staff with regard to consumers' service needs? (5) How can an administrator advocate for immigrants and their children?

## EXERCISES

1. Interview an administrator at a social service agency. Ask about her or his philosophy with respect to management, leadership, and supervision. How does she or he embrace consumer input and feedback and use the feedback in the administration of the agency?
2. Enter a conversation with a classmate. Ask for his or her perceptions concerning your potential for leadership. Why does this person think you would be a good administrator? What would be some of your challenges in assuming an administrative role? Consider entering a similar discussion with your academic advisor.
3. Ask a faculty member in your program for the program's or school's administrative story. Who founded the social work program at your college or university? Identify the basic values and theoretical underpinnings of social work education at your college or university. How does the administration of your school or program embrace the strengths perspective?
4. Visit the Career Development Office at your college or university or review https://www.myperfectresume.com/build-resume/choose-template. If you desire an administrative position, what aspects of your resume would you highlight? How would you indicate in your resume a commitment to consumers and their participation in your administrative activities?
5. Ask your class instructor, academic advisor, field instructor, or coach for feedback on your performance. How did you receive this feedback and what did you do with the provided information? Why do you think feedback is a critical aspect of supervision and personal growth and reflection?

## ONLINE RESOURCES

- U.S. Small Business Administration (https://www.sba.gov/advocacy): The Office of Advocacy is an independent voice for small business within the federal government, the watchdog for the Regulatory Flexibility Act (RFA), and the source of small business statistics. Advocacy advances the views and concerns of small business before Congress, the White House, the federal agencies, the federal courts, and state policymakers.
- American Council on Education (http://www.acenet.edu/news-room/Pages/Toolkit-Resources-for-Administrators.aspx): Designed to provide assistance to administrators in creating, implementing, evaluating, and sustaining career flexibility policies and practices for faculty and also contains additional resources.
- U.S. Department of Health and Human Services (https://www.hhs.gov/programs/

social-services/homelessness/resources/index.html): Funds several resource centers and activities that provide valuable information for consumers, providers, and policymakers.

- Social Work Administrator—Social Work License Map (https://socialworklicensemap.com/become-a-social-worker/social-worker-careers/social-work-administrators-researchers-planners-and-policymakers): Highlights administrators as decision makers, concerned about the well-being of a total system. Provides information on social work schools and career opportunities.
- *Administration in Social Work* (https://www.researchgate.net/journal/0364-3107AdministrationinSocialWork): A highly respected, peer-reviewed journal that has provided timely, relevant information to human services administrators, managers, and educators for more than a quarter century.

# 9 Policy Practice, Political Persuasion, and Advocacy

## LEARNING OBJECTIVES

After reading this chapter, you should be able to:

1. Define and explain policy practice in social work
2. Describe the applicability of the problem-solving model, the strengths perspective, and empowerment in policy practice
3. Articulate the importance and use of advocacy in policy practice
4. Identify how social workers can influence the political process and legislative change
5. Describe and explain the importance of professional skills in policy practice

## POLICE PROFILING OF PERSONS OF COLOR

Ken is a social worker at St. Peter's social service agency. His primary role is to assist consumers in securing meaningful employment. Most of the people served by St. Peter's live within a 2-mile radius of the agency. St. Peter's is located in an urban setting plagued by poverty, crime, violence, poor housing, unemployment, and challenging transportation connectivity.

In the past few weeks, several of Ken's male consumers have expressed concern about racial profiling. In particular, it appears that police officers are routinely stopping and questioning African American males for no particular reason. The mayor and chief of police have publicly stated that the area surrounding St. Peter's needs to be "cleaned up." Merchants and store owners have been complaining to politicians about vagrancy. Indeed, police patrols have been stepped up, and in recent weeks, there has been an appreciable increase in the number of misdemeanor violations given to local residents of color.

Consumers of services are livid. They seek an immediate end to racial profiling. Consumers of color can barely walk down streets or wait at a bus stop without being harassed, let alone seek employment. In their zeal to satisfy local businesspeople, it appears that the mayor and police chief have created an unofficial campaign to rid the streets of racial minorities.

Ken has facilitated two community meetings in reaction to the present situation. Consumers agree that police actions constitute an affront to their human dignity and believe that it is time to start thinking strategically and politically and get involved in local politics. There is a general concern that many people do not realize or understand what is happening. Additional information and documentation are needed, and consumers have begun the process of making contacts with community leaders and elected officials to raise consciousness and better assess the situation. Consumers have begun seeking ways to place the issue of racial profiling on various public agendas. The official name of the newly formed community group to combat racial profiling in Ken's service community is Citizens Committed to Dignity for Persons of Color.

# POLICY PRACTICE, POLITICAL PERSUASION, AND ADVOCACY

It has been noted throughout previous chapters that social work has always had a dual focus: individuals/families *and* the environment within which they live. An essential concern of the profession is improving the conditions that affect individuals and families. This dual focus is often summarized as *person-in-environment.* This connection demonstrates that policy practice and advocacy, which affects the environment, in turn has a direct effect on individuals. Policy practice is not just a desirable activity for social work; it is an essential activity if social work is to achieve its historic mission.

One of the early social work leaders, Porter Lee, described social work as "cause and function," where the *function* of social work might typically be seen as individual work and the *cause* as the social advocacy role for producing larger scale change. In his presidential address at the National Conference in 1929, Lee concluded,

> In the last analysis, I am not sure that the greatest service of social work as a cause is contributed through those whose genius it is to light and hand on the torch. I am inclined to think that in the capacity of the social worker, whatever his/her rank, to administer a routine functional responsibility in the spirit of the servant in a cause is the explanation of the great service of social work. (p. 20)

Later formulations have described "the cause in function" as shifting the focus to a more substantiated type of advocacy that is derived from and pertinent to the individual (Lee, 1929).

Policy practice, political persuasion, and advocacy have always been central themes in macro practice. An early example was the settlement house movement at the beginning of the 1900s, which was closely connected with the Progressive Era, a time of intense social reform activity. Jane Addams and others from Hull House intervened at multiple levels of government to promote social justice (Levine, 1971; Lundblad, 1995). They were heavily involved with the Chicago Civic Federation, an influential local political advocacy organization (Linhorst, 2002). Through involvement in this organization and other activities, Hull House participants supported the establishment of the Cook County Juvenile Court, which served as a model for the nation. Furthermore, their advocacy efforts at the federal level led to passage of national child labor legislation (Linhorst, 2002).

This chapter explores policy practice, the political process, and advocacy. Of particular interest is the promotion of social change through policy analysis, formulation, and development, as well as advocacy using various orientations (e.g., strengths perspective, empowerment, problem solving, person-in-environment). Consumer empowerment via political involvement is explored in relationship to the population group or groups being served by the social worker. Various forms of legislative and political participation are examined, including testifying, lobbying, promoting ordinances and laws, connecting with political action committees (including social work's Political Action for Candidate Election committee, commonly referenced as PACE), electing social workers to political office, serving as staff members for officeholders, and networking with politicians.

### Time to Think 9.1

Racial profiling by police officers is a complex, multifaceted phenomenon. For example, profiling could involve citations of a number of types—arrests for traffic violations, vagrancy, and other violations of the law. Attention to detail is often an important asset when examining policing and practices. Contemplate ways to differentiate perception from social facts when documenting racial profiling. How might consumers of services shed light on the techniques, practices, and ploys used in racial profiling in their community? How might the voices of consumers be compromised or heightened as a result of racial factors? Using this chapter's opening vignette, what could be the role of Citizens Committed to Dignity for Persons of Color in this process?

## DEFINING SOCIAL POLICY

**Social policy** involves statements of "what ought to be" and defines what services will be delivered, who consumers are, and what roles social workers will assume. As principles of action, policies translate a government's sense of responsibility to citizens and the world at large (Tice & Perkins, 2002). Because policies are normative and grounded in values, social context, and time period, they are influenced by the interests of various stakeholders, which often involves disagreement and tension (Meenaghan & Washington, 1980). The dynamics of policy include broad categories ranging from taxation to health care and environmental protection. Indeed, the boundaries of social policy are unclear; however, policies encompass a core of ideologies, sets of beliefs, that tend to polarize us (Axinn & Levin, 1992). For example, priorities regarding children are often compared to and contrasted with imports associated with people who are older, or the needs of the poor are presented as being in conflict with those of the middle class.

Contextual factors and an array of political processes shape specific policies in each historical era (Jannson, 2001). Such processes are influenced by laws, rules, regulations, and budgets. Aspects of social policies can be found in the following:

- Constitutions that define social policy powers of the local, state, and federal governments
- Public policies or laws enacted in local, state, or federal legislatures

**FIGURE 9.1**

The Legislative Process

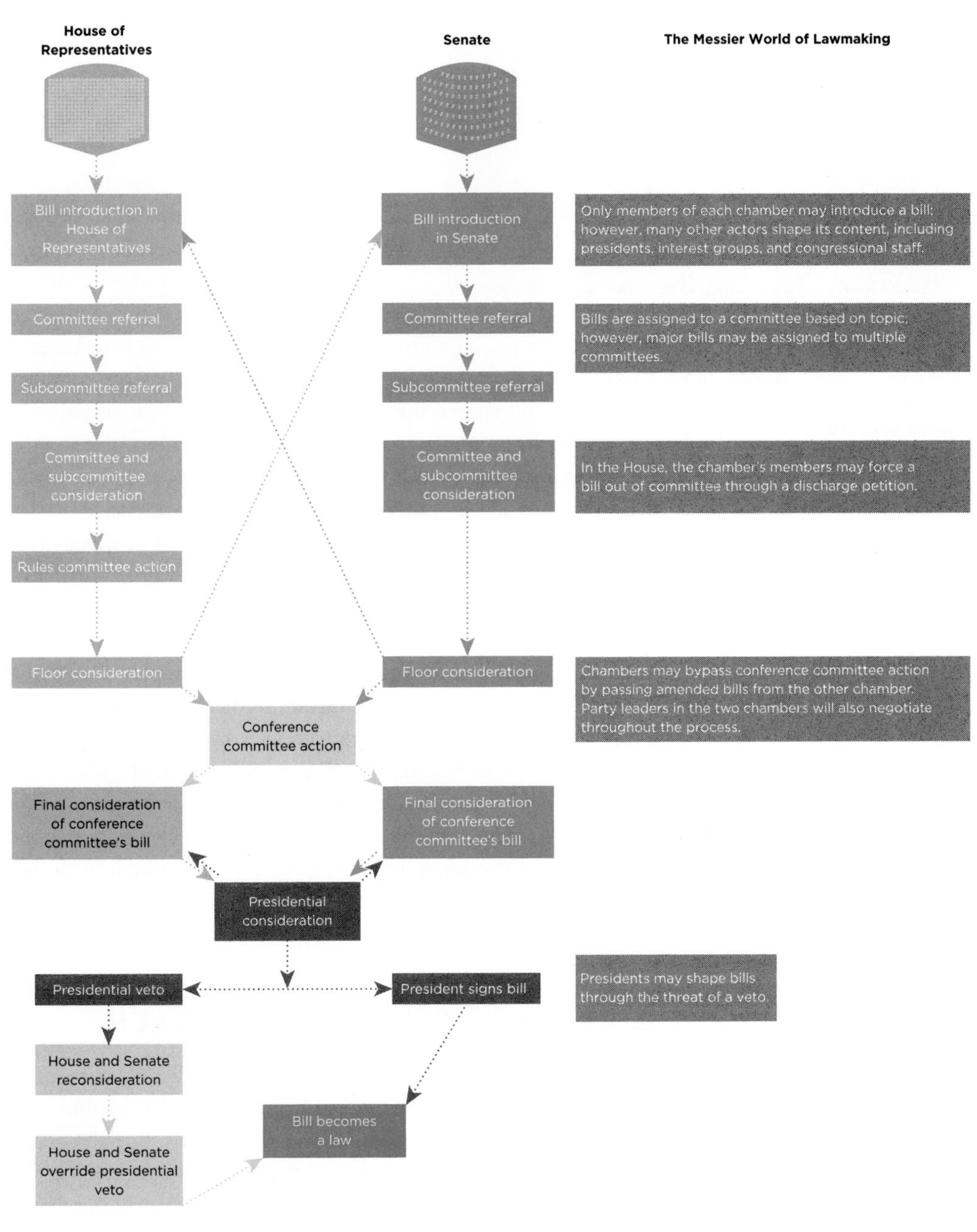
House of Representatives
Senate
The Messier World of Lawmaking
Bill introduction in House of Representatives
Bill introduction in Senate
Only members of each chamber may introduce a bill; however, many other actors shape its content, including presidents, interest groups, and congressional staff.
Committee referral
Committee referral
Bills are assigned to a committee based on topic; however, major bills may be assigned to multiple committees.
Subcommittee referral
Subcommittee referral
Committee and subcommittee consideration
Committee and subcommittee consideration
In the House, the chamber's members may force a bill out of committee through a discharge petition.
Rules committee action
Floor consideration
Floor consideration
Chambers may bypass conference committee action by passing amended bills from the other chamber. Party leaders in the two chambers will also negotiate throughout the process.
Conference committee action
Final consideration of conference committee's bill
Final consideration of conference committee's bill
Presidential consideration
Presidential veto
President signs bill
Presidents may shape bills through the threat of a veto.
House and Senate reconsideration
Bill becomes a law
House and Senate override presidential veto

*Source:* Abernathy (2019), p. 336.

- Court decisions that overrule, uphold, and interpret statutes
- Budgets and funding allocations that demonstrate societal values and priorities

Bloomberg/Contributor/Getty Images

**PHOTO 9.1** Understanding the role of government is essential to social work practice and policy.

- Stated objectives that specify missions and goals
- Rules and procedures that define how policies will be implemented at the local, state, and federal levels (Jannson, 2001, pp. 18–19).

Social policy development occurs on many levels (e.g., within organizations, communities, and nations). Much of social policy is the result of government decisions. This point is demonstrated in Figure 9.1, which displays the legislative pathway that a bill travels to become a social policy and law. Two primary groups participate in the passage of policy into law: the legislature and special interest groups. Policy work is often completed by legislators who are appointed to committees and subcommittees on the basis of their particular interests. Committees are the loci of testimony on issues, and legislative hearings provide for official testimony from the public.

Special interest groups fall into two broad categories based on their activities. Political action committees (PACs) influence the composition of legislatures before elections. Lobbyists exert pressure between elections to gain legislative actions for their interests (Tice & Perkins, 2002). The National Education Association (NEA) and the American Medical Association (AMA) are examples of powerful special interest groups that influence policies relevant to their membership.

Of course, legislative branches of government such as the U.S. Senate and House of Representatives may be reluctant to advance and vote on a legislative bill if the president of the United States has announced intent to not support or sign the legislation. This was the case with the passing of U.S. budget legislation in the early months of 2019 when President Trump signaled his unwillingness to sign a budget bill that did not include a border wall. This stalemate in budget legislation resulted in the longest shutdown of the U.S. government in modern history.

## THE PROBLEM-CENTERED APPROACH

To understand the implications and effects of social welfare policies and to influence the development of those decisions, social workers must be familiar with the policymaking process from the problem-centered approach. Social workers involved in macro practice operate in both the political and the policy arena. The provision of benefits and services to people to meet basic needs, including housing, income, food, and health care, is regulated by social policy. Thus, society's response to social problems often comes by means of social policy. The traditional approach to policy development involves unraveling a problem in a series of processes. In problem-centered policy development, problem definition is the cornerstone of policy design (Chapin, 1995; Tice & Perkins, 2002).

To demonstrate the **problem-centered approach to policy development**, follow these steps:

1. Consider at least six social issues facing our nation, such as access to health care, mental health, substance use, or homelessness.
2. Identify population groups at risk and affected, giving special attention to relevance of human diversity.
3. Decide on the "real" or "root" cause of the issues.
4. Explore societal and community responses to these issues.
5. Define the services designed to address the issues.
6. Consider how people and their communities are labeled in order to receive the services.

As this exercise illustrates, the problem-centered approach involves a series of processes intended to address an entanglement of problems, issues, and values that typically combine to make policy development a complex web of activities. Thus, social policy occurs on many levels and reflects a variety of government choices and decisions affecting not only basic needs but also opportunities for and the rights of people to advance in life.

Although social policy is often developed in response to social problems, the relationship between problems and policies is not simple. For instance, a social issue is often only labeled as a problem when it affects a significant number of people or gains the attention of influential, powerful people. Consequently, social policies reflect the social and personal values of those with decision-making capabilities (Tice & Perkins, 2002).

Problem identification is a basic aspect of the process of understanding human needs and priorities. Problem definition creates a source of knowledge that can be used in assessing current policy trends and implementing new policies and programs. Finally, problem definition reflects commonly held beliefs and values about our environments (Karger & Stoesz, 1998). Expanding on problem identification, consider a number of steps:

1. *Identify the policy or program goal and needed change.* What is wrong with the current policy? How does this affect communities? Organizations? Groups? Individuals? How can it be improved? It is an important first step to know as much as possible about the current policy. Find out what needs it addressed at the time of its inception and how those needs may have changed. Who advocated for the implementation of the policy? What would they say about the proposed change? What role does human diversity play in advocating for change?
2. *Identify the values related to the problem/human need.* Why is this change desirable? Have various levels of society that might be affected been consulted? Is it ethical? Have diverse populations been considered?
3. *Analyze the current situation or operation—"the actual."* What is currently in place? Who is affected? How can it be improved? Investigate the situation from the perspectives of communities, organizations, groups,

and individuals. Notice the impact at the different levels. Who benefits from the situation? Does anyone suffer from it?

4. *Determine "the ideal" policy program or service provision.* How does the proposed change improve the system? Why is it better? What are the elements of this program or provision that make it ideal? Are the effects of this policy program or provision beneficial to all? How so?
5. *Identify options.* Can this policy be implemented in different ways? What are the fundamental principles? Are there many plans or courses of action, or is it more restrictive? Who supports the change? Who are the opponents of the change? What are the points of opposition?
6. *Choose the best or most feasible option or alternative.* What is most likely to be implemented at this time? Are there any future changes that might affect this policy? How can this policy have the most crucial impact?
7. *Implement the modified policy or program through an action plan.* What steps need to be taken to implement the change? What groups or organizations would be advocates in this process? How will the public know about the proposed change? Pritzker and Lane (2016) offer, "To facilitate social change, the social work profession needs social workers who can lead political efforts and a social work population capable of engaging with politics and empowering clients to leverage their political voices" (p. 81).
8. *Evaluate the change.* What is different as a result of the change? Were there unexpected implications? Were any problems created by the change? Has it been accepted? Criticized? Have the benefits been reaped?

## THE POLICY PROCESS FROM A STRENGTHS PERSPECTIVE

With the problem-centered approach to policy development as a backdrop, it is time to shift attention to an examination of the strengths perspective for policy design. In essence, the strengths perspective suggests that many of the barriers that confront people "come from educational, political, and economic exclusion based on demographics rather than individual characteristics" (Tice & Perkins, 2002, p. 5; Rappaport, Davidson, Wilson, & Mitchell, 1975). **Using strengths in policy practice** challenges social workers to identify and create opportunities that nurture the growth and capabilities of people in their environments. Thus, policy development from a strengths perspective highlights the potential for community and large-scale change rather than perceived deficits or weakness.

If social policy is to reflect the reality of its intended recipients and if self-determination is paramount, consumers must be included in the strengths approach to policy. What are the responsibilities of social workers? According to Chapin (1995), social workers must ensure that the voices of clients are both heard and understood by policymakers and must focus on the common needs and strengths of people rather than their deficits. However, Reisch and Jani (2012) emphasize sensitivity to and understanding the importance of participation in politics and political environment in practice. They state,

> During the past several decades, social work practice in the USA and the industrialised world has become increasing politicized—a consequence of political-economic, ideological, demographic and cultural changes. . . . It influences how all participants in the service process define needs, implement alternative strategies of helping and evaluate their effectiveness. (Reisch & Jani, 2012, p. 1132)

## The Strengths Perspective and Policy Analysis

The strengths approach, examined in depth in Chapter 2, advances a **policy analysis framework** that incorporates the unique strengths of individuals and communities while addressing human needs. Charlotte Towle's (1945/1987) *Common Human Needs* provides a foundation for the framework by suggesting that social policy is a tool for helping people meet their basic needs. As Tice and Perkins (2002, p. 12) conclude, an emphasis on human need suggests that social workers should recognize:

- People with similar needs are nevertheless confronted with different barriers to meeting their needs.
- Highlighting common needs instead of social problems eliminates labels based on deficiencies or pathologies.
- With human needs as the basic criteria, people do not have to be described as deficient to justify receiving benefits and services.
- The social work values of self-determination and respect for worth and dignity are operationalized by a focus on human needs.
- Recognizing common human needs supports the conceptual core of the strengths perspective whereby social workers collaborate with people as opposed to exerting the power of knowledge or institutions.
- Human needs involve communities as a resource that offers opportunities for growth and development. (Chapin, 1995; Saleebey, 1992; Tice & Perkins, 1996, 2002; Towle, 1945/1987)

As designed by Tice and Perkins (2002, p. 13), Table 9.1 integrates the traditional problem-centered approach to policy development with the strengths perspective. Saleebey (1992) describes the strengths perspective as a collaboration of ideas and techniques rather than a theory or paradigm. It "seeks to develop abilities and capabilities in clients" and assumes that "clients already have a number of competencies and resources that may improve their situations" (Saleebey, 1992, p. 15; Tice & Perkins, 2002, p. 11). When applied to policy and macro practice, the strengths perspective addresses common human needs and barriers to meeting such needs rather than community or individual deficits, weaknesses, or pathologies.

**TABLE 9.1**

Comparison of the Problem-Centered and Strengths Approaches to Policy Development

| Policy Process | Problem-Centered Approach | Strengths Approach |
|---|---|---|
| Identify the problem(s) or issue(s) | • A condition or situation is identified and labeled as a "problem" to be corrected in the context of a beginning step in policy development. Values of and self-determination by consumers of services are important and determining factors for moving forward. | • Barriers associated with meeting common needs are identified as well as the assets of consumers of services for setting agendas and determining relevant issues for advancing a policy initiative. |
| | • "Problem" impacts the quality of life for a large group of the economically/socially powerless and typically includes assessment and research describing, specifying, and prioritizing needs.<br>• Problem definition is influenced by identified and agreed-upon values.<br>• Political ideology affects problem identification, and people in positions of power exert influence in problem definition. | • Issues to be addressed are identified and negotiated with interested and relevant people in a fashion that identifies, includes, and uses the strengths of consumers of services.<br>• Stories and observation of ordinary people are sought, valued, and included in defining and prioritizing issues.<br>• Recognition and value are given to the passion, knowledge, and experience of consumers of services and people in need when coping with and confronting barriers to produce social change. |
| Formulate policy alternatives | • Thorough gathering of information and knowledge is essential.<br>• Existing data sources (e.g., government and agency sources) are often valuable.<br>• Professional associations and commissioned research projects through grants can be important sources of data.<br>• Professional policymakers and researchers are considered the experts and viewed with authority.<br>• Involves organized activities to identify and include legislative and elected officials as well as other influential stakeholders. | • Knowledge accumulation focuses on the strengths of the individuals and their experiences and stories.<br>• Qualitative and consumer-driven forms of data collection are considered tools to assist people and stakeholders as makers in identifying and addressing issues.<br>• Consumers of services are collaborators in information collection, research efforts, and policy development.<br>• The environment (social, psychological, and biological) is scanned to identify strengths and assets that support policy development and people in their ability to move forward in a relationship to identified issues.<br>• Consumers of services work to identify and introduce formal and informal resources to support policy development and implementation.<br>• A concerted effort is made to identify how consumer needs can be met through policy development in ways endorsed and supported by consumers. |

| Policy Process | Problem-Centered Approach | Strengths Approach |
|---|---|---|
| Legitimize policy | • Special interest groups garner resources (e.g., money and people) to influence the process of passing bills into law.<br>• Social welfare advocacy groups make a concerted effort to endorse or confront issues/programs.<br>• Research findings and the perspectives of experts are used to support efforts.<br>• Information is organized and for distribution and dissemination (e.g., publications, pamphlets, announcements, media postings, blogs, e-mails, texts). | • Consumer abilities and strengths are embraced and used to provide real-life context, knowledge, and passion to issues.<br>• Consumers are consulted and included in information gathering, research, and promotional efforts with a focus on promoting (e.g., publications, pamphlets, announcements, media postings, blogs, e-mails, texts) the perspectives and voices of consumers. |
| Evaluate policy | Universities, government, and commissioned entities conduct and evaluate studies. | Consumer abilities and strengths are considered included in evaluative research studies and processes. |

*Source:* From *Faces of Social Policy: A Strengths Perspective,* 1st edition, by C. Tice/K. Perkins, © 2002.

Policy development from a strengths perspective negotiates needs and barriers by soliciting input from people, the eventual consumers of services. This is primarily accomplished through the worker-consumer relationship, collaborative knowledge building, linking people with existing resources and services, and advocating for services when they do not exist. Consequently, the process of social policy development becomes more inclusive by considering problems ranging from the personal through the external environment and interweaving these two dimensions in a circular fashion (Gutierrez, Parsons, & Cox, 1998; Tice & Perkins, 2002, pp. 12–13).

Table 9.1 describes how problem-based and strengths-oriented policy development compares and recognizes different ways of thinking and acting. Both orientations are valuable in prompting insight and are often complementary in policy practice.

The strengths perspective can be used to conceive a new understanding of the relationship between social workers, consumers, and policy development. When policymakers move beyond seeing themselves as the experts, more attention is paid to community outreach to provide voice to and perspective from diverse groups. Policy developed from a strengths perspective should be evaluated according to the extent to which policies reflect the ideas and needs of people in their communities. Thus, social workers are challenged to develop strengths not only in individuals but also in communities.

It is at this juncture that empowerment comes into play. Empowerment represents a means of accomplishing policy and community development by conceptualizing two key elements: giving community members the authority to make decisions and choices and facilitating the development of the knowledge and resources necessary to exercise these choices (Zippay, 1995, p. 266).

Read the following case study and apply the strengths perspective framework to its analysis. How did the analysis support empowerment? What aspects of the analysis were most difficult for you?

## FORMING A COALITION

Betty James works at a local domestic violence shelter that receives significant funding from the state human services agency. A bill has been introduced in the state legislature that would require domestic violence shelters to share all of their records with the state agency. After discussions with staff and consumer of services representatives, many concerns have been raised about the purpose of such disclosure and the ability to maintain client confidentiality. The state government has experienced a shortfall in income in this fiscal year because of a financial downturn and resultant reduction in income from taxes. Despite a 5% increase in the number of clients this year, the state has informed Betty's agency that it can expect a reduction in the state allocation. Consider the following questions:

1. How would Betty help develop a coalition with other agencies?
2. How could or should consumers of services be involved?
3. How might Betty contact legislators? What could she present?

4. Should discussions be held with the state agency? If so, how should this be accomplished?
5. How could support from consumers of services, the community, groups associated with the agency, or churches be secured?
6. How might diversity be a factor? For example, might organizations advancing the rights of and services for women assume a special role?
7. What and who should Betty's group prepare for testimony before legislative hearings?

## THE ADVOCACY PRACTICE AND POLICY MODEL AND POLICY PRACTICE

In Chapter 4, the advocacy practice and policy model (APPM) offered four major tenets for consideration when advocating for change in practice. In the context of policy practice and political persuasion, **political access** is particularly relevant and is thus examined in depth in the following sections and paragraphs of the present chapter. However, it is important to point out that *economic and social justice, human rights and needs,* and *supportive environment* remain key factors when contemplating social work practice in relationship to policy practice and political persuasion.

For example, Weiss-Gal and Gal (2008) suggest that the social-economic orientations and professional values of social workers can contribute to their perceptions of policy practice as well as involvement in social welfare policy practice. Take a moment to reflect, does or should the active involvement of social workers in policy practice hinge on the social worker's alignment with professional values and beliefs emphasizing *economic and social justice?* Are professionals and consumers more likely to play meaningful roles in policy formation and development if they are committed to and have a passion to advance economic and social justice for all? Indeed, many instances of policy practice and legislative reform are rooted in individual and collective experiences involving various forms of economic and social injustice (e.g., various forms of discrimination, oppression, and deprivation).

### Time to Think 9.2

For consumers of services and social workers, is it possible that the desire to become active in policy practice and political persuasion is grounded in personal economic and social need and/or experiences of injustice? Is your interest in social work practice rooted in any such personal connection to economic and social injustice? Consider discussing with your social work classmates, field instructors, and faculty members the advantages and disadvantages of emotional attachments to causes when engaged in policy practice and advocacy.

In order for policy practice and political persuasion to occur in social work practice, a *supportive environment* is also needed. Resources necessary can include the ability to dedicate time, support from a supervisor and employing agency, technological means for communication, the involvement of consumers of services, expertise in writing policies and legislative acts, and the ability to garner endorsements from key stakeholders and leaders. A supportive environment also takes into account a conducive political climate for change in and with an organization, community, or society. Rush and Keenan (2014) suggest that social workers consider that "welfare contexts enable and constrain the manner in which social work is practiced" (p. 1436). Contextual factors could include the presence of dominant ideological beliefs—supportive or in opposition to policy change and the role of social workers in political persuasion.

Last but not least, consideration of *human rights and needs* of consumers is an important and ongoing focus in policy practice and political persuasion, particularly as described and articulated by consumers of services. For a variety of reasons, it is vital to understand that consumers of services may not be at a time in their lives to participate in policy development and political persuasion. Consumers immersed in struggles related to their own rights and needs are often overwhelmed, requiring sensitivity and respect from social workers about the ability of consumers to participate in policy development and political persuasion. For example, for a person struggling with housing, one's immediate need centers on acquiring a safe shelter, not necessarily advocating for policy development and human rights. Timing is a key consideration for the participation and utilization of the strengths of consumers in policy development and political activities, especially with cause advocacy as compared to case advocacy.

## KNOWING THE POLITICAL PROCESS

If social workers are to engage in policy practice, they need to have a general knowledge of practice and specific training in advocacy techniques. The political knowledge base should include political institutions, the policy process, current economic and social conditions, the positions of political players, and related areas (Delli Carpini & Keeter, 1996). Unfortunately, "politics" is often viewed negatively. The public conception often is that politics is manipulative and dishonest. Politicians are perceived as untrustworthy. The news media launch investigations into the moral character of politicians and often expose unsavory aspects of their past. In recent years, social media have become a popular and loosely regulated and untrustworthy forum for influencing public attitudes and thinking about politicians, policies, and legislation. Indeed, in 2018, one of the lead national stories involved Russian interference with national elections, including the 2016 presidential election. It is also important to note that the term *politics* is also used in a more informal fashion to describe the manipulation of interpersonal relationships involving influence and power, particularly in the workplace.

This type of negative thinking and the bombardment of information about political issues can stimulate, limit, and slant our views about and interest in becoming part of the political process. The use of critical thinking and skepticism concerning the accuracy and validity of various forms of news and information sharing is important. Whatever we think of politics, however, the political process influences everyday life for social workers and clients alike. Public policy and funding are part of the political process. Social workers need to be aware of politics and participate in the political process to maximize their effectiveness. To opt out of political processes is to turn important decisions over to other people who may have less knowledge, less self-interest, or a lesser commitment.

Tom Williams/Contributor/Getty Images

**PHOTO 9.2** Attorney General Jeff Sessions testified before a house Judiciary Committee on November 14, 2017, where he fielded questions about Russian meddling in the 2016 election.

Although politics is often viewed negatively, many politicians are honest and struggle to reconcile competing interests. They want to achieve the best results in difficult situations. As Reisch (2000) notes,

> If we continue to regard electoral politics as choosing between the "lesser of two evils," if we continue to see electoral participation as an "either/or" strategic decision, it is inevitable that we will become disheartened and drop out of the dialogue over the future of our society. . . . Making effective choices, however, requires us to assess the current political climate carefully, affirm our commitment to the values we profess, and ally ourselves with other forces, locally and globally, that share our vision and goals. (p. 293)

## THINKING AND ACTING POLITICALLY

For social workers to have maximum impact on behalf of consumers and communities, it is important to think politically. Most policies have come about as a result of political processes. When social workers neglect to engage in **thinking politically** about the politics of social welfare policy, the needs of consumers and their communities are left out of the policy development process. Social workers, according to Domanski (1998), are in a unique position to increase the political salience of social issues. To make a difference, it is important that social workers be aware of social issues, their political implications, and the political process. Reisch (2000, p. 294) suggests that social workers consider several crucial questions to launch their political thinking:

- What political strategies can create change in the era of globalization?
- How can politics confront the isolation experienced by urban and rural communities and the marginalization of their populations?
- What will be the roles of the public, private, and nonprofit sectors in the provision of income maintenance and social services?

- What roles will social workers play in the social welfare nexus as the relationships among the government, nonprofit, and for-profit organizations change dramatically?
- Who should bear the economic and social costs of rapid economic and technological changes?
- Can a welfare state exist if all of the essential services are not provided or if services are provided by nongovernmental organizations?

As these queries suggest, it is important that social workers stay abreast of the political climate in their jurisdiction, the state, and the nation. Often the election of a new politician to a key position can have a major impact on funding allocations. This may also be the catalyst for new initiatives and opportunities to explore new areas of interest. A politician's agenda may focus on an area of social service that has been neglected in the past, opening up opportunities for funding and new programs. This shift in spending may have an impact on current programs, which may see a loss in available funds. Whether political change threatens funding or broadens possibilities, social workers should be aware of the possibility of future changes.

Social workers can do a number of things to become part of the political process. The most basic act is simply to *register and vote.* This is a very simple process and has become easier in recent years. Not to vote is to opt out of the political process and one's role in a democracy. Most social workers get involved by voting, advocating, and keeping informed of political issues, while only a few consider themselves activists or attend public hearings (Domanski, 1998).

*Getting involved in political activities* on behalf of a party or a particular candidate is another way to support the political process. Campaigns depend on the support of staff and volunteers for success in elections and implementation of political agendas. Tasks may range from answering phones and distributing flyers to assisting in speech preparation and hosting events. Some restrictions may be placed on federal workers by the Hatch Act, which limits certain political activities for individuals whose salaries are supported by federal funds (Thompson, 1996). Social workers should review and conform to organizational, state, and federal policies and laws regulating and restricting involvement and participation in political activities, especially during work hours.

*Helping consumers to get involved* and to increase their political awareness is one way of empowering individuals. Encouraging consumers to register and vote, emphasizing their potential to contribute to their community, invites feelings of importance and connectedness. Social workers should further develop consumers' connection to their community by emphasizing the political context in which they live and offering suggestions to get consumers involved in political activities.

Fortune, Mingun, and Cavazos (2007) suggest that the practicing of various professional skills can be impactful in relationship to practice outcomes in social work education. For social work educators and students, practicing and role-playing skills and appropriate actions to engage consumers of services in political involvement are a consideration in field education, practice coursework, and skill-based seminars and workshops.

## INFLUENCING THE POLITICAL PROCESS

Social workers possess knowledge and skills for **influencing politics**. Strategies that can be used by social workers include advocacy, networking, lobbying, coalition building, using the media, using technology, participating in political action committees, and taking part in campaigning efforts.

To be effective, social workers should be aware of the basics of the **legislative process** and of the groups that influence legislation. Some of these are briefly discussed next.

### Getting Information About Legislative Proposals

Sources of legislative information include the following:

- Web-based resources such as National Association of Social Workers (NASW) legislative alerts, the National Priorities Project (www.nationalpriorities.org), and the Electronic Policy Network (www.movingideas.org)
- Websites such as www.politicalinformation.com and www.policylibrary.com
- Periodicals such as the *Congressional Quarterly Weekly Report*
- Newsletters from organizations that deal with specific issues
- Social advocacy groups
- Trade associations or coalitions of service agencies, which are interested in policy proposals that will affect their member organizations, including groups that are concerned with, for example, the collective needs of voluntary child welfare agencies or those of hospitals
- Coalitions interested in policy developments
- Newspaper indexes

### Using Information From Policy Groups

In every state and nationally, organizations study current policy and make recommendations for modification of policies to better serve clients. These groups issue position statements and advocate for changes. Frequently, these groups have websites or issue newsletters. A comprehensive list of advocacy groups can be found on the Electronic Policy Network website at www.movingideas.org. Membership in such groups is beneficial for fueling initiatives to change legislation, gaining information, and networking.

### Tracking Proposed Legislation

It is useful to know how a particular piece of legislation is moving through the legislative process. A bill, once introduced by a member, will be referred to a committee, which, it is hoped, will schedule hearings on the bill. Once the committee votes the bill out, it will be dealt with by the legislative body in which it was introduced. At each step, there are opportunities to influence the process. By tracking the legislation, a social worker or groups of social workers can target their efforts more effectively. More specifically, when considering how social workers can provide input to legislative committees and bodies, Weiss-Gal (2013) identifies the value of "placing matters on the agenda, providing information, providing explanations, expressing opinions and making suggestions, and commenting on the manner of the discussion" (p. 304).

## Time to Think 9.3

Take a moment and identify an issue, need, or type of social-economic injustice that you would be willing to advocate for a new policy, piece of legislation, or program. Which of the many activities examined in this section of the book would you be willing to devote time and energy? Hamilton and Fauri (2001) indicate, in their examination of political participation, that social workers embrace "a range of activities from voting to campaigning, but the most politically active respondents were engaged in professional associations" (p. 321). Since the publication of these findings, do you believe social workers have become more involved in the use of social media and technology or other forms of political advocacy? If so, how?

### Building Relationships With Legislators and Their Staff

An agency should develop and maintain contacts with legislators to gain their support. These relationships are significant for sharing ongoing information and in times of crisis, when a legislator's support could benefit the agency or when the need arises for letters of support. Agency leaders should strive to maintain contacts by calling legislators regularly and sending them letters, agency newsletters (hardcopy or electronic), and media spotlights about agency successes or events. Legislators should receive invitations to agency functions, such as annual meetings and public relation events. Some agencies gear regular meetings toward legislators to inform them of current social issues that affect the agency and its clients and that pertain to legislative proposals.

When asking for help, it is advisable to have developed an established relationship with key legislators, politicians, and stakeholders. If possible, identify how each legislator and her or his staff members best communicate with her or his constituents. For example, does the legislator use a Twitter account, e-mail, and so on or rely on mail and phone calls?

## Obtaining Funding

When legislation is passed that will potentially benefit a cause, the budget is the next crucial issue of concern. Funding is typically handled separately from the regular passage of bills. The allocation of funding will contribute to determining how the effort can be implemented. It is important to note that legislators have at times passed policies and pieces of legislation involving mandates without designating financial support. Such practices place the onus of implementation of such a policy or legislation on entities ill prepared to support such action. For example, the passing of required home visits to protect an at-risk population group (e.g., children and older adults) might seem like good legislation. However, if local agencies can't afford such practices, then agency finances could become compromised and result in cuts in other forms of services.

## Lobbying

**Lobbying** is the process of influencing legislation. It encourages leaders to consider issues of great importance to individuals and organizations. The late Sheldon Goldstein, who served as the executive director of the National Association of Social Workers, described a number of principles he learned while involved in legislative advocacy in Illinois:

- Legislators want to say "yes" to constituents, all things being equal.
- On the other hand, legislators hate controversial proposals. Individuals and groups have long memories if a legislator has voted against their proposals. As legislators have said, "Friends come and go but enemies accumulate."
- Voters, not dollars, vote. Letters and calls from a legislator's constituents are taken very seriously—much more seriously than efforts of paid lobbyists. Often a few letters or calls will determine a legislator's vote.
- Bills are most easily killed in committee.
- Choose a bill's sponsors carefully.
- Tell the truth. (Goldstein, 1990)

When meeting with an elected official in person, keep in mind that representatives need both *opinions* and *information*. Two issues are of primary importance to legislators: (1) the *cost* of the proposed bill and subsequent services and (2) the intended *outcome* or social impact of the policy (Brueggemann, 1996, p. 359).

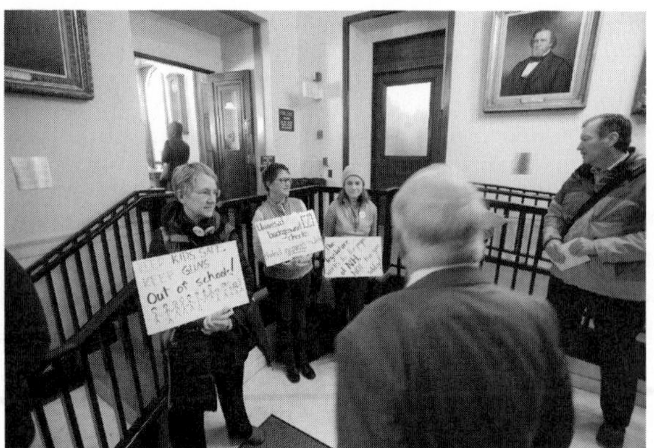

**PHOTO 9.3** Antigun lobbyists greet lawmakers in the New Hampshire state house, on January 2, 2019. Lobbying is part of advocacy action.

Written material, consumer comments, and other supportive material should be made available to legislators whenever possible.

Dear and Patti (1981) suggest a number of "empirically based tactics," which include introducing the bill early or before the session, getting multiple sponsors (particularly influential legislators), securing majority-party support and support of the governor, and trying to get open committee hearings and testimony at these hearings. Not surprisingly, bills that have low fiscal impact have the support of the majority party and are not controversial will generally have the best chance of passage.

As you become more familiar with the state legislative processes, there are a number of things that you may find striking. One is the sheer volume of legislation. Many legislators deal with thousands of bills in a session. It is impossible for any legislator to have detailed knowledge about either the subject matter of all the bills or the specific provisions of the bills themselves. In practice, this means that legislators have to rely on other members or on outsiders to provide guidance on how to act on specific proposals. Second, many lobbyists try to influence legislative decisions in ways that are favorable to their group's interests. Third, legislative committees are crucial to the outcome of bills because many bills are modified in—or never emerge from—committee. The final vote on a bill may be largely a formality, as decisions about bills are largely made in committee, by lobbying, or by recommendations of legislative leaders.

## PROFESSIONAL SKILLS IN POLICY PRACTICE

At this point, the importance of social workers engaging in the broad range of activities considered "political" should be obvious. What **policy practice skills** are necessary to participate in the political process of policy development?

### Communication

Communication skills are crucial to the effect that social work discussions will have on consumers and on public- and private-sector policymakers. As stated by Gummer (1990),

> The first step in any policy process is to see the issues one is concerned with are placed on the public or private agenda. The capacity to determine which items go on, and which are excluded from, the policy maker's agenda is an important and much sought-after source of power. (p. 107)

Communication also plays an essential role in correcting errors in policy thinking (Burch, 1991). Social workers can frame social welfare issues in ways that reflect social work's professional interests. Furthermore, social workers may have opportunities to testify at legislative hearings. Should this opportunity arise, the following may be useful to consider:

- It is important to be aware of your audience and the actors (e.g., politicians, political aides and staff members, other advocates). What arguments will appeal to each?
- It is often ineffective to argue for a position individually using a moral standpoint alone. Recommendations should be reasonable and responsible and address fiscal considerations: Why does this proposal make good fiscal or business sense?
- Human interest stories in addition to statistics and other factual information can be helpful. Be aware that overuse of statistics or "facts" may be boring.
- The use of academic language or professional jargon can be off-putting as well as talking down to legislators.
- It is helpful to anticipate counterarguments and be ready to answer critical questions or include responses to potential concerns in your presentation.
- Consider role-play and critique your presentation before an official meeting. It might be helpful to have someone play the role of devil's advocate, using potential counterarguments or questions.
- Consider preparing a written presentation as a guide. However, it is often impractical and ineffective to read such a script word for word. Yet a brief handout for distribution to officials many be helpful and appropriate.
- When making a formal presentation, it is wise to be prepared to modify your presentation. Hearings may fall behind schedule, and presenters often have to shorten or change presentations to conform to conditions or rules.
- Hearing settings can be rather hectic, with several things going on at the same time, requiring presenters to be prepared, stay focused, and be flexible. It is important for advocates and lobbyists to be clear about what is desired from legislators. When seeking support of a particular bill, people should state from the outset of the presentation the desired goal(s), which are briefly recapped at conclusion.

Presenters will want to be mindful about the appropriate and effective use of technology when making presentations. Attention to detail, prompting interests, and connectivity to causes, length, and people requiring accommodations are but a few noteworthy considerations.

- In order to be prepared, it is helpful to identify explicit short- and long-term goals and key strategies when communicating with key actors.
- Haynes and Mickelson (2006) suggest social workers "be honest and factual whenever a legislator or legislative aide is contacted . . . remember that straightforward presentations with data generally provide the most persuasive approach" (p. 103).

### Collaboration

Domanski (1998) suggests that collaboration demonstrates the importance of power in numbers while diversifying the support for social welfare programs. When collaborating with consumers, community members, and other policy stakeholders, "skills of negotiation, a willingness to compromise, and an understanding of the incremental nature of the U.S. social welfare policy reform are important tools" (p. 161). Social workers acting as collaborators encourage and facilitate open and honest exchange of ideas, plans, and resources, and they enable consumers and community members to jointly define their separate interests by mutually identifying changes that may be needed to achieve common purposes (Garner & Orelove, 1994, p. 63).

### Assessment

For policy development from a strengths perspective, social workers must conduct a holistic rather than a diagnosis assessment. Consumer knowledge and motivation are the basis of such an assessment, as opposed to professional expertise. Strengths assessment focuses on optimizing community resources. As stated by Saleebey (1997), "Acquisition of natural community resources is predicated on the belief that including consumers in the decision about who or what entity provides the service will promote adherence to the form and direction of the help received" (p. 125).

Three principles define an assets-based approach to assessment (Saleebey, 1997, pp. 205–206). First, social workers begin with the resources that are present in the community rather than what is lacking or what a community and its citizens need. Second, the assessment is internally focused. It is essential that social workers know what is going on in the community and with its residents, as well as what individual and group capabilities exist. Finally, the process is relationship driven.

### Critical Thinking

**Critical thinking** involves the dual process of "identifying and challenging assumptions" and "imaging and exploring alternatives." Policy development requires thinking rationally to address social issues by building on unique strengths. However, social workers must be reminded that there is more to policy development than calculated rationality. In other words, efficiency does not always result in the best social policy. Policy formation and development is also an emotional issue for many people, rooted in one's values, passions, and previous experiences. For example, do not necessarily assume that a politically conservative Republican necessarily opposes or is ambivalent about LGBTQ legislative rights. Such a legislator may have an emotional attachment or been moved by an emotional plea or understanding to such rights via a personal or family relationship.

Policy development from a strengths perspective requires synthesis: the integration of various needs and values. This means first seeking to *understand.* Too often, social workers' own agendas and need to be heard can make it extremely difficult to give undivided attention to the needs and wants of others (Timpson, 2002).

## ETHICAL CONSIDERATIONS

The National Association of Social Workers (NASW) 2017 *Code of Ethics* confirms the responsibility of social workers to promote social welfare and advocate for adequate living conditions, fulfillment of human needs, and social justice (p. 29). Furthermore, social workers "should engage in social and political action that seeks to ensure that all people have equal access to the resource, and employment, services, and opportunities" in relationship to basic human needs (p. 30). Indeed, policy development, legislative change, advocacy, and political persuasion to advance the interests and needs of vulnerable and exploited populations are signature aspects of practice that differentiate social workers from other professionals.

However, commitments to social and political action do not come without ethical peril. For example, the 2017 revision of the NASW *Code of Ethics* included changes and new language regarding the use of modern technology in practice. The development of policies involving technological use in relationship to consumers of services (clients) was affirmed. Social workers are required to notify and seek approval from consumers about the use of informed consent when technology is used to communicate. Consider for a moment the possible ill effects and exploitation of the unauthorized use in political action and policy practice of pictures, recordings (video and audio), and the identity and images of consumers without knowledge and consent. Life in the age of YouTube clips and cell phone recordings presents both opportunities and challenges for helping professionals, educators, and members of the general public.

SAGE edge™ Visit **www.edge.sagepub.com/ticemacro** to help you accomplish your coursework goals in an easy-to-use learning environment

## SUMMARY

The better social workers understand the functioning of government and the process of policy development, the greater the likelihood of exerting influence over social programs and services. This chapter examines policy development from a number of orientations to promote advocacy efforts and the empowerment of consumers for policy change. Although a variety of suggestions and ideas have been offered for use in social work practice, the use of critical thinking in collaboration with the thoughts of consumers, colleagues, and supervisors is a crucial component. In reality, policy practice, political persuasion, and advocacy are complex, interrelated processes that require thought, reflection, and meaningful conversation with appropriate others.

Ideally, this framework of policy analysis offered in this chapter will encourage macro social workers to envision themselves and consumers as political actors with the capacity to influence and affect the United States' course of action. It is through thoughtful thinking and action that the unique human needs and social issues of individuals, groups, and communities can be effectively addressed.

## TOP 10 KEY CONCEPTS

critical thinking 222
influencing politics 217
legislative process 217
lobbying 219
policy analysis framework 209
policy practice skills 220
problem-centered approach to policy development 206
social policy 204
thinking politically 215
using strengths in policy practice 208

## DISCUSSION QUESTIONS

1. Consumer participation and influence concerning policy formation and development is often affected by power and privilege. Discuss how various forms of diversity (e.g., race, gender, social-economic status, age) are important factors for consideration when promoting the voices of consumer in advocacy efforts and political persuasion, especially in the areas of experience, passion, emotion, and determination.
2. Is policy and legislative change a rational process? Identify nonrational aspects involved with policy development, advocacy, and political persuasion efforts.
3. In policy practice, is it possible to use the strengths perspective and problem solving simultaneously? If so, identify and discuss examples.
4. As suggested earlier, politics and political persuasion are often viewed negatively. What are some ethical standards and boundaries for adherence by social workers? Identify checks and balances that social workers can adopt to promote a sound ethical compass in policy practice.

## EXERCISES

1. Research a legislative proposal through Internet and media sources. Eventually, identify and read the original legislative bill and any subsequent amendments. Track the progress of the legislative initiative, both its support and opposition. Were consumer groups involved in the legislative process? Was the bill ever enacted? Why or why not?
2. Join an e-mail list, blog, or online discussion group dedicated to social advocacy. Assess the involvement and participation of consumers of services. How could the system be improved (e.g., inclusiveness, website development and administration, etc.)?
3. Contact one of your legislators in support of or opposition to a pending bill of interest that you have researched. Ask the legislator about the possibility of you providing additional information and perspective about the merits of the bill. Could consumers be involved in any such reach-out and education?
4. Identify an elected legislator in your district that aligns with and has voted in favor of legislation benefiting a client population group. Consider attending a fundraiser for the legislator and intentionally meet people, including the legislator. Be attentive to who attended the event and their demographic and social-economic characteristics.
5. Attend a neighborhood, residential life, or residents' council meeting. During and after the meeting:
    - Review the meeting agenda, listen to the meeting's discussion, and read previous meeting minutes.
    - List at least three issues that were labeled as problems for the membership.
    - Investigate what measures were taken to address these problems. Did policy statements result from the identified problems?

## ONLINE RESOURCES

- Political Action for Candidate Election (PACE) is social work's political action committee and is endorsed by the National Association of Social Workers (NASW). PACE is dedicated to support for candidates who support the NASW's political agenda. Visit https://www.socialworkers.org/Advocacy/Political-Action-for-Candidate-Election-PACE to learn more information about PACE, congressional voting records, and advocacy efforts.
- Readers might be surprised to learn what are the top political action committees (PACs) in the United States and what they spend to influence elections. See https://www.thoughtco.com/biggest-political-action-committees-3367778.
- Visit http://www.ncsl.org/bookstore/state-legislatures-magazine/federalism-hot-legislative-issues-2018.aspx to review the top legislative issues according to the National Conference of State Legislatures.
- The United Nations Entity for Gender Equality and the Empowerment of Women provides ideas for influencing legislators and policymakers at http://www.endvawnow.org/en/articles/121-influencing-legislators-or-other-policy-makers-.html.

# 10 Using Technology in Social Work Practice

## LEARNING OBJECTIVES

After reading this chapter you should be able to:

1. Define advances in technology and social media
2. Describe the possible use of technology by social workers
3. Apply the advocacy practice and policy model to technology
4. Consider ethical issues associated with technology
5. Explore the future use of technology in practice

## ROSE GRABANIA EMBRACES TECHNOLOGY

Rose has been a social worker for well over 30 years. Throughout her career, Rose has been instrumental in organizing community-based voter registration drives, public education on policy initiatives associated with health care and wellness programs, and a reading partnership for both children and older adults. In the past, Rose did her organizing work primarily through face-to-face encounters, petitions, forums, boycotts, meetings, and lobbying.

Over the past decade, Rose has come to realize that technology plays a huge part in a changing society. The increase of information available to people and the speed of communication patterns have altered the traditional methods Rose used to initiate social change. Consequently, Rose has gradually integrated more technology into her traditional macro practice strategies. For example, she used e-mails and text messages in conjunction with websites to advocate in the last political campaign. She successfully raised money for a children's camp by using an online funding drive.

What concerns Rose is the ongoing need to enhance her technology literacy and competence while considering how technology and social media affect her relationships and interactions with consumers. In many ways, Rose sees new relationship possibilities along with an array of ethical considerations.

## ADVANCES IN TECHNOLOGY AND SOCIAL MEDIA

Social workers began using technology in their practice in the late 1980s and early 1990s (McNutt, 2018). Personal computers, computer networks, and technology centers supported the Internet development and provided a set of tools for social workers to use across consumer systems (Schuler, 1996). As listed in

Table 10.1, the digital, online, and other electronic technology offer a landscape of practice options.

There are three basic approaches when considering the integration of technology with social work practice—proactive, reactive, and rejection. Ideally, the majority of social workers will decide to be proactive and positive in their reaction to the acquisition of new knowledge (Belluomini, 2013). A proactive stance requires reading about current technologies that affect evidence-based practices, consumer populations, advocacy actions, ethics, agency processes, and strengths-based solutions. Furthermore, macro social work necessitates remaining up-to-date on technologies affecting groups, communities, and organizations. To a degree, this can be accomplished through online services that include articles of interest to educate practice. Examples include www.socialworker.com/, www.socialworktoday.com, and www.socialworkblog.org.

There are situations in which the approach to technology might be reactive. This is when critical thinking about technology and its impact is especially essential. For example, Snapchat could capture a particular community or agency in a negative light and place the entity at risk for funding, harm, stereotyping, or stigma. Indeed, university officials likely attempt to monitor the usage of social media in relationship to the oppression of and discriminatory comments toward students. Similarly, membership by a social worker on Facebook or other social media platforms makes public a profile that might be better kept private from consumers and their communities.

Rejecting technology involves a decision against its use because the tool will not enhance the quality of life for consumers and communities. Misinformation and cyberbullying are examples that could influence a social worker to reconsider the value of technology in practice. Even the use of e-mail under some circumstances can come under scrutiny as being informal, brief, subject to misuse and viewing by others, and too spontaneous. If technology holds the potential of negatively impacting consumers or affecting their privacy, social workers are obligated to anticipate the negative consequences of social media and technological exposure.

**TABLE 10.1**

Web 2.0 Technology-Based Techniques

| | |
|---|---|
| Blogs and microblogging | Image sharing (Flickr) |
| Wikis | Video sharing (YouTube) |
| Social media (Facebook, Twitter, Instagram, Snapchat) | Virtual worlds (Second Life) |
| Meetups | Storify |
| Podcasts | |

*Source:* Adapted from McNutt (2018, p. 140).

## Time to Think 10.1

Review the opening case and consider how technology and social media could be used to enhance Rose's organizing activities. What specific features of technologies could you see Rose using and why? Who could serve as a resource person, mentor, source of encouragement, and role model for Rose? Identify and describe organizing strategies that would combine traditional methods of organizing with technological applications.

## THE USE OF TECHNOLOGY BY SOCIAL WORKERS

A strength of the social work profession is its ability to adapt new methods and models to address social, economic, and environmental issues. With an open mind to innovation, technology offers social workers new and effective ways of advancing communication, delivering services, and working with consumers in communities while pushing or enhancing the boundaries of traditional practice (Reamer, 2013).

Technological services and intervention provided to consumers are often called "telehealth," "e-therapy," "online therapy," or "online counseling." The contemporary application of technology in practice is multifaceted and can include the use of psychoeducation websites, phone apps, self-guided interventions, supportive electronic communities, online hotlines, chat sites, and professional online forums and listservs (Dombo, Kays, & Weller, 2014).

### Websites

**PHOTO 10.1** Social media are a tool for social work policy and practice.

Social workers have access to a variety of websites designed to inform and guide assessment, planning, networking, organizing, evaluation, and administration. For example, www.people.uncw.edu defines social change strategies focused on individuals, groups, and organizations. This site also defines and applies the role of change agents in relation to settings and goals.

Principles of community organizing are found at www.icpj.org, where the relationship between organizing and activism is concisely described. The fundamentals of grassroots organizing are found at www.commorg.wisc.edu, including 10 rules for effective community organizing. Highlighted in the rules is the need for group formation and community leadership development to help ensure goal achievement.

Of course, the challenge in using websites involves the reader deciphering the validity, objectivity, and value of website content. Website content needs to be viewed with skepticism and critical thinking. Workers should give special attention and scrutiny to the sources for information.

## Social Media

Social workers can use **social media** to build partnerships and collaborations with people who share common interests, goals, and activities. In 2004, Mark Zuckerberg launched Facebook, a free **social networking** site that allows members to post profiles and upload photos and videos. With approximately 2.23 billion users, Facebook is the most popular social network used to connect and share online.

Social workers who use Facebook and other forms of social media such as blogs, message boards, or Twitter must be careful and responsible about sharing personal or consumer information. Discussion on any public arena opens the possibilities for inappropriate disclosures. Indeed, the onus is undoubtedly on the social worker to protect consumers by constructing boundaries that protect privacy and emphasize respectful engagement (Young, 2013).

## E-mail

Electronic mail, e-mail, involves people exchanging messages using electronic devices. First introduced in the 1960s by Ray Tomlinson, the e-mail of today came to the general public in the mid-1970s. The substantial growth of the use of e-mail has made a tremendous impact on the norms that influence socialization and how we come to understand both private and public information (Bratt, 2010).

One result of e-mail is the possible disconnect between "real-life interactions and the perceived anonymity of the online world" (Bratt, 2010, p. 341). The notion of "friending" makes establishing and maintaining relationships across consumer systems appear easy. Online friendships have few of the relationship components associated with the traditional concepts of a friend. For example, loyalty, shared experiences, common beliefs, and trust are not necessarily a part of "friending." Consequently, the embedded complexity is that social workers do not have personal relationships with consumers but rather connect at a professional level.

Given that e-mail occurs in a professional setting, certain **e-mail etiquette** should be followed. Table 10.2 outlines some guidelines for e-mail communication.

## Texting

Texting or text messaging, also called short message service (SMS), is an exchange of brief written messages or comments between mobile phones or portable devices (Kuhns, 2012). Texting is an extremely casual way of exchanging information; consequently, it is essential that social workers be aware of the context of communication. Texting provides social workers with a fast and easy form of communication, but we are reminded that words can be misspelled,

**TABLE 10.2**
Professional E-mail Etiquette

| | |
|---|---|
| 1. | Include a clear, direct subject line. Examples of a good subject line include "Meeting date changed," "Quick question about your presentation," or "Suggestions for the proposal." |
| 2. | Use a professional e-mail address, most likely an agency e-mail address. E-mail addresses should always convey the sender's name, so that the recipient understands who sent the e-mail. |
| 3. | Think twice before hitting "reply all." Refrain from hitting "reply all" unless everyone on the list needs to receive the e-mail. |
| 4. | Include a signature block. Readers should receive some information about the sender, such as full name, title, agency name, and contact information, which should include a phone number. |
| 5. | Use professional salutations. Don't use laid-back, colloquial expressions like, "Hey you guys," "Yo," or "Hi folks." |
| 6. | Use exclamation points sparingly. Exclamation points should only be used to convey excitement. |
| 7. | Be cautious with humor. Humor can easily get lost in translation without the right tone or facial expressions. |
| 8. | Know that people from different cultures speak and write differently. Miscommunication can easily occur because of cultural differences, especially in the writing form when we can't see one another's body language. Tailor messages to the receiver's cultural background or based on the depth of the relationship. |
| 9. | Reply to e-mails—even if the e-mail was intended for someone else. Here's an example reply: "I know you're very busy, but I don't think you meant to send this e-mail to me. And I wanted to let you know so you can send it to the correct person." |
| 10. | Proofread every message. Recipients will notice, and perhaps judge, any mistakes that are made. |
| 11. | Add the e-mail address last. Avoid sending an e-mail accidentally before the e-mail has been completed and proofread. |
| 12. | Double-check that the correct recipient has been selected. It's easy to select the wrong name, which can be embarrassing to senders and to the accidental recipient. |
| 13. | Keep fonts classic like Times New Roman. For business correspondence, keep fonts, colors, and sizes classic. |
| 14. | Nothing is confidential—so write accordingly. A basic guideline is to assume that others will see what is written, so don't write anything that shouldn't be seen by everyone. |

misconstrued, or misinterpreted. Additionally, the use of emojis, symbols, and graphic representations is open to multiple interpretations and alternate meanings. The following questions should be considered: Is texting the best way to communicate one's thoughts to another person? Are there differences in what is said over text versus in person? What needs to be remembered is that texting remains a more impersonal and short-worded mode of communication. Furthermore, it is important to note that the platform is more secure and more accessible.

## Time to Think 10.2

Consider your use of texting and e-mail. How conscious are you of how you convey your thoughts and ideas via these forms of communication? Have you ever received or sent a message that you regretted or felt dismayed over? If so, what action did you take to correct the incident? What if your texting or e-mail comments were subpoenaed and disclosed via court proceeding? Would damaging or embarrassing content be revealed?

## ADVOCACY SUITES

Social workers can link consumers to elected officials, educational material, and advocacy strategies through a comprehensive online system. An example of such a system is Maryland Learning Links (www.marylandlearninglinks.org) that compiles information and resources on mental/behavioral health, policy/leadership, evaluation/assessment, and other topics relevant to individuals, communities, and organizations. The National Council of Nonprofits (www.councilofnonprofits) offers social workers and the general public a site with advocacy tools and lobbying strategies for local, state, and federal actions.

The availability of advocacy suites expands social work's resources and facilitates state-of-the-art interventions based on human rights standards. Thus, the suites help create public policy and programs that respect, protect, and fulfill the values of social work as seen in social, economic, and environmental justice.

The speed, effectiveness, intensity, and global nature of technology clearly present new and ever-changing opportunities for social workers as we struggle to adapt to new approaches to practice and policy. The profession understands that technology is here to stay and will exponentially increase, generating profound social action and change.

## THE ADVOCACY PRACTICE AND POLICY MODEL AND TECHNOLOGY

With the rise of high-speed Internet connections and web-enabled cell phones, social workers and consumers find it easier to find and access information and resources. What is the role of the advocacy practice and policy model (APPM) in this ever-changing environment? The flexibility of the framework, comprising economic and social justice, a supportive environment, human needs and rights, and political access, is adaptable and agile to meet the demands of new media and forms of communication.

Throughout this book, the needs and strengths of consumers and communities are recognized as vital components to social work practice. It is useful to conceive technology, much like other resources or interventions, in the context of social work values and ethics. Technology keeps consumers and professionals updated on the issues at hand, mindful of consumers' role in the change process, and current with evidence generated from research that informs practice.

Indeed, many social workers would argue that technology supports educational advancement and research agendas. From this foundation of knowledge and skills, social workers are better equipped to respond to consumers and community situations in a timely fashion. By establishing robust systems of communication, supported by technology, social workers can engage with consumers when assessing a community, or any other social system, from a multitude of perspectives, including the strengths orientation.

Many social workers would agree that technology literacy is intricately linked to elements of advocacy. Technology has created greater access to information that informs practice and provides educational venues to people who previously had only limited access. Thus, technology itself becomes a tool of intervention and change. By sharing technological knowhow, social workers and consumers join forces in partnerships and broad-based coalitions. It can be argued that technology helps to create and nurture lines of communication, relationships, and communities beyond the barriers of time and space.

## Economic and Social Justice

In an increasingly interconnected and technological society and world, individuals, groups, communities, and organizations use and rely on social media and other digital technology to locate information, communicate, and access services (Tooley, 2015). It can be argued that the Internet is an important factor for fostering social justice because it enables anyone to participate in the global economy, obtain education and training, and network.

As advocates for universal access to the Internet, social workers would help to end the isolation so many people experience, especially those in rural areas and developing nations (Dobson, 1997). Technology in the context of economic and social justice recognizes that free Internet is critical because it is the technology that we use to connect and share knowledge with each other. Consequently, there is a need to prioritize investment in the national and global infrastructure to help ensure meaningful access to the Internet for all. This kind of thinking is fundamental to the values of social work and the principles of equity and justice.

The APPM recognizes that social justice encompasses economic justice. Economic justice, which affects individuals as well as societal order, encompasses the moral principles that ideally guide social policies and the creation of societal institutions. The problem of unequal access to technology is only a small part of inequality in the United States; however, it is a good place to start. Universal access to the Internet challenges the barriers of language and customs, and it is easier to provide than other services like health care or housing (Dobson, 1997). Additionally, the Internet opens space for communication that will minimize the isolation experienced by economically challenged people and poverty-stricken countries.

The elements associated with the notion of **universal Internet** are depicted in Figure 10.1. As indicated, both social work values and moral principles are critical to social and economic justice as they relate to equity and equality.

**FIGURE 10.1**
Social and Economic Justice

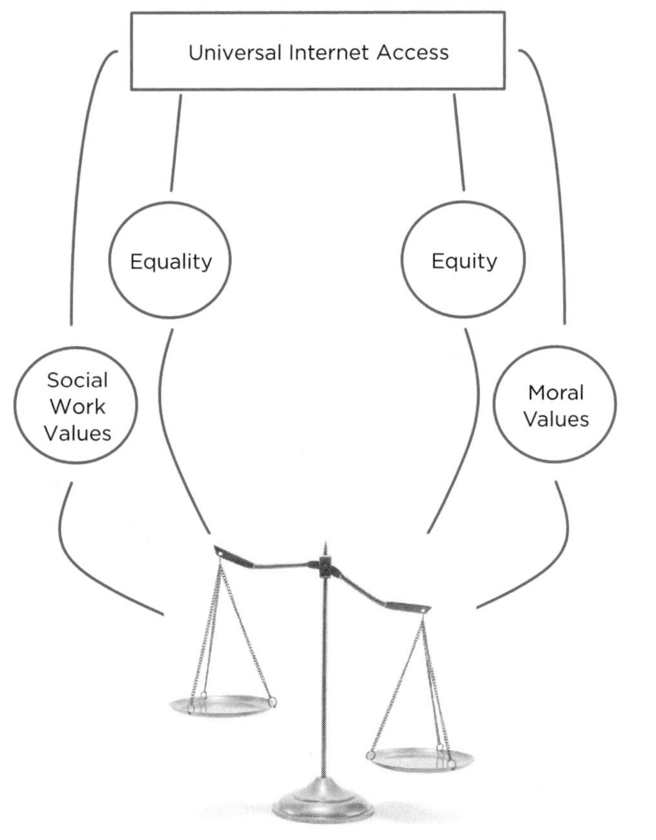


When considering the tenet of economic and social justice, social workers should consider the following questions:

- How can economic opportunities become more broadly distributed?
- Is economic justice about more than just income and wealth?
- How can prosperity be shared across households, regions, and sectors of the economy?
- What is the relationship between concepts of human rights and economic and social justice?
- How does social and economic justice celebrate aspects of diversity?

## Supportive Environment

The speed and intensity of digital technology has changed the societal and work environment. These changes require an understanding of the current and future of technological developments. Specifically, the professional of social work needs to revisit and possibly revise concepts related to communication patterns, social systems, relationships, and resources that surround a person. Within this framework, the APPM supports an environment that nurtures creativity in the context of privacy, equality, and equity.

The digital environment includes the use of computers, Internet networks, and various forms of social media, including texting. This environment, by its very nature, allows users to engage with each other almost instantaneously and with near anonymity. The expansion of communication opportunities also has challenges associated with ethics, privacy, and security that require ongoing attention. Furthermore, the range of information available through technology requires users to scan the environment to find pertinent data, to discern good information from bad, and to stay relevant in the face of rapidly changing discoveries.

As seen in Figure 10.2, the elements of an environment supportive of technology are complex and require vigilant monitoring and adjustments. The tenets of

**FIGURE 10.2**
Elements of a Supportive Environment

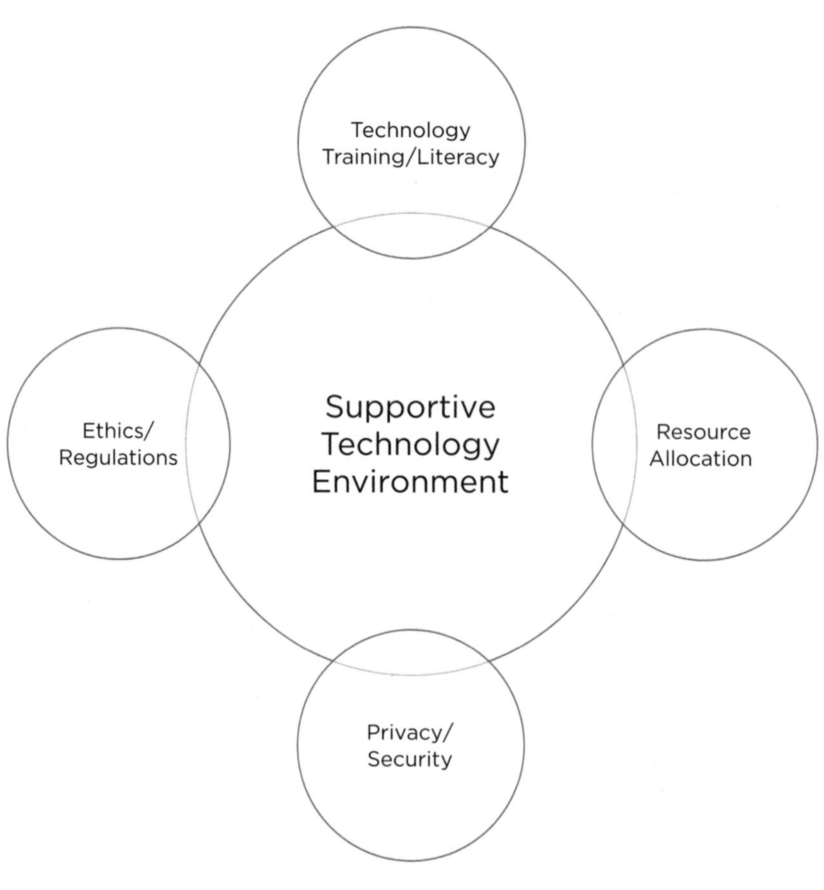

the APPM and its conceptualization of advocacy help to ensure an environment that supports ethical and effective practice and policy development.

## Human Needs and Rights

According to the World Economic Forum (Hickin, 2017), a not-for-profit foundation, there are three ways in which technology can address human needs and address rights.

1. Online learning and the right to education:
   Globally, approximately 120 million children do not attend school. Technology is emerging as a major asset to help ensure that children have access to education.
2. Big data distribution:
   There is a vast amount of data available on environmental conditions, migration, and conflict situations. Cloud computing and big data analysis can use this data to analyze key trends and provide early warnings related to critical issues, aiding the prevention and rapid repose to humanitarian disasters.
3. Protecting the supply chain:
   An estimated 30 million people are currently in forced labor across multiple industries from electronics to fishing. Technology can be used to enable transparency in supply chains from sourcing through to customer purchase.

The complexities of these issues are significant. What becomes obvious when considering social institutions, social class, changes in the value systems, and employment settings is the **intersectionality of technological innovations** (see Figure 10.3) with inequality and resource scarcity. These interlocking systems speak to the need for social workers to understand systems of power and advocate on behalf of those marginalized nationally and internationally.

## Political Access

Social work practice coupled with the access to the power base of politics has changed with the emergence of Web 2.0 techniques and the subsequent use of social media, particularly Facebook and Twitter (Germany, 2006; Guo & Saxton, 2015; McNutt, 2018). When advocating for social causes, these technical tools introduce a relations-building element into the process of online organizing, which can enhance consumer participation, friend and fund raising, and the dissemination of information and viewpoints to political allies and decision makers.

According to the APPM, the technology-based tools available to social workers add strength and options that address many challenges to social

**FIGURE 10.3**
Intersectionality of Technological Innovations

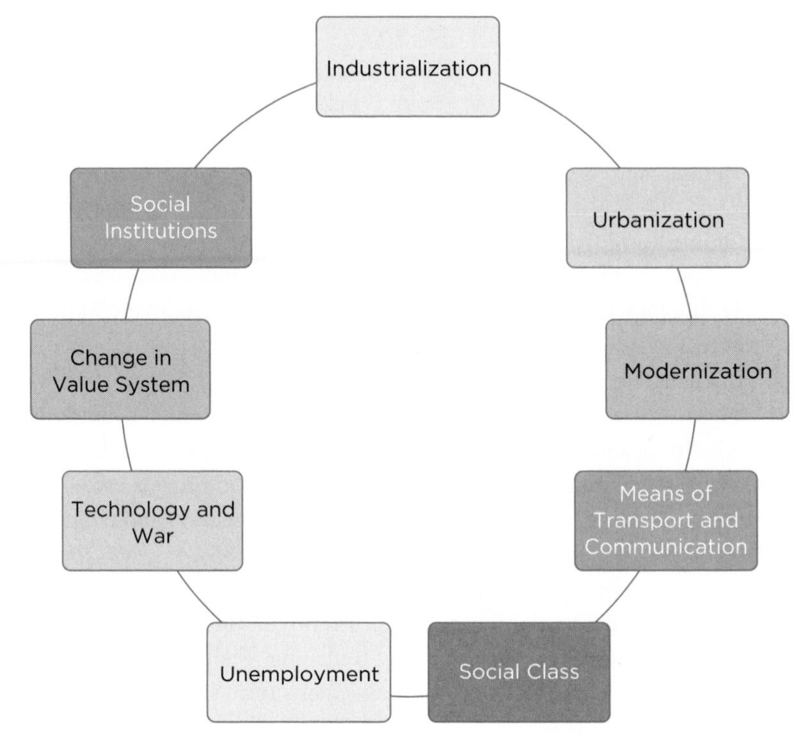


*Source:* Provided by SociologyGuide.com.

change. In contrast to more traditional tools and strategies, technology options are vast and growing. The dynamic nature of the APPM complements the growing use of technology and the increase in knowledge of how advocacy strategies work, structurally improve organizations, and address issues of social justice.

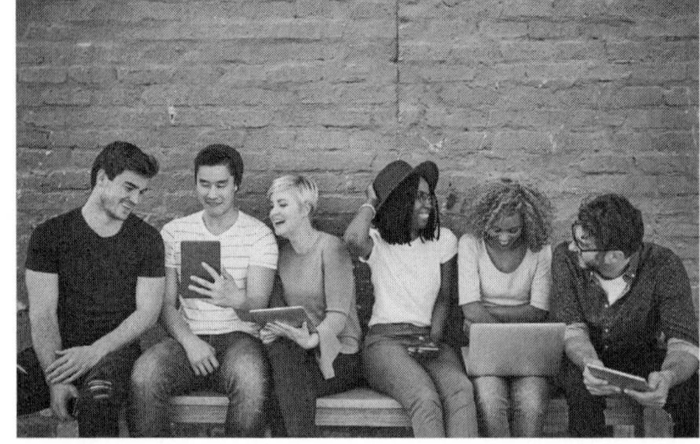

©iStockphoto.com/PeopleImages

**PHOTO 10.2**
Ethics must govern the use of social media.

In keeping with social work values and goals, technology standards are needed to address ethical regulations. Specific technology standards that protect the integrity and privacy of consumers and social workers include adherence to the *Code of Ethics,* compliance with laws that protect consumers' rights regarding data transmission and storage, recognition of cultural and social contexts, and verification of identity. Furthermore, it is imperative that social workers use technology to remain proficient in their field of practice while enhancing consumer accessibility to technology.

## Time to Think 10.3

After reading the table of technology standards, consider why the profession of social work is focused on both the use of technology and ethical regulations (NASW, 2017). How do the standards offer protection to social workers and consumers alike? Why do you think communities are included in the standards?

## ETHICAL ISSUES ASSOCIATED WITH TECHNOLOGY

Technology has altered our homes, workplace, relationships, and communication patterns. The widespread availability of technology brings new and challenging ethical issues to the forefront for social workers. Understanding the most critical ethical issues that arise from technology will help us to better understand how to address them in a proactive manner. Table 10.3 outlines practical considerations where using technology in practice.

### Confidentiality

Between using online forums, social media, and other technologies, social workers are collecting and have available to them a lot of sensitive information. Some of

**TABLE 10.3**
Ethical Social Media Use

| | |
|---|---|
| A. | To minimize the potential for the social media concerns previously described, it would be prudent for practitioners to first take an in-depth look at the content of their online identity and then consider taking appropriate security precautions with their own personal information and identity. |
| B. | Practitioners should become familiar with the privacy settings on their personally controlled social media sites and adjust them so as to limit undesired access by clients to personal information (Guseh et al., 2009, p. 585; Lehavot, et al., 2010, p. 164; Luo, 2009, p. 21). |
| C. | Practitioners are advised to conduct a personal Google search in order to gain awareness of what anyone, including a client, might find out about them. If inaccurate or clinically inappropriate information is found on a website, the practitioner should submit a request to the site's manager to have the information removed, if possible (Luo, 2009, p. 21). |
| D. | One way to help control the information a client might find is to create a professional website with relevant links and to possibly purchase a domain name, both of which would help to reduce misrepresentation online (Luo, 2009, p. 21), while also providing an avenue through which to bring in potential clients (Malamud, 2011). |
| E. | Practitioners should discuss online privacy issues openly with their clients and suggest more appropriate means of communication (e.g., telephone) indicating that it benefits both clinician and client to respect professional boundaries (Lehavot et al., 2010, p. 165; Luo, 2009, p. 21). |

*Source:* Voshel and Wesala (2015).

this information is about consumers and the communities where they live. Social workers understand their obligation to protect consumer **privacy** and **confidentiality**. Furthermore, they are familiar with mandatory reporting laws related to abuse and neglect (Reamer, 2013).

Digital technology and other forms of social media have added a new layer to issues of consumer confidentiality. For example, social workers must be diligent in thwarting the hacking of records and other breaches of confidentiality. They also maintain strict adherence to the Health Insurance Portability and Accountability Act (HIPAA) and the Family Educational Rights and Privacy Act (FERPA) that focus on consumer confidentiality by providing specific guidelines for practice.

The National Association of Social Workers' *Code of Ethics* (NASW, 2017) provides compelling statements regarding confidentiality for practice across systems:

## 1.07 Privacy and Confidentiality

(l) Social workers should protect the confidentiality of clients' written and electronic records and other sensitive information. Social workers should take reasonable steps to ensure that clients' records are stored in a secure location and that clients' records are not available to others who are not authorized to have access.

(m) Social workers should take reasonable steps to protect the confidentiality of electronic communications, including information provided to clients or third parties. Social workers should use applicable safeguards (such as encryption, firewalls, and passwords) when using electronic communications such as e-mail, online posts, online chat sessions, mobile communication, and text messages.

(n) Social workers should develop and disclose policies and procedures for notifying clients of any breach of confidential information in a timely manner.

(o) In the event of unauthorized access to client records or information, including any unauthorized access to the social worker's electronic communication or storage systems, social workers should inform clients of such disclosures, consistent with applicable laws and professional standards.

(p) Social workers should develop and inform clients about their policies, consistent with prevailing social work ethical standards, on the use of electronic technology, including Internet-based search engines, to gather information about clients.

(q) Social workers should avoid searching or gathering client information electronically unless there are compelling professional reasons, and when appropriate, with the client's informed consent.

(r) Social workers should avoid posting any identifying or confidential information about clients on professional websites or other forms of social media.



### Organizing Online

Franco, a social worker with an urban not-for-profit agency, is organizing an online holiday toy drive for children in the community where he works. As a result of his organizing strategies, Franco has contact information on both contributors to the drive, as well as those in need of toys. Throughout the drive, Franco has used his agency's e-mail address; however, people participating in the drive have searched and found Franco's personal Facebook page and asked to "be friended." Franco feels torn: He wants to reach out and establish community partnerships, but he understands that Facebook is not the appropriate venue. What do you think Franco should do in this situation? What obligation does Franco have to report the situation to his agency supervisor?

## Boundaries and Dual Relationships

Ethical issues related to professional boundaries and **dual relationships** are common and multifaceted. There are three basic reasons why boundary issues are particularly critical to social workers: (1) protection of the intervention process, (2) protection of consumers from exploitation, and (3) protection of social workers from liability (Dewane, 2010).

The use of digital technology has introduced new and complicated boundary issues. Specifically, consider the use of Facebook by a social worker who is asked by a consumer, present or past, to be "friends." Or what if consumers have access to the postings of a social worker where personal information is learned? In situations such as these, it is helpful to consider Reamer's (2001) typology of dual relationships.

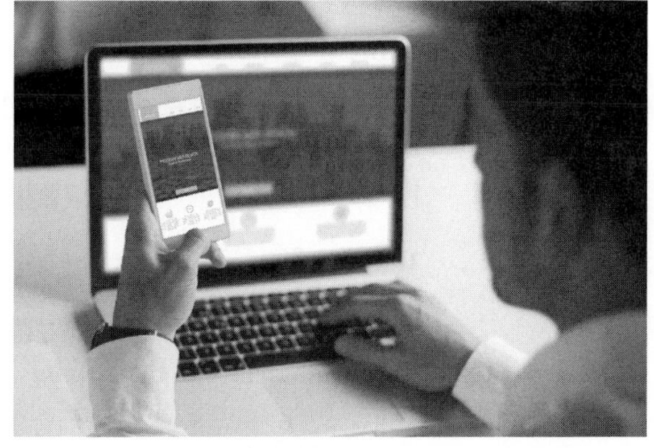

©iStockphoto.com/milindri

**PHOTO 10.3** Informed consent is essential when using social media.

Reamer (2001) proposes a typology of the following five categories of dual relationships in social work that include the following:

- **Intimacy**—in which physical contact is made
- **Personal benefit (monetary gain)**—involves an exchange of money between a social worker and a consumer
- **Emotional/dependency needs**—where a social worker gains emotional support from a consumer
- **Unintentional/unplanned relationships**—in small communities, social workers may cross the path of consumers, which is not inherently unethical but requires skillful handling
- **Inadvertent situations**—meeting a consumer by chance in a store or at an event
- **In a technological way**—the use of social media may contribute to unintentional communications and forming of relationship
- **Altruism**—dual relationships form because of social workers wanting to help a consumer

Deciding whether to enter into a second relationship includes the following:

- How will this secondary relationship change the power differential or take advantage of a power differential in the relationship?
- How long will this relationship last? Is it a one-time occurrence or expected to last indefinitely?
- How will ending one relationship affect the other relationship?
- How much will objectivity be impaired?
- What is the risk of exploitation?
- Would such a second relationship constitute or approach a violation of ethical or legal standards? (Dewane, 2010)

## Ethical Considerations

As indicated in the typology, not all dual relationships are unethical. The challenges in the digital age are not easily solved, but the *Code of Ethics* (NASW, 2017) provide helpful guidelines in the 1.06 *Conflicts of Interest* section:

**1.06 Conflicts of Interest**

a. Social workers should be alert to and avoid conflicts of interest that interfere with the exercise of professional discretion and impartial judgment. Social workers should inform clients when a real or potential conflict of interest arises and take reasonable steps to resolve the issue in a manner that makes the clients' interests primary and protects clients' interests to the greatest extent possible. In some cases, protecting clients' interests may require termination of the professional relationship with proper referral of the client.

b. Social workers should not take unfair advantage of any professional relationship or exploit others to further their personal, religious, political, or business interests.

c. Social workers should not engage in dual or multiple relationships with clients or former clients in which there is a risk of exploitation or potential harm to the client. In instances when dual or multiple relationships are unavoidable, social workers should take steps to protect clients and are responsible for setting clear, appropriate, and culturally sensitive boundaries. (Dual or multiple relationships occur when social workers relate to clients in more than one relationship, whether professional, social, or business. Dual or multiple relationships can occur simultaneously or consecutively.)

d. When social workers provide services to two or more people who have a relationship with each other (for example, couples, family members), social workers should clarify with all parties which individuals will be considered clients and the nature of social workers' professional obligations to the various individuals who are receiving services. Social workers who anticipate a conflict of interest among the individuals receiving services or who anticipate having to perform in potentially conflicting roles (for example, when a social worker is asked to testify in a child custody dispute or divorce proceedings involving clients) should clarify their role with the parties involved and take appropriate action to minimize any conflict of interest.

e. Social workers should avoid communication with clients using technology (such as social networking sites, online chat, e-mail, text messages, telephone, and video) for personal or non-work-related purposes.

f. Social workers should be aware that posting personal information on professional Web sites or other media might cause boundary confusion, inappropriate dual relationships, or harm to clients.

g. Social workers should be aware that personal affiliations may increase the likelihood that clients may discover the social worker's presence on Web sites, social media, and other forms of technology. Social workers should be aware that involvement in electronic communication with groups based on race, ethnicity, language, sexual orientation, gender identity or expression, mental or physical ability, religion, immigration status, and other personal affiliations may affect their ability to work effectively with particular clients.

h. Social workers should avoid accepting requests from or engaging in personal relationships with clients on social networking sites or other electronic media to prevent boundary confusion, inappropriate dual relationships, or harm to clients.

In summary, the *Code of Ethics* is vital to social workers in redefining and maintaining appropriate relations with consumers and their communities and organizations. They provide a clear demarcation between the professional and private life of all involved parties.

## Time to Think 10.4

Tutu has worked as the director of a women's homeless shelter for several years. In her capacity, she has come to know a number of women, some of whom stay in touch with her after they leave the shelter and establish residency in their private homes. Ashley was a resident of the shelter for approximately 6 months, during which time she was pregnant. When she left the shelter and moved into her own apartment, Ashley gave birth to a daughter, Grace. Ashley has asked Tutu to participate in Grace's baptism and to serve as Grace's godmother. What should Tutu do given the standards of professional boundaries and dual relationships?

### Informed Consent

As advocates, lobbyists, policy analysts, or organizers, social workers may provide services, such as consultations or education, electronically. As stated in the *Code of Ethics* (NASW, 2017) below, social workers have the ethical duty to ensure that consumers and community partners fully understand the nature of the services to be provided. This can be difficult if the consumer is not initially seen face-to-face when consent could be explained.

**1.03 Informed Consent**

(a) Social workers should provide services to clients only in the context of a professional relationship based, when appropriate, on valid informed consent. Social workers should use clear and understandable language to inform clients of the purpose of the services, risks related to the services, limits to services because of the requirements of a third-party payer, relevant costs, reasonable alternatives, clients' right to refuse or withdraw consent, and the time frame covered by the consent. Social workers should provide clients with an opportunity to ask questions.

(b) In instances when clients are not literate or have difficulty understanding the primary language used in the practice setting, social workers should take steps to ensure clients' comprehension. This may include providing clients with a detailed verbal explanation or arranging for a qualified interpreter or translator whenever possible.

(c) In instances when clients lack the capacity to provide informed consent, social workers should protect clients' interests by seeking permission from an appropriate third party, informing clients consistent with the clients' level of understanding. In such instances social workers should seek to ensure that the third party acts in a manner consistent with clients' wishes and interests. Social workers should take reasonable steps to enhance such clients' ability to give informed consent.

(d) In instances when clients are receiving services involuntarily, social workers should provide information about the nature and extent of services and about the extent of clients' right to refuse service.

(e) Social workers should discuss with clients the social workers' policies concerning the use of technology in the provision of professional services.

(f) Social workers who use technology to provide social work services should obtain informed consent from the individuals using these services during the initial screening or interview and prior to initiating services. Social workers should assess clients' capacity to provide informed consent and, when using technology to communicate, verify the identity and location of clients.

(g) Social workers who use technology to provide social work services should assess the clients' suitability and capacity for electronic and remote services. Social workers should consider the clients' intellectual, emotional, and physical ability to use technology to receive services and the clients' ability to understand the potential benefits, risks, and limitations of such services. If clients do not wish to use services provided through technology, social workers should help them identify alternate methods of service.

(h) Social workers should obtain clients' informed consent before making audio or video recordings of clients or permitting observation of service provision by a third party.

(i) Social workers should obtain client consent before conducting an electronic search on the client. Exceptions may arise when the search is for purposes of protecting the client or other people from serious, foreseeable, and imminent harm, or for other compelling professional reasons.



Perhaps it is helpful to consider the concept of **informed consent** as a way to empower consumers. Specifically, by asking consumers for permission before offering services or engaging them in forms of technology, they have the right to refuse or indicate their choices. Thus, informed consent lends dignity and equality to the professional relations while recognizing the rights of consumers.

## Time to Think 10.5

Have you been asked to sign an informed consent? Why and what did you consider as you signed the form? If you have not had the opportunity to participate in informed consent, what situations do you imagine might occur in your life when you would need to do so? Who does informed consent protect and why?

## FUTURE USE OF TECHNOLOGY IN SOCIAL WORK PRACTICE

The Grand Challenges for Social Work Initiatives (Academy of Social Work and Social Welfare, 2009) focuses creative thought and action on emerging issues relevant to the lives of individuals, families, and communities in the context of social justice. Included in the Grand Challenges for Social Work Initiatives is the topic of harnessing technology for social good.

As stated by Academy of Social Work and Social Welfare members Berzin, Singer, and Chan (2015), Information and Communication Technology (ICT) is transformational and offers the ability to embolden new opportunities to rethink social work practice. As the world becomes more reliant on technology, social work is increasingly challenged to use technological advancements and digital advances for social good. Indeed, programs and services would become more available to people who are often excluded from the social service system because of geography, transportation, and scheduling barriers (Berzin et al., 2015).

Unfortunately, there is a dearth of empirical research on how technology can influence social work practice and policy (Ceranoglu, 2010). The need for research to inform the use of technology in practice and policy is but one issue that the social work profession must address as we move further ahead in the application of technology to practice. Other issues to consider are as follows:

1. Ensuring that social work students are kept abreast of technological advances through their courses and field education enrollment
2. Encouraging social work faculty to gain competency in technology and to maintain a skill set in the area
3. Advocating for structural support for and student, staff, and faculty training in technology at colleges and universities
4. Supporting local, state, and federal funding sources to conduct research on the efficiency and effectiveness of various types of technology in relationship to the common good of all
5. Establishing interdisciplinary working relationships with programming and technology companies to offer input on how and why computer platforms and devices are creative

6. Participating and involving consumers on boards of programming and technology companies to provide input on design, research, and product distribution feedback
7. Funding innovation in technology in schools of social work, agencies, and community organizations so as to enhance the ability for intersectionality of technological tools across systems
8. Advocating for universal Internet to ensure that all people and communities have access to technology in an equal fashion
9. Introducing technology to children early in school settings across all sectors of society along with accompanying ethical standards
10. Networking with the local, state, and federal political structures in such a way that elected officials are readily available to communicate across all systems and with all segments of the population
11. Advocating for robust federal privacy policies and regulatory standards of enforcement

SAGE edge™ Visit **www.edge.sagepub.com/ticemacro** to help you accomplish your coursework goals in an easy-to-use learning environment

## SUMMARY

The digital age is here to stay! Social work education and practice need to incorporate digital literacy in pedagogical approaches and practice skill development, supported by **ethical standards** and evidence-based research. Additionally, we must be mindful that advocacy, related to the access and support of social media, should be in the forefront of consumer interactions as it relates to privacy, confidentiality, and the allocation of resources (Hitchcock, Sage, & Smyth, 2018).

This chapter highlights how the APPM, along with professional social work organizations, offer innovations in technology and the subsequent monitoring and enforcement of networks. As a vital element of the change process, technology in all its forms is a viable tool to challenge social injustices by intersecting core social work values with consumer strengths and needs.

## TOP 10 KEY CONCEPTS

confidentiality 238
dual relationships 239
e-mail etiquette 229
ethical standards 245
informed consent 243
intersectionality of technological innovations 235
privacy 238
social media 229
social networking 229
universal Internet 232

## DISCUSSION QUESTIONS

1. What elements of a federal privacy policy would you like to enact to protect your personal information on sites like Google? Discuss the implications of such a policy on you as a social worker employed as a community organizer or lobbyist.
2. Informed consent is an essential component in the use of technology with consumers. Consider how you would gain informed consent from a consumer who did not speak your first language and had minimal reading skills.
3. You are a social worker in a rural food bank. One of the people who frequents the food bank asked that you "friend" him on Facebook. How would you respond and why?
4. You are working on a voter registration drive in a major metropolitan area. Part of the drive process involves educating people to knock on neighborhood doors, talk about the importance of voting, and offer registration forms for completion. While you are training volunteers on the process, with PowerPoint slides and handouts, several people in the class are texting on their phones. How would you respond to this situation?
5. How does the advocacy practice and policy model apply to the need for adequate training opportunities in technology offered by colleges and universities for students, staff, and faculty?

## EXERCISES

1. Interview a student who is majoring in computer science. Ask about his or her skill set, career plans, and thoughts on future developments in technology. Reflect upon the provided answers in the context of your social work plans. What are the points of intersectionality between the two of you?
2. Review Table 10.2 and list the missteps you have made when e-mailing and how you went about making the necessary corrections.
3. Review the technology and/or social media policies of your social work program. Where are they published, how are you trained on them, how do they relate to your work with consumers, and what occurs if a policy is violated?
4. Discuss with a faculty member in your program his or her thoughts on technology as a tool for teaching, advocacy, and practice. How did the faculty member rate their competence in technology? What surprised you about the faculty member's comments and why?
5. Explore your community to discover where people go to use computers who do not have them at home. Visit a homeless shelter to see if computers are available there and, if so, to what degree they are used. What did your exploration tell you about access to technology, power, and privilege?

## ONLINE RESOURCES

- American Academy for Social Work and Social Welfare (http://aaswsw.org/): An honorific society of distinguished scholars and practitioners dedicated to achieving excellence in the field of social work and social welfare through work that advances social good. The academy offers articles on social work practice and technology.
- Federal Trade Commission (https://www.ftc.gov/): A government organization that works to protect consumers by preventing anticompetitive, deceptive, and unfair practices, including those related to technology, privacy, and confidentiality.
- *The New Social Worker*: The Social Work Careers Magazine (http://www.socialworker.com): An online magazine that provides articles about social work practice, including trends in technology and career opportunities.
- NASW, ASWB, CSWE, and CSWA Standards for Technology (https://www.socialworkers.org/includes/newIncludes/homepage/PRA-BRO-33617.TechStandard): A pamphlet compiled by the National Association of Social Workers, Association of Social Work Boards, Council on Social Work Education, and the Clinical Social Work Association on the use of technology in social work.
- *Journal of Technology in Human Services* (https://www.tandfonline.com/toc/wths20): A peer-reviewed journal that provides relevant information on the various applications of technology in human services.

# 11 Informing Macro Practice With Research

## LEARNING OBJECTIVES

After reading this chapter, you will be able to:

1. Discuss evidence-based practice along with research
2. Distinguish the benefits of using quantitative versus qualitative analyses
3. Explore ethical dilemmas involved with research strategies
4. Articulate how to infuse research findings into macro practice

## AARON EMPLOYS QUANTITATIVE AND QUALITATIVE RESEARCH METHODS

Aaron has worked on a neighborhood planning council and has been involved with an action and citizen-based community planning review team. His team recently disseminated a comprehensive report to New Jersey Governor Murphy, called "Atlantic City: Building a Foundation for a Shared Prosperity" (n.d.). This report is based on 5 months of fact finding, consultation, and quantitative/qualitative analysis. The report's multifold goals are to provide a historical background, recommend steps for progress to address chronic challenges, and provide a framework for shared prosperity. The review team spoke with stakeholders comprising casino owners, parents of children in Head Start, public employees, business leaders, union members and young entrepreneurs, elected leaders, and civic activists. National experts knowledgeable of Legacy Cities were also a part of the process. A six-pronged shared vision for prosperity resulted in the following recommendations: (1) focus on the fundamentals of government; (2) build a diverse economy based on the principle of shared prosperity; (3) build effective partnerships between government, philanthropic, and nongovernmental anchor institutions; (4) improve the amenities that affect the quality of life for current members and can attract new residents; (5) build on Atlantic City's strengths; and (6) address social challenges and create pathways to opportunity. Atlantic City is considered a distressed city where over a third of its citizens, including 10,000 children, live below the poverty line, and it has one of New Jersey's highest rates of infant mortality. Additionally, Atlantic City has been hit extremely hard by the national foreclosure crisis. Aaron's review team members have included in their report figures that illustrate New Jersey and Atlantic City poverty rates and unemployment rates over time. This report's strategic vision urges Atlantic City to use a new strategic approach based on the model of 24 other small "Legacy Cities" found in seven states. Key findings that resulted from the review team's research report included the following: (1) Atlantic City faces significant public health challenges, (2) significant health disparities exist for black residents, and (3) men of all races/ethnicities have higher rates of mortality than women. The methodology used by Aaron and his review team members included existing data from the New Jersey Department of Health (NJSHAD), the U.S. Census Bureau's American Community Survey data, and so on. Aaron also serves as a social work professor at a nearby university, where he is able to include students in his research methods, practice, and fieldwork classes to be involved in Atlantic City's revitalization process.

## WHAT IS EVIDENCE-BASED RESEARCH MACRO PRACTICE?

Evidence-based practice (EBP) involves applying clinical evidence and research to decisions made about practice interventions. Historically, social workers have long assessed client system issues and consumers in organizations and communities, based on facts; however, using research and clinical findings helps practitioners across multiple fields of practice make better macro-level decisions. The National Association of Social Workers (NASW) notes how using EBP helps social workers use cultural aspects and empirically based interventions across their levels of practice (NASW, n.d.). Social workers are change agents who require flexibility, critical thinking, and theoretical and evidence-based best practices, as they evaluate social service programs, tackle community or societal issues, and interpret results for future applications to consumers (Netting, Kettner, McMurty, & Thomas, 2017, p. 106).

Inherently, an evidence-based approach is critical and continuously questions if certain practices or policies are effective. The EBP approach has emerged, along with a growing body of research evidence and increasingly sophisticated research techniques, and guides human service organizations, communities, and policymakers. As well, an evidence-based approach provides evidence that shows which practice interventions and programs are effective.

Photo taken by Michel G.

**PHOTO 11.1** Research is used to highlight and address chronic community challenges.

Evidence takes many forms—observations of consumers or a client system, surveys about service delivery strategies, or a needs assessment in impoverished communities. EBP considers diversity and differences that can lead some organizations or communities to disproportionately suffer from issues that human service workers try to alleviate, such as discrimination or inequality. Sometimes standard research methods used in agency research result in misleading or false conclusions and require modification. For example, quantitative research approaches can yield number data that simply counts how many services were delivered; however, qualitative research approaches may offer word data that attends to the voices of those who receive said services and reveals what consumers feel about the quality of provided services.

Six basic steps are involved in the research process: problem formulation, research design development, data collection, data analysis, drawing conclusions, and public dissemination of results (Monette, Sullivan, DeJong, & Hilton, 2014, pp. 8–9). First, a practical, narrowly defined, methodologically doable, and ethically and financially appropriate research question requires formulation. Second, a viable research design requires development that spells out the stages of the research process. Third, decisions are made about what kinds of data will be collected and how. Will **pretests** (preliminary data-gathering techniques to discern adequacy) or pilot studies (small-scale trial runs) be used? Fourth, data analysis using statistical tools can be used to confirm or refute empirical realities. Fifth, conclusions are drawn and can be expressed in a summarized form (e.g., descriptive study) or with hypotheses or statements (e.g., predictive and explanatory research) that lead to weak or strong findings or results. In evaluation research, drawing conclusions may involve judging the adequacy or effectiveness of an organization or program and any modifications that may help improve conditions. Sixth, the most crucial stage of the research process is publicly disseminating results through a report, book, publications, or presentation to a professional organization or community. This last stage ensures that newly created knowledge can be used by others to make programmatic changes or build and conduct future research.

One of the most important ideas in a research project is the **unit of analysis**. The unit of analysis is the specific element or object whose characteristics are going to be described or explained, and it is the data researchers collect. Many units of analysis exist, and five are commonly used in human services research. The unit of analysis is the major entity that a researcher analyzes, and a unit could be the following:

- Artifacts
- Geographical units (census tract, state, town)
- Groups, organizations, and communities
- Individuals (e.g., consumers, organizational staff)
- Social interactions (arrests, divorces, dyadic relations)

Macro social workers often study and work with large systems like organizations as a unit of analysis, because formal organizations are specifically created groups designed to achieve particular goals. Corporations, government bureaus, prisons, schools, and human service agencies are examples. Sometimes researchers study communities, for example, to learn about best program practices. For example, a director of a substance use center might think that an organization that uses SMART recovery instead of a 12-step program may better serve consumers, especially if organizational communication is democratic, open, and transparent instead of closed and rigid. Even though consumers using substances engage in a successful recovery, only organizations can have a success rate.

To study success rates of substance use programs, researchers might use either qualitative or quantitative approaches in their studies.

### Time to Think 11.1

The report disseminated by Aaron's community planning review team, noted in the opening case study, discovered public health indicators and added them as an appendix to the report. These largest causes of mortality in New Jersey are heart disease, cancer, unintentional injury, stroke, chronic lower respiratory disease, homicide, mortality due to gun violence, suicide, diabetes, hypertension and kidney disease, liver disease, HIV/AIDS, infant mortality, and chlamydia (the only nonmortality indicator included in the report). For black men, the mortality rate due to heart disease greatly exceeds that of white men, and the rate for black women greatly exceeds that of white women. For mortality due to homicide or gun violence, rates for black men exceed all other groups. For Hispanic men, however, rates for many causes of mortality are actually lower than for both black and white men (except unintentional injury), and the same low rates are also found for Hispanic women (except for diabetes). The Hispanic health paradox has intrigued the review team. What might be happening in Atlantic City across races/ethnicities that might serve as risk or protective factors that can be studied through quantitative or qualitative research? What implications does this review team's evidence-based research have for social workers employed in Atlantic City and people living there? What kinds of evidence do researchers need to examine?

## The Logic of Scientific Inquiry

Scientific research is predicated on particular tenets that distinguish it from other forms of inquiry (e.g., philosophical or theological). The scientific pursuit of knowledge involves a rational and systematic process for pursuing knowledge involving a topic, a comprehensive literature review, the formulation of a hypothesis or theory for testing, a specified methodology, and an analysis and reporting of findings. In research articles, typically examined for publication through blind peer review, manuscripts end with a discussion/conclusion section examining the limitations of the research as well as the need for subsequent research. Social scientists build upon previous research in a cumulative manner in an effort to replicate prior research findings and advance knowledge. It is the findings from a body of research that provides social workers with confidence when considering and engaging in best practices.

At the heart of research is the struggle for objectivity, an attempt to eliminate bias and influence in the research process. Although objectivity is an ideal state, social scientists approach research in a way designed to thwart subjectivity and pressure from others. Objectivity is sought through adherence to formulated rules and procedures that guide research and by the provision of checks and balances (e.g., entertaining divergent perspectives or worldviews). Indeed, skepticism is deemed a desirable and healthy attribute to the extent that researchers question and challenge one another with respect to their adherence to scientific principles in research.

## QUANTITATIVE VS. QUALITATIVE ANALYSES

**Qualitative research** involves data in the form of descriptions, narratives, pictures, or words. By contrast, **quantitative research** uses counts, numbers, and measures of things (Berg & Lune, 2012; Monette et al., 2014). Many research projects incorporate both approaches and then make choices as to whether to use cross sections (a snapshot in time) or longitudinal (gathering data over time) research. **Measurement** techniques and measurement levels require consideration too. Will verbal reports, observations, or archival records be used? Will measures used be at the nominal, ordinal, interval, or ratio level of measurement (Monette et al., 2014, pp. 105–113)? How will reliability and validity be assessed? How will cultural humility be regarded?

### Quantitative Analysis

**Quantitative analysis** (QA) is a technique to understand behavior by using math or statistics, measurement, and research. Researchers who use quantitative analysis try to represent a particular reality in terms of a numerical value, and they use such analyses for measurement, performance evaluation, or valuation of an organization's productivity and effectiveness. They may also use QA to evaluate a community's needs or to predict real-world events. Quantitative analysis gives researchers tools to analyze and examine current, past, and anticipated future events. Any subject involving numbers may be quantified; therefore, social scientists like macro social workers find QA beneficial.

Large organizations, community planners, and governments rely on quantitative analysis to make economic policy decisions or other monetary decisions. Employment figures are commonly tracked, investment opportunities for organizations and communities are analyzed, and organizations evaluate success of service delivery programs created for consumers.

Methods used in quantitative analysis may be described as either descriptive or inferential. **Descriptive methods** analyze and summarize data to describe what is found in an existing data set. An example might be to look at unemployment rates in a city and describe the population's characteristics by gender, race, and ethnicity. Aaron and his review team mentioned in the opening case study most likely used such methods. **Inferential methods** analyze and summarize data to make estimates about a larger body of data. For example, a sample of incomes of people who live in southern New Jersey versus northern New Jersey could be examined to estimate and infer, from this sample data, the mean income of the larger population of the United States.

### Qualitative Analysis

The goals of **qualitative** data **analysis** may be to describe, evaluate, and explain phenomena, as well as to understand by generalizing beyond the data to more abstract and general concepts or theories, people, groups, or organizations. Qualitative research recognizes how abstraction and generalization are matters of degree and emphasizes context to better understand groups, organizations, and communities; it also emphasizes inductive reasoning more than deductive reasoning. Social work researchers may display qualitative data, in figures and tables, to let word data describe an issue or thematic story.

The term *qualitative methods* is relatively new. While there is no single definition, qualitative methods often share common features, such as flexibility, holism, naturalism, and insider perspectives. Epistemological debates continue among qualitative researchers, and the diverse methodological approaches they employ often reflect the influence of constructivist critiques. **Constructivism** is a paradigm or worldview that posits learning is an active, constructive process. People actively construct or create their own subjective representations of objective reality. The basic approaches—ethnography, grounded theory, case studies, narrative, phenomenological, and action research—exemplify fundamentals of data collection and analysis, the role of theory, standards for rigor, ethical issues, and social work values used by macro-level researchers. Rapid growth in the popularity of qualitative methods ensures that they will play a key role in the social work professions' knowledge development in the future (Connolly, 2003; Padgett, 2013). Table 11.1 illustrates how to display qualitative data to highlight policy areas with related descriptions and issue examples.

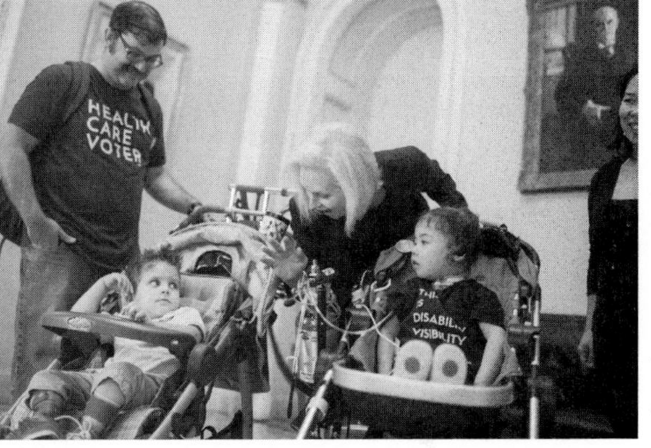


Tom Williams/Contributor/Getty Images

**PHOTO 11.2**
Life conditions are a part of the political realities. Senator Kirsten Gillibrand, D-NY, meets a family whose children have special medical needs.

**TABLE 11.1**
Ways to Illustrate Qualitative Data

| Issue Examples | Descriptions | Policy Areas |
|---|---|---|
| Medicaid expansion, minimum wage, reproductive choices | Representing vulnerable and oppressed people in the wider community | Health disparities and economic and social justice |
| Capital punishment, hate crimes, immigration | Advocating for diversity; opposing biased or discriminatory legislation | Explicit and implicit bias |
| Charitable choices, religion in public schools, school vouchers | Separating church and state; stopping public policy from being unduly influenced by idiosyncratic religious tenets or views | First Amendment |
| Gun control | The right to carry a gun, use it to protect oneself with or without a permit or license; the access to firearms to any person | Second Amendment, stand-your-ground law |

## Time to Think 11.2

Imagine you are a member of a program development task force and research team that is preparing to apply for a funding grant. In your community, there exists a documented number of 400 school dropouts, and some of these dropouts are runaway youth. The task force is considering how to best provide services to help people obtain medical care, search for employment, find shelter, reunify families, and deliver daycare and after-school programs. The task force decides to divide into two groups. One group plans to use *quantitative analysis* to develop an idea statement that can be used in the grant proposal, and they plan on writing approximately five pages. The second group wants to use *qualitative analysis* to develop their idea statement, and they envision offering approximately five to eight more pages to the grant writing effort. Divide into small groups and try to write an idea statement that requires quantitative evidence and analysis; then try to write another idea statement using qualitative evidence and analysis (Brueggemann, 2014, p. 349).

## ETHICAL DILEMMAS IN RESEARCH STRATEGIES

A fair amount of tension exists between the roles of social worker and social work researcher because of the researcher's dual roles and boundary issues (Landau, 2008). Ethical dilemmas vary depending upon if the research is being carried out in a therapeutic framework (settings where consumers receive social work services) or a nontherapeutic framework (community members). In therapeutic settings, consumers may be confused about interactions and boundaries. In nontherapeutic settings, research on vulnerable populations like the homeless or older adults in long-term care settings may not appear so voluntary. In qualitative research, especially participant observation, consent is given once. However, to be truly ethical, consent should be continually negotiated, in the form of "process consent" (Landau, 2008, p. 574). What makes research "ethical" is not so much its procedures or design but the researcher's individual actions, commitments, and decisions (Haverkamp, 2005).

### Organizations

An exciting role for a macro social worker may be that of a **social entrepreneur**, who may be instrumental in facilitating the creation of a new social service organization. Think for a moment about the ways macro social workers can begin a new social organization. Consider the ethical dilemmas related to hiring, funding, management, and political influence. Whether an organization is designed to help people with developmental disabilities, the homeless, or people who have suffered domestic violence, some group of people had to envision how to best help these target populations, and research had to guide them (Lindorff, 2007). Directors of organizations have to deal with nepotism in hiring practices. They have to lead and manage by modeling integrity, and they must avoid conflicts of interest when funding involves political influences from the outside. Research related to hiring practices, leadership style, budget types, and political lobbying could be fodder for research studies and reports to ensure organizations act as ethically as possible.

### Communities

Community planning and evaluation requires community research, and it is a vital way to improve community engagement, refine services, and strengthen a democratic process among citizens. Macro social workers who participate in community planning play crucial roles across multiple fields of social work.

At its core, community planning is a process by which citizens/consumers join, sometimes along with macro social workers, to assess community needs and strengths, as well as to create proposals to make communities better. Before community planning can occur, research in the form of assessment, planning, and strategizing is required. Without proper planning, social work administrators are unable to fulfill their organization's mission or the future needs of their consumers (Daugherty & Atkinson, 2006).

Macro social workers can place themselves strategically within communities to train and educate citizens/consumers in civic affairs. They can also work ethically to persuade local government entities to include neighborhood members as active consumers amid the planning process. In this role, macro social workers can teach consumers about budgets, agency operating procedures, and federal, state, and local program requirements and policies. Social workers can collaborate with consumers to get information about private or public plans that might affect their neighborhoods and locale. Community planning groups consisting of macro social workers and consumers can comment on city/community-initiated plans and public services, critique plans, assemble reports to local government entities, and provide feedback. Consumer feedback is especially important to elicit from communities of people who have historically had fewer resources, less power, and less opportunities to influence plans created by government bureaucracies or powerful business entities. Macro social workers best help vulnerable communities improve when they serve as liaisons between staff, community politicians, and neighborhood planning groups. In this role, they can help consumers access contacts to best help them navigate complex governmental bureaucracies. As liaisons and active collaborators with consumers, macro social workers help to write reports and proactively present plans to local officials for future implementation.

### Societal

Global, international, or societal empowerment must be considered and studied so that exploitive global market society and intergovernmental organizations, like the International Monetary Fund or World Bank, are understood, in an effort to help consumers in large systems. An important goal of macro social workers is to employ social action models to help indigenous people around the world obtain empowerment via grassroots social organizations, nongovernmental organizations, and international social movements. For example, today people from the Middle East—the "Arab Spring"—are taking responsibility for their future by overthrowing autocratic governments and refusing to follow dictators (Bailey, 1988; Bruggemann, 2014, p. 39).

## INFUSING RESEARCH FINDINGS INTO MACRO PRACTICE

Macro social workers can infuse findings from research they have conducted into multiple forms of organizational, community, and societal practice. Once a planning group is coordinated, through recruiting committed consumers/community members, using public forums, running focus groups, holding meetings, and forming the group and orienting members on rules, boundaries, values, and so on, a methodological approach needs to be selected. Subsequently, political realities, cultural differences, and ways to disseminate findings and advocate for change are considered.

### Placing Research on the Agenda

When macro social workers place organizational, community, or societal issues on agendas, they must begin with defining the planning issue. Identifying common issues can help consumers and social workers avoid pitfalls. For example, an existing vacant lot behind a public library might be a wonderful space for a community garden plot. Eliciting dialogue about how to develop an idea about creating a community garden may evolve into a clear-cut set of joint actions for group members to address.

While agenda items in the form of solutions are sometimes obvious, there are other times when barriers and pitfalls must be dealt with first. For example, real causes may not be identified if issues are prematurely labeled. Options must be left open when planning and identifying issues. Sometimes consumers, politicians, and even social workers can come to meetings with possible solutions already fixed in their minds. Such set-in-stone mind-sets may be problematic if not every stakeholder/consumer is brought along in the process of planning and conducting research. Pitfalls may be circumvented by asking good questions—ask who, what, when, why, and how questions to obtain evidence-based information. Explore multiple questions in relation to a community, organizational, or societal issue.

Decision-making techniques such as brainstorming can be used. Brainstorming can explain rules and the purpose of gathering and placing an item on a research agenda so feedback may be collated in a systematic and sensible fashion. Employing brainstorming can reduce dominating cliques, domineering people, or group dependency on a particular authority figure. Rules of brainstorming might include (1) expressiveness (express any idea that comes to your mind), (2) nonevaluation (no criticism is permitted), (3) quantity (the more ideas the better), and (4) building (try to build on other people's ideas) (Brueggemann, 2014, p. 187).

Reverse brainstorming, which is a technique to consider negative consequences, may also be used. Nominal group technique (NGT) is another viable approach where consumers form a group in name only, with a structured series of steps so every member has equal input. The NGT offers a way to generate information about a particular issue, elicit responses from consumers (by using a round-robin strategy), discuss ideas, and establish priorities using a rank-ordering mathematical process. NGT yields a conclusion, considers multiple alternatives, and encourages participation and discussion (Miley, O'Melia, & DuBois, 2017).

## Political Realities in Organizations, Communities, and Society

Sometimes social or consumer movements employ research or research strategists to bolster their influence or evaluate their effectiveness. Understandably, researchers, consumers, and social workers, in organizations, communities, and society, are all influenced by political realities. Macro social workers use advocacy-based and empowerment approaches to engage people in social advocacy, social movements, and transformational politics. **Social advocacy** involves forming alliances with advocacy organizations and consumer groups to enhance capacity and make a difference in the policy arena. Social workers advocate for the development of empowering policies throughout the agenda-setting, formulation, implementation, evaluation, and revision stages of the policy process. **Social movements**, amid communities and society, as exemplified in the past 40 years, have come in the form of civil rights, women's equality, disability rights, and justice for the LGBTQ community. These movements have resulted in significant increases in political power, legal rights, government resources, and in some cases enhanced socioeconomic status for consumers who were previously marginalized (Brueggemann, 2014, p. 38). Examples of such activism continue in the form of the "Occupy" movement, "Me Too" movement, and outrageous public and congressional sentiments and incivility over the confirmation of Supreme Court Justice Brett Kavanaugh. Research can play a vital role in assessing the influence of politics or political sway in social movements and events.

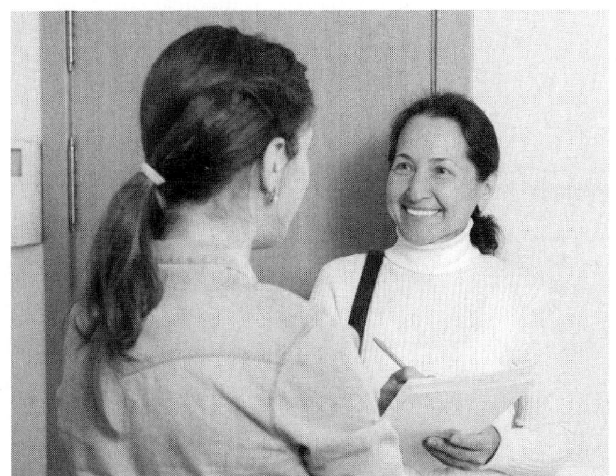

©iStockphoto.com/JackF

**PHOTO 11.3** Qualitative research informs the practice of social work.

## Addressing Cultural Competence: Diversity and Difference

Examples of how research has related to diversity issues and also influenced health care, public, and social policies are those of the gay rights movement involving marriage rights and the military. The gay rights movement has been steadily becoming more powerful and the military has abandoned its failed "don't ask, don't tell" discriminatory policy. Slowly, gay men and lesbian women are making progress, state by state, in their quest to marry. Research has been collected along the way to show the desire of consumers/citizens for marriage equality and more. Additionally, the labor movement is in some ways gaining strength despite challenges by conservative politicians who wish to crush collective bargaining. Research is collected in state, educational, and other bargaining units to drive decisions about advocacy.

**Transformational politics** conveys the idea that systems, albeit organizations, communities, or society, require courage, creativity, and vision to chart a course and focus on a future that is empowering for all. Amid the process to empower, the practice of cultural humility ought to be evidenced in the hearts and minds of politicians, consumers, and macro social workers. Important questions that culturally competent and humble members of planning processes can ask include the following: What should happen? How can we best get there from here? What should be? What will be? (Brueggemann, 2014, p. 38). And, why aren't more diverse consumers included in our research?

Social workers have a long tradition of saying "start where the client/consumer is." When a macro social worker tunes into and tries to engage a community, organization, or wider population, their efforts will be rewarded if they are culturally competent and give ample attention to multiple cultural perspectives. Amid research processes, oftentimes the macro social worker will not resemble the values and cultural mores of the population or larger systems they are trying to change. Cultural competence involves learning from consumers, acknowledging and dismissing stereotypes, and fostering self-determination (Netting et al., 2017, p. 65). In addition to becoming culturally competent, and as previously covered in Chapter 3, medical educators Tervalon and Murray-Garcia (1998) stress how cultural humility ought to be the core goal of cross-cultural practice, no matter the size of the system.

Three human diversity issues are involved in research writing: (1) curtailing bias against particular groups in reports, (2) avoiding the use of exclusive language in reports, and (3) considering which consumers and community members get to see the results of a report. Biases in writing that may stereotype ought to be attended to throughout the research process. Exclusive language can be avoided by minimizing the use of only the male pronoun and using descriptors of cultural groups that are recognized by the group itself. For example, avoid using the term *Mexican American* in New Mexico because it may offend people who view themselves as Spanish Americans with little connection to Mexico. Accuracy can be acquired by not lumping groups of people all together under one label. Again, advocates who come from a feminist perspective think that sharing results with participant consumers is just another dimension of how "the researcher and subject can work in different ways to explore a 'truth' that they mutually locate and define" (Davis, 1986, p. 45).

## Time to Think 11.3

Husband and wife researchers Link and Phelan (2001, p. 367) have contributed research where they suggest that stereotypes occur and stigmatization exists when five particular elements collide: (1) identifying and labeling human differences; (2) cultural values and differences connect labeled consumers to negative stereotypes; (3) a separation of "them" versus "us" evolves, thereby categorizing consumers as a group; (4) consumers in the labeled group lose status and are discriminated against; and (5) once stigmatized, a labeled population fails to gain access to resources and is subsequently excluded and disempowered (adapted from citation in Netting et al., 2017, p. 68). Consider these elements, and then identify and discuss how environmental and structural forces affect organizations, communities, and society in such a way that these larger systems become stereotyped and stigmatized. Consider the opening case study set in the Atlantic City context.

The opening case study alludes to the steps that Aaron and his review team members took to develop their research agenda. The team (1) worked with consumers in the community, (2) prioritized problems, (3) translated problems into needs, (4) evaluated the levels of intervention required for each need, (5) established goals, (6) specified objectives, (7) specified action steps, and (8) formalized a contract (Marlow, 2011, p. 26). Their practice efforts involved engagement, assessment, planning, implementation, evaluation, termination, and follow-up. The last step in practice and also research is that of follow-up or dissemination and use of the research findings. What are we going to do given the recommendations the researchers have supplied?

Unfortunately, this stage tends to be the most neglected in social work practice; however, dissemination of research findings is crucial. Dissemination can occur in multiple ways, including (1) publishing a report and distributing it to organizations nationally and internationally, (2) distributing data results electronically to multitude venues (e.g., webpages, blogs, wikis), or (3) orchestrating a community forum.

The final human diversity issue related to research writing is who ought to get a copy of the results. Increasingly, macro social workers who are also researchers think that findings need to be given to consumers and study participants—such sharing of at least parts of a report is critical to participatory or action research (Marlow, 2011, p. 302). Research results can be empowering to consumers and study participants.

### Using Research Findings to Advocate for Change

Macro social workers involved in organizational, community, or societal planning can employ multiple approaches that yield particular results. Such approaches may include the needs/services, the deficit/problem approach, the asset/strengths approach, or an advocacy-based approach (Brueggemann, 2014, pp. 184–185; Cox, Tice, & Long, 2019).

## DISSEMINATION OF RESEARCH FINDINGS

A community forum can be a wonderful vehicle to disseminate research results. Essentially, a community forum can publicize a meeting or series of meetings to which consumers or community members are invited. Once created, a community forum can serve to get input for the initial development of a research question or set of questions, to develop a project, and to disseminate findings.

Examples of multiple approaches to planning that involve research are listed in Table 11.2, along with the pros and cons of each approach. The Appendix includes a table that outlines the relevant sections of the NASW (2018) *Code of Ethics* intended to guide macro social workers and researchers in their work with consumers across all systems.

Standards found in the revised version of the *Code of Ethics* (NASW, 2018) outline numerous ways research enhances social work practice. For example, in Section 5.02, *Evaluation and Research* is addressed. Such information about Section 5.02 is found in the Appendix. Section 6 substantially addresses how social workers use research as part of their ethical responsibility to the larger

**TABLE 11.2**
Approaches to Research and Their Pros and Cons

| Approach | Pros | Cons |
|---|---|---|
| Needs/services | Focus on individual needs and service gaps | Misses developing community strengths, leadership, or ways to improve communities, organizations, society |
| Deficit/problem | Still focuses on how systems include people who may become dysfunctional or stunted and traditional rational problem solving | Focuses too much on systems defects in community service provision, tends to rely on expert specialists instead of engaged consumers, only sees deficits |
| Asset/strengths | Identifies consumers/community potential for social bonds and participatory democracy and creates concrete positive projects to improve neighborhoods and improve consumers' skills | May miss identifying real needs and problems with community resources or people's strengths |
| Advocacy based | Considers economic and social justice, human needs and rights, political perspectives, and environmental contexts | May miss as strong a focus on empowerment and strengths |

society (e.g., 6.01 Social Welfare; 6.02 Public Participation; 6.03 Public Emergencies; 6.04 Social and Political Action).

Research about advocacy efforts in social work macro practice and policy efforts is greatly needed. Earlier chapters addressed the four interlocking components of the APPM, and the subsequent table and section illustrate the APPM's utility in informing macro practice when studying the large system issue of poverty. Specifically, Table 11.3 highlights how the APPM can be used to configure viable strategies to use research to explore macro social work practice issues. Four advocacy tenets are applied: (1) economic, environmental, and social justice; (2) human needs and rights; (3) political access; and (4) supportive environment. Note the possibilities for quantitative and qualitative research studies to inform macro practice while studying poverty concerns of clients, organizations, and communities.

**TABLE 11.3**
Applying the APPM to Inform Macro Practice With Research

| Advocacy Tenets | Qualitative Research | Quantitative Research |
|---|---|---|
| Economic, environmental, and social justice | Conduct in-depth interviews with people living in poverty to record verbatim responses and analyze word data to learn about their experiences with social welfare agencies. | Assess how the power structure within selected organizations and/or communities has changed to address inequality issues by collecting and analyzing statistical data. |
| Human needs and rights | Interview leaders of governmental organizations to learn how they have shown their commitment to human rights. Record responses and analyze emerging themes. | Analyze existing data and create items in a new survey research tool to evaluate how organizations, governments, and multilateral institutions have shown their commitment to human rights. |
| Political access | Interview an available sample of people and ask them about their voter registration status. Record their verbatim responses and analyze themes. | Compare and contrast existing archived data about voting practices across states from the Northeast and Southwest to discern descriptive and inferential statistical findings. |
| Supportive environment | Interview 50 mothers who use community day-care options and record word data about their experiences. | Conduct a secondary data analysis on the types of training programs that currently exist in the community, in an effort to discern which programs still require development and implementation. |

Visit **www.edge.sagepub.com/ticemacro** to help you accomplish your coursework goals in an easy-to-use learning environment

## SUMMARY

In this chapter, the power of using quantitative and qualitative research methods in macro social work practice was dovetailed with how to effectively create research agenda items, implement research in a culturally humble way, and disseminate findings to best help organizations, communities, and society. The opening case study prodded students to consider how officially orchestrated planning councils can responsibly collaborate with consumers and macro social workers and sponsors (e.g., foundations, social agencies, city councils, mayors' offices, and planning commission entities) to engage in decision making, local responsibility, and grassroots democracy to plan futures, based on evidence-based research collected and evaluated in a culturally competent and humble manner.

## TOP 10 KEY CONCEPTS

constructivism 253
descriptive methods 252
inferential methods 252
qualitative analysis 252
quantitative analysis 252
social advocacy 257
social entrepreneur 254
social movements 257
transformational politics 258
unit of analysis 250

## DISCUSSION QUESTIONS

1. Imagine you are the director of a substance use treatment center, and you have been asked to write a grant proposal to seek funding for a new opioid treatment unit. What steps would you take to assess and justify the need for this special unit and programming? What quantitative or qualitative research methodologies would you use? How will you ensure that the structure of this unit is carried out ethically and financially sensibly?
2. How do people's subjective notions affect how they create a research problem? How differently might you perceive an issue/phenomenon, depending upon if you take a "quantitative approach" versus a "qualitative approach"?
3. How can macro social workers engage action-social planning groups for change using advocacy-based and empowerment-oriented processes? Consider the role of the social worker, the sponsoring agency, the recruitment of consumers, use of public forums, and use of focus groups.
4. What, if any, community-based planning initiatives exist in the town or city where you reside? Who are some citizen/consumer planners you could work with to design and execute research to help a community thrive? Consider the opening case study—the review team that sponsored the Atlantic City initiative.
5. How can macro social workers use their interpersonal skills, empathy, and reflection in their activities with large systems?

## EXERCISES

1. Divide the class into two groups. One group will role-play being members of a foster parent organization that has been asked to give the Department of Health and Human Services (DHHS) suggestions for research priorities. What research issues would Group 1 study from a quantitative approach? What research problems would Group 2 study from a qualitative approach?
2. Search for the term *participatory action research* and describe the advantages to both the researcher and the participant in conducting this type of research.
3. Imagine you were asked to evaluate a program in which you are working (e.g., field placement, paid work setting, etc.). How would you justify the significance of your research to another person/student?
4. Divide into small groups and imagine you are members of an action-social community planning committee. How will you press for grassroots involvement of consumers who want to insert their values and ideas in policy decisions and implement new initiatives in the community? Explore how your team will substantively consider the following aspects related to community planning and implementation (modified from Brueggemann, 2014, pp. 177–179):
    - Gain consumers'/citizens' trust
    - Collaborate with consumers/neighborhood participants (e.g., local access, resource development, skill building)
    - Understand varying personal agendas (e.g., motives such as academic study, curiosity, altruism, financial gain, professional duty, neighborliness, protection of interests)
    - Accept multiple issues
    - Accept limitations
    - Accept varied commitments (e.g., varying life priorities; informal rules of operation)
    - Accept different types of processes (e.g., coalition boards, citizens advisory boards)

## ONLINE RESOURCES

- Social Work Search (http://www.sociaworksearch.com): This site has links to research and statistics topics.
- University of Michigan Social Work Library—Guide to EBP Research (http://hsl.lib.umn.edu/learn/ebp): Provides a tutorial on evidence-based practice as used by health-care professionals.

# Evaluating Macro Change

## LEARNING OBJECTIVES

After reading this chapter, you should be able to:

1. Describe what evaluating macro change involves
2. Understand funding sources related to research evaluation.
3. Explore the relevance of participatory research and policy-practice
4. Articulate ethical issues and considerations involved with evaluating macro change

## JESSICA EVALUATES MACRO CHANGE

Jessica is a social worker employed by the Community AIDS Research Consortium. Her responsibilities include serving as the co-chair of the AIDS clinical trials program's community advisory board, recruiting and counseling study participants, and participating in multiple community-based organizations' efforts to educate and train others about the human immunodeficiency syndrome and acquired human immunodeficiency virus (HIV/AIDS). Jessica also sits on important state and national boards and committees where she collects and analyzes data, writes grants, and engages in action research, where consumers of services become involved in research to promote practical findings to enhance the lives of people. Every 5 years, Jessica and her colleagues are required to resubmit a competitive grant proposal to acquire continued funding. While working with the Community AIDS Research Consortium, for the past decade, Jessica has engaged in both quantitative and qualitative approaches to research. She encourages consumers of services to assist with defining the purposes of and planning for various research projects. Jessica also assists her research team members, and consumers appreciate and consider four categories of social research—descriptive, explanatory, exploratory, and evaluative. In recent years, Jessica's research has evaluated which clinical trial recruitment strategies have been most successful, described demographics of attendees at community educational forums, explored service delivery needs of study participants, and explained differences in program outcomes across multiple states in the Northeast.

## WHAT IS EVALUATION?

Evidence-based macro practice critically challenges social workers to delve into a scientific understanding of the various aspects of community organization, management, and planning and large-scale change. Social workers who work with and within large systems interact with complex forces that require tools

©iStockphoto.com/nd3000

**PHOTO 12.1** Scientific inquiry is critical to social work practice and policy.

to function and develop insight about the interactions between staff, agencies, consumers, and the even larger systems (e.g., community and societal factors) that affect the field of social work. Social work professionals must appreciate and understand multiple factors, including human diversity, consumer advocacy, skills essential to running meetings effectively, handling community conflict, and managing both time and stress. At the heart of the social work process—whether at the individual, family, group, organizational, community, or societal level—is a commitment to improve the lives of people through the purposeful and professional use of one's self. Professionals who choose to engage in macro social work practice will be involved in more than just a 9 to 5 job. Macro-oriented social workers seek ways, using research data and findings, to empower consumers of services to enrich organizations, neighborhoods, and communities and improve quality of life (Murari & Guerrero, 2013).

Leaders, administrators, managers, and social workers rely on empirically supported models of practice to guide program and policy development, manage service systems, empower communities, and prompt various forms of social change. Macro practitioners may be involved with writing grant proposals, developing action plans, mobilizing grassroots organizations, community building, and national legislative campaigns, to mention just a few activities. Macro practice efforts and actions can help communities and organizations enhance service delivery and improve social and environmental conditions for consumers of services.

Specifically, there exists a dearth of rigorous research on many kinds of macro practice interventions and the results of organizational, community, and societal change. Additionally, much of the research investigating the influence of efficacy of programs, projects, policies, and legislation employs case studies and surveys offering insight and ideas, but often limitations regarding the generalizability of findings. Furthermore, more research is needed to better understand how culture influences service providers and service effectiveness (Hemmelgarn, Glisson, & James, 2010).

In contrast, a rich research literature exists examining leadership, specifically leader-member exchange and transformational leadership (Bass & Avolio, 2006; Northouse, 2013). Extensive literature also exists on burnout and compassion fatigue. Macro practitioners would be well advised to immerse themselves in the rich content examining burnout, which guides one on how to reduce feeling stressed and maintain healthy work-life balance (Schaufeli, Leiter, & Maslach, 2009).

## Traditional Approaches to Social Research

Usually, social research is categorized as one of four types. Schutt (2018) summarizes these types of research as follows:

- *Descriptive research:* At first, researchers simply want to define what they are studying and describe the social phenomena of interest.
- *Exploratory research:* Researchers try to discover how people get along in specified settings, what meanings they give to their actions, and what issues concern them.
- *Explanatory research:* The focus gradually shifts to the causes and effects of the phenomenon.
- *Evaluation research:* Special attention is given to whether particular policies and programs help to alleviate issues and problems.

People conducting **descriptive research** collect data with the intent to better describe social phenomena. In macro social work practice, this could involve collecting data describing a community, an organization, a service population (e.g., teenagers, older adults, and clinical trial study participants), social conditions (e.g., poverty, health literacy, opportunity or lack of opportunity, or homelessness), and social actions (e.g., collaboration, discrimination, recruitment, and types of support). When considering specific kinds of social phenomena, consumers of services often find themselves uniquely equipped to facilitate an advanced understanding and description of influences and occurrences. For example, who better to "brainstorm" and identify factors related to economic opportunity in a community than consumers of services who have experienced a degree of upward mobility?

In addition, social workers possess a rich tradition of documenting needs, opportunities, and characteristics of people being served through descriptive research. Funding sources often require such information (e.g., community needs assessments and consumer profiles). For social workers and consumers alike, descriptive data facilitate the identification of population groups at risk and allow for a differential assessment of the availability of resources, barriers, and opportunities by consumer groups.

In **exploratory research**, the primary focus is on formulating or refining definitions of actions, concepts, conditions, and issues. To initiate a preliminary grasp of a phenomenon, situation, or circumstance, a beginning characterization of what is occurring is required. Consumers of services have expertise in providing these kinds of understandings and conceptual breakthroughs.

If you are interested in learning about the distinct culture and areas of strength of a particular social service agency, ask for a depiction of this organization from the perspective of consumers. They will often be able to identify specific qualities and characteristics that differentiate a given human service organization from its social counterparts. Without consumer insight, the sense of discovery in exploratory research is often compromised.

One of the most difficult and complicated types of research is **explanatory research**. Examining the causes and effects of social phenomena is a complex matter, as establishing causality involves addressing three important prerequisites—establishing that the factors under consideration are correlated (change together), determining time order (the causal factor occurs prior to the outcome factor), and accounting for other factors that could be affecting the outcome factor. For example, communities typically change as a result of technological innovation, changes in leadership, variations in the availability of resources, and population shifts. Understanding the relevance, time order, and relationship among these and other relevant factors in producing community-level change is greatly enhanced when incorporating the views of consumers.

While social workers regularly engage in many forms of research, **evaluation research** is especially important in macro social work practice. Program and policy development are common forms of macro-level intervention in social work practice. Hence, the ability to weigh the successes and limitations associated with social programs and policies is fundamental to documenting macro-level change.

Particularly in the current age of accountability, administrators, professionals, and consumers alike are very interested in evaluating the effectiveness of social programs and services and policy initiatives. Americans want to know "how much bang for the buck" will I receive? Politicians, government watchdog organizations, and special interest groups often place intense pressure on administrators and service providers to demonstrate the efficacy of programs and policies.

Royse (2011) suggests that program evaluation has traditionally sought to address the following kinds of issues:

1. Are consumers being helped?
2. Is there a better (e.g., cheaper, faster) way of doing this?
3. How does this effort or level of activity compare with what was produced or accomplished last year? (Did we achieve our objectives?)
4. How does our success rate compare with other agencies' success rates?
5. Should this program be continued?
6. How can we improve our program?

*Source: Research Methods in Social Work,* 6th edition, by Royse, p. 284, 2011.

Royse (2011) provides useful and important questions for study. For the social worker interested in implementing a strengths perspective, however, additional consideration ought to be given to identifying concrete mechanisms for including the insights and perspectives of consumers in evaluating social change. For example, how best might consumers be involved in defining criteria for program continuation? How can consumers give narrative (qualitative) feedback to improve programming?

The effectiveness of any program, service, law, or policy needs to be contemplated and approached from multiple vantage points, especially from that of the consumer, even though this is a potentially unpopular and politically charged stance. Measuring the success of any program or policy through the eyes and perception of consumers—using consumers' ideas about the process and criteria needed to evaluate success—is an imperative in macro social work practice. Consumer-directed research represents as valuable and worthy a source of discovery as any other scientific endeavor.

### Time to Think 12.1

As a macro-level social worker, Jessica is involved in a collaborative fashion with designing, implementing, and evaluating research being conducted about clinical trial outcomes and research about HIV-infected consumers' satisfaction with their study experience and how organizations are responding to their service delivery needs. After working for the Community AIDS Research Consortium for the past 10 plus years, imagine and identify ways Jessica has been able to advance the voices of consumers to inform research studies. As examples, she has been actively involved in identifying and documenting the effect of macro change involving various populations at risk, organizational practices, community resources, and national policies. As a social worker, what are potential challenges and hurdles that Jessica has likely faced when working with community officials, administrators, and other researchers with research projects?

## FUNDING SOURCES AND RESEARCH

The interests of funding sources, accreditation bodies, administrators, board members, legislators, and politicians are routinely imposed on helping professionals when evaluating program delivery and policy implementation. In these instances, social workers are required to produce documentation and statistics describing how consumers use service delivery (e.g., units of service by type and number of minutes). This information typically involves a detailed analysis of consumer characteristics or demographics (e.g., age, gender, race, socioeconomic status) and the ability of consumers to meet or maintain eligibility requirements. Administrators are highly invested in identifying and tracing measures of consumer usage and worker production. This kind of information is used to demonstrate staff utilization and to justify the deployment of resources in the delivery of services.

Research emphasizing consumer attributes and units of service tends to emphasize cost efficiency and can be accounting oriented. This type of data collection is typically time-consuming and is frequently viewed by practitioners as an accountability requirement dictated by funding sources. In fact, in conjunction with the expectations of funding sources, cost analyses by type of consumer group are often used by administrators as a basis for pinpointing allocation or reallocation of resources.

## Time to Think 12.2

A stipulation of program funding is program evaluation. The ABCs of program evaluation are the following:

**A**lways expect funding sources to mandate program evaluation.

**B**e prepared to advocate for consumer participation in program evaluation.

**C**are needs to be taken to ensure that evaluation is approached in a participatory manner.

Unfortunately, program evaluation driven by the requirements of government and funding sources often neglects a primary question: How do consumers define quality programming? Consider and identify consumer perspectives concerning the effectiveness of program delivery, services, organizational practices, and policies that are especially valuable when considering evaluative processes and procedures.

Royse (2011) suggests the need for **program monitoring**: "measuring the extent to which a program reaches its target population with the intended interventions" (p. 288). Of course, program monitoring is not meant to be the sole prerogative of directors and managers. Guidance can be derived from multiple sources, particularly from consumer groups: "There is no assumption that staff or the administration know best." To the contrary, consumer input and feedback are essential components of comprehensive, high-quality program monitoring.

In social work research, the "basic desire to know has been intensified [at times compromised] by the pressure for more accountability in the human services" (Monette, Sullivan, DeJong, & Hilton, 2014, p. 7). Single-subject designs and other empirical practice models give social workers and consumers a structure for reevaluating and documenting consumer improvement and achievement, especially on a micro level (case by case). Although these techniques have been valuable sources of empowerment and advocacy for many consumers, it behooves consumers and social workers to continue to raise the standard when it comes to consumer participation in research. This is especially true in assessing conditions and evaluating planned change in relation to large-scale change and larger social systems. Indeed, it ought to be anticipated that consumers and community leaders will differ in their assessments of the merits of macro-level change.

### Unit of Analysis: Organizations, Communities, and Society

An important part of creating and modifying a research problem is deciding which unit of analysis to use. Units of analysis are the specific elements or objects with characteristics researchers want to describe or explain, and they are also the objects about which data will be collected. Multiple units of analysis exist. There

**TABLE 12.1**
Possible Units of Analysis in Research When Evaluating Macro Change and Practice

| Unit of Analysis | Example | Possible Variables | Research Problem |
|---|---|---|---|
| Organizations | Adolescent treatment facilities | Auspices, funding level, size, type of programs or services implemented | Do public agencies serve more minority and lower socioeconomic status consumers than private agencies? |
| Communities | Geographical units | Town, state, census tract | Which communities provide the most affordable housing options? |
| Society | Developed country vs. a Third World country | Social interactions (arrests, crime rate, divorces, poverty level) | What accounts for differences citizens experience in public safety? |

are five typical ones used in human service research: individuals, groups, organizations, programs, and social artifacts. Other units of analysis are used when studying documents. This chapter focuses on three units of analysis, as illustrated in Table 12.1, that are typically used in macro practice: organizations, communities, and society.

At times, macro social work practitioners and researchers deal with *organizations* as the unit of analysis. Formal organizations are intentionally created groups that are designed to achieve some particular goals. Examples of formal organizations include government bureaus, human service agencies, schools, prisons, unions, and corporations. For example, a social worker may think and observe that organizations that serve adolescent consumers need to adapt more technology and different kinds of communication structures, so they would use "organization" as the unit of analysis to study different communication strategies and technological advances used across different organizations.

Research in macro social work can also focus on *communities* or *societies* as alternate units of analysis. For example, communities in the Northeast may vary from those in the Southwest regarding available and affordable housing options. Also, regarding societies, international social workers may study how India or Costa Rica differ from the United States and United Kingdom in their policies and outcomes related to arrests for particular crimes or dealing with extremely low levels of poverty.

## Decision Making in Evaluative Research

With regard to macro-level change, social workers require knowledge and skills in "establishing ongoing systems and mechanisms to monitor and improve outcomes . . . the planned or unplanned end result of an intervention, treatment and/or process" (Neuman, 2003, pp. 8–9).

In its most basic form, this involves helping to create a strategy and process for evaluating the effectiveness of efforts to create social change.

In human services, many professionals are familiar with the work of the United Way of America (UWA) in promoting outcome measurement in nonprofit agencies. For the UWA, a major emphasis has involved promoting "the use of outcome measurement as an aid to communicating results and funding decisions within its network of member United Ways" (Fischer, 2001, p. 562). Although many human service agencies continue to struggle to identify resources to fund outcome evaluations, several helpful publications are available to help practitioners (see, e.g., Rossi, Freeman, & Lipsey, 1999). Also, the UWA produced its own guide to help agencies manage the task of outcome evaluation (Hatry, van Houten, Plantz, & Greenway, 1996).

No single model exists for developing a comprehensive outcomes management program to measure the effectiveness and influence of social intervention. Instead, think of outcome evaluation as a process whereby professionals and consumers form outcomes, develop a strategy or plan, review internal data sources, review external data sources, design a framework and finalize outcomes, standardize terms and collection procedures, determine a report format, develop guidelines for data management, present the evaluation program for support, implement the evaluation program, and evaluate the results (Neuman, 2003, pp. 10–17).

It is vital that specific outcome measures be viewed by both consumers of services and professionals as acceptable indicators of influence and change. Cheetam (1992) differentiates between "service-based measures" focusing on quality of service and "client-based services" emphasizing the effects of service (or social intervention) on quality of life. Hence, the perspective of the consumer is crucial to determine measures and outcomes.

Regarding empowerment, advocacy, and strengths-based outcome evaluation, Jonson-Reid (2000) suggests that community-based research can be improved in the following ways. Professionals ought to consider: "(1) researching how a project defines community empowerment; (2) using a theory-based framework to connect program definitions, components, and measures; and (3) understanding the relationship of time to the use of the program outcome" (p. 57). These suggestions seem appropriate both for designing a process of outcome evaluation and also operationalizing concepts into measures. Thoughtful consideration needs to be given to the role of consumers and other stakeholders in shaping outcome evaluation, deeming the appropriateness of theoretical frameworks, and judging the relevance of time.

In the case of community-building efforts, special attention needs to be given to what residents and consumers of services believe constitute the purposes of projects or programs and agreed-on gauges for success. Jonson-Reid (2000) indicates that "clear definitions and theory-based connections between program components, outcomes, and measures should be accompanied by realistic time frames" (p. 74).

## Advocacy Strategies Related to Evidence-Based Macro Practice

The dynamic advocacy practice and policy model (APPM) may assist macro social workers in evaluating macro change in an evidence-based manner, considering human needs and rights, supportive environment(s), political access, and economic/social justice (Cox, Tice, & Long, 2019, p. 70). As examples, at the *organization level of analysis,* regarding economic and social justice, researchers may analyze how well is this organization securing needed resources for consumers. At the *community level of analysis,* regarding supportive environments, the macro practitioner might analyze how well a community's organizations are creating supportive environments to foster collaborations and generate solutions. Regarding evidence-based advocacy and macro-based research at the societal level, a social worker might consider political access by analyzing how well policymakers and politicians look beyond consumers'/citizens' situations to assess structural and systemic issues that contribute to the existence of private troubles.

## PARTICIPATORY RESEARCH AND POLICY AND PRACTICE

Conceived by administrators, politicians, and research consultants, **participatory research** is the opposite of authoritative or expert-based approaches. This is a process whereby "all participants (especially consumers) are afforded opportunities to reflect on programs, projects, and policies, the mission and aims of the organization and their own and others' involvement in change efforts. Evaluation is something done with people, not *on* people" (Finn & Jacobson, 2003, p. 335).

Participatory research directly challenges traditional beliefs and practices conserving authority and power in the research process. It elevates consumers to a coresearcher or coevaluator status. Credence and legitimacy are given to the capacities of consumers to conceptualize and develop measures to assess their social circumstances and conditions.

Participatory research is closely aligned with the strengths perspective, empowerment theory, and the APPM (Cox et al., 2019). Emphasis on the abilities and talents of consumers to understand their own lives and to shape research in a way that accurately assesses and evaluates their lived realities employs a strengths-based approach and orientation. Promoting consumers as active participants in research processes and securing consumer ownership in decision making in research as "coinvestigators" are illustrations of empowerment and advocacy.

### Types of Participatory Research

One way of thinking about some of the virtues of participatory research is to view it as a particular form of **grounded research**. Glaser and Strauss (1967) describe grounded research as an inductive process where conceptual distinctions, hypothesis, and theory formulations are derived from data. From their perspective, important insight for decision making in research comes from "grounded" sources—the experiences and perceptions of humans (consumers) in everyday life.

Glaser and Strauss (1967) explain how "awareness contexts" exist in the social world (p. 83). **Awareness contexts** can be thought of a situations or circumstances in which people experience varied degrees of visibility and understanding of what is going on. Here, the ability to know is contingent on one's consciousness and ability to comprehend the meaning of actions, language, gestures, and behavior.

For example, have you ever experienced a social situation, like a party, gathering, meeting, or event, where you engaged in interaction or conversation with others and struggled to understand what was happening? You might have felt like an outsider while others seemed able to follow and adhere to the rules, terms, and conditions surrounding the social interaction and discourse. Your first experience at a professional conference, political rally, board meeting, or protest demonstration may have evoked an uneasy feeling of not being "in the know."

In social research, decision makers are confronted with the challenging task of posing questions, hypotheses, and theories in conjunction with specific social contexts (e.g., rural vs. urban context, social-economic surroundings, and demographic characteristics). This constitutes a challenge at every stage of the research process. Consider the complexity of trying to identify the attributes of any single concept or measure in a research project without an astute awareness of social context. Consider how the term *homelessness* differs for people in a densely populated, racially diverse, and economically challenged African urban area as compared to homelessness in a rural, predominantly Caucasian small town.

As another example, geographic communities and neighborhoods in urban areas are often defined by corporation limits. Yet, in rural areas, community identity is often a matter of township or county affiliation. These types of distinctions are relevant for researchers to contemplate when determining the appropriate geographical context for examining topics such as homelessness. However, understanding the meaning of belonging to a specific city, township, town, or county will necessitate special insight and thought about the meaning of concepts, behaviors, and actions from people who actually live there.

There are many good and rational reasons why consumers of services ought to be fully vested in research processes. Their insight and expertise about contextual awareness and understanding in relation to particular communities, neighborhoods, and organizations constitute such a justification. Yet, ever more important, the integrity of social research rests on analytical thought, critical reflection, and the ability to entertain states of being from multiple vantage points. This broader and more encompassing way of thinking relies on the ability to embrace participatory research and to use thinking that extends beyond professional expertise and the intellectual origins and imagination of social scientists.

Participatory research can take multiple forms. The following bulleted items illustrate different types of participatory research, accompanied by some ideas on how consumers can become involved. Of course, the key to true participatory research is for consumers to assess and make informed decisions concerning their level of involvement and potential for making contributions in the research process. This is very different from having scientific experts delegate duties to consumers or allowing scientists to make unilateral decisions about how consumers can best contribute to research.



**PHOTO 12.2** Focus groups are components of participatory research.

Participatory research is particularly important and challenging when examining macro or large-scale change. Policy, legislative, and program changes will affect many people and various constituencies. This means that various special interest groups will be positioning themselves and vying to affect decision making. To help ensure adequate consumer participation, consumers need to be involved in every phase of a research project.

The notion of a **research team** needs to be embraced in a broad and inclusive fashion with each of the following types of participatory research. The basic assumption is that the team approach extends to consumers, embraces diversity of person and thought, and offers a mechanism for critical reflection and contemplation. This allows for the experiences and awareness of consumers to come forward in evaluating the results, or potential results, of large-scale social change. "Critical reflection is a structured, analytic, and emotional process that helps us examine the ways in which we make meaning of circumstances, events, and situations. . . . Posing critical questions is key to critical reflection" (Finn & Jacobson, 2003, p. 355).

Particular vocabulary is important to understand when trying to understand how to evaluate macro change using research. For example, differences exist across advisory groups and focus groups. Social-historical analyses differ from surveys and program evaluations. And still, policy and legislative analyses are completely different entities than case studies and field studies.

- *Advisory groups:* It is not unusual to have an advisory group attached to research projects. **Advisory groups** can help guide research processes, be a helpful resource in decision making, and serve in a consultative role. Although these groups are typically loaded with experts and professionals, it is important to recruit consumers who show interest in research and evaluation and who feel comfortable speaking out in an advisory group context.
- *Focus groups:* Scientists often struggle with developing and refining the research question. The **focus group** helps develop the research question since it provides suggestions about the definitions of the question and other issues regarding planning the research. The focus group format is a somewhat flexible strategy for collecting information and data from a group of people at one time and place. Facilitators initiate discussion on a subject to elicit insights, perspectives, and data from consumers of services. Anticipate high levels of participation and strong reactions from consumers when examining important topics.
- *Social-historical analyses:* Societies, communities, programs, services, and agencies function in a social-historical context. In assessing and evaluating strengths and areas to be strengthened, it is often important to document and collect data with respect to historical information and events. In any form of **social-historical analysis**, digging up the social remains of the past, a key question involves who is asked to remember and describe the factual events and provide documents (e.g., letters,

memos, records, minutes, and photographs). Consumers provide an enlightened and unique vantage point for describing the past.

- *Surveys:* Survey research is typically conducted to collect information concerning beliefs, attitudes, and behaviors. **Surveys** provide leaders and politicians with a gauge of public sentiment and the opinions of various constituency groups. Deciding which questions are to be asked, how, and to whom will have a pronounced effect upon findings. The validity of measures—the extent to which they measure what they purport to measure—is of the essence. Surveys can be especially helpful in conducting program or project evaluation. Consumers can be important team members by providing contextual awareness for questionnaire construction and in refining data collection techniques. In addition, they are a crucial population to poll concerning program or policy effectiveness.
- *Program evaluations:* Royse (2011) identifies several distinct types of program evaluation. They include patterns of use (Who is being served?), formative evaluation (How can the program be improved?), consumer satisfaction (How satisfied are consumers with the program?), outcome evaluation (Does the program reach its goals?), and cost-effectiveness (Is the program cost-effective in helping consumers?) (pp. 258–268). It is difficult to imagine devising a system for evaluating social service programming without significant ownership and buy-in from consumers. Consumers need to be active participants in determining program goals and evaluative outcomes, as well as in the process of completing program evaluation. Again, a research team with significant consumer participation would seem to be a promising format.
- *Policy and legislative analyses:* Social workers often work with consumers to assess the need for policy formulation and development. Two examples of this are community needs assessments and agency (organizational) profiles. In these instances, information is gathered to advise and influence policymakers and legislators. Additionally, consumers can serve as catalysts for evaluating the effectiveness (both successes and detrimental effects) of legislative and policy initiatives. In both cases, consumers are important participants in developing the process and criteria and adding a unique perspective for use in **policy/legislative analysis**.
- *Case studies:* These are often useful to analyze and describe a particular community, organization, event, program, or social unit in great depth. Although case studies are notorious for their weaknesses with respect to generalizability, they provide important information in flushing out the how, where, why, and when of social phenomena. Consumers constitute a valuable source of information for determining the nature of programs, organizations, and communities. Consumers can also provide valuable leads concerning data sources.

- *Field studies:* Some social processes need to be studied as they happen and in a relatively undisturbed fashion. In these instances, researchers seek to understand how events and actions unfold in their natural settings. This kind of research involves acquiring a sense of social context, an understanding of how actions develop and take place. Hence, if a social worker seeks to understand a particular community, then she or he needs to know how it really functions. This will necessitate direct observation and a level of immersion in the community. This often requires the involvement of consumers. It is their expertise that often allows researchers access to the everyday workings and activities of a community that may be invisible to the casual eye.

## A Participatory Research Case Examined: Welfare Reform

A case in point for the relevance of participatory research involves the Personal Responsibility and Work Opportunity Reconciliation Act of 1996. This historic piece of social legislation resulted in significant changes in the ways communities address the needs of the poor. Enacted in a spirit of "new federalism," with the intention of promoting self-sufficiency and reducing federal spending on public assistance, this law shifted social responsibility from the federal government to the states and local communities. Additionally, time restrictions were placed on receipt of aid—hence, the change of title from Aid for Dependent Children (AFDC) to Temporary Assistance to Needy Families (TANF).

> In essence, states were directed to develop strategic plans for using Temporary Aid to Needy Families (TANF) block grant monies that are consistent with federal guidelines and mandates concerning work requirements and payment levels. States, in turn, ask local areas (often counties) to create service delivery plans compatible with federal and state regulations, to address the needs of local constituents. The net result is a proliferation of state and local initiatives, each unique in name and substance, that reinforce the two main federal directives emphasizing employment and time limits of financial assistance. (Long, 2000, p. 63)

It is important to note that this type of service delivery has profound implications for policy and program evaluation. The creation of customized programs by state and county produced a myriad of programs (frequently called "family or children come first" initiatives) across our nation. Each program was unique in its specific goals and objectives. Decentralization and local control allowed states and counties appreciable latitude in assessing the success of welfare reform. Consequently, counties were challenged to develop individualized strategies for evaluating their program goals and desired outcomes.

As a result of federal mandates and prevailing belief systems (e.g., fiscal responsibility, self-sufficiency, the work ethic, and pressures for state or local control), many programs approached evaluation in terms of budgetary relief, cost-effective utilization of services, reduction in the number of people on welfare rolls, and various back-to-work ratios (Kilty & Meenaghan, 1995). These "accounting" types of criteria fit nicely with public and political concerns for reducing spending on welfare and for encouraging work. Meanwhile, consumer-oriented interests—such aspects as self-actualization, quality family time, and basic needs (e.g., food, medical care, and utilities)—were often overlooked or overshadowed in community-based research plans.

**PHOTO 12.3** Consumer participation is vital to decision making.

For many counties, it became relatively simple to rely on traditional measures of success, focusing on reducing welfare rolls and transitioning people toward available forms of employment. Although many counties developed advisory or planning boards to monitor TANF programs, political appointees and administrators were often overrepresented on these boards. The idea of embracing and including the voices of consumers in developing program goals, objectives, and measures of success was not always fashionable.

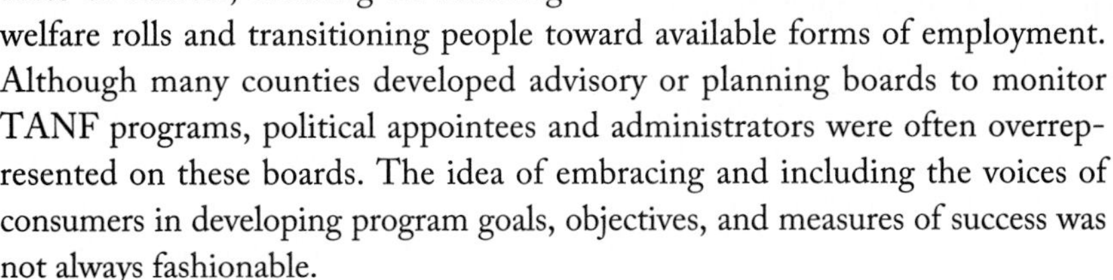

Long (2000) suggests that a comprehensive study of the effects of welfare reform would include consumer-driven criteria. From the perspective of TANF recipients, factors to be considered in an analysis of the success of welfare reform would likely include the employment market (e.g., the kinds of jobs available and their wages and benefits), the prospect of worker satisfaction, the availability of affordable child care, the presence of social support (e.g., family, friends, and groups), the availability of affordable and efficient transportation to and from work, the existence of safe housing, the effects on family preservation, options for medical insurance, and support from local organizations (e.g., social services, churches, and employers).

A thorough examination of how the lives of consumers have changed as a result of welfare reform would also include the use of multiple research methodologies, both quantitative and qualitative. Consumers could assist in the design and implementation of focus groups, case studies, surveys, and field research. Indeed, it is difficult to imagine how one could effectively describe and document the impact of welfare reform without the active participation of recipients.

Interestingly, one descriptive analysis of the impact of welfare sanctions found that only 10% of former recipients felt they were better off as a result of welfare reform (Lindhorst, Mancoske, & Kemp, 2000). As one might have anticipated, consumers in this study pointed to the disruptive effect of welfare reform on family life. When asked, consumers described the following kinds of struggles: changes in living arrangements, inability to pay rent, disruption in phone service, reliance on food banks or kitchens, separation of children from their caregiver, homelessness, and involvement with foster care (p. 195).

Clearly, looking at welfare reform from a consumer's perspective means considering factors that are very different from those posed by politicians and government leaders. People who are sanctioned as a result of welfare reform know firsthand the consequences of the legislation. Thoughtful reflection by consumers should be considered a source of enlightenment and discovery in research.

## Criticism of Participatory Research

Many criticisms have been leveled against participatory research. Most center on the idea that the involvement of laypeople (e.g., nonresearchers, politicians, lobbyists, and consumers of services) in the research process interjects subjectivity and bias, thereby compromising a major tenet of logic scientific inquiry—objectivity. Traditionalists believe that in the quest to more fully understand the relevance of culture and context, consumer participation in research can taint findings and, knowingly or unknowingly, push a project in a certain direction. Participatory research provides an opportunity for persuasion and influence that could unduly influence methodology and findings.

Over the past several decades, there has been a rich body of literature (e.g., Beresford, 2000, 2007; Beresford & Boxall, 2012; Beresford & Croft, 2001, 2004) examining the relevance and usefulness of consumer, sometimes referred to as "service user," participation in research. Consumers of services can offer valuable experiential knowledge in conventional research projects, collaborative research (consumers working jointly with traditional researchers), and user research (consumer-led and controlled research) (Beresford, 2007, pp. 333–334). Consumer participation in research can involve

> all keys aspects of research including: the origin of research; the accountability of the research; who undertakes the research; research funding; research design and process; dissemination of research findings; action following from research. (Beresford, 2000, p. 495)

Some social scientists argue that participatory research is just another name for action research, where there is a specific intent to engage consumers in research as a means of improving social conditions. In **action research**, a major and explicit goal of consumer participation is to guide or structure research in a manner that leads to practical outcomes for improving circumstances or overcoming oppressive conditions for people. Because action research is aimed at remedying social issues and/or enhancing people's lives, acquisition of knowledge is not intended to be the sole intent of the research. Instead, consciousness raising and persuading others to adopt a particular way of thinking are often implicit, if not explicit, goals.

## Consumer Participation in Research

Participatory research need not be action research, however. Participatory research allows for the abilities and talents of consumers to come forward in the research process. The primary goal of having consumers participate as coresearchers is to offer their expertise, based on experience and knowledge, which can include the development of hypotheses, theories, and models, based on the viewpoints and firsthand knowledge of consumers, for testing (Beresford & Croft, 2001). Participatory research can (but may not necessarily) mean that participants are engaged in an attempt to create social change that favors their interests.

## Participatory Research and Advocacy

The strengths perspective (Saleebey, 2002, 2012) offers basic tenets that are helpful to consider when using participatory research to involve consumers of services. These include the following:

- Membership
- Dialogue and collaboration
- Strengths of systems of various sizes
- Helping consumers discover their abilities and resources

**TABLE 12.2**

Applying the Advocacy Policy and Practice Model Through Participatory Research to Evaluate Macro Change

| APPM Tenet | Participatory Research | Macro Change |
|---|---|---|
| Human needs and rights | How can consumers of services lend experience, perspective, and viewpoints about the specific needs and rights of population groups for study? | How might consumer participation in research inform and influence decision making regarding human needs and rights with policies, program development, legislation, and social work practice? |
| Economic and social justice | How can consumers of services help identify social and economic factors for consideration in research? | How can social and economic conditions be better understood and affected through consumer participation in change efforts? For example, how can the voice(s) of consumers be powerful in influencing decision makers? |
| Supportive environments | Consumers are keenly aware of elements supportive or unsupportive in their living environments. Consumers can identify key individuals, groups of people, organizations, and conditions both as units of analysis. | Focus on the consideration of supportive environments can prompt descriptive and exploratory research to identify areas for strengthening (e.g., the presence of urban food deserts and the lack of affordable transportation) in support of consumer health and well-being. |
| Political access | Consumer participation in research can often depend on the endorsement, validation, and support of key politicians or decision makers aligned with such politicians. Building relationships and alliances with politicians can be a key factor for advancing consumer participation, viewpoints, and influence in research. | The awareness and validation of politicians, political party members, and a political base in participatory research can initiate a beginning level of support (e.g., endorsement, funds, and voting) for macro-level change (e.g., policy development, projects, and new programs) in conjunction with research findings. |

In addition, the dynamic APPM (Cox et al., 2019) offers a four-pronged advocacy approach for identifying and understanding tenets of advocacy that can be useful when contemplating participatory research in relationship to macro-level change. As a brief illustration of the usefulness of the four APPM principles with participatory research and macro change, consider Table 12.2.

## Time to Think 12.3

Identify a research question involving a contemporary social issue and population group that interests you for social work practice. Examples might include the sexual harassment of women, underemployment of racial minorities, homelessness for people experiencing mental health challenges, and the absence of treatment services in your community for people wanting help with substance issues. How could consumers of services, past and present, become involved in participatory research? Using exploratory research as an example, how might consumers be able to identify concepts, trends, behaviors, actions, and conditions that others participating in a research endeavor would lack knowledge? Would all consumers be willing, expected, or considered for participation in research? Identify consumer strengths (e.g., leadership, verbal communication, insightfulness, emotional state, etc.) that would be valuable when encouraging and selecting consumers to become involved in participatory research.

## Advocacy and Strengths-Oriented Measures in Macro-Level Change

When approaching research from either an advocacy policy-practice focus or strengths-based manner, multiple areas can be identified for further exploration and study. In each of these cases, emphasis is given to building the abilities and capacities of larger systems. Although the following is not an exhaustive list, it provides several themes for discussion among research team members when conceptualizing the evaluation of large-scale change.

- *Assets:* Groups of people, organizations, communities, and societies consist of assets. These are positive features or resources that help to sustain and promote the well-being of a social system. For a group of people, it could be a sense of cohesiveness or "we-ness." Communities often possess a degree of pride. For a society, an asset could be adaptability. When evaluating social change, attention ought to be given to the potential for strengthening salient assets and advocating for economic and social justice.
- *Capabilities:* Larger social systems also possess abilities and potentials. These often go unrecognized or unrealized. Saleebey (2002) suggests this to be "especially true of marginalized communities where individuals and groups have had to learn to survive under difficult and often rapidly changing conditions" (p. 236). When studying social change, the

research team needs to weigh the degree to which human and social capacity is actualized. This includes both formal entities (e.g., agencies, churches, and schools) and informal associations (e.g., neighborhood groups).

- *Rights:* One indicator of macro-level change involves the formation or development of laws and policies that advance or protect the rights of people. For example, many Americans have been disappointed that an equal rights amendment for women has never been passed in the United States. Such a piece of national legislation could have established guidelines and standards for the fair and equitable treatment of women. Such a law could have been a source of inspiration for women, as the Americans with Disabilities Act (ADA) has been for persons experiencing disabilities. Evaluating human needs is just as important as evaluating human rights.
- *Opportunities:* When conceptualizing structural change, one should think in terms of the creation of widespread opportunities for groups of people. These can be thought of as opportunity pathways or highways, where large numbers of people experience newfound access to information, power, resources, and decision-making processes. At the organizational level, opportunity could be measured by recognized membership, for example. Opportunities are also affected by political access and the decisions of policymakers and politicians.
- *Accomplishments and goal attainment:* Larger social systems (e.g., groups, organizations, and communities) often set goals for themselves. This could involve reducing absenteeism and truancy in schools or creating additional jobs or businesses in an area. Many times, state and national competitions establish measurable criteria for evaluating organizational or community progress and recognizing accomplishments. These can be useful markers of large-scale social change, especially when such goals are formed and established with the input of consumers. For example, consumers of services often value full-time employment that includes a livable wage, medical benefits, and opportunities for childcare. Meanwhile, politicians and business leaders can be satisfied with simply creating and reporting part-time and minimum-wage jobs without medical or day-care provisions.

## ETHICAL CONSIDERATIONS

As indicated earlier in this chapter, fundamental principles of research include objectivity, replication, the accumulative nature of findings, and the value of discovery. Participatory research provides opportunities to both inform research processes and procedures as well as produce checks and balances to thwart bias. However, ethical boundaries exist with regard to protecting consumers and society, which include premises of confidentiality and prohibitions against falsifying and/or misrepresenting research procedures, data, and findings, to name just a few prohibitions.

The direct personal involvement of a field or macro social worker in the social lives of consumers raises many ethical dilemmas. Dilemmas arise when a researcher or evaluator is alone in the field, organization, or community and has little time to make a moral decision. Although evaluators may be aware of general ethical issues, such dilemmas arise unexpectedly in the course of observing and interacting in macro systems. Four particular ethical issues in field research, for example, are deception, confidentiality, involvement with deviants, and publishing reports.

Deception involves the issue of being covert or overt in conducting research. Some field sites or activities can only be studied covertly, even though covert research is really not preferable or easier to do than overt research because of the challenges of maintaining a front and the constant fear of getting caught.

Confidentiality is a moral obligation the evaluator promises his or her consumer participant. Sometimes an evaluator or researcher cannot quote a person, such as a vulnerable stakeholder or community leader. One strategy instead of reporting the source of an informant is to document evidence that says the same thing and uses a document instead as the source of information.

Researchers who conduct research on deviants who engage in illegal behavior face added challenges. Researchers can experience a dilemma in building trust and rapport with deviants, while not violating their own personal moral standards.

Publishing reports can also create dilemmas regarding the right of privacy and the right to know. A researcher does not publicize consumer secrets, violate privacy, or harm reputations. However, some researchers will simply ask consumers to examine a report to verify its accuracy and to approve of their portrayal in print. For marginalized groups (e.g., substance users, prostitutes, etc.), this may not be possible, but researchers must always respect member privacy.

Social work researchers, much as social work practitioners, sign an oath to conduct themselves in accordance with a code of conduct—for social workers, the principles and standards identified in the National Association of Social Workers' (2018) *Code of Ethics*. Indeed, failure to abide in ethical conduct in research can yield profound and damaging consequences for consumers of services. And, for social work researchers, reprimands and potential expulsion from the profession can occur as a result of misconduct.

---



---

## SUMMARY

Understanding social change with larger systems is a multifaceted proposition. The unit of analysis could be a characteristic or attribute of a group of people, organization, community, or society. The composition of the research team, including their backgrounds, expertise, and predispositions, will have a powerful effect on the research process and subsequent findings.

In this chapter, you are challenged to embrace a somewhat nontraditional view of research. The primary focus has been on finding ways to identify and consider the use of the strengths of consumers to become participants and team members in research involving macro-level change. This is true of all kinds of research, including descriptive, exploratory, explanatory, and evaluative.

A participatory approach to research demands the active involvement of consumers in methodological decisions as well as throughout the research process. Consumers are viewed as experts in their own right, as they possess unparalleled knowledge, direct experience, and a unique orientation to issues and problems. Grounded information is often crucial to the formation of concepts, hypotheses, and theories in the research process. Consumers need not be viewed merely as subjects for study but as potential coinvestigators and valued members of a research team. This is true regardless of the methodology employed (e.g., case study, survey, or field research).

## TOP 10 KEY CONCEPTS

action research 278
awareness contexts 272
descriptive research 266
evaluation research 267
explanatory research 266
exploratory research 266
grounded research 272
participatory research 272
program monitoring 269
research team 274

## DISCUSSION QUESTIONS

1. Discuss with your classmates your interest or lack of interest in research. As a social worker, how would you envision yourself becoming involved in research projects and involving what topics? Who might be a research mentor for you (e.g., a faculty member, field supervisor, or other researcher)? And, could you see yourself participating in a research team that produces a published research article?
2. Is there a fine line between consumers influencing and unduly swaying research? Consider action research in this realm. Discuss what you believe might be inappropriate behaviors by social workers and consumers.
3. Your social work education program is involved in program evaluation through the assessment of student learning via practice behaviors and competencies. Most likely, as a student in field education, your field supervisor will be or has conducted an evaluation of your abilities when working with consumers of services. What are your thoughts about this process at your university, and have you been actively involved in program evaluation for your program? If so, how? If not, why not? How is the voice of students important in evaluating your educational program's effectiveness?

## EXERCISES

1. Ask a social worker engaged in research for her or his views on participatory research and the use of consumers of services as coinvestigators. What types of arguments are provided for or against the use of consumers in the research process? Does

her or his views represent a strengths- or advocacy-based orientation in relationship to consumer participation or a more traditional stance concerning the conduction of research?

2. Request a copy of an agency's program evaluation standards as prescribed by a funding source (e.g., United Way, grant funder, or allocation board). What kind of information is mandated? Are the standards geared toward effectiveness or efficiency? Does this constitute descriptive, exploratory, explanatory, or evaluative research? How are consumers included in decision making with respect to the research process? Do consumers serve a program-monitoring function? Are consumers considered in any fashion as members of the evaluation team?

3. Contact your local county Department of Human Services and inquire about efforts in your county to evaluate the success of TANF. What kind of research strategy has been employed? What criteria have been used to measure the success of welfare reform at the local level, and who determined such criteria? Was insight solicited from consumers in order to acquire contextual awareness of the consequences of welfare reform? Why or why not?

4. Identify a recent policy or legislative initiative that has been undertaken in your community. Was a community assessment completed to gather relevant data and to gauge public sentiment? Were consumers of services in your community involved in designing or conducting any of this research (e.g., focus groups, surveys, and/or social-historical analysis)?

## ONLINE RESOURCES

- To learn more about a contemporary effort to advance participatory research, examine the website participatesdgs.org. The Participate initiative began in 2012 and involves the promotion of participatory research examining the plight of economically deprived and marginalized people in 29 countries.
- The Social Work Policy Institute at socialworkpolicy.org provides a useful review of various resources for examining and promoting best practices and ethical conduct in social work research.
- The Centers for Disease Control and Prevention at cdc.gov/eval/standards/index.htm has advanced a set of 30 standards for use in assessing the quality of evaluation activities. A primary goal of these standards is to support culturally competent evaluation practices.

# Advocacy for Human Rights and Social, Economic, and Environmental Justice

## ADVOCACY AND REFUGEE SERVICES

Maria is employed as a social worker in a refugee center located in a border state of the United States. She recognizes that immigrants and refugees face unique challenges due to immigration policies and the mind-set of some citizens and politicians. In the context of the legal and social statutes of migrants, Maria recognizes that her ability to provide much-needed social services and ensure community well-being is significantly affected. This is especially the case in relation to policies that limit family visitation and family reunification. Even more complicated are immigrant and "mixed-status" families in which members include combinations of citizens and noncitizens.

A particularly difficult situation for Maria is when she recognizes that a migrant worker is experiencing employment exploitation. Reporting such a grievance to enforcement agencies could be seen as a potentially deportable offense rather than an opportunity to seek justice. Maria also understands that the consequences of advocating for immigrants, including those with mixed status, could result in the separation of families. In such a work environment, Maria struggles to find a balance in her professional values, the political realities, and her personal moral code of conduct.

## LEARNING OBJECTIVES

After reading this chapter you should be able to:

1. Define the values of social work from a historical perspective
2. Describe the need for political activism
3. List practical considerations for promoting for human rights and social, economic, and environmental justice
4. Describe right and left political leanings
5. Apply the advocacy practice and policy model (APPM) to domestic and global social justice issues
6. Define advocacy strategies for human rights and social, economic, and environmental justice across borders

The national and international political landscape challenges social work to remain true to the values and ethical considerations that are central to the profession. These values—a commitment to human dignity, human welfare, and social justice—remain essential characteristics of the practice of social work, much as they have been throughout the history of the profession.

This chapter considers the core values and ethics of social work in relation to consumer participation, empowerment, advocacy, and dominant American values, including individualism, self-interest, work, and materialism. The strengths perspective is considered in light of social work's values and the prevailing political conservatism. Students are encouraged to not only apply

Pacific Press/Contributor/Getty Images

**PHOTO 13.1** Social worker speaks with unaccompanied minor immigrants in Calabria.

rational thinking in practice but also embrace a strong sense of social-political activism in relationship to personal and professional value systems.

## VALUES BASE OF SOCIAL WORK

As illustrated throughout this book, social work is a values-based profession committed to enhancing positive life conditions across consumer systems (Pak, Cheung, & Tsui, 2016; Reamer, 1990). Defined as the qualities, meanings, and intentions by which we order our lives, values are the premises and assumptions on the basis of which we make decisions (Brueggemann, 1996; Pak, Cheung, & Tsui, 2016). Values provide the foundation for social work practice and establish a course of action for the profession (Loewenberg & Dolgoff, 1992; Simmons, 2010). Social work has embraced **historic social work values** that imply that people have the right to be respected and that social workers should not discriminate against people and communities because of race, ethnicity, gender, sexual orientation, religion, country of origin, or socioeconomic class.

Rapp and Poertner (1992) stated that the collective philosophy of social work, coupled with individual philosophies, and the broader social context are all important sources of values. Core social work values are respect for the dignity and uniqueness of the individual and client self-determination. Compton and Galaway (1979), Hepworth and Larsen (1982), and Frunza and Sanu (2017) suggest the professional's cardinal values include the following:

1. People should have access to resources.
2. Every person is unique and has inherent worth.
3. People have a right to freedom.
4. Society and the individual citizen have mutual responsibility for the realization of these values.

One can see that consumer participation, self-determination, and confidentiality lie at the heart of social work practice. It is important to note, however, that the implementation of these values may vary on the basis of priorities and objectives (e.g., as influenced by funding, organizational context, administrators, and vested interest groups). Additionally, policies must be in place to support the professional values and protect consumers from legal implications (e.g., infringements on confidentiality).

It should be noted that social workers do not expect the same behavior of their consumers that they expect of themselves. One of social work's virtues is that it has advocated allowing others to do and say certain things that social workers might not say or do. In social work practice, values are often seen as affecting the choice of objectives and goals. Values surface when purpose is addressed. The tradition speaks of the profession as value laden but sees the ethical "oughts" as separate from the "knowns." Consequently, *values* and *ethics* are not interchangeable terms. Values are concerned with what is good and desirable, whereas ethics address what is right and correct—typically as defined by a profession.

If "doing the right thing" on behalf of consumers is a distinguishing feature between effective social workers and those who are ineffective, it is important to examine what "doing the right thing" means (Lewis, Lewis, Packard, & Souffle, 2001). In this book, doing the right thing involves social workers making judgments within a framework of professional values, supported and operationalized by a code of ethics. Professional values give social workers a direction in pursuit of effectiveness. They provide a steady direction for the pursuit of social work interventions.

## Time to Think 13.1

Read over the case study on Maria and her work in a refugee center located in a border state. What value systems are in conflict and why? How do you recommend that Maria addresses the many challenges she has providing serves to migrants and mixed-status families? What role do the state's resident and elected officials have in value clarification and subsequent service provision? Does it matter if Maria's city is a sanctuary city? If so, why?

Reamer (1998) and Pumphrey (1959) provided one of the earliest and most influential categorizations of social work's core values, placing them in three groups of values-based objectives. The first group emphasized the relationship between the values operating in the culture at large. This group was concerned with the compatibility between struggling for social justice and social change, as well as addressing basic human needs and the broader culture's values. The second category dealt more narrowly with social work's perception of its own values, particularly the ways the profession interpreted and implemented its values and encouraged ethical behavior. The final category emphasized social workers' relationships with specific groups and individuals served by social workers, particularly understanding and responding to clients' values. Of specific importance was the potential for conflict among competing values.

In this chapter, **advocacy** and the strengths perspective embrace social work values by incorporating consumers' abilities, voices, viewpoints, knowledge, and skills in the helping process. Said another way, regardless of their level of functioning, the severity of their life circumstances, and the magnitude of the problems that need to be overcome, consumers and their communities need to be seen as having the ability to resolve their problems. As social workers, we support the empowerment of consumers by expecting and recognizing their strengths and facilitating the necessary change efforts. Thus, practicing from a **strengths perspective** supports empowerment for individuals' well-being and the environmental factors that influence it. In this way, social work's understanding of the interaction between people and their environment is directly guided by the values.

Underpinning social work values is the sense that people have certain basic needs related to housing, food, education, safety, and medical care. In other words, services and the environment help to shape the opportunities and privileges available to people. During the Progressive Era, the era of the settlement movement, and the Great Depression, social workers saw all too often that social and economic problems were linked to the hardship faced by individuals and families. Today, people's suffering may at times may be less visible, but misery remains part of daily life for segments of people living in the United States. Unfortunately, the link between environmental factors and individual and community opportunities is often less apparent, but the relationship exists even in this time of unprecedented consumerism.

It is important to point out that although professional values can have a powerful and meaningful influence in guiding the rational and analytical thoughts of practitioners, advocating with consumers for **human rights** and social, economic, and environmental rights also involves political aspects and influences as well as elements of power and control (Meenaghan, Kilty, Long, & McNutt, 2013). The influence of special interest groups in shaping individual and social perceptions through the use of social media, advertisements, and various forms of privileged communication (e.g., conversations, consultation, and social events) requires recognition. Typically, the functions of special interest and political groups for influencing policy narratives involve "the articulation of interests," "attempts to influence decision makers in light of those interests," "coalition building," development of "an agenda by related interest groups," and efforts "to ensure future support or prevent erosion of critical support from a coalition of interest groups" (Meenaghan, Kilty, Long, & McNutt, 2013, p. 89).

## POLITICAL ACTIVISM

How do social workers engage in political activism? They might begin by canvassing door-to-door for a particular cause, candidate, elected official, or program. Another common form of **activism** is organizing public meetings or rallies and writing articles or editorials for a newspaper or a community newsletter. In all cases, activism requires creativity, energy, passion, innovation, and commitment.

In systems of government such as in the United States, conventional politics includes election campaigning, voting, passing laws, participation in political action committees (PACs), use of social media, and lobbying politicians. Action outside of these arenas might include coalition building, boycotts, neighborhood organizing, marches, and sit-ins. Thus, the boundary between activism and conventional politics is often fuzzy and depends on the circumstances (Martin, 2007).

Social workers recognize that the activism and conventional politics sometimes operate side by side as seen in the environmental and peace movements alongside a green party. It is also possible for social workers to speak of activism inside an organization, such as a government department or a political party. If a social worker organizes to challenge a decision or try to alter the usual decision-making process, this can be called activism, although it is much less visible than activism in public places. Table 13.1 lists different methods and activities for engaging in political activism.

**TABLE 13.1**
Areas of Activism

| Method | Activity |
|---|---|
| Public protest | • Rally<br>• March<br>• Public meeting |
| Protest and persuasion | • Speeches<br>• Slogans<br>• Banners<br>• Picketing<br>• Protest disrobing<br>• Vigils<br>• Singing<br>• Marches<br>• Teach-ins |
| Noncooperation | • Religious excommunication<br>• Rent strike<br>• Boycott |
| Intervention | • Sit-in<br>• Setting up economic and political institutions |

## Time to Think 13.2

**Values and Activism**

Brian, a social worker, works in a community center and organizes both advocacy efforts and community-based educational programs for older people. The center is located in an upper-middle-class neighborhood consisting primarily of professionals. Brian has been asked to begin integrative programming for older people with psychiatric conditions, including depression and schizophrenia. His current program consumers are resistant to the idea, as are many of the community residents; however, his board of directors is supportive of the new venture.

What social work values appear to have a bearing on this case? How might Brian persuade the current consumers and community members through activism methods while taking advantage of a much-needed program opportunity for people with mental illness?

## POLITICAL LEANINGS

**Political leanings** are often described in terms of left and right positioning. Broadly speaking, the right is thought to be conservative and in keeping with a capitalist system of government. In contrast, the left is described as more progressive in ideology with leanings toward socialism. Another way of considering the terms is that conservatives tend to want a smaller federal government and less spending on social welfare, whereas liberals want to expand the role of government to include more programs and services with a broad, universal perspective of human need in mind. It is important to keep in mind that this terminology can only loosely be applied since activism and political ideology are multidimensional concepts and often do not comfortably fit within the left-right classification system (Martin, 2007).

It is possible to see activism as a spectrum from the local to the global, both geographically and in relation to the person. Local activism is often about protecting the quality of life of a family or small community, such as when local citizens campaign for better schools or hospitals or against a factory or freeway. Resistance to program and service delivery in one's local community is sometimes disparagingly called NIMBY (not-in-my-back-yard) activism, which was referenced earlier in Chapter 7.

A broader focus brings concern for groups subject to disadvantage or discrimination, including women, ethnic minorities, the poor, and people with disabilities. Much activism is carried out by people in these groups, supported by some from more privileged groups. For example, some men are profeminist activists and some able-bodied people advocate on behalf of those with physical challenges.

Pacific Press/Contributor/Getty Images

**PHOTO 13.2** Promoting social, economic, and environmental justice engages public education.

As indicated by Figure 13.1, a number of political ideologies can be seen as interlocking in terms of their philosophic frameworks, beliefs, and actions. Furthermore, it is possible to view political philosophies as a broad spectrum from the local, state, to federal governments and globally. For social workers, a broader political focus highlights concern for disenfranchised groups or issues of discrimination and exploitation. Activism within the political environment is usually designed to readjust the distribution of goods and services as well as power in decision making. The direction that resources and power are distributed is often highly related to political leanings.

**FIGURE 13.1**
Political Philosophies

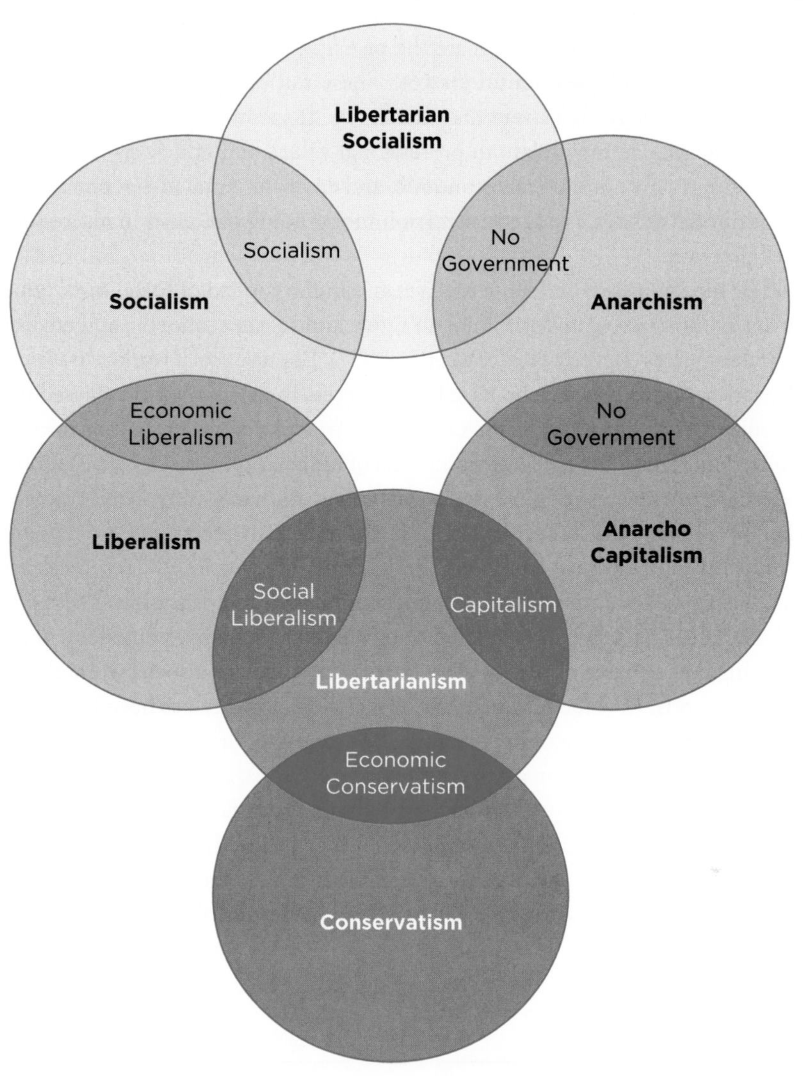


## Time to Think 13.3

Examine Figure 13.1 once again and explore some political ideologies that are unfamiliar to you. How are the political ideologies similar or in contrast to your way of thinking and how and why? Also consider countries that have such ideologies as part of their governance. Contrast and compare the political ideologies and subsequent government to the United States in terms of citizen participation and the comprehensive provision of social services.

## HUMAN RIGHTS AND SOCIAL, ECONOMIC, AND ENVIRONMENTAL JUSTICE

Embedded in social work values are the principles of human rights and **social, economic, and environmental justice**. These notions are particularly crucial to macro practice from a strengths perspective. It seems important to highlight these principles as they relate to professional values and ethics. In this discussion, human rights and social, economic, and environmental justice should each be considered as both a goal and focal point for guiding processes in macro social work practice.

The idea of justice or a sense of fairness is in the context of social work values, especially those associated with human rights and social, economic, and environmental resources (Beverly & McSweeney, 1987). Because social workers traditionally work with consumers who have limited access to resources and are faced with prejudice and discrimination, the challenge is to replace injustice with justice. As depicted in Figure 13.2, the overriding goal of human rights and social, economic, and environmental justice is full and equal participation in society that is equitable, whereby all members feel physically and psychologically secure.

Historically, the most common criteria for distributing limited resources have been the principles of equality, need, contribution, and compensation. These principles at times have been interpreted to mean actual equality, with all recipients acquiring equal shares of the distributed resources, such as a social worker's time or public funds. In some instances, the principle of equality has been interpreted to mean merely equality of opportunity—for example, that resources or services are made available to all on a first-come, first-served basis.

Although some philosophers have argued that the principles of equality should guide the distribution of limited resources, others believe that the extent of one's current need should be the primary determinant or that there is an obligation to distribute resources based on the extent of one past's contributions. Controversy

**FIGURE 13.2**
Goals of Human Rights

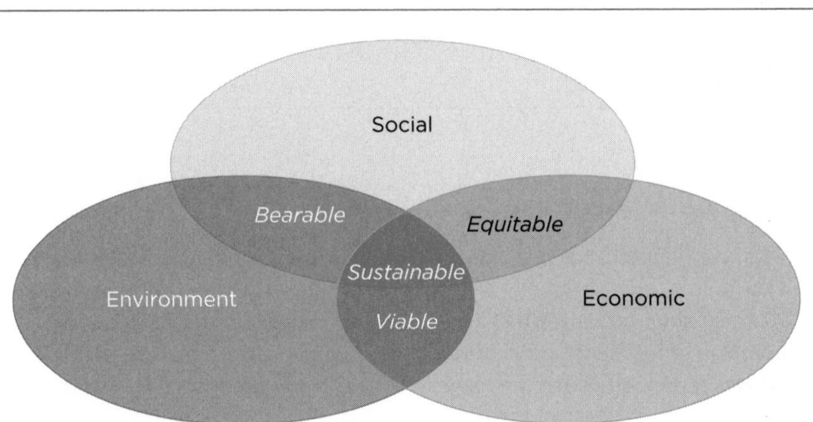

about which criteria should be used to distribute scarce resources properly has persisted for centuries. Although it is unlikely that this controversy will be settled easily, if at all, it is important for social workers to be sensitive to it.

**Principles of justice in social work practice** reflect philosophical frameworks. For example, Walz and Ritchie (2000) suggest that Mahatma Gandhi's theory of nonviolent social change and the pursuit of social justice complement social work practice. Gandhi's methods of social service and social action combine micro and macro practice.

Gandhian theory highlights social justice as fairness to people, with a particular focus on those people who are disadvantaged. In a similar manner, Rawls, in his seminal work, *A Theory of Justice,* argues that we can best construct our moral vision of a good or a just society by trying to imagine its internal arrangement from behind a "veil of ignorance," which obscures our own current status (such as income) or personal access to opportunities (Rawls, 1971, p. 85). Rawls concludes that if people are aware of their current status, they are likely to want to maintain the same societal structure even if it means that inequalities will continue (Jansson, 1998; Polack, 2004). Building on the work of Rawls, it can be said that the process of justice involves using the professional self as an instrument to challenge inequalities and support social reform as part of our professional role.

Embedded in this discussion of human rights and social, economic, and environmental justice is the concept of professional power. People depend on professional services to help them gain control over their lives during times of trouble and distress. The power to intervene carries with it unique responsibilities to society that are not connected to other kinds of work. The ethics of professional practice are directly related to the use and abuse of power. According to Manning (1997), every decision and action taken by social workers communicates a message to society about what social work values and, indirectly, what society values (Lundy & van Wormer, 2007; Manning, 1997). The social work pioneer, Charlotte Towle (1969), discussed the moral function of social work as social conscience—a sense of what is right or good. Thus, Towle conceptualized the profession as the "conscience of the community . . . using head, heart, and hand" to do social work (p. 14).

Similarly, it can be argued that social work as a profession has a public duty to make the invisible visible—to show the underside of a system that seems to work adequately (Jennings, Callahan, & Wolf, 1987; Miller, Hayward, & Shaw, 2012). The foundation of this endeavor is the values and purpose of the profession that direct ethical issues.

C. Wright Mills (1956) suggested that there are **power elites** who control the needed resources in societies. Furthermore, these power elites play instrumental roles in three primary institutions: the government, the military, and corporations. Mills (1956) claims that these hierarchies of power are the key to understanding modern industrial societies. The sheer power accumulated by the power elites dictates not only that their interests will be served over the good of society but also that interests of the elites become the interests of common people. For example, if the power elite concludes that tax reductions will be of benefit to them, taxes will be reduced even at the cost of increased national debt. Mills suggests that it is common experiences and role expectations that produce people of similar character and values.

According to Mills, power in U.S. society is found at two levels. The vast majority of people are at the bottom of society's hierarchy. As might be expected, people at this level are largely economically dependent and often economically and politically exploited. For instance, they are employed in positions with little chance of advancement and have few opportunities to gain economic ground even with a lifetime of diligent work. In other words, this group of people holds little power.

Between the masses and the power elite, Mills (1956) describes a middle level of power comprising local leaders and special interest groups. Although vocal, these groups have minimal impact on the real source of society's power. The nation's politicians and elected officials fall into this group, according to Mills (1956). The U.S. Congress and political parties are a reflection of this middle-level power. Issues are debated and policies are approved, but the power elite maintains control over legislators and legislation. As a result, it should not be surprising that many people have lost their faith in the political system to the point that they do not vote or follow political events. Indeed, as indicated by Pew research, voter turnout for 2016 continued to be low by international standards, despite a record turnout (Desilver, 2018; Krogstad & Lopez, 2017). For all practical purposes, many disenfranchised Americans have become alienated from the U.S. political and governance systems.

## Time to Think 13.4

To apply Mills's theory to current events, take some time to read a newspaper article that describes a policy debate or social issue. Assess who you think are the power elite, the politicians, and the general public. Then consider the following questions: (1) How is the balance of power maintained? (2) What could be done to shift the power base? (3) What would be the intended consequences? (4) What might be the unintended consequences?

## APPLY THE ADVOCACY PRACTICE AND POLICY MODEL (APPM)

Application of the advocacy practice and policy model (APPM) is important in the context of human rights and justice because many of the issues that confront our consumers, including poverty, unemployment, homelessness, hunger, inadequate health care, and unequal and inadequate education, exist due to human rights injustices in the social, economic, and environmental systems (Segal, Gerdes, & Steiner, 2004). Social workers engaged in macro practice, such as administration, policy analysis, and program development, who want to ensure justice have sought to serve as advocates and to create and sustain empowering policies, programs, and services. By combining social work values and ethics in support of social justice, social work practices create a reinforcing environment that will

- Identify the valued outcome for consumers in the public policy that directs and supports the program
- Identify the values outcomes for consumers as described in the program design
- Identify other values important to producing desired consumer outcomes
- Identify worker-directed values required to maintain staff morale and produce consumer outcomes
- Anticipate value conflicts and assist staff to make decisions in light of these conflicts
- Use as many vehicles as possible to communicate these values to consumers, staff, and other constituents (Rapp & Poertner, 1992, p. 178; Reisch & Jani, 2012)

Applying a strengths perspective in advocacy efforts can be helpful but not necessarily intuitive, particularly when considering larger social systems. Table 13.2 identifies and describes how organizational and community aspects derived from the strengths perspective can be useful in the context of advocating for and advancing various forms of social justice.

**TABLE 13.2**

Characteristics of the Strengths Perspective in the Context of Social Justice

| |
|---|
| • Organizations and communities can learn and retain information. |
| • The role of the social worker is to transfer knowledge and skills useful to organizations and communities. |
| • Organizations and communities are the experts on their own experiences. |
| • Social workers facilitate the competencies of organizations and communities by transferring advocacy, mediation, and political skills. |
| • Intervention strategies help communities and organization perceive their conditions in a broader societal context and help connect individual matters to the environmental conditions. |
| • Organizations and communities gain from consciousness-raising activities associated with political power and economic growth and development. |
| • All organizations and communities deserve respect and acceptance for their strengths, including resilience. |
| • Collaboration, cooperation, and egalitarian partnerships strengthen the fiber of organizations and communities. |
| • Networks are crucial to the health of organizations and communities. |
| • Communities and organizations should emphasize cooperative and interdependent activities for the accomplishment of goals related to social justice. |

*Source:* Adapted from Cox and Parsons (1994, pp. 39, 94, 100–101).

## Time to Think 13.5

You are the director of a social work department in a rural community hospital. As part of your work, you review the reason for admissions to the hospital. It has come to your attention that an increasing number of alcohol-related injuries and accidents are associated with teens and people well over the age of 65. There are no substance abuse programs in the tricounty region. However, approximately 110 miles from your hospital, there is a prosperous city with a drug and alcohol treatment unit.

Use the following situation to consider change that extends beyond an individual or group of consumers. As you think about the change effort, list the policies, organizations, and systems that will be affected by the change. What interventions will you use to initiate the change effort? How does your work reflect the values and ethics of social work and the strengths of consumers in their communities? What are the justice issues involved?

Macro practice entails public education as an integral element of interventions with strategies tailored to (1) political decision makers, (2) decision makers of foundations, (3) other potential private funding sources, (4) the public at large, (5) consumer-supported action groups, and (6) ongoing staff and consumer education (Gutierrez, Parsons, & Cox, 1998; Guttmann, 2006). Problem solving in this context is viewed as part of a sociopolitical movement. For instance, the director of a homeless shelter who is committed to social justice connects the problems of consumers to the larger political aspects of the nation's housing stock. Table 13.2 defines other characteristics of practice that combine a strengths perspective with a social justice orientation. As is apparent, these characteristics require long-term communication, diligence, and education with consumers, staff, volunteers, and the general public.

A vital step for social workers is developing their own power on the personal (individual) level. This first requires recognizing one's personal powers. As individuals working in organizations and communities, social workers need to analyze their power, individually and collectively, in the workplace and strategize how to use any such power to rally around issues of social justice. A third step involves identifying allies in the organization or community and finding how social workers can work with these allies to meet common goals of the community and social change.

Figure 13.3 depicts the change process and the possible roles of social workers. Critical to the process involves forming problem definitions that intersect collaborations with consumers, organizations, and community partners. The action plan necessities some form of activism that also involves organizations and communities through interface with consumers. What is significant to note is the roles of monitoring and evaluation in the change process. Progress and results of the change action are typically derived through monitoring and evaluation. This feedback informs social workers as to the practice and policies that were instrumental in addressing the designated injustices and how effective and efficient the course of activism was in the context of desired goals.

**FIGURE 13.3**
The Art of Change and the Act of Social Justice

*Source:* Provided by the Center for Economic and Social Justice.

**FIGURE 13.4**
Advocacy Practice and Policy Model (APPM)

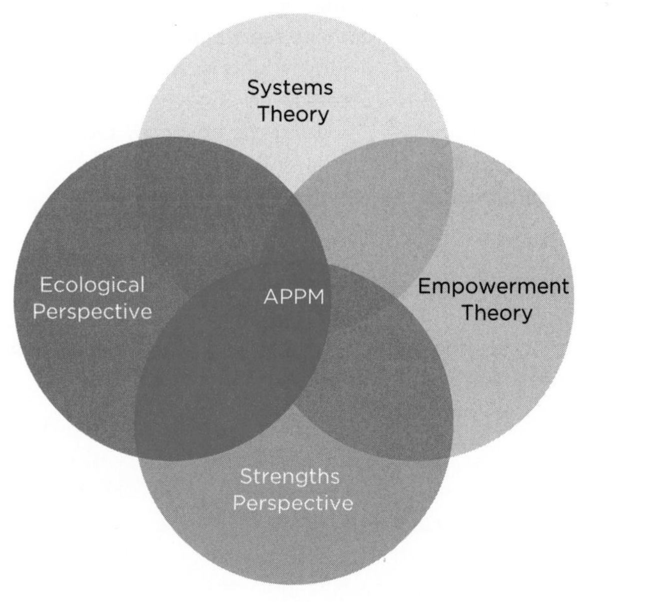


*Source:* Cox, Tice, & Long (2019, p. 67).

Social work activism will continue, in current campaigns like those associated with health-care coverage and gun control, and will likely branch out into new issues and using new strategies. And, although activism may decline when institutionalization or structural change is seen to address social problems, new problems will keep being brought to attention.

The APPM, depicted in Figure 13.4, with its four dynamic, interlocking tenets, highlights the importance activism and advocacy hold within the social work profession (Cox, Tice, & Long, 2019). Considering the APPM allows social workers to assess and evaluate how their practice and policy initiatives address issues related to human rights and social, economic, and environmental justice. By motivating and guiding advocacy, the APPM also provides social workers with guideposts to consider and assess the intersections of diversity and the influence of the four tenets on specific justice issues. For example, environmental justice has an impact on the living conditions of people in their communities while affecting health conditions. Thus, the intent of the APPM is to enhance comprehensive, critical thinking about broad issues that filter down into community-related and individual concerns.

## Advocacy Pertaining to Gun Violence

Marco lives in a city in which gun violence is prevalent. Almost every weekend, at least two people are killed and several others are wounded on the city streets by individuals and gangs with guns. Employed as a social work administrator of a health clinic in the city, Marco sees, on a regular basis, the devastating results of the violence on individuals, families, and communities. Also, he witnesses how the violent acts affect his staff because they often know both the victims and perpetrators.

A long-term advocate for health services, Marco feels the need to extend his community activism and advocacy to address the influence of gun violence on the city's social, economic, and environmental conditions. He has come to see that prevention of gun violence is a human rights issues that must be addressed across levels of government.

Using the advocacy practice and policy model (APPM) and the consumers of the health clinic, how can Marco

**Questions**

1. Gain political access to influence policy development and public education on gun violence and protection?
2. Evaluate how human needs and resources intersect the violence that occurs in the city and the medical needs of victims and perpetrators?
3. Assess what advocacy strategies could be used to educate the general public in the city and state about social and economic factors related to violence, in particular, gun violence?
4. Define the elements of a supportive environment relevant to consumers and staff of the health clinic, victims of violence, and those that perpetrate violence?

## ADVOCACY STRATEGIES FOR HUMAN RIGHTS AND SOCIAL, ECONOMIC, AND ENVIRONMENTAL JUSTICE

Social work **advocacy strategies** are often an ongoing and ever-evolving process. Sometimes they are proactive—with consumers, communities, and organizations working to address issues that have not gained widespread public attention. However, many times strategies are reactive, wherewith consumers, communities, and organizations try to challenge or change issues that negatively affect life conditions.

Listed below is a step-by-step process, adapted from Mahoney (2014), when considering the development of advocacy strategies. It should be noted that advocacy for change depends on much more than just dedicated people working together for a common cause. It is important to develop a deeper understanding of the issue, including research to analyze who has power. Remember, advocacy is about power—who can influence things that matter. Social workers and all others involved in challenging injustices must recognize where the power lies and how to most effectively influence or confront it, as well as the consequences to consumers and others of provoking people in power.

1. Establish goals. Social workers routinely consider who to inform or educate, what policy or legislation needs changing, and the compilation of a list of supporters for future actions.
2. With consumers, it is important to define the criteria and guidelines for the goals and to devise a communication system to keep stakeholders informed of strategies, progress, areas to address, and goal revision.
3. Communication with consumers and advocates is vital to learn how soon they want to be notified of emerging issues and which topics are of the highest interest. Social workers seek knowledge about the investment of consumers in current issues and causes.
4. Social workers seek research and track human rights issues that affect consumers, their communications, and organizations. Research can be saved and shared with consumers using various venues, including social media and public forums.
5. Identifying resources in relationship to financial, technology, and human capital is important. Estimates of

Drew Angerer/Staff/Getty Images

**PHOTO 13.3** Activism takes many forms. Family members of those killed by gun violence attend a news conference to demand action for gun violence on December 6, 2018.

resource and expenditures are valuable as well as tools for automating work and saving time. Social workers become keenly aware of partnerships, affiliates, and internal relationships as well as gaps in resources and possible sources for plugging such holes.

6. The development of messaging and talking points can be key. Drafting sample language for letters and e-mails to be sent to and from consumers and to stakeholders (e.g., elected officials) is often helpful.

   A communication plan for online, offline, grassroots, and grasstops actions should be considered. It is important to consider how many e-mails, which social media channels, and what webpages are needed as well as the appropriateness of an advocacy day, a flash mob, or a press conference. Effectiveness can be enhanced by identifying grassroots advocates, their location, and how to reach them (e.g., online communication, social sites, or offline messaging). Top-level legislative influencers should be identified and considered for prioritization. Advocacy works best when it involves a combination of activities at multiple levels.

7. The training of consumers as advocates on the reasons why addressing an issue is important and how change is possible is a key component. Social workers can explore coaching consumers on the talking points of the advocacy issue and agenda.

*Source:* Adapted from Mahoney, C. (2014). Retrieved from http://www.votility.com/blog/effective-advocacy-strategies-in-9-steps.

Once an advocacy strategy or plan is established, there is a sense of direction and how to move forward in concert with consumers and others invested in addressing the issue. Such planning encourages confidence, and that confidence provides a sense of power and control. The progression of moving from a need to a plan of advocacy action is provided in Table 13.3.

What is important to keep in mind is that promoting change in practice, policy, and power relations requires a systematic and critical approach to planning and monitoring advocacy. More often than not, the pathway to change is not straightforward or immediate. Persistence, creativity, and extensive partnerships are needed to address the challenging issues of justice.

Across the globe, there are various forms of social, economic, and environmental injustices confronting humanity, suitable for political activism involving social workers (see, e.g., Mmatli, 2008). These issues include unemployment, poverty, various forms of inequality and discrimination, homelessness, abuse of human rights, civil conflicts, war, pollution, global warming, and toxic living conditions. Also, Felderhoff, Hoefer, and Watson (2015) suggest that although social workers may be more active in political activism and issues than members

**TABLE 13.3**
Action Steps

| Goal | Action Steps |
|---|---|
| By December 2019, provide the agency with data on consumers' and service providers' views about mental health needs, including the availability of emergency and preventive services, as well as avenues for public education. | By February 2019, the agency's subcommittee (comprising staff and consumers) will design and distribute informed consents from consumers and service providers for surveys on availability of emergency and preventive services, as well as avenues for public education. |
| | By April 2019, the agency's subcommittee will secure informed consent from consumers and service providers to distribute the survey. |
| | By June 2019, the agency's subcommittee will prepare a survey to distribute to consumers and service providers. |
| | By July 2019, the agency's subcommittee will distribute the survey. |
| | By September 2019, the agency's subcommittee will summarize the results and prepare a report. |
| | By November 2019, the chair of the agency's subcommittee will communicate the results of the survey to the agency staff, consumers, elected officials, and the general community. |

*Source:* Adapted from The Community Tool Box of the Center for Community Health and Development at the University of Kansas. Retrieved from https://ctb.ku.edu/en.

of the general public, social workers have room for improvement (e.g., voting, encouraging others to vote, "attending protests, marches, or demonstrations; serving on a local elected or appointed board; and organizing contributions to candidates") (p. 34).

Visit **www.edge.sagepub.com/ticemacro** to help you accomplish your coursework goals in an easy-to-use learning environment

## SUMMARY

Creating opportunities for change and innovation in practice and policy that support human rights and social, economic, and environmental justice requires considerable reflection and thought. It also requires a broad-based understanding of the needs and wants of consumers. A persistent question is, How can social workers use their knowledge, power, and skills in working with consumers to effect change? Also required is optimism regarding human and social potential. Social workers must believe that transformable meaningful change is possible and work from an empowerment and strengths perspective to facilitate participatory and sustainable change. A positive focus not only on the strengths and possibilities that exist in the world but also on the strengths and possibilities of the profession is a much-needed element in the change process.

Much of what was presented in this chapter addresses awareness, critical thinking, and social action to achieve human rights and social, economic, and environmental justice through the advocacy actions as seen in social work practice and policy. Social workers need to be relentless in an attempt to shape society and the distribution of resources according to the social consciousness of the profession.

## TOP 10 KEY CONCEPTS

activism 288
advocacy 287
advocacy strategies 299
historic social work values 286
human rights 288
political leanings 290
power elites 293
principles of justice in social work practice 293
social, economic, and environmental justice 292
strengths perspective 287

## DISCUSSION QUESTIONS

1. Given the current political climate, what areas of activism seem most likely to be successful and why?
2. In reference to Figure 13.1, how would you describe your political beliefs? Please provide examples of why.
3. In your lifetime, how has the power of people influenced a practice, policy, event, or decision? Explain why you think this was the case.
4. As a social worker in a community-based health clinic, you have identified that consumers are interested in information regarding the opioid crisis. However, the clinic's administrator considers the topic to be beyond the purview of the clinic's mission. Using Figure 13.4, explain the steps you would take to gain support for a public education series on the topic.
5. Discuss how the advocacy practice and policy model could be applied to human rights or social, economic, or environmental justice confronting you and your community. What tenet of the model seems most relevant to the issue and why?

## EXERCISES

1. Consider the groups and organizations on your campus and their activities. Are any of their activities geared toward human rights and social, economic, and environmental justice? If, so in what way? If there is no such activism on your campus, please consider why that is the case.
2. Review Table 13.1 and consider what skills you have that could be used in relation to activism activities. Please explain how you came to your decision.
3. Review a national newspaper and list the articles that address human rights and social, economic, and environmental justice. What are the prevailing themes of the articles? Are the themes domestic or international? Is there intersectionality of the themes? What issues do you find to be most urgent and require immediate attention?
4. Throughout the chapter, references are made to "consumers." Please list the

times when you have been a consumer of services and felt as though your needs and wants were recognized. What did you gain from this sense of empowerment and why?

5. Although there are national organizations advocating for changes in gun control, few changes have been made at any level of government. Apply the chapter's context on Mills (1956) to explain why this is the case.

## ONLINE RESOURCES

- National Advocacy Groups (http://www.theseedsnetwork.com/features/advocacy/national-organizations/): A comprehensive listing of national groups dedicated to advocacy on behalf of a particular group or social issue.
- Immigrants Advocate Network (https://www.immigrationadvocates.org/): Provides resources and public education of human rights issues related to immigrants and immigrant communities.
- *Advocacy Handbook for Social Workers* (https://c.ymcdn.com/sites/www.naswnc.org/resource/resmgr/Advocacy/Advocacyhandbook.pdf): Written by Dan Beerman, ACSW, LCSW Professor at North Carolina Agriculture & Technical State University and University of North Carolina–Greensboro Joint Master of Social Work Program. Revisions by Doaw Xiong, BSW, Intern National Association of Social Workers–North Carolina.
- The Advocates for Human Rights (https://www.theadvocatesforhumanrights.org/mechanisms): Monitors and reports abuses to the United Nations (through the Advocates' special consultative status with the United Nations Economic and Security Council) and regional human rights organizations.
- United Nations on Women (http://www.endvawnow.org/en/articles/104-developing-an-advocacy-strategy.html): Defines international advocacy strategies to address issues related to women, including education, employment, health care, and assault. Provides educational information for use in schools and public forums.
- *National Association of Social Workers Social Justice Priorities 2016–2017*. (http://www.socialworkblog.org/wp-content/uploads/NASW-Social-Justice-Priorities-2016-17.pdf): The publication lists the five national social justice priorities the organization is committed to working on in the designated timeframe.

# 14 Assessing Your Macro Practice Skills

## LEARNING OBJECTIVES

After reading this chapter, you will be able to:

1. Appreciate and recognize macro social work as a lifelong calling
2. Engage in self-assessment via reflection and feedback regarding practice abilities and skills with large systems
3. Explore strengths in macro practice roles, including self-advocacy
4. Understand the value of networking, partnerships, and collaboration
5. Articulate the need to stay current through reading

## HIRING PARAPROFESSIONALS

Allyson Crawford is a social work supervisor in a child protection unit at the county cabinet for children and family services. She has eight social workers and four social work assistants under her authority. As caseloads have swelled, the agency has decided to hire additional protective service workers. The cabinet is currently experiencing a fiscal crunch, as the county has not passed new monies for services to children in 5 years. As a result, county administrators have approved the hiring of three new social work assistants in Allyson's unit but no additional social workers.

Allyson, other professional social work administrators, and the agency's consumer council firmly believe that the new hires should be professional social workers. Asking paraprofessionals to assume professional positions and perform professional duties is inappropriate, irresponsible, a possible violation of state law, and arguably unethical. Allyson and others fear the harmful consequences of such action for consumers. Allyson worries she will be held responsible for any incompetent actions of people under her supervision.

Allyson has quickly entered into discussions with members of the consumer council, other supervisors, the unit social workers, members of her local chapter of the National Association of Social Workers (NASW), empathetic administrators at the agency, and multiple others to assess and strategize about her personal power as well as the power of consumers and professionals. To date, most agree that the hiring of new paraprofessionals presents a huge liability issue for Allyson, the organization, the county, and public officials.

## MACRO PRACTICE AS A LIFELONG CALLING

Macro social workers have a lifelong mission to become more knowledgeable of the extent of life challenges and barriers facing consumers requiring services. Comprehending varying levels of vulnerability for economic strain is important to effectively plan and provide services in and to organizations, communities, and society at large. Many of the *Grand Challenges* for social work focus on financial stability and poverty reduction (Long, 2018; Williams, 2016). Therefore, adding a robust poverty research agenda will enhance what macro social work professionals have to offer consumers in larger systems.

The list of human rights, economic, environmental, psychological, and social challenges requiring social work research and macro practice responsiveness is considerable (Williams, 2018). In small and larger systems, two areas requiring research include racial inequality and poverty. Research needs to examine the precise causes that lurk behind racial disparities and racial differences and move beyond race as a mere predictor. For example, research is needed demonstrating best practices for affirmative action and advancement of diversity and inclusion in organizations. Research describing the effects of gentrification and redlining in communities is also needed. Additionally, minimal attention has been given to understanding aspects of poverty across the life span. Knowledge about the percentage of Americans in poverty and how assets and income differ across age, ethnicity, gender, and race in organizations, communities, and society will identify specific needs and population groups at risk and enhance the ability to effectively serve consumers of services through program and policy development. Such research on poverty holds promise for advancing capabilities for both direct and indirect social work practice (Williams, 2018, p. 68).

Disenfranchised consumers and populations are confronted with multiple insecurities, especially financial insecurity. Health-care insecurity continues to put U.S. consumers and populations in the United States in struggles for their life and quality of life. Vulnerable consumers worry about how they will afford good-quality health care as they age and possibly face financial devastation if and when they become ill. Disenfranchised consumers also face physical and social insecurity (e.g., mistrust, stress, and skepticism), which can undermine access to services, housing, or nutrition. Macro social work researchers can focus on how interventions and programs can promote, mitigate, and/or moderate such insecurities and woes.

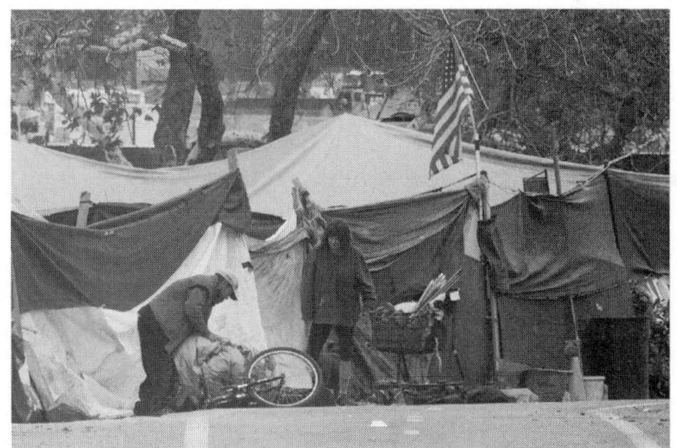
ROBYN BECK/Contributor/Getty Images

**PHOTO 14.1** Macro social work bridges individual needs with national and global issues.

In this section, multiple situations are mentioned wherein quantitative, qualitative, or participatory action research would be useful to proactively respond to issues such as health-care disparities, poverty, or economic, environmental, or social injustices. Responding to these issues will persist and consequently require social workers to maneuver on the macro level. Macro-level interventions require social workers to revisit their "calling" to be advocates for human rights and social justice. Interventions must be assessed and social worker's use of self in engaging with large systems also requires assessment.

## Time to Think 14.1

Consider the case study featuring Allyson and her supervisory work in child and family protection. If you were Allyson, how would you think through the following issues?

1. Identify how the misuse of paraprofessionals as substitutes for professionals may be detrimental to consumers, the agency, and professionals or an asset. How could consumers and professionals work together to document and provide information to substantiate harmful consequences?
2. How does this case example help elucidate the role of power in decision making? Although administrators at the agency appear empathetic concerning the staffing situation, is it not crucial to identify who has the power to rectify the situation? Is there a "power elite" in the county that dictates decisions? How can the strengths of consumers, professionals, and concerned others be used to influence key decision makers? Given those in power, what types of information would be compelling?

## ENGAGING IN SELF-ASSESSMENT

Assessing available resources across consumer systems helps macro social workers and consumers achieve change efforts, choose strategies to promote consumers' strengths and advocacy efforts, and activate environmental resources. To assess one's work and progress, social workers can consider the array of resources systems in the physical and social environment and ask the following: How do they function as resources? What cultural resources support social workers? The **competency self-assessment** found in Table 14.1 can help with the self-assessment process.

### Using Reflection to Assess and Enhance Macro Practice Skills

Engaging in self-assessment is an important endeavor for macro social workers. Table 14.1 provides a tool to assess some competencies that are relevant to work with consumers and large systems.

Through the process of engaging in self-assessment and evaluating competency levels, students completing the items related to the rating scale in Table 14.1 have the opportunity to rate themselves as 1s (beginning competence level), 3s (intermediate competence level), or 5s (advanced competence level). Obviously, students would want to have 5s in each category; however, this result will not likely always occur. For example, in assessing the ability to assess "physical environment" for a consumer-in-environment perspective, a 1 rating may be expected from a newly minted BSW graduate and indicate his or her ability as a macro social worker to merely generally describe the community, workplace, or home of a consumer. A social worker with an admitted "calling to do macro social work," even though he or she has not practiced very long, may be able to reach a 3 rating,

**TABLE 14.1**

Competency Self-Assessment

Use the scale below to rate your achievement level on the concepts or skills presented in this book.

| 1 | 2 | 3 | 4 | 5 |
|---|---|---|---|---|
| I can accurately describe the concept/skill | | I can consistently identify the concept/ skill when analyzing macro practice work | | I can competently employ the concept/skill in my macro practice work |

*Distinguishes macro social work assessment from an advocacy and strengths-based viewpoint:

__________ Recognizes economic, environmental, and social justice in the allocation of resources

__________ Locates resources in complex situations

__________ Collaboration with community and organizational partners (stakeholders)

*Contextualizes assessment from a consumer-in-environment viewpoint by assessing

__________ Organization/community structures

__________ Interactions between consumers and organizations/communities

__________ Thoughts and feelings in the context of organizations and communities

__________ Cultural factors/influences on consumers linking with large systems

__________ Physical environment

__________ Political environment

*Verbalizes how social work tools are relevant to macro practice with large systems:

__________ Group assessment

__________ Organizational assessment, including *force field analysis* (forces helping to achieve or hindering going toward a goal)

__________ Community and neighborhood assessment, including focus groups

*Describes techniques for macro social work professionals to enhance assessment:

__________ Interviews significant consumers/community leaders/administrators/elected politicians

__________ Contacts professionals in organizations, communities, society

__________ Observation (a technique of field research by which an investigator or participant observer studies the life of a group by sharing in its activities)

*Defines procedures for social workers to record documentation:

__________ Documentation formats, including organizational and community policies

__________ Ethical and legal considerations in documentation

*Source:* Modified from page 150, Ex 10.7 in 2009 Pearson Education, Inc. Publishing as Allyn & Bacon Instructor's Manual and Test Bank for *Generalist Social Work Practice: An Empowering Approach*, 6th ed. (Miley, O'Melia, & DuBois, 2009).

thereby signifying this social worker can consistently identify the concepts and skills required to help consumers navigate within and outside of their community, workplace, or home. These social workers may know community leaders, agency directors, and nuances about neighborhoods. And a 5-rating may reveal more advanced competence in assessing the "physical environment" because macro social workers self-rated as 5s are likely able to integrate more interprofessional and intersystem knowledge when evaluating their assessments and interventions. Social workers who rate themselves as 5s may understand "physical environment" broadly and in depth by assessing the built environment, structural environment, and sustainable environment issues.

## Time to Think 14.2

What potential resource systems might you explore to assess how a community system consumer has defined a direction to improve relationships between citizens/consumers of color and the police force? Broadly consider how economic, environmental, and internal community resources might help reach the goal of assessing resource capabilities. Consider further how the community where you live or work offers resources to explore. Think about how cultural assessments reveal how cultural identity affects consumer interactions with larger systems and how cultural elements internalized by consumers contribute to diversity within any social system or larger society.

### Accepting and Using Feedback

When macro social workers use feedback from research, data, reports, leaders, administrators, and so on, they can help consumers reflect on changes needed in their lives and the organizations, communities, and society in which they work and live. Feedback provides a dynamic and continuous stream of communication. Some information fits well with how an organization or a community does something. The system assimilates such feedback, thereby reinforcing the status quo. Contrarily, incompatible information forces the organization or community to change to accommodate discrepancies. Essentially, two forms of feedback exist: (1) information that maintains the current equilibrium and (2) information that induces change toward a new equilibrium.

Macro social workers give both types of **feedback**. They offer reinforcing feedback to maintain existing strengths and advocacy efforts. For example, when a social worker facilitates a townhall meeting and the diverse views of all the consumers in attendance are accepted, such an approach encourages continued respect for diversity. By contrast, social workers might also introduce system-altering feedback to disrupt perplexing patterns or allow for new possibilities. When a social worker confronts a consumer committee about how funding has been unequally allocated, the social worker gives feedback to disrupt the status quo and seek a newer and fairer way to distribute funds. Macro social workers have to offer feedback sensitively as they work toward the desired goals of interest to consumers, organizations and communities.

### Expanding and Improving a Macro Skill Base

Forming empowering, strengths-based, and advocacy-oriented relationships and partnerships with consumers in large systems—such as groups, organizations, and communities—requires an array of skills. Trusting relationships must be built between consumers and organizations, neighborhoods, and communities. Social workers also help consumers increase their power through cohesive development and leadership distribution. In other words, macro social workers facilitate feelings of power in as many consumers in large systems as they can, especially consumers who feel disempowered or oppressed.

Macro social workers make direct connections with consumers and work to accept their contributions, no matter how active they are in partnering with larger systems. The goal of the macro social worker is rather simple—they collaborate with consumers and systems to resolve difficult, challenging, complex, and controversial situations. Social workers require proficiency and competency in resource networking, client advocacy, and facilitating macro-level change within organizations, communities, and society.

## RECOGNIZING STRENGTHS IN MACRO PRACTICE ROLES

This book about macro social work practice has emphasized the importance of an advocacy-based policy-practice model. Hence, Figure 14.1 illustrates the advocacy practice and policy model (APPM) in relation to the range of four domains that require social work professionals to step up and be active advocates. First, in the domain of economic, environmental, and social justice, practitioners are reminded to be vigilant when assessing funding issues and realities within organizations, communities, and society. As well, this domain highlights the need to be involved with decision-making efforts and assess and address public health and resource needs.

Second, in the human needs and rights domain, professionals ought to advocate for equality and the dissipation of health disparities. Social workers can help consumers become active participants on community councils and active advocates for access to health services and housing services. Shelter is a basic human need, so practices such as redlining and gentrification require ongoing monitoring.

Third, macro social workers must promote a supportive environment. In doing so, public health concerns, social movements in the making, and the revitalization of communities and creation of new organizations require vigilance.

Fourth, the domain of political access urges macro social workers to be aware of local, state, and federal policies, laws, and statutes. Understanding the nuances of "who has the power" in organizations and communities, relative to the conservative to liberal continuum or spectrum, helps facilitate and evaluate work with large systems. Figure 14.1 illustrates the application of the advocacy policy-practice model in relation to multiple macro social work practice roles.

**FIGURE 14.1**
Applying the APPM

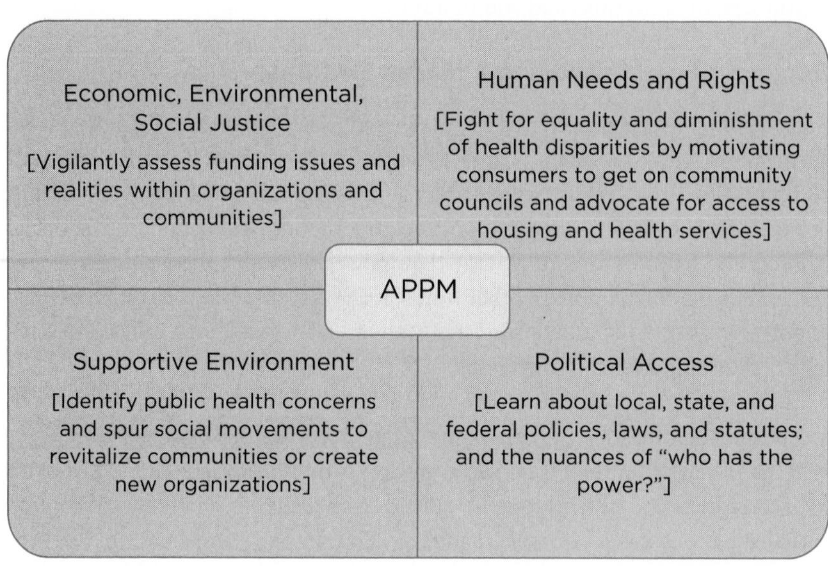

Economic, Environmental, Social Justice
[Vigilantly assess funding issues and realities within organizations and communities]
Human Needs and Rights
[Fight for equality and diminishment of health disparities by motivating consumers to get on community councils and advocate for access to housing and health services]
APPM
Supportive Environment
[Identify public health concerns and spur social movements to revitalize communities or create new organizations]
Political Access
[Learn about local, state, and federal policies, laws, and statutes; and the nuances of "who has the power?"]


Social workers can expand and improve their skill base if cognizant of how to apply the APPM to multiple macro practice roles. Figure 14.2 further illustrates multiple **macro social work roles** and skill sets across organizations, communities, and society. The roles of educator, enabler, mediator, integrator/coordinator, general manager, analyst/evaluator, broker, facilitator, initiator, negotiator, mobilizer, and advocate are foremost in the repository of skills that professionals require. To assess how well to intervene and then evaluate work across levels, the macro social worker must be aware of what steps to take when working with consumers in organizations, communities, and the larger society.

Figures 14.3, 14.4, and 14.5 provide steps to **assessing macro social work** practice. Three important steps are involved in macro social work at the organizational level. For example, when social workers are involved with organizations, during Step 1, they assess the connections the agency or organization has with its wider community, note sociocultural artifacts, and consider possible funding and/or referral sources. During Step 2, the organization's capacity inside requires assessment, such as the following: (1) What leadership style is being used? (2) Which services are provided? (3) How are the programs and structure of the organization? (4) How adequate is the technology being used? and (5) What personnel policies, practices, and procedures are being used? For Step 3, an effective macro social worker will explore the cultural humility and competency levels that exist within the organization by determining the following: (1) How healthy are external relations? (2) How diverse, friendly, and healthy are staff? and (3) How culturally relevant are the available programs and services?

Three important steps are involved in macro social work at the community level, too. For example, when social workers are involved with communities,

**FIGURE 14.2**
Macro Social Work Practitioner Skill Set and Roles

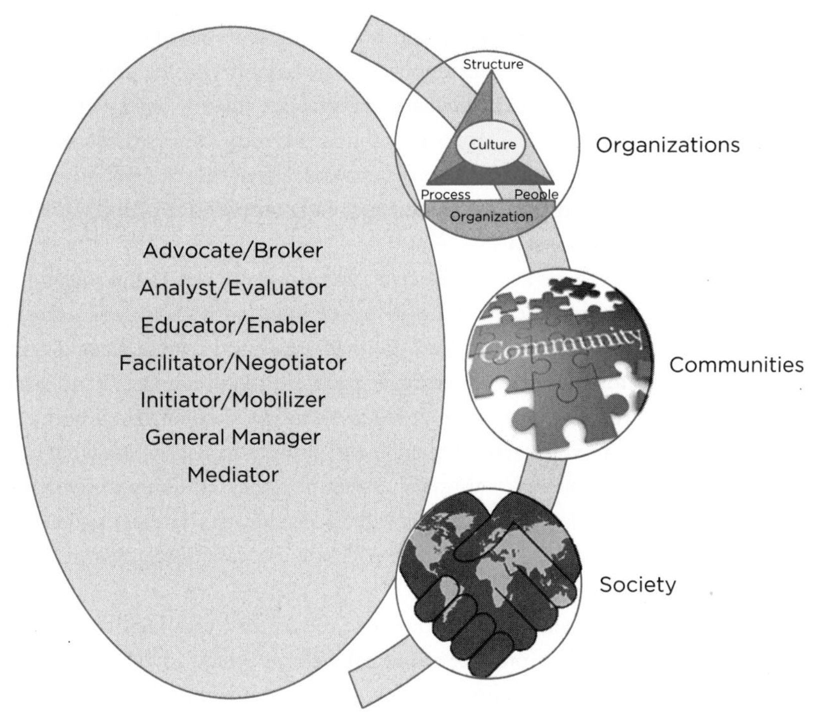


**FIGURE 14.3**
Assessing Macro Social Work With Organizations Framework

Step 1: Examine organization to assess relationships

- Learn about the organization and its environmental relationships
- Identify sociocultural artifacts
- Note funding and referral sources

Step 2: Assess organization's capacity inside

- What leadership and management approaches are used?
- Which programs and services are offered?
- How is the overall structure of the organization and its programs?
- How adequate and functional are technology/technical resources?
- What personnel policies, practices, and procedures exist?

Step 3: Explore cultural humility and competency

- How healthy are external relations?
- How diverse, healthy, and friendly are workers/staff?
- To what extent are programs and services offered culturally relevant and appropriate?

during Step 1, they identify the focal community. This identification involves ascertaining community boundaries, learning the history of the community and its consumers, and collaborating with consumers. During Step 2, the data and information about the community require obtainment. Data about consumers and targeted population needs becomes important, and identifying helpful information about data sources is key. For Step 3, an effective macro social worker will assess assets, capacity, and the structure of a community. They assess such by discerning power sources and assessing differences, strengths, assets, and values. In addition, they assess existing helpful linkages and observe control and influence aspects, as well as available services.

Yet another three steps are involved in macro social work at the societal or global level. For example, when social workers are involved with societies, during Step 1, they must assess economic and political feasibility issues. They do this by understanding how urgently a particular problem requires redress and what resources are important. During Step 2, macro social workers involved with any society must choose an approach for change and simultaneously assess what personnel policy, practice, or policy approaches require consideration and selection. For Step 3, effective macro social workers will discern which strategies and tactics to use. By so doing, they will assess which collaborative tactics are most relevant and consider campaign strategies.

Social workers, in their roles of advocates, educators, and facilitators, may accomplish advocacy policy-practice via social welfare/policy advocacy-oriented organizations, such as health maintenance organizations, neighborhood civic associations, or service club entities like the Rotary, Lions, or Kiwanis clubs or League of Women Voters (Brueggemann, 2014, pp. 304–305). To make social changes or ensure social justice at the community, state, and national levels, as analysts,

**FIGURE 14.4**

Assessing Macro Social Work With Communities Framework

Step 1: Identify focal community

- Ascertain community boundaries
- Learn about the community's history and consumer characteristics
- Collaborate with consumers/focal community population

Step 2: Obtain information and data on community

- Collect data about consumers/targeted population's needs
- Identify helpful information and data sources

Step 3: Assess assets, capacity, and structure

- Discern sources of power and resource availability
- Assess differences, strengths and assets, and values
- Examine service delivery aspects
- Discern existing and helpful linkages
- Observe control and influence aspects, as well as services available

**FIGURE 14.5**
Assessing Macro Social Work With Society/Societies Framework

Step 1: Assess economic and political feasibility

- How urgently must the problem be addressed?
- What resources must be considered?

Step 2: Choose an approach for change

- What personnel policy, practice, or policy approach ought to be selected?

Step 3: Discern which strategies and tactics to use

- Which collaborative strategies and tactics might be best and most relevant?
- What campaign strategies require consideration?

evaluators, or mobilizers, social workers may be involved and seek board membership with a community or nation's political and policy advocacy organizations, activist community organizations, and civil and human rights organizations. As enablers and initiators in social advocacy organizations, social workers can work expeditiously and perhaps bypass formal, unwieldy, and time-consuming political processes by convincing government officials to act in the best interests of consumers who may not have powerful lobbyists or corporate sponsors in their back pockets.

**PHOTO 14.2** Advocacy uses organizations to achieve social justice goals.

The United States has nearly 2 million nonprofit organizations that account for approximately 5% of gross domestic product. By 2052, an estimated $6 trillion will flow directly to social organizations. At the same time, a new generation of business leaders, philanthropists, and social entrepreneurs—including macro social workers—is creating new types of hybrid social enterprises (Brueggemann, 2014, p. 312). Such initiatives often identify creative and innovative ways to link, establish, and develop partnerships between for-profit and nonprofit entities to address consumer, organizational, community, and societal needs and problems. For example, Cincinnati-based grocery giant Kroger has been expanding its unsold-food programs to distribute goods to community foodbanks across the nation. Kroger has also been a longstanding leader for partnering with nonprofit organizations to provide employment for people with developmental challenges.

## ADVOCACY STARTS WITH SELF

Since social work's beginnings, the profession has noted the importance of relationship and **conscious use of self**. Self is a function of relationship with others, and the self is constantly created, maintained, and re-created (Arnd-Caddigan

& Pozzuto, 2008). The qualities of awareness, genuineness, and honesty are significant to building relationships, and the self is a process in interaction. The use of self requires attention to an unpredictable and unfolding process, not simply a narrow focus on particular techniques or outcomes. "Knowing the real self is the pre-condition to using the self in social work," and searching for the "self" sets the foundation for a vibrant, loving, and caring society and facilitates the realization of goals important to the social work profession (Kaushik, 2017, p. 28).

Involvement with research and work with large systems requires social workers to be lifelong learners when it comes to the refinement of macro social work practice skills. While nationally, few Boards of Social Work Examiners include specific continuing education requirements for practice with large systems, these skills are important to advocating for consumers and working effectively with organizations, with communities, and in society. Macro social workers must stay current with research findings, legislation, and administrative and organizational practices. Research-informed practice remains a lifelong requirement for any social worker engaged in macro practice. To summarize a few points from earlier chapters about research (a method of systematic investigation or experimentation), social workers conduct research to test theories about human behavior and the social environment and to document evidence of the effectiveness of intervention strategies. Therefore, basic **research literacy** is required. Macro social workers must know about the research process, research terminology, and concomitant ethical issues. Social workers must critically analyze research studies and conduct formal research themselves for the purpose of program development and policy analysis.

It is worth noting that participation and using the contributions of practicing social workers in various forms of practice-informed research can be challenging. As noted by Rowan, Richardson, and Long (2018), "Examples in social work literature of social workers using practice experiences to inform scientific inquiry are not plentiful, as practitioners are usually positioned as consumers rather than co-producers of research" (p. 15). Furthermore, practice-prompted and informed research manuscripts may face unique scrutiny by reviewers, editorial board members, and editors in the publication review process (Rowan et al., 2018). Indeed, lack of sensitivity toward the publication of research involving new and previously underdocumented population groups and needs could be in part an artifact of an overall lack of appreciation for the potential contributions of practitioner knowledge and wisdom in the research process.

Social workers do indeed consciously use themselves as instruments of change and advocacy. When macro social workers take on a research role with large systems, they must be aware of the pros and cons, advantages and disadvantages between different research approaches, as previously covered—quantitative deductive approach or qualitative inductive approach. Two subsequent sections illustrate how these two approaches flow differently.

## Quantitative vs. Qualitative Research Processes

Earlier chapters covering informing macro practice with research and evaluating macro change elaborated on the logic of scientific inquiry and distinguished between quantitative and qualitative approaches. Macro social workers must be

**FIGURE 14.6**
Quantitative Research Process Flow

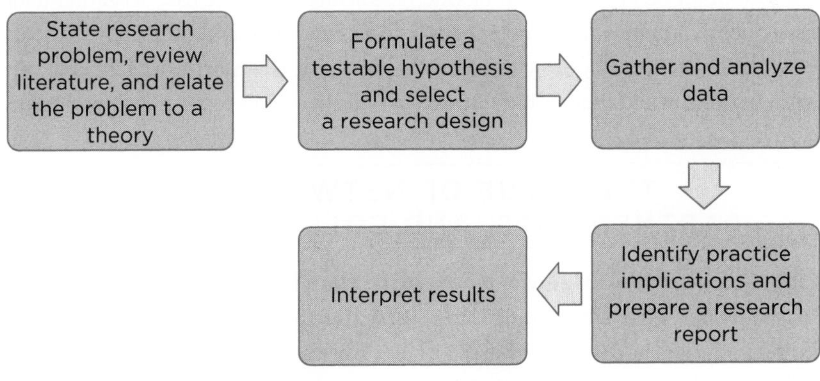


cognizant of research-informed processes, specifically **quantitative and qualitative research process flows**. The flowchart in Figure 14.6 illustrates how researchers wishing to evaluate macro change by using a quantitative approach would proceed. Sometimes a research question or hypothesis about a large system can be easily articulated, and empirical literature can be found to contextualize subsequent research. Once a question or hypothesis is developed, researchers would choose a design and gather data. Data analysis would ensue and results would be interpreted, thereby producing an eventual report for dissemination.

When macro social workers, who are also researchers or evaluators, do not choose to start from a research or hypothesis, they could employ a qualitative research process. This process would not begin with locating existing literature or testing a hypothesis. Rather, researchers using a qualitative approach would be more interested in building theory than testing a theory or hypothesis. Action research, participatory research, grounded theory, and naturalistic inquiry are options such researchers might use. Figure 14.7 shows how data would be collected in raw form. For example, sitting in an agency meeting, attending a community

**FIGURE 14.7**
Qualitative Research Process Flow

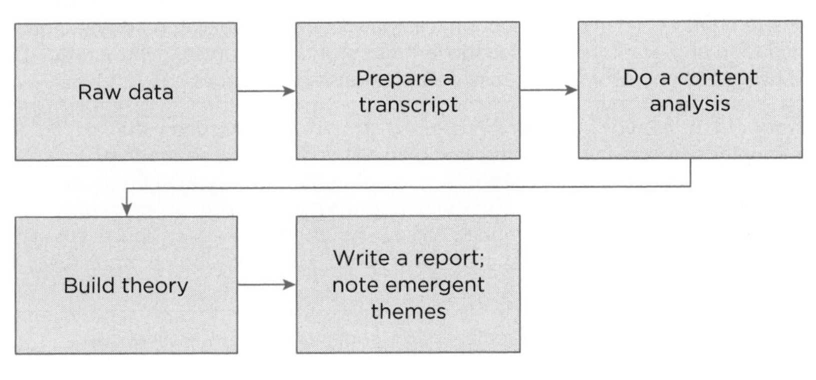

forum, or observing and participating in a social movement might present opportunities to collect data in vivo—in the field, from the ground up. Raw data in the form of notes might be kept, or audio or video recordings could be used to gather data. Subsequently, themes would emerge as data are analyzed, and ultimately, a theory would be built regarding how to proceed. The eventual report would include verbatim word data and themes rather than statistical analyses or simply numeric data.

## THE VALUE OF NETWORKING, PARTNERSHIPS, AND COLLABORATIONS

Table 14.2 illustrates an array of **macro social work functions** with the associated skills and knowledge areas required to work with larger systems. The use of critical thinking, the will and wherewithal to be a healthy leader and administrator, and the ability to realize what you know and what you still need to learn about organizations, communities, and society are part and parcel of being a competent professional social worker. Such a professional who networks, partners, and collaborates will be best prepared to conduct and analyze research, create and run organizations, assess, evaluate and intervene in communities, and be aware of societal trends, movements, policies, and needs.

**TABLE 14.2**
Self-Assessing Macro Social Work Functions and Skills

| Social Work Functions | Skills and Knowledge to Assess |
|---|---|
| Administration | Conventional managerial leadership, federal regulations dealing with administration, classics in administration theory, general vs. social administration, supervision, decision making, budgeting, finance, administering the human side of organizations, functions of the executive, program evaluation, program logic evaluation models |
| Critical thinking | Learning theory, rational problem solving, social change, social thinking, sociocultural premises, using journals and research, theory of social problems, working with groups, social leadership |
| Practice with organizations | History and theory of organizations, basic philanthropy, fundraising and giving, getting started, working with boards and staff, social enterprise development; management, leadership and economics; foundation fundraising resources, foundation and grant information; government funding sources; contracting; writing grants and proposals; grassroots fundraising resources |
| Practice with communities | History of community; community research; social work practice with communities; community building; sociology of community; community theory; communitarianism; modern classics in neighborhood and community organizing, history of community organizing, community organizing: theory and practice; social work community organizing; the Saul Alinsky approach; community organization with specific communities; faith-based community organizing |
| Practice with societies | Social policy, social advocacy, social action, social critique, interest group liberalism, the good society |

Meenaghan, Kilty, Long, and McNutt (2013) pose the following important, reflective questions helpful for social workers contemplating placing research abilities and skills into action:

> Which questions (and whose questions) should be stressed? Which interests are served by which program designs? Who should participate and at what points in designing and studying interventions—creation, collection, interpretation, and so on? (p. 303)

©iStockphoto.com/asiseeit

**PHOTO 14.3**
Social workers are involved in lifelong learning.

## STAY CURRENT THROUGH READING

Social work education does not stop with graduation. **Continuing education** is part of the continuum of social work education, which can include an associate's degree in human services and professional social work education at the undergraduate, graduate, and doctoral levels. Because social work knowledge and skills change and evolve, and state licensing boards require continuing education, macro social workers must keep abreast of changing knowledge and intervention strategies by reading and participating in continuing education. Congress (2012) has cited Rooney's (1988) three levels of continuing education effectiveness:

- Level 1—whether theory and skills are learned
- Level 2—whether social workers are able to practice those skills at the end of their training
- Level 3—whether social workers will practice these skills when they return to their jobs

Social work professionals emphasize the importance of continuing educations for all licensed and credentialed practitioners. Also, keeping abreast of the most recent literature and research in one's area of expertise and scope of practice can be challenging. Fortunately, modern search tools and electronic access to published documents have made scholarly works more readily available. Indeed, one of the very first thoughts for social workers in keeping in touch with best practices should involve a review of literature to capture and read what the most recent research suggests.

This chapter has conceptualized macro social work practice as a lifelong commitment for social workers that requires engaging in competency self-assessments and understanding the utility of research-informed practice. Competency self-assessment tools can be used to assess what further training and education may be required to sharpen macro social work functions, roles, and skills.

Macro social workers are actively involved with organizations, communities, and society at the national and international levels. International social workers may help with economic and community development projects in developing countries through the United Nations or International Red Cross and International Social Services (ISS). Student experiences with the Peace Corps, other service-oriented volunteer corps, and international educational experiences can be very informative and supportive of developing a macro-oriented social work outlook. Macro social workers can also link with social justice and advocacy organizations such as Amnesty International and Human Rights Watch to fight against unjust imprisonment, torture, or other human rights violations (Brueggemann, 2014, p. 437). At the policy level, social workers can help to reduce pollution and end international conflict with the goal of creating a sustainable social and natural environment.

Perhaps a hallmark of international social work is the ability to engage people or consumers no matter where you are. Macro social work, too, is all about learning how to engage people by building trust, developing strengths, stimulating empowerment, and employing advocacy policy-practice. Macro social workers are called to assess and then facilitate the challenge of perceptions, stimulate reflection, encourage sensible decision making, develop and implement plans, and provide training, education, and leadership.



## SUMMARY

Throughout this text, readers have been urged to identify sources of information to help them in their work with large systems and consumers. Macro social workers can acquire much knowledge from collaborating with key informants, case managers, and focus group participants. Also, reviewing case study content, diaries, journals, internal case records, minutes from employee meetings, billing records, and the most recent literature and research can be informative. The advocacy policy and practice model (APPM) can be especially instrumental in guiding macro social workers to use direct observation and learn by participant observation what occurs in community and national forums that can be used to foster change. Macro social work is important work because organizations, communities, and societies are diverse, vary in power structures and technological advancements, and need attention so that economic, environmental, and social justice are continually advocated for.

## TOP 10 KEY CONCEPTS

assessing macro social work 310
competency self-assessment 306
conscious use of self 313
continuing education 317
feedback 308
macro social work functions 316

macro social work roles 310
qualitative research
process flow 315
quantitative research
process flow 315
research literacy 314

## DISCUSSION QUESTIONS

1. What roles might macro social workers commonly assume in the development and promotion of social organizations, especially with micro-oriented employment?
2. In the opening vignette, social worker positions were being replaced by paraprofessionals. Through discussion with classmates, identify several viable macro social work ideas and options to pursue in relationship to this personnel matter. How might your personal and/or professional comfort level be challenged with each idea and option?
3. Macro social work is a field that lauds authentic personal relationships, altruism, compassion, and reciprocal communication. By contrast, modern complex organizations often eliminate altruism and compassion, require nonpersonal relationships, use one-way communication, and rely on depersonalized, quantitative statistics. What ethical dilemmas might occur as social workers inject personal feelings, compassion, and values into an impersonal organizational system? How will you cope with such dilemmas?
4. It is imperative to cite and validate information sources when posing ethical dilemmas involving social justice. Consider how in the opening case study, "caseloads had swelled" at Allyson's agency. What does this mean with regard to the actual number of cases and the severity of issues in the people being served? What types of information would be important to document the need for additional professionals? Remember, this is a child protection agency. (Note: Consider the NASW *Code of Ethics* and your state statutes for protecting children.)

## EXERCISES

1. Ethical statements reflect personal and professional values. Ask the listed professionals to identify the relevant ethical principle for each of the following societal values. How do your findings compare to the ethics for social work practice? What are the similarities between professionals?

| Professions | Lawyer | Physician | Clergy | Psychologist | Banker |
|---|---|---|---|---|---|
| Social justice | | | | | |
| Freedom | | | | | |
| Life orientation | | | | | |
| Privacy | | | | | |
| Individual choice | | | | | |
| Equality | | | | | |

2. Read a national newspaper for several days and collect at least two articles that highlight a professional who has acted in accordance with or in opposition to the rules of professional ethics. Consider the situation, the particular values and ethics involved in the situation, and the actions of the professional. What would you do in a similar situation? Also, review Abramson's (1984) definition of "ethical dilemma":

   An ethical dilemma or moral quandary is one in which there are conflicts and tensions concerning the right and the good, when choosing one course of action will uphold one moral principle while violating another. (p. 129)

3. Go to the following selected organizational resources and learn more about evidence-based practice:
   - Campbell Collaboration
   - Social Care Institute for Excellence
   - SAMHSA Guide to Evidence-Based Practices
   - Swedish Institute for Evidence-Based Practice

## ONLINE RESOURCES

- Business and Human Rights (www.business-humanrights.org)
- Corporate Critic online (www.ethicalconsumer.org)
- Corporate Watch (www.corporatewatch.org)
- Endgame Research Services (www.endgame.org)
- Multinational Monitor (www.multinationalmonitor.org)

# Appendix

## NASW CODE OF ETHICS STANDARDS RELATED TO RESEARCH

**5.02 Evaluation and Research**

(a) Social workers should monitor and evaluate policies, the implementation of programs, and practice interventions.

(b) Social workers should promote and facilitate evaluation and research to contribute to the development of knowledge.

(c) Social workers should critically examine and keep current with emerging knowledge relevant to social work and fully use evaluation and research evidence in their professional practice.

(d) Social workers engaged in evaluation or research should carefully consider possible consequences and should follow guidelines developed for the protection of evaluation and research participants. Appropriate institutional review boards should be consulted.

(e) Social workers engaged in evaluation or research should obtain voluntary and written informed consent from participants, when appropriate, without any implied or actual deprivation or penalty for refusal to participate; without undue inducement to participate; and with due regard for participants' well-being, privacy, and dignity. Informed consent should include information about the nature, extent, and duration of the participation requested and disclosure of the risks and benefits of participation in the research.

(f) When using electronic technology to facilitate evaluation or research, social workers should ensure that participants provide informed consent for the use of such technology. Social workers should assess whether participants are able to use the technology and, when appropriate, offer reasonable alternatives to participate in the evaluation or research.

(g) When evaluation or research participants are incapable of giving informed consent, social workers should provide an appropriate explanation to the participants, obtain the participants' assent to the extent they are able, and obtain written consent from an appropriate proxy.

(h) Social workers should never design or conduct evaluation or research that does not use consent procedures, such as certain forms of naturalistic observation and archival research, unless rigorous and responsible review of the research has found it to be justified because of its prospective scientific, educational, or applied value and unless equally effective alternative procedures that do not involve waiver of consent are not feasible.

(i) Social workers should inform participants of their right to withdraw from evaluation and research at any time without penalty.

(j) Social workers should take appropriate steps to ensure that participants in evaluation and research have access to appropriate supportive services.

(k) Social workers engaged in evaluation or research should protect participants from unwarranted physical or mental distress, harm, danger, or deprivation.

(l) Social workers engaged in the evaluation of services should discuss collected information only for professional purposes and only with people professionally concerned with this information.

(m) Social workers engaged in evaluation or research should ensure the anonymity or confidentiality of participants and of the data obtained from them. Social workers should inform participants of any limits of confidentiality, the measures that will be taken to ensure confidentiality, and when any records containing research data will be destroyed.

*(Continued)*

(Continued)

(n) Social workers who report evaluation and research results should protect participants' confidentiality by omitting identifying information unless proper consent has been obtained authorizing disclosure.

(o) Social workers should report evaluation and research findings accurately. They should not fabricate or falsify results and should take steps to correct any errors later found in published data using standard publication methods.

(p) Social workers engaged in evaluation or research should be alert to and avoid conflicts of interest and dual relationships with participants, should inform participants when a real or potential conflict of interest arises, and should take steps to resolve the issue in a manner that makes participants' interests primary.

(q) Social workers should educate themselves, their students, and their colleagues about responsible research practices.

**6. SOCIAL WORKERS' ETHICAL RESPONSIBILITIES TO THE BROADER SOCIETY**

**6.01 Social Welfare**

Social workers should promote the general welfare of society, from local to global levels, and the development of people, their communities, and their environments. Social workers should advocate for living conditions conducive to the fulfillment of basic human needs and should promote social, economic, political, and cultural values and institutions that are compatible with the realization of social justice.

**6.02 Public Participation**

Social workers should facilitate informed participation by the public in shaping social policies and institutions.

**6.03 Public Emergencies**

Social workers should provide appropriate professional services in public emergencies to the greatest extent possible.

**6.04 Social and Political Action**

(a) Social workers should engage in social and political action that seeks to ensure that all people have equal access to the resources, employment, services, and opportunities they require to meet their basic human needs and to develop fully. Social workers should be aware of the impact of the political arena on practice and should advocate for changes in policy and legislation to improve social conditions in order to meet basic human needs and promote social justice.

(b) Social workers should act to expand choice and opportunity for all people, with special regard for vulnerable, disadvantaged, oppressed, and exploited people and groups.

(c) Social workers should promote conditions that encourage respect for cultural and social diversity within the United States and globally. Social workers should promote policies and practices that demonstrate respect for difference, support the expansion of cultural knowledge and resources, advocate for programs and institutions that demonstrate cultural competence, and promote policies that safeguard the rights of and confirm equity and social justice for all people.

(d) Social workers should act to prevent and eliminate domination of, exploitation of, and discrimination against any person, group, or class on the basis of race, ethnicity, national origin, color, sex, sexual orientation, gender identity or expression, age, marital status, political belief, religion, immigration status, or mental or physical ability.

*Source:* Adapted with permission from *Code of Ethics* (2018, pp. 7–27). Copyright 2018, National Association of Social Workers, Inc., NASW *Code of Ethics*.

# Glossary

**Action research:** Has a specific intent to engage consumers in research as a means of improving social and environmental conditions, and it's another name for participatory research by scientists. A major and explicit goal of consumer participation is to guide or structure research in a manner that leads to practical outcomes for improving circumstances or overcoming oppressive conditions.

**Activism:** Efforts and activities attempting to shift power and resources, as well as encourage large-scale change.

**Administration:** The process of leading, supervising, creating, assessing, directing, and educating groups of individuals to achieve stated objectives and goals in organizations.

**Administrative roles:** Spheres of influence that include leadership, decision making, mediation, collaboration, and political involvement.

**Administrative tasks:** Working as an individual or in a team and engaged in activities of planning, human resource development, supervision, resource allocation, and evaluation.

**Advisory group:** Consumers or professionals who possess special knowledge and expertise by virtue of them being stakeholders in a large system or community and possessing needed knowledge and experience.

**Advocacy:** Representing, defending, and organizing around the needs and rights of individuals, small groups, communities, and organizations through direct interaction and intervention strategies.

**Advocacy practice and policy model (APPM):** A model of social work practice and policy that encompasses systems theory, empowerment theory, an ecological perspective, and a strengths perspective in order to adequately address the needs of individuals, groups, communities, and organizations.

**Advocacy strategies:** Ideas and approaches designed to influence rights, resource allocation, and decision making.

**Assessing macro social work:** To determine and measure the effectiveness of a social work professional's interventions with large systems.

**Asset building:** Investing in building resources, strengths, and the potential of individuals, communities, and organizations.

**Association for Community and Social Administration (ACOSA):** A membership organization formed in 1987 to promote teaching, research, and social work practice in the areas of community organization and social administration.

**Awareness contexts:** Can be thought of a situations or circumstances in which people experience varied degrees of visibility and understanding of what is going on. The ability to know is contingent on one's consciousness and ability to comprehend the meaning of actions, language, gestures, and behavior.

**Broker:** A person who negotiates to build bridges that enhance building consensus, partnerships, and additional resource allocation.

**Built and natural environments:** The space in which the objective and subjective features of the physical environment exist, in which people live, work, and play.

**Campaign strategy:** Directly working with political organizations or communities in implementing a plan or approach to achieve a stated goal.

**Charity Organization Society (COS):** Beginning in the 19th century, Charity Organization Society (COS) was formed to improve the life conditions of people. COS focused on direct factors and causes of poverty at the individual level, including poor work habits and addiction.

**Civil Rights Act of 1964:** This landmark legislation made it illegal to discriminate on the basis of race, gender, ethnicity, color, religion, or national origin. It prompted change in voter registration and voting requirements and made it illegal to discriminate in employment and in public places such as schools, parks, transportation, and restaurants—places we often take for granted today.

***Code of Ethics:*** A code established for all social workers to abide to that addresses social workers' conduct and responsibility, including their responsibility to clients/consumers, colleagues, and employers.

**Collaboration:** Working together in partnership to achieve a stated goal.

**Community:** Groups of people with a common characteristic or interest living together within a larger society.

**Community-based practice:** Emphasizes how communities provide a network of care, support, membership, and celebration.

**Community-based service delivery:** Providing services to consumers where they live and interact with others.

**Community building:** The process of improving a community based on its strengths, not its weaknesses, and the initiative of community members.

**Community development:** A planned approach to improving the standard of living and well-being of disadvantaged populations.

**Community organizing:** Uniting a community through collaborations, partnerships, and organizations to work together to solve social problems.

**Community practice:** The process of understanding and assisting the local community to evaluate, plan, and coordinate efforts to provide for the community's well-being.

**Community well-being:** Any sort of cultural, social, political, and economic conditions a community establishes that will allow for the community to be successful.

**Competency self-assessment:** Any individual development process starts with the employees carrying out a self-assessment of their competencies using their job profile to help identify key areas of focus.

**Comprehensive planning:** Attempts to bring about large-scale change quickly. This is often less practical and can be unrealistic.

**Confidentiality:** The important notion that social workers must keep any information about their consumers private unless there is a need to know.

**Conscious use of self:** A term defining the social worker as the "instrument" purposely used to promote change with client systems. It affects the development of an effective helping relationship, the medium through which change occurs in social work practice. The term describes the skill of purposefully and intentionally using the social worker's motivation and capacity to communicate and interact with others in ways that facilitate change. *Conscious use of self* requires attention to an unpredictable and unfolding process, not simply a narrow focus on particular techniques or outcomes.

**Constructivism:** A paradigm or worldview that posits learning is an active, constructive process.

**Consumer:** A person who is self-directed and engages in social work services.

**Consumer participation:** Mindful and concerted efforts to actively involve the participation, perspectives, and voices of consumers of services in social planning.

**Contest strategy:** A plan that builds on consumer, community, and organizational strengths and resources to gain a desired goal.

**Continuing education:** Training taken by social workers and other professionals who have already completed the formal education required to enter the field. Most professions require employees to keep up with current knowledge by attending specific additional training in a time frame. Continuing Education (CE) is part of the continuum of social work education, which can include an associate degree in human services and professional social work education at the undergraduate, graduate, and doctoral levels.

**Critical thinking:** Identifying and challenging ideas and assumptions and imagining and exploring alternative ways of thinking and acting.

**Cultural competence:** A set of attitudes, skills, behaviors, and policies enabling individuals and organizations to establish effective interpersonal and working relationships that supersede cultural differences.

**Cultural humility:** The ability to maintain an interpersonal stance that is other oriented in relationship to aspects about cultural identity that are most important to that person. It requires an understanding of one's self on a deep level plus a critical examination of power and privilege.

**Cyber activism:** Using the Internet to promote activism and advocacy. This can include raising awareness through social media or creating online communities geared toward the conversation of a specific issue or topic.

**Decision making:** The cognitive process or act of choosing between two or more courses of action.

**Descriptive methods:** Analyze and summarize data to describe what is found in an existing data set.

**Descriptive research:** Collecting data with the intent to better describe social phenomena. When considering specific kinds of social phenomena, consumers of services often find themselves uniquely equipped to facilitate an advanced understanding and description of influences and occurrences.

**Difference:** Condition or degree of being unlike, dissimilar, or diverse. Synonyms for the term *difference* include *dissimilarity, unlikeness, divergence, variation, distinction,* and *discrepancy.*

**Direct practice:** Social work activities that require direct interaction with individuals, families, and small groups. Examples of direct practice include counseling, case management, assessment, and referrals.

**Diversity:** Connotes variety rather than homogeneity. Refers to the range of personnel who represent people from varied backgrounds, cultures, ethnicities, races, viewpoints, and minority populations.

**Dual relationships:** When a person has more than one type of relationship with another person, including personal, business, or formal relationships.

**Dynamic advocacy model:** A model of social work practice and policy cited throughout the book that encompasses systems theory, empowerment theory, an ecological perspective, and a strengths perspective in order to adequately address the needs of individuals, groups, communities, and organizations.

**Eclectic approach:** Sees the value in and draws upon the use of various outlooks and perspectives for use in intervention and practice.

**Ecological perspective:** Acknowledging the biological environment, along with the social environment, as important and intersecting aspects of a person's life.

**E-mail etiquette:** Rules that one must follow regarding sending and receiving e-mails. It could include using a signature at the end of an e-mail or using formal sentences and wording.

**Empowerment:** Focuses on the ability of people to gain control and power over their lives. More specifically, refers to consumers' ability to exert influence over decision-making processes and their desired outcomes, both in service interventions and in regard to the development of policies, programs, and legislation.

**Empowerment approach:** Social work practice that goes beyond providing people with services and resources. It approaches social work as a way to empower and give voice to people to access resources on their own.

**Empowerment theory:** A way of making change by empowering those who are directly affected. Supports the voice, dignity and equality of people. Also see **empowerment.**

**Environmental justice:** Refers to people having the right to clean food, soil, air, water, and green space and the right to influence how humankind interact with each element. Two recurring themes focus upon how degradation is equally shared across all communities and demographic groups and how there is equal inclusion in decision-making processes that evolve into environmentally related actions and policies.

**Ethical dilemma:** A situation in which two or more professional ethical values are in conflict. In an ethical dilemma, any of the possible actions or responses the social worker can make inevitably require mediation, communication, and negotiation.

**Ethical issues:** Dilemmas that occur for administrators that could risk a consumer's private information and involves conflicts of interest or political decisions.

**Ethical principles:** The ethical principles are based on social work's core values of service, social justice, dignity and worth of the person, importance of human relationships, integrity, and competence.

**Ethical standards:** Rules intended to generate trust, good behavior, equality, dignity, truthfulness, fairness, and kindness.

**Evaluation research:** Gives researchers the ability to weigh the successes and limitations associated with social programs and policies.

**Evidence-based practice:** The integration of evidence into social work practice to create services that best cater to clients' needs.

**Explanatory research:** Examines the causes and effects of social phenomena, as establishing causality, and involves addressing three important prerequisites—establishing that the factors under consideration are correlated (change together), determining time order (the causal factor occurs prior to the outcome factor), and accounting for other factors that could be influencing the outcome factor.

**Explicit bias:** Refers to people's conscious attitudes and beliefs about a group or person.

**Exploratory research:** The primary focus is on formulating or refining definitions of actions, concepts, conditions, and issues. Without consumer insight, the sense of discovery in exploratory research is often compromised.

**Facilitator:** Anyone who brings people together, builds consensus, and acts to help a process achieve goals.

**Feedback:** Transmitting information about the results of an action. This permits an objective evaluation of the action's effectiveness. It permits modifications for the action to increase likelihood of success. Feedback provides a dynamic and continuous stream of communication.

**Focus group:** A form of survey research called group-depth interviews because they are like in-depth interviews with a number of people at the same time.

**Formal organizations:** Have a definitive structure and an established decision-making process. It is easy to identify membership and the chain of command and authority in a formal organization.

**For-profit organization:** Companies and businesses that charge people or government agencies for services and products in order to acquire and accumulate profit.

**Geographic communities:** Groups of people living in a defined geographic location.

**Grand Challenges for Social Work:** Represent a dynamic social agenda, focused on improving individual and family well-being, strengthening the social fabric, and helping create a more just society.

**Grounded research:** An inductive process where conceptual distinctions, hypothesis, and theory formulations are derived from data. From a grounded researcher's perspective, important insight for decision making in research comes from "grounded" sources—the experiences and perceptions of humans (e.g., consumers) in everyday life.

**Historic social work values:** Values that imply that people have the right to be respected and that social workers should not discriminate against people and communities because of race, ethnicity, gender, sexual orientation, religion, country of origin, or socioeconomic class.

**Holistic assessment:** Evaluating and collecting data on a situation or problem from a multidimensional perspective.

**Human rights:** Opportunities, liberties, and capabilities deemed to be necessarily available for all humans.

**Implicit bias:** Refers to the stereotypes or attitudes that affect humans' understanding, actions, and decisions in an unconscious manner.

**Improvement team:** A group or committee of consumers of services to discuss improvement ideas at an organization (e.g., social service agency).

**Inclusion:** Bringing together and harnessing diverse forces and resources in a beneficial way. It is commonly the practice of diversity by creating an environment of respect, involvement, connection. It combines involvement and empowerment, where the inherent worth and dignity of all people are recognized.

**Incremental planning:** Involves smaller step-by-step changes that will occur over an extended time period.

**Indirect practice:** Social work activities that indirectly affect individuals, families and small groups, groups, and communities and organizations. Examples of indirect practice include policy analysis, advocacy, community action, and development and management of services.

**Inferential methods:** Analyze and summarize data to make estimates about a larger body of data.

**Influencing politics:** Activities, means, and ways used to sway and affect policy formation and development.

**Informal organizations:** Can simply be a fluid group of people with similar needs or interests who come together to solve a problem (a block club, neighbors who exchange childcare, volunteers who maintain a food pantry, etc.).

**Informed consent:** Consent given with full knowledge of potential risks and benefits before information is given or released.

**Inputs:** Include resources such as money and people. These inputs come through *processes* in a coordinated fashion to achieve the goals established for the organization.

**Inreach:** Refers to a conscious, concerted, and active process of reaching or tapping into consumer groups, organizations, and associations for participation in social planning.

**Institutional change:** Encompasses actions and activities in the planning process directed at creating macro-level change (e.g., program development, policy formation, and legislative initiatives).

**Interprofessional practice:** Where professionals from a variety of disciplines work together in a collaborative fashion to address client needs.

**Intersectionality:** The interconnected nature of social categorizations (e.g., class, gender, race) regarded as creating overlapping and interdependent systems of discrimination or disadvantage.

**Intersectionality of technological innovations:** Addressing the diversity between technological inventions, including which communities have access to them and why.

**Invisible diversity traits:** Invisible traits of a person that could connote his or her identity. Examples include thinking styles, education, and beliefs.

**Legislative process:** The basic process and steps of how social policies and legislation are introduced and passed, recognizing how individuals and groups of people influence legislative enactment.

**Lobbying:** The process and activities associated with influencing legislation and policies.

**Lobbyist:** A person who strategically works with legislators to influence policy making.

**Locality development:** An aspect of macro practice that involves working at the community level with members of the community who are directly affected and involved in all change efforts.

**Macro social work functions:** Practical roles social work professionals engage in to facilitate the healthy well-being of organizations, communities, and society.

**Macro social work practice:** Approaching the practice of social work on a larger scale that often involves communities, organizations, and national and international issues. Macro social work encompasses practices such as social work research, community-based education initiatives, program development for communities, program evaluation, policy analysis and advocacy, nonprofit administration and leadership, and organizational development.

**Macro social work roles:** The practical ways social workers assume to improve the functioning of large systems.

**Marketing:** In human services, this term refers to comprehensive approaches examining consumer strengths and discernment in order to identify and promote ways of moving forward in responding to the hopes and needs of consumers.

**Mary Richmond (1861–1928):** A social work practitioner, teacher, and theoretician who formulated the first comprehensive statement of principles of direct social work practice. Richmond founded Charity Organizations. She also wrote the first social work book, *Social Diagnosis*, in 1917.

**Measurement:** The process of describing abstract concepts in terms of specific indicators by the assignment of numbers or other symbols to these indicants, in accordance with rules.

**Mediating structures:** Institutions that serve as a buffer in between individuals and larger institutions, organizations, or communities.

**Mediator:** A go-between or a buffer in an argument who seeks conflict resolution by acknowledging and bridging differing positions.

**#MeToo movement:** Starting on social media as a viral post on Twitter, an international movement against sexual harassment and sexual assault.

**Mission:** A stated overall purpose of an organization. A mission statement constitutes a summary of the current activities and philosophical premises surrounding the work of the organization. The mission statement describes why the agency is important, who is served, and the reason for the agency's existence. A well-written mission statement reflects the unique identity and distinct attributes (competencies) of the agency and allows the reader to differentiate this agency from other, similar organizations.

**Mutual-aid groups:** Groups of people who work together to develop supportive and trustworthy relationships, identify and use strengths, and/or develop new ones in order to meet individual and/or collective goals.

**National Association of Social Workers (NASW):** The national organization that represents social workers.

**NIMBY phenomenon:** An acronym for "not in my backyard," which captures the sentiment of community members to thwart the implementation of programs and policies promoting the rights of consumers of services in their specific community.

**Nonplace communities:** Based on associations and affiliations rather than a geographic location.

**Nonprofit organizations:** Private organizations granted special tax status and designation, often receiving and spending funds to address the organization's mission-driven needs involving specified population groups.

**Online advocacy:** Using electronic communication technologies such as social media, e-mail, and blogs for various forms of activism and advocacy to enable large and/or specific audiences to promote change.

**Open systems:** Systems that both give to and draw from elements external to themselves.

**Organization:** A group of people intentionally organized to accomplish a common goal or set of goals.

**Organizational change potential:** The attempt to gauge and assess the potential for change in an organization.

**Organizational culture:** Involves a sense of organizational identity involving assumptions and values that influence decision making, actions, and communication in the organization.

**Organization developer:** A role that facilitates organizational improvement and change, particularly through information and feedback from key constituent groups and stakeholders.

**Organizational development:** Efforts to improve and enhance the effectiveness of an organization.

**Organizational politics:** Recognizes the conflict and debate within organizations in attempts to gain power and control.

**Outputs:** Are tangible results produced by the processes in the system such as services for consumers.

**Participatory research:** The process whereby all participants (especially consumers) are afforded opportunities to reflect on programs, projects, and policies; the mission and aims of the organization; and their own and others' involvement in change efforts.

**Person-in-environment:** This perspective highlights the importance of understanding an individual and individual behavior in relationship to the environmental context in which that person lives and acts.

**Policy analysis framework:** An organized and structured set of concepts and ideas to analyze and break down policies and the process of policy formation and development.

**Policy and legislative analyses:** An evaluation of laws, statutes, and regulations important to understanding sociopolitical issues.

**Policy practice skills:** The capabilities placed into action to influence policies, legislation, politicians, and policymakers.

**Political access:** Building means and the ability to communicate with and approach politicians to influence and effect social change.

**Political Action for Candidate Election (PACE):** Part of the National Association of Social Workers (NASW), PACE is a political action committee that supports candidates from any party who support NASW's policy agenda.

**Political leanings:** Often described in terms of left and right positioning. Broadly speaking, the right is thought to be conservative and in keeping with a capitalist system of government. In contrast, the left is described as more progressive in ideology with leanings toward socialism.

**Political power:** Strategies, organizations, and actions that focus on influencing policy development and implementation.

**Populations-at-risk:** Populations with access and functional needs that may interfere with their ability to access or receive social services.

**Power elite:** A term coined by C. Wright Mills referencing a relatively small number of people who control the needed resources in a society and exercise instrumental roles and influence over entities such as the government, military, and corporations.

**Power imbalances:** The disproportion of power between workers and service users stems from the unethical uses of power based on social class, gender, race, sexualities, and ability and needs to be reflected on by the social work professional.

**Pretest:** A preliminary application of the data-gathering technique to assess the adequacy of that technique.

**Principles of justice in social work practice:** Reflect philosophical frameworks.

**Privacy:** The act of secluding oneself or specific information about oneself shared through interpersonal communication or social media.

**Private agencies:** Are funded and supported by private monies (e.g., donations and contributions) and typically focus on smaller, targeted populations groups and services that are consistent with the mission and identity of the funding source(s).

**Private trouble:** An issue or problem that is dealt with privately. This term is often considered more of an individual issue.

**Problem-centered focus:** This approach emphasizes the identification and statement of consumer problems and deficits when considering assessment and intervention models for change.

**Professional use of self:** Social workers develop a professional identity based on their education and training to act through a sense of self as a profession in accordance with the profession's Code of Ethics.

**Program evaluation:** Analyzing social work programs and practices as a way to assess and determine effectiveness and goal attainment.

**Program monitoring:** Measures the extent to which a program reaches its target population with the intended interventions, and consumer input and feedback are essential components.

**Public agencies:** Are typically funded and supported through public, taxpayer dollars and often implement a wide range of programs serving a large number of consumers. Support and policies are often dictated by governmental mandates and laws.

**Public issue:** An issue or crisis that involves the public or that is viewable to the public as a whole.

**Public organizations:** Government agencies typically serving a large number of people with various needs.

**Qualitative analysis:** Describes, evaluates, and explains phenomena and endeavors to understand by generalizing beyond the data to more abstract and general concepts or theories, people, groups, or organizations.

**Qualitative research:** Research that focuses on data in the form of words, pictures, descriptions, or narratives.

**Qualitative research process flow:** Dynamic assessment and evaluation strategy used by social work researchers to collect, analyze, and interpret number data to inform policy practice.

**Quantitative analysis:** A technique to understand behavior by using math or statistics, measurement, and research. Used to represent a particular reality in terms of a numerical value, macro social work researchers may use such analyses for measurement, performance evaluation, or valuation of an organization's productivity and effectiveness.

**Quantitative research:** Research that uses numbers, counts, and measures of things.

**Quantitative research process flow:** Dynamic assessment and evaluation strategy used by social work researchers to collect, analyze, and interpret word data to inform policy practice.

**Research literacy:** Ability to access, interpret, and critically evaluate primary literature

**Research team:** The backgrounds, expertise, and predispositions of people on a research team will have a powerful effect on the research process and subsequent findings. The team approach extends to consumers, embraces diversity of person and thought, and offers a mechanism for critical reflection and contemplation. This allows for the experiences and awareness of consumers to come forward in evaluating the effect, or potential effect(s), of large-scale social change.

**Roles for social workers in community practice:** Social workers work directly with individuals and small groups, assessing their needs and referring them to the appropriate resource within the community.

**Self-help groups:** Also known as mutual aid societies, they are founded by people with common or similar problems (e.g., alcoholism, divorce, health challenges, interpersonal violence) to provide help and support to members of the group.

**Settlement houses:** One of the most influential organizations in the history of American social welfare, settlement houses, such as Addams's Hull House, were houses where residents learned and observed first-hand from members of the community that the house was located in.

**Social action:** Emphasizes collective empowerment taken by an individual or group to make real change within a community or organization.

**Social advocacy:** Involves forming alliances with advocacy organizations and consumer groups to enhance capacity and make a difference in the policy arena.

**Social, economic, and environmental justice:** A set of moral principles that encompass equal and equitable opportunities for all individuals in order for them to live their best life.

**Social entrepreneur:** An individual who is instrumental in facilitating the creation of a new social service organization.

**Social environments:** Acknowledges importance of individuals, families, groups, organizations, communities, and society and people's homes and financial resources, as well as the laws and expectations that govern social behaviors.

**Social-historical analyses:** Evaluation of all possible future costs and benefits of one or more intervention plan that considers historical events linked to a community's social well-being.

**Social justice:** A value of social work that maintains that all people deserve and should have access to the same rights and resources.

**Social media:** Websites and applications that enable users to create and share content or to participate in social networking.

**Social movements:** Movements in communities and society that have resulted in significant increases in political power, legal rights, government resources, and in some cases enhanced socioeconomic status for consumers who were previously marginalized.

**Social networking:** Using social media to connect and interact with others.

**Social planning:** The application of problem-solving techniques and data-driven methodologies to creating, developing, integrating, and delivering human services.

**Social policy:** Often viewed as a statement of what ought to be, it defines what services will be delivered and for how long, who the consumers are, and what roles social workers will assume.

**Social systems:** Recognizes groups of organized people and recognizes the importance of formal, informal, and societal systems in our lives.

**Social work values:** Part of the social work *Code of Ethics,* the core values of the social work profession include service, social justice, dignity and worth of the individual, importance and centrality of human relationships, integrity, and competence.

**Society for Social Work Research (SSWR):** Founded in 1994 as an independent organization dedicated to the advancement of social work research. SSWR works collaboratively with other organizations and groups, including faculty in schools of social work, master's/doctoral students, and research staff in public and private agencies who are committed to improving support for research among social workers.

**Strategic planning:** An activity typically associated with community practice, community organizing, and leadership in human services. People collectively explore assets and areas for improvement, development of plans of action, and the evaluation of the effectiveness of policies and programs.

**Strengths:** A range of talents that can be used to one's advantage.

**Strengths perspective:** A way of practicing social work by acknowledging the strengths, skills, ideas, and possibilities of all consumers.

**Supervision:** Provides direction, education, feedback, and support while acknowledging successful achievement in tasks and goals.

**Supportive environment:** Relies on a focus on human relationships and the dignity and worth of individuals.

**Surveys:** Collection of data by questioning members/consumers in a population.

**Sustainable development:** It involves long-term thinking when examining programs and services designed to meet the needs and concerns of consumers.

**SWOT analysis:** A popular approach to structure strategic planning emphasizing the strengths, weaknesses, opportunities, and threats for a social unit (e.g., organization or community).

**Systems theory:** Used by social workers to understand problems within human systems and to conceptualize a process of change to address them in a holistic fashion. Recognizes the interconnectedness of human behavior and physical and mental wellness in the context of the environment.

**Task environment:** When examining how an organization relates to its external environment, an examination of important relationships with funding sources, collaborators, competitors, regulators, consumers, and the general public takes place.

**Theoretical foundation of the APPM:** Incorporates systems theory, empowerment theory, strengths perspective, and an ecological perspective to frame the model for effective social work practice and policy.

**Thinking politically:** Recognizing that policies come about as a result of political processes, thought and analysis of the politics of social welfare policy are needed as well as how to engage consumers of services in the policy development process.

**Transactions:** Communications, both positive and negative, with others in the environment. These are used to foster dialogue and collaboration to strengthen support systems.

**Transformational politics:** Conveys the idea that systems, albeit organizations, communities, or society, require courage, creativity, and vision to chart a course and focus on a future that is empowering for all.

**Unit of analysis:** The specific element or object whose characteristics are going to be described or explained, and it is the data researchers collect.

**Universal Internet:** The notion that access to the Internet is a basic right that everyone should have worldwide.

**Using strengths in policy practice:** Identifying and creating opportunities that nurture the growth and capabilities of people in their environments for policy formation and development.

**Value base:** Involves a range of beliefs and standards that shape how one views appropriate behaviors and action.

**Visible diversity traits:** Visible traits of a person that could connote his or her identity. Examples include hair color, skin color, ways of dressing or acting, and so on.

**Vision:** An image of how an organization should be working (functioning). A vision statement is a future-oriented document that is aspirational in nature. It identifies where the agency *wants* to be. Much like a compass, the vision statement serves as a guide to direct planning, organizational activities, and decision making. The vision statement can be used to show the way for organizational changes and program development.

# References

## Chapter 1


Abramovitz, M. (1989). *Regulating the lives of women: Social welfare policy from colonial times to the present.* Boston, MA: South End.

Axinn, J., & Levin, H. (1975). *Welfare: A history of the American response to need.* New York, NY: Dodd, Mead.

Azzopardi, C., & McNeill, T. (2016). From cultural competence to cultural consciousness: Transforming to a critical approach to working across differences in social work. *Journal of Ethnic & Cultural Diversity in Social Work, 25*(4), 282–299.

Cancian, M. (2001). Rhetoric and reality of work-based welfare reform. *Social Work, 46,* 309–314.

Council on Social Work Education. (2015). Educational Policy and Accreditation Standards (EPAS). Retrieved from http://www.cswe.org/getattachment/Accreditation/Standards-and-Policies/2015-EPAS/2015EPASandGlossary.pdf.aspx

Cox, L. E., Tice, C. J., & Long, D. D. (2019). *Introduction to social work: An advocacy-based profession* (2nd ed.). Thousand Oaks, CA: Sage.

Federico, R. C. (1973). *The social welfare institution.* Lexington, MA: D. C. Heath.

Friedlander, W. A. (1976). *Concepts and methods of social work.* Englewood Cliffs, NJ: Prentice Hall.

Garvin, C. D., & Cox, F. M. (1995). A history of community organizing since the Civil War with special reference to oppressed communities. In J. Rothman, J. Erlich, & J. Tropman (Eds.), *Strategies of community intervention.* Itasca, IL: F. E. Peacock.

Garvin, C. D., & Tropman, J. E. (1992). *Social work in contemporary society.* Englewood Cliffs, NJ: Prentice Hall.

Glisson, C. A. (1994). Should social work take greater leadership in research on total systems of service? Yes. In W. Hudson & P. Nurius (Eds.), *Controversial issues in social work research.* Boston, MA: Allyn & Bacon.

Harrington, M. (1962). *The other America: Poverty in the United States.* New York, NY: Penguin.

Haynes, K. S., & Holmes, K. A. (1994). *Invitation to social work.* New York, NY: Longman.

Hill, K. M., Erickson, C. L., Donaldson, L. P., Fogel, S. J., & Ferguson, S. M. (2017). Perceptions of macro social work education: An exploratory study of educators and practitioners. *Advances in Social Work, 18*(2), 522–542.

Hollis, F. (1972). *Casework: A psychosocial therapy.* New York, NY: Random House.

Johnson, Y. M. (1999). Indirect work: Social work's uncelebrated strength. *Social Work, 44,* 323–334.

Long, D. D. (2000). Welfare reform: A social work perspective for assessing success. *Journal of Sociology and Social Welfare, 27,* 61–78.

McMillen, J. C. (1999). Better for it: How people benefit from adversity. *Social Work, 44,* 455–468.

Mellinger, M. (2017). What drives advocacy? An exploration of value, mission and relationships. *Journal of Policy Practice, 16*(2), 145–165.

National Association of Social Workers. (2017). *Code of ethics.* Washington, DC: NASW Press. Retrieved from https://www.socialworkers.org/About/Ethics

Perlman, H. H. (1957). *Social casework: A problem-solving process.* Chicago, IL: University of Chicago Press.

Perlman, R., & Gurin, A. (1972). *Community organization and planning.* New York, NY: John Wiley.

Pierce, D. (1989). *Social work and society: An introduction.* New York, NY: Longman.

Piven, F. F., & Cloward, R. A. (1982). *The new class war: Reagan's attack on the welfare state and its consequences.* New York, NY: Pantheon.

Reisch, M. (2016). Why macro practice matters. *Journal of Social Work Education, 52*(3), 258–268.

Reisch, M., & Gorin, S. H. (2001). Nature of work and future of the social work profession. *Social Work, 46,* 9–19.

Richmond, M. E. (1917). *Social diagnosis.* New York, NY: Russell Sage Foundation.

Roberts, R. W., & Northen, H. (1976). *Theories of social work with groups.* New York, NY: Columbia University Press.

Romanyshyn, J. M. (1971). *Social welfare: Charity to justice.* New York, NY: Random House.

Rothenberg, P. S. (1998). *Race, class, and gender in the United States: An integrated study*. New York, NY: St. Martin's.

Rothman, J. (1964). An analysis of goals and roles in community organization practice. *Social Work, 9*, 24–31.

Rothman, J. (1974). *Planning and organizing for social change: Action principles from social science research*. New York, NY: Columbia University Press.

Rothman, J. (1995). Approaches to community intervention. In J. Rothman, J. Erlich, & J. Tropman (Eds.), *Strategies of community intervention*. Itasca, IL: F. E. Peacock.

Rothman, J., Erlich, J. L., & Teresa, J. G. (1976). *Promoting innovation and change in organizations and communities*. New York, NY: John Wiley.

Suppes, M. A., & Wells, C. C. (2003). *The social work experience: An introduction to social work and social welfare*. Boston, MA: McGraw-Hill.

Trattner, W. I. (1989). *From poor law to welfare state: A history of social welfare in America*. New York, NY: Free Press.

Weil, M. (1996). Model development in community practice: An historical perspective. *Journal of Community Practice, 3*(3–4). Retrieved from https://doi.org/10.1300/J125v03n03_02

Williams, D. J. (2016). The future of effective social work practice: Broadening multidisciplinary collaboration and increasing flexibility. *Social Work, 61*(4), 363–365.

## Chapter 2

Austin, M. J., Anthony, E. K., Knee, R. T. & Mathias, J. (2016). Revisiting the relationship between micro and macro social work practice. *Families in Society: The Journal of Contemporary Social Services, 97*(4), 270–277.

Blundo, R. (2001). Learning strengths-based practice: Challenging our personal and professional frames. *Families in Society: The Journal of Contemporary Human Services, 82*, 296–304.

Bronfenbrenner, V. (1979). *The ecology of human development*. Cambridge, MA: Harvard University Press.

Brueggemann, W. G. (1996). *The practice of macro social work*. Chicago, IL: Nelson-Hall.

Chapin, R. K. (1995). Social policy development: The strengths perspective. *Social Work, 40*, 506–514.

Compton, B. A., & Galaway, B. (1994). *Social work process*. Pacific Grove, CA: Brooks/Cole.

Cowger, C. (1994). Assessing client strengths: Clinical assessment for client empowerment. *Social Work, 39*, 262–268.

Cox, L. E., Tice, C. J. & Long, D. D. (2019). *Introduction to social work: An advocacy-based profession* (2nd ed.). Thousand Oaks, CA: Sage.

Donaldson, L. P., Hill, K., Ferguson, S., Fogel, S., & Erickson, C. (2014). Contemporary social work licensure: Implications for macro social work practice and education. *Social Work, 59*(1), 52–61.

Ezell, M., Chernesky, R., & Healy, L. (2004). The learning climate for administration students. *Administration in Social Work, 28*, 57–76.

Franklin, C., & Jordan, C. (1992). Teaching students to perform assessment. *Journal of Social Work Education, 28*, 222–241.

Germain, C. (1979). *Social work practice: People and environments*. New York, NY: Columbia University Press.

Germain, C. (1991). *Human behavior in the social environment*. New York, NY: Columbia University Press.

Germain, C., & Gitterman, A. (1980). *The life model of social work practice*. New York, NY: Columbia University Press.

Graybeal, C. (2001). Strengths-based social work assessment: Transforming the dominant paradigm. *Families in Society: The Journal of Contemporary Human Services, 82*, 233–242.

Gutheil, I. (1992). Considering the physical environment: An essential component of good practice. *Social Work, 37*, 391–396.

Gutierrez, L. M. (1995). Understanding the empowerment process: Does consciousness make a difference? *Social Work Research, 19*(4), 220–237.

Hepworth, D., & Larsen, J. A. (1990). *Direct social work practice: Theory and skills* (3rd ed.). Pacific Grove, CA: Brooks/Cole.

Hoefer, R. (2012). *Advocacy practice for social justice*. Chicago, IL: Lyceum Books, Inc.

Kirst-Ashman, K. K., & Hull, G. (1999). *Understanding generalist practice*. Chicago, IL: Nelson-Hall.

Kirst-Ashman, K. K., & Hull, G. (2001). *Macro skills workbook: A generalist approach*. Pacific Grove, CA: Brooks/Cole.

Kretzmann, J. P., & McKnight, J. L. (1993). *Building communities from the inside out: Toward finding and mobilizing a community's assets*. Evanston, IL: Northwestern University Center for Urban Affairs and Policy Research.

Landon, P. (1999). *Generalist social work practice.* Dubuque, IA: Eddie Bowers.

Long, D. D., & Rosen, I. (2017). Social work and optometry: Interprofessional practice revisited. *Health and Social Work, 42,* 117–120.

Magnusson, D., & Allen, V. L. (1983). *Human development: An interactional perspective.* New York, NY: Academic Press.

McBeath, B. (2016). Re-envisioning macro social work practice. *Families in Society: The Journal of Contemporary Social Services, 97*(1), 5–14.

Miley, K. K., O'Melia, M., & DuBois, B. (2001). *Generalist social work practice: An empowering approach.* Boston, MA: Allyn & Bacon.

Payne, M. (1997). *Modern social work theory* (J. Campling, Consulting Ed.). Chicago, IL: Lyceum Books.

Pincus, A., & Minahon, A. (1973). *Social work practice: Model and method.* Itasca, IL: F. E. Peacock.

Pritzker, S., & Applewhite, S. R. (2015). Going "Macro": Exploring the careers of macro practitioners. *Social Work, 60*(3), 191–199.

Rapport, J. (1990). In praise of the paradox: A social policy of empowerment over prevention. *American Journal of Community Psychology, 9,* 1–25.

Rees, S. (1991). *Achieving power.* Sydney, Australia: Allen & Unwin.

Reynolds, B. (1951). *Social work and social living: Explorations in philosophy and practice.* Silver Springs, MD: National Association of Social Workers.

Rodwell, M. (1987). Naturalistic inquiry: An alternative model for social work assessment. *Social Service Review, 61,* 231–246.

Rothman, J. (2012). *Education for macro intervention: A survey of problems and prospects.* Unpublished manuscript, Association for Community Organization and Social Administration, Lynwood, IL.

Saleebey, D. (1992). *The strength perspective in social work practice.* New York, NY: Longman.

Saleebey, D. (1996). The strengths perspective in social work practice: Extensions and cautions. *Social Work, 41,* 296–305.

Saleebey, D. (1997). *The strength perspective in social work practice.* New York, NY: Longman.

Saleebey, D. (2006). *The strength perspective on social work practice* (4th ed.). Boston, MA: Allyn & Bacon.

Schriver, J. M. (1998). *Human behavior in the social environment.* Boston, MA: Allyn & Bacon.

Shulman, L. (1979). *The skills of helping individuals and groups.* Itasca, IL: F. E. Peacock.

Solomon, B. (1976). *Black empowerment: Social work in oppressed communities.* New York, NY: Columbia University Press.

Specht, H., & Courtney, M. E. (1994). *Unfaithful angels: How social work has abandoned its mission.* New York, NY: Free Press.

Tice, C. J., & Perkins, K. (1996). *Mental health issues: Building on the strengths of older adults.* Pacific Grove, CA: Brooks/Cole.

Tice, C. J., & Perkins, K. (2002). *The faces of social policy: A strengths perspective.* Pacific Grove, CA: Brooks/Cole.

Towle, C. (1965). *Common human needs* (Rev. ed.). Silver Springs, MD: National Association of Social Workers.

Van Berg, J., & Grealish, E. M. (1997). Finding family strengths. A multiple-choice test. *The Community Circle of Caring Journal, 1,* 8–16.

Warren, R. (1978). *The community in America* (3rd ed.). Chicago, IL: Rand McNally.

Weick, A., Sullivan, W., & Kisthardt, W. (1989). A strengths perspective for social work practice. *Social Work, 34,* 350–354.

## Chapter 3

Buzzelli, M. (2008). *Environmental justice in Canada—It matters where you live.* Ottawa, Ontario: CPRN.

Cross, T. L., Bazron, B. J., Issacs, M. R., & Dennis, K. W. (1989). *Towards a culturally competent system of care: A monograph on effective services for minority children who are severely emotionally disturbed.* Washington, DC: Georgetown University Center Child Health and Mental Health Policy, CASSP Technical Assistance Center. Retrieved from http://csmha.umaryland.edu/how/cultural_competency_2001

Devore, W., & Schlesinger, F. G. (1981). *Ethnic-sensitive social work practice.* St. Louis, MO: Mosby.

Dewane, C. (2017, September 10). Environmental social work: A call to action, SWHELPER. Retrieved June 22, 2018, from https://www.socialworkhelper.com/2017/10/09/environmental-social-work-call-action/

Dominelli, L. (2012). *Green social work: From environmental crisis to environmental justice.* Cambridge, UK: Polity.

Dominelli, L. (2013). Environmental justice at the heart of social work practice: Greening the profession. *International Journal of Social Welfare*, *22*, 431–439.

Duffy, A. M. (2001). A critique of cultural education in nursing. *Journal of Advanced Nursing*, *36*, 487–495.

Fairburn, J., Butler, B., & Smith, G. (2009). Missing inaction: Gender in international environmental law. In C. Blerta, I. Dankelman, & J. Stern (Eds.), *Powerful synergies: Gender equality, economic development, and environmental sustainability* (pp. 29–41). United Nations Development Programme. Retrieved from http://www.undp.org/content/undp/en/home/librarypage/womens-empowerment/powerful-synergies.html

Fisher-Borne, M., Cain, J. M., & Martin, S. L. (2015). From mastery to accountability: Cultural humility as an alternative to cultural competence. *Social Work Education*, *34*(2), 165–181.

The 5 worst states for LGBT people. (2014, November 24). *Rolling Stone*. Retrieved February 4, 2019, from https://www.rollingstone.com/politics/news/the-5-worst-states-for-lgbt-people-20141124

Fong, R., & Furuto, S. (Eds.). (2001). *Culturally competent social work practice: Skills, interventions and evaluation*. Boston, MA: Allyn & Bacon.

Furlong, M., & Wight, J. (2011). Promoting "critical awareness" and critiquing "cultural competence": Towards disrupting received professional knowledges. *Australian Social Work*, *64*, 38–54.

Gray, M., Coates, J., & Hetherington, T. (2013). Overview of the last ten years and typology of environmental social work. In M. Gray, J. Coates, & T. Hetherington (Eds.), *Environmental social work* (pp. 1–28). New York, NY: Routledge.

Green, J. (1995). *Cultural awareness in the human services: A multi-ethnic approach* (2nd ed.). Toronto, Canada: Allyn & Bacon.

Jani, J., Pierce, D., Ortiz, L., & Sowbel, L. (2011). Access to intersectionality, content to competence: Deconstructing social work education diversity standards. *Journal of Social Work Education*, *47*(2), 283–301.

Lum, D. (1986). *Social work practice and people of color: A process-stage approach*. Monterey, CA: Brooks/Cole.

Mailhot, J. (2015). *Green social work and community gardens: A case study of the north central community gardens*. Retrieved June 22, 2018 from https://brage.bibsys.no/xmlui/bitstream/handle/11250/2385188/Mailhot.pdf?sequence=1

Marsiglia, F. F., & Kulis, S. (2009). *Diversity, oppression, and change*. Chicago, IL: Lyceum.

McIlvaine-Newsad, H., & Porter, R. (2013). How does your garden grow? Environmental justice aspects of community gardens. *Journal of Ecological Anthropology*, *16*(1), 69–75.

McKibben, B. (2010). Earth: Making a life on a tough new planet. *Social Work*, *61*, 256–268. doi:10.1080/03124070802178275

Nesmith, A., & Smyth, N. (2015). Environmental justice and social work education: Social workers' professional perspectives. *Social Work Education*, *34*(5), 484–501. http://dx.doi.org/10.1080/02615479.2015.1063600

Ortega, R. M., & Faller, K. C. (2011). Training child welfare workers from an intersectional cultural humility perspective: A paradigm shift. *Child Welfare*, *90*(5), 27–49.

A Philadelphia apartment building may be a national model for low-income LGBT seniors. (2014, September 14). *The Washington Post*.

Philly hospitals among the most LGBT-friendly in the nation. (2018, April 6). *Philadelphia Gay News*. Retrieved from http://www.epgn.com/news/local/13267-philly-hospitals-among-most-lgbt-friendly-in-the-nation

Ramsay, S., & Boddy, J. (2017). Environmental social work: A concept analysis. *British Journal of Social Work*, *47*(1), 68–86.

Reisch, M. (2013). Community practice challenges in the global economy. In M. O. Weil, M. Reisch, & M. L. Ohmer (Eds.), *The handbook of community practice* (2nd ed., pp. 47–71). Thousand Oaks, CA: Sage.

Rudman, L. A. (2004). Social justice in our minds, homes, and society: The nature, causes, and consequences of implicit bias. *Social Justice Research*, *17*(2), 129–142.

Sue, D. W., Bernier, J. E., Durran, A., Feinberg, L., Pedersen, P., Smith, E. J., & Vasquez-Nuttall, E. (1982). Position paper: Cross-cultural counseling competencies. *The Counseling Psychologist*, *10*, 45–52.

Sue, S. (1998). In search of cultural competence in psychotherapy and counseling. *American Psychologist*, *53*, 440–448.

Teixeira, S., & Krings, A. (2015). Sustainable social work: An environmental justice framework for social work education. *Social Work Education*, *34*(5), 513–527.

Tervalon, M., & Murray-Garcia, J. (1998). Cultural humility versus cultural competence: A critical distinction in defining physician training outcomes in multicultural education. *Journal of Health Care for the Poor and Underserved*, *9*(2), 117–125.

Toribo, J. (2018). Implicit bias: From social structure to representational format. *THEORIA, 33*(1), 41–60.

Where does Philadelphia rank in the top LGBT-friendly cities in U.S.? (2017, October 11). *CBS Philly.*

## Chapter 4

Cox, L. E., Tice, C. J., & Long, D. D. (2019). *Introduction to social work practice: An advocacy model* (2nd ed.). Thousand Oaks, CA: Sage.

Delany, C. (2006). The tools and tactics of online political advocacy: Online politics 10. Retrieved from http://www.epoltics.com

Gamble, D. N. (2011). Advanced concentration macro competencies for social work practitioners: Identifying knowledge, values, judgment, and skills to promote human well-being. *Journal of Community Practice, 19,* 369–402.

Garcia, B., & Van Sorest, D. (2006). *Social work practice for social justice: Cultural competence in action.* Alexandria, VA: Council on Social Work Education Press.

Hoefer, R. (2012). *Advocacy practice for social justice* (2nd ed.). Chicago, IL: Lyceum Books.

Hoefer, R., & Jordan, C. (2008). Missing links in evidence-based practice in macro social work. *Journal of Evidence-Based Social Work, 5*(3–4), 549–568.

Jansson, B. S. (1998). *Becoming an effective policy advocate: From policy practice to social justice.* Pacific Grove, CA: Brooks/Cole.

Long, D. D., Tice, C. J., & Morrison, J. D. (2006). *Macro social work practice: A strengths perspective.* Belmont, CA: Brooks/Cole Cengage Learning.

McBeath, B. (2016). Re-envisioning macro social work practice. *Families in Society, 97,* 5–14.

Meenaghan, T. M., Washington, R. O., & Ryan, R. M. (1982). *Macro practice in human services: An introduction to planning, administration, evaluation and community organizing components of practice.* New York, NY: Free Press.

National Association of Social Workers. (2018). *Code of ethics.* Retrieved from socialworkers.org

Netting, F. E. (2005). The future of macro social work. *Advances in Social Work, 6*(1), 51–59.

Netting, F. E., O'Connor, M. K., Cole, P. L., Hopkins, K., Jones, J. L., Kim, Y., . . . Wike, T. L. (2016). Reclaiming and reimagining macro social work education: A collective biography. *Journal of Social Work Education, 52*(2), 157–169.

Pritzker, S., & Applewhite, S. R. (2015). Going "macro": Exploring the careers of macro practitioners. *Social Work, 60*(3), 191–199.

Queiro-Tajalli, I., Campbell, C., & McNutt, J. (2003). International social and economic justice and on-line advocacy. *International Social Work, 46,* 149–161.

Reamer, F. G. (1993). *The philosophical foundation of social work.* New York, NY: Columbia University Press.

Reisch, M. (2016). Why macro practice matters. *Journal of Social Work Education, 52*(3), 258–268.

Schneider, R. L., & Lester, L. (2001). *Social work advocacy: A new framework for action.* Belmont, CA: Brooks/Cole.

Walker, J., Jr. (1991). *Mobilizing interest groups in America: Patrons, professions and social movements.* Ann Arbor: University of Michigan Press.

## Chapter 5

Acker, J. (1990). Hierarchies, jobs, bodies: A theory of gendered organizations. *Gender & Society, 4*(2), 139–158.

Alinsky, S. (1969). *Reveille for radicals.* New York, NY: Vintage.

Argyris, C., & Schon, D. A. (1996). *Organizational learning II.* Reading, MA: Addison-Wesley.

Bolman, F. G., & Deal, T. E. (2013). *Reframing organizations* (5th ed.). San Francisco, CA: Jossey-Bass.

Brager, G., & Specht, H. (1973). *Community organizing.* New York, NY: Columbia University Press.

Brueggemann, W. G. (2002). *The practice of macro social work.* Chicago, IL: Nelson-Hall.

Burns, T., & Stalker, G. M. (1961). *The management of innovation.* London, UK: Tavistock.

Busch, M., & Hostetter, C. (2009). Examining organizational learning for application in human service organizations. *Administration in Social Work, 33*(3), 297–318.

Council on Social Work Education (CSWE). (2015). Educational policy and accreditation standards. Retrieved from http://www.cswe.org/File.aspx?id=41861

Deal, T. E., & Kennedy, A. A. (1982). *Corporate cultures: The rites and rituals of corporate life.* Reading, MA: Addison-Wesley.

Deming, W. (1982). *Out of crisis.* Cambridge: Massachusetts Institute of Technology, Center for Advanced Engineering Study.

Drucker, P. F. (1954). *The practice of management.* New York, NY: Harper.

Etzioni, A. (1964). *Modern organizations.* Englewood Cliffs, NJ: Prentice Hall.

Evans, T. (2013). Organisational rules and discretion in adult social work. *The British Journal of Social Work, 43*(4), 739–758.

Feinstein, K. W. (1987). Innovative management in turbulent times: Large-scale agency change. In F. M. Cox (Ed.), *Macro practice: Strategies of community organization.* Itasca, IL: F. E. Peacock.

Furman, R., & Gibelman, M. (2013). *Navigating human service organizations* (3rd ed.). Chicago, IL: Lyceum.

Giddens, A. (1979). *Central problems in social theory.* Berkeley: University of California Press.

Gummer, B., & Edwards, R. L. (1985). A social worker's guide to organizational politics. *Administration in Social Work, 9*(1), 13–21.

Habermas, J. (1971). *Knowledge and human interests.* Boston, CA: Beacon.

Harrison, M. (1987). *Diagnosing organizations: Methods, models, and processes.* Newbury Park, CA: Sage.

Hepworth, D. H., & Larsen, J. A. (1993). *Direct social work practice.* Pacific Grove, CA: Brooks/Cole.

Jaskyte, K. (2010). An exploratory examination of correlates of organizational culture. *Administration in Social Work, 34*(5), 423–441.

Katz, D., & Kahn, R. L. (1966). *The social psychology of organizations.* New York: John Wiley.

Katz, D., & Kahn, R. L. (1978). *The social psychology of organizations.* New York: John Wiley.

Kirst-Ashman, K. K., & Hull, G. H., Jr. (2001). *Macro skills workbook: A generalist approach.* Pacific Grove, CA: Brooks/Cole.

Lee, J. A. B. (1994). *The empowerment approach in social work practice.* New York, NY: Columbia University Press.

Lewis, J. A., Lewis, M. D., Packard, T., & Souflee, F. (2001). *Management of human service programs.* Pacific Grove, CA: Brooks/Cole.

Long, D. D. (2004). Introduction to social welfare. In A. L. Sallee (Ed.), *Social work and social welfare.* Peosta, IA: Eddie Bowers.

March, J. G., & Olsen, J. P. (1976). *Ambiguity and choice in organizations.* Bergen, Norway: universitetsforlaget.

Maynard-Moody, S. (1987). Program evaluation and administrative control. In F. M. Cox (Ed.), *Macro practice: Strategies of community organization.* Itasca, IL: F. E. Peacock.

McGregor, D. (1960). *The human side of enterprise.* New York, NY: McGraw-Hill.

Morgan, G. (1986). *Image of organizations.* London, UK: Sage.

Morse, J., & Lorsch, J. (1970). Beyond theory Y. *Harvard Business Review, 45,* 61–68.

Mosley, J. (2013). Recognizing new opportunities: Reconceptualizing policy advocacy in everyday organizational practice. *Social Work, 58*(3), 231–239.

National Association of Social Workers (NASW). (2008). *Code of ethics of the National Association of Social Workers.* Washington, DC: Author.

National Association of Social Workers. (2017). *Code of ethics.* Washington, DC: NASW Press. Retrieved from https://www.socialworkers.org/About/Ethics

Netting, J. E., Kettner, P. M., & McMurtry, S. L. (1998). *Social work macro practice.* New York, NY: Longman.

Netting, F. E., Kettner, P. M., McMurtry, S. L., & Thomas, M. L. (2017). *Social work macro practice* (6th ed.). Boston, MA: Pearson.

Neugeboren, B. (1991). *Organization, policy, and practice in the human services.* New York, NY: Haworth.

Olsen, M. E. (1978). *The process of social organization; Power in social systems* (2nd ed.). New York, NY: Holt, Rinehart, and Winston.

Ott, S. J. (1989). *The organizational culture perspective.* Pacific Grove, CA: Brooks/Cole.

Payton, R. L., & Moody, M. P. (2008), *Understanding philanthropy: Its meaning and mission.* Bloomington: Indiana University Press.

Perrow, C. (1979). *Complex organizations: A critical essay* (2nd ed.). Glenview, IL: Scott, Foresman.

Pfeffer, J. (1981). *Power in organizations.* Marshfield, MA: Pitman.

Raeymaeckers, P., & Dierckx, D. (2013). To work or not to work? The role of the organizational context for social workers' perceptions on activation. *The British Journal of Social Work, 43*(6), 1170–1189.

Rappaport, J. (1985). The power of empowerment language. *Social Policy, 16*(2), 15–21.

Rieman, D. S. (1992). *Strategies in social work consultation: From theory to practice in the mental health field.* New York, NY: Longman.

Robbins, S. (1992). *Essentials of organizational behavior* (3rd ed.). Englewood Cliffs, NJ: Prentice Hall.

Rothman, J., & Tropman, J. E. (1987). Models of community organization and macro practice: Their mixing and phasing. In F. M. Cox, J. L. Erlich, J. Rothman, & J. E. Tropman (Eds.), *Strategies of community intervention: Macro practice* (4th ed., pp. 353–372). Itasca, IL: F. E. Peacock.

Savio, G. (2017). Organization and stigma management. *Sociological Perspectives, 60*(2), 416–430.

Schein, E. (1985). *Organizational culture and leadership*. San Francisco, CA: Jossey-Bass.

Schein, E. H. (2010). *Organizational culture and leadership* (4th ed.). San Francisco, CA: Jossey-Bass.

Senge, P. M. (1990). *The fifth discipline: The art and practice of the learning organization*. New York, NY: Doubleday.

Simon, B. L. (1994). *The empowerment tradition in American social work: A history*. New York, NY: Columbia University Press.

Simon, H. A. (1957). *Administrative behavior* (2nd ed.). New York, NY: Macmillan.

Solomon, B. (1976). *Black empowerment: Social work in oppressed communities*. New York, NY: Columbia University Press.

Stanley, T., & Lincoln, H. (2016). Improving organizational culture—The Practice Gains. *Practice, 28*(3), 199–212. doi:10.1080/09503153.2015.1087491

Taylor, F. W. (1911). *The principles of scientific management*. New York, NY: Harper.

von Bertalanffy, L. (1950). An outline of general systems theory. *British Journal for the Philosophy of Science, 1*(2), 493–512.

Walmsley, G. L., & Zald, M. N. (1973). *The political economy of public organizations*. Lexington, MA: Lexington Books.

Weber, M. (1947). *The theory of social and economic organizations* (A. M. Henderson & T. Parsons, Trans.). New York, NY: Macmillan. (Original work published 1924)

Weick, K. E. (1995). *Sensemaking in organizations*. Thousand Oaks, CA: Sage.

## Chapter 6

Brady, S. R., & O'Connor, M. K. (2014). Understanding how community organizing leads to social change: The beginning development of formal practice theory. *Journal of Community Practice, 22*, 210–228.

Checkoway, B. (2013). Social justice approach to community development. *Journal of Community Practice, 21*, 472–486.

Community Matters. (2018). Setting up a community action group. Retrieved from https://communitiesmatter.suicidepreventionaust.org/content/set-community-action-group

Community Outreach and Resident Education (CORE). (2018). *Take action on Flint water*. Retrieved from https://www.michigan.gov/flintwater

Cox, L. E., Tice, C. J., & Long, D. D. (2019). *Introduction to social work practice: An advocacy model* (2nd ed.). Thousand Oaks, CA: Sage.

Dover, M. A. (2017). Human need. Retrieved from http://www.oxfordbibliographies.com/view/document/obo-9780195389678/obo-9780195389678-0067.xml

Fanning, J. (2018). Understanding the role of social work. Retrieved from https://mswonlineprograms.org/job-duties-and-responsibilities-of-social-workers

Gamble, D. N. (2011). Advanced concentration macro competencies for social work practitioners: Identifying knowledge, vales, judgment and skills to promote well-being. *Journal of Community Practice, 19*, 369–402.

Gamble, D. N., & Weil, M. (2010). *Community practice skills: Local to global perspective*. New York, NY: Columbia University Press.

Hardcastle, D. A., Powers, P. R., & Wenocur, S. (2015). *Community practice: Theories and skills for social workers*. Ipswich, MA: EBSCO Publishing.

Harrington, M. (1974). *The other America: Poverty in the United States*. New York, NY: Macmillan.

Lyon, L. (1987). *The community in urban society*. Chicago, IL: Dorsey.

Lysack, M. (2012). Building capacity for environmental engagement and leadership: An ecosocial work perspective. *International Journal of Social Welfare, 21*, 260–269.

Midgely, J. (1995). *Social development: The developmental perspective in social welfare*. London, UK: Sage.

Morrison, J. D., Howard, J., Johnson, C., Navarro, F. J., Plachetka, B., & Bell, T. (1998). Strengthening neighborhoods by developing community networks. In P. L. Ewalt, E. M. Freeman, & D. Poole (Eds.), *Community building: Renewal, well-being, and shared responsibility*. Washington, DC: NASW Press.

Naparstek, A. J. (1999). Community building and social group work: A new practice paradigm for American cities. In H. Bertcher, L. F. Kurtz, & A. Lamont (Eds.), *Rebuilding communities: Challenges for group work*. New York, NY: Haworth.

National Association of Social Workers. (2017). *Code of ethics*. Washington, DC: NASW Press. Retrieved from https://www.socialworkers.org/About/Ethics

Netting, E. E., Kettner, P. M., & McMurtry, S. L. (2001). Selecting appropriate tactics. In J. E. Tropman, J. L. Erlich, & J. Rothman (Eds.), *Tactics and techniques of community intervention*. Itasca, IL: Peacock.

Perlman, R., & Gurin, A. (1972). *Community organization and social planning*. New York, NY: Wiley.

Richmond, M. E. (1955). *Social diagnosis*. New York, NY: Russell Sage Foundation. (Original work published 1917)

Rothman, J. (1979). Three models of community organization practice, their mixing and phasing. In F. M. Cox, J. L. Erlich, J. Rothman, & J. C. Tropman (Eds.), *Strategies of community organization* (3rd ed.). Itasca, IL: Peacock.

Taylor, S. H., & Roberts, R. W. (1985). *Theory and practice of community social work*. New York, NY: Columbia University Press.

Warren, R. B., & Warren, D. I. (1977). *The neighborhood organizer's handbook*. Notre Dame, IN: University of Notre Dame Press.

Weil, M. O. (1996). Community building: Building community practice. *Social Work, 41*(5), 481–499.

## Chapter 7

Altpeter, M., Schopler, J. H., Galinsky, M. J., & Pennell, J. (1999). Participatory research as social work practice: When is it viable? *Journal of Progressive Social Work, 10*(2), 31–53.

Bromley, R. (2003). Social planning: Past, present, and future. *Journal of International Development, 15*, 819–830.

Delgado, M. (2000). *Community social work practice in an urban context: The potential of a capacity-enhancement perspective*. New York, NY: Oxford University Press.

DiNitto, D. (2000). *Social welfare: Politics and public policy*. Boston, MA: Allyn & Bacon.

Dudley, J. R. (1978). Is social planning social work? *Social Work, 23*(1), 37–41.

Jones, E. R., & Harris, W M. (1987). A conceptual scheme for analysis of the social planning process. *Journal of the Community Development Society, 18*(2), 18–41.

Kahn, S. (1991). *Organizing: A guide for grassroots leaders*. Silver Spring, MD: NASW Press.

Kotler, P. (1982). *Marketing for nonprofit organizations* (2nd ed.). Englewood Cliffs, NJ: Prentice Hall.

Kotler, P., Ferrell, O. C., & Lamb, C. (1987). *Strategic marketing for nonprofit organizations: Cases and readings*. Englewood Cliffs, NJ: Prentice Hall.

O'Melia, M. (2002). From person to context: The evolution of an empowering practice. In M. O'Melia & K. Miley (Eds.), *Pathways to power: Readings in contextual social work practice* (pp. 1–14). Boston, MA: Allyn & Bacon.

Piat, M. (2000). The NIMBY phenomenon: Community residents' concerns about housing for deinstitutionalized people. *Health and Social Work, 25*(2), 127–138.

Ramon, S. (1999). Collective empowerment: Conceptual and practical issues. In W. Shera & L. Wells (Eds.), *Empowerment practice in social work: Developing richer conceptual foundations* (pp. 38–49). Toronto: Canadian Scholars Press.

Rapp, C. A. (1998). *The strengths model: Case management with people suffering from severe and persistent mental illness*. New York, NY: Oxford University Press.

Saleebey, D. (2002). The *strengths perspective in social work practice*. Boston, MA: Allyn & Bacon.

Staples, L. (1984). *Roots to power: A manual for grassroots organizing*. New York, NY: Praeger.

Stoner, M. R. (1986). Marketing of social services gains prominence in practice. *Administration in Social Work, 10*(4), 41–52.

Watson-Thompson, J., Fawcett, S. R., & Schultz, J. A. (2008). Differential effects of strategic planning on community change in two urban neighborhood coalitions. *American Journal of Community Psychology, 42*, 25–38.

Whitmore, E., & Wilson, M. (1997). Accompanying the process: Principles for international development practice. *International Social Work, 40*(1), 57–74.

Zachary, E. (2000). Grassroots leadership training: A case study of an effort to integrate theory and method. *Journal of Community Practice*, 7(1), 71–93.

## Chapter 8

Asamoah, Y. (1995). Managing the new multicultural workforce. In L. Ginsberg & P. Keys (Eds.), *New management in human services* (2nd ed.). Washington, DC: NASW Press.

Bailey, D. (1995). Management: Diverse workplaces. In R. Edwards (Ed.), *Encyclopedia of social work* (19th ed.). Washington, DC: NASW Press.

Bliss, D. L., Pecukonis, E., & Snyder-Vogel, M. (2014). Principled leadership development model for aspiring social work managers and administrators: Development and application. *Human Services Organizations: Management, Leadership & Governance, 38*, 5–15.

Briggs, H. E., & McBeath, B. (2009). Evidence-based management: Origins, challenges, and implications for social service administration. *Administration in Social Work, 33*, 242–261.

Brueggemann, W. G. (1996). *The practice of macro social work.* Chicago, IL: Nelson-Hall.

Cowger, C. D. (1994). Assessing client strengths: Clinical assessment for client empowerment. *Social Work, 39*(3), 262–268.

Cox, L. E., Tice, C. J., & Long, D. D. (2019). *Introduction to social work: An advocacy-based profession* (2nd ed.). Thousand Oaks, CA: Sage.

DiTomaso, N., Post, C., & Parks-Yancy, R. (2007). Workforce diversity and inequality: Power, status and numbers. *The Annual Review of Sociology, 33*, 473–501.

Dolgoff, R., Harrington, D., & Loewenberg, F. M. (2011). *Ethical decisions for social work practice* (9th ed.). Belmont, CA: Brooks/Cole.

Flynn, J. P. (1985). *Social agency policy: Analysis and presentation for community practice.* Chicago, IL: Nelson-Hall.

Frahm, K. A., & Martin, L. L. (2009). From government to governance: Implications for social work administration. *Administration in Social Work, 33*, 407–422.

Garner, H. G., & Orelove, F. P. (1994). *Teamwork in human services: Models and applications across the life span.* Boston, MA: Butterworth-Heineman.

Gilliam, C. C., Chandler, M. A., Al-Hajjaj, H. A., Mooney, A. N., & Vakalahl, H. F. O. (2016). Intentional leadership planning and development: The collective responsibilities to educate more social work leaders. *Advances in Social Work*, 17(2), 330–339.

Gummer, B. (1991). *The politics of social administration: Managing organizational politics in social agencies.* Englewood Cliffs, NJ: Prentice Hall.

Gummer, B., & Edwards, R. L. (1985). The enfeebled middle: Emerging issues in education and social administration. *Administration in Social Work, 12*(3), 13–23.

Hardcastle, D. A., Wenocur, S., & Powers, P. R. (1997). *Community practice: Theories and skills for social workers.* New York, NY: Oxford University Press.

Hasenfeld, Y., & English, R. A. (1974). *Human services organizations.* Ann Arbor: University of Michigan Press.

Healy, L., Havens, C., & Pine, B. (1995). Women and social work management. In L. Ginsberg & P. Keys (Eds.), *New management in human services* (2nd ed.). Washington, DC: NASW Press.

Hoefer, R., & Sliva, S. M. (2014). Assessing and augmenting administrative skills in nonprofits: An exploratory mixed methods study. *Human Services Organizations: Management, Leadership & Governance, 38*, 246–257.

Homan, M. S. (2016). *Promoting community change: Making it happen in the real world* (6th ed.). Belmont, CA: Brooks/Cole.

Jani, J. S., Osteen, P., & Shipe, S. (2016). Cultural competence and social work education: Moving toward assessment of practice behaviors. *Journal of Social Work Education, 32*(3), 311–324.

Johnson, H. W., McLaughlin, J. A., & Christenson, M. (1982). Interagency collaboration: Driving and restraining forces. *Exceptional Children, 48*, 395–399.

Kadushin, A. (1985). *Supervision in social work* (2nd ed.) New York, NY: Columbia University Press.

Katz, D., & Kahn, R. (1978). *Social psychology of organizations* (Rev. ed.). New York, NY: John Wiley.

Kretzmann, J., & McKnight, J. (1996). Assets-based community development. *National Civic Review, 85*(4), 23–27.

Lauffer, A. (1981). The practice of social planning. In N. Gilbert & H. Specht (Eds.), *Handbook for social services.* Englewood Cliffs, NJ: Prentice Hall.

Lewis, J. A., Lewis, M. D., Packard, T., & Souflée, F. (2001). *Management of human service programs.* Pacific Grove, CA: Brooks/Cole.

Madden, R. (2003). *Essential law for social workers.* New York, NY: Columbia University Press.

MorBarak, M. E. (2000). The inclusive workplace: An ecosystems approach to diversity management. *Social Work, 45*(4), 339–352.

National Association of Social Workers. (2017). *Code of ethics.* Washington, DC: NASW Press. Retrieved from https://www.socialworkers.org/About/Ethics

Netting, F. E., Kettner, P. M., & McMurtry, S. L. (1998). *Social work macro practice* (2nd ed.). New York, NY: Longman.

Netting, F. E., Nelson, H. W., Borders, K., & Huber, R. (2004). Volunteer and paid staff relationships: Implications for social work administration. *Administration in Social Work, 28*(3/4), 68–89.

Neugeboren, B. (1991). *Organization, policy, and practice in human services.* New York, NY: Haworth.

Packard, T., Patti, R., Daly, D., Tucker-Tatlow, J., & Farrell, C. (2008). Cutback management strategies: Experience in nine county human service agencies. *Administration in Social Work, 32*(1), 55–75.

Patti, R. (1977). Patterns of management activity in social welfare agencies. *Administration in Social Work, 1*(1), 5–18.

Pfeffer, J. (1981). *Power in organizations.* Boston, MA: Pitman.

Poulin, J. (Ed.). (2000). *Collaborative social work: Strengths-based generalist practice.* Itasca, IL: F. E. Peacock.

Raney, A. F. (2014). Agility in adversity: Integrating mindfulness and principles of adaptive leadership in administration of a community mental health center. *Clinical Social Work Journal, 42,* 312–320.

Rapp, C. A., & Poertner, J. (1992). *Social administration: A client-centered approach.* New York, NY: Longman.

Reamer, F. G. (2005). Documentation in social work: Evolving ethical and risk-management standards. *Social Work, 50*(4), 325–334.

Reisch, M., & Gambrill, E. (1997). *Social work in the 21st century.* Thousand Oaks, CA: Pine Forge Press.

Reynolds, B. (1987). *Social work and social living.* Silver Spring, MD: National Association of Social Workers. (Original work published 1951)

Saleebey, D. (1997). *The strengths perspective in social work practice.* New York, NY: Longman.

Saleebey, D. (2013). *The strengths perspective in social work practice* (6th ed.). New York, NY: Pearson.

Shera, W., & Bejan, R. (2017). A post-master's advanced diploma and a MSW specialization in Social Service Administration: Design, delivery, and assessment of outcomes. *Human Services Organizations: Management, Leadership & Governance, 41*(3), 240–251.

Shulman, L. (1993). *Interactional supervision.* Washington, DC: NASW Press.

Skidmore, R. A. (1990). *Social work administration: Dynamic management and human services* (2nd ed.). Englewood Cliffs, NJ: Prentice Hall.

Tsui, M.-S., & Cheung, F. C. H. (2009). Social work administration revisited. *Journal of Social Work,* 9(2), 148–157.

Unguru, E., & Sandu, A. (2017). Supervision. From administrative control to continuous education and training of specialists in social work. *Revista Romanecasca pentru Educatie Multidimensionala, 9*(1), 17–35.

Watson, L. D., & Hegar, R. L. (2013). The tri-sector environment of social work administration: Applying theoretical orientations. *Administration in Social Work, 37,* 215–226.

Williams-Gray, B. (2014). Preparing for social service leadership: Field work and virtual organizations that promote critical thinking in administrative practices. *Journal of Teaching in Social Work, 34,* 113–129.

Wimpfheimer, S. (2004). Leadership and management competencies defined by practicing social work managers: An overview of standards developed by the network for social work managers. *Administration in Social Work, 28*(1), 45–56.

## Chapter 9

Abernathy, S. F. (2019). *American government: Stories of a nation* (2nd ed.). Washington, DC: CQ Press.

Axinn, J., & Levin, H. (1992). *Social welfare: A history of the American response to need.* New York, NY: Longman.

Brueggemann, W. G. (1996). *The practice of macro social work.* Chicago, IL: Nelson-Hall.

Burch, H. (1991). *The whys of social policy: Perspective on policy preferences.* New York, NY: Praeger.

Chapin, R. K. (1995). Social policy development: The strengths perspective. *Social Work, 40*(4), 506–514.

Dear, R., & Patti, J. (1981). Legislative advocacy: Seven effective tactics. *Social Work, 26,* 289–296.

Delli Carpini, M. X., & Keeter, S. (1996). *What Americans know about politics and why it matters.* New Haven, CT: Yale University Press.

Domanski, M. D. (1998). Prototypes of social work political participation: An empirical model. *Social Work, 43*(2), 156–168.

Fortune, A. E., Mingun, L., & Cavazos, A. (2007). Does practice make perfect? Practicing professional skills and outcomes in social work field education. *The Clinical Supervisor, 26,* (1/2), 239–263.

Garner, H., & Orelove, E. P. (1994). *Teamwork in human services.* Boston, MA: Butterworth-Heinemann.

Goldstein, H. (1990). Strengths or pathology: Ethical and rhetorical contrasts in approaches to practice. *Families in Society, 71*(5), 267–275.

Gummer, B. (1990). *The politics of social administration: Managing organizational politics in social agencies.* Englewood Cliffs, NJ: Prentice Hall.

Gutierrez, L., Parsons, R. J., & Cox, E. O. (1998). *Empowerment in social work practice: A sourcebook*. Pacific Grove, CA: Brooks/Cole.

Hamilton, D., & Fauri, D. (2001). Social workers' political participation: Strengthening the political confidence of social work students. *Journal of Social Work Education, 37*(2), 321–332.

Haynes, K. S., & Mickelson, J. S. (2006). *Affecting change: Social workers in the political arena*. New York, NY: Pearson.

Jannson, B. S. (2001). *The reluctant welfare state: American social welfare policies—past, present, and future*. Pacific Grove, CA: Brooks/Cole.

Karger, H. J., & Stoesz, D. (1998). *American social welfare policy*. New York, NY: Longman.

Lee, P. R. (1929). Social work: Cause and function. *National Conference of Social Work, Proceedings, 56*, 3–20.

Levine, D. (1971). *Jane Addams and the liberal tradition*. Madison: State Historical Society of Wisconsin.

Linhorst, D. M. (2002). Federalism and social justice: Implications for social work. *Social Work, 47*, 201–222.

Lundblad, K. S. (1995). Jane Addams and social reform: A role model for the 1990s. *Social Work, 40*, 661–669.

Meenaghan, T. M., & Washington, R. O. (1980). *Social policy and social welfare*. New York, NY: Free Press.

National Association of Social Workers. (2017). *Code of ethics*. Washington, DC: NASW Press. Retrieved from https://www.socialworkers.org/About/Ethics

Pritzker, S., & Lane, S. (2016). Political social work: history, forms, and opportunities for innovation. *Social Work, 62*(1), 80–82.

Rappaport, J., Davidson, W., Wilson, M., & Mitchell, A. (1975). Alternatives to blaming the victim or environment: Our places to stand have moved the earth. *American Psychologist, 30*, 525–528.

Reisch, M. (2000). Social workers and politics in the new century. *Social Work, 45*(4), 293–297.

Reisch, M., & Jani, J. S. (2012). The new politics of social work practice: Understanding context to promote change. *British Journal of Social Work, 42*, 1132–1150.

Rush, M., & Keenan, M. (2014). The social politics of social work: Anti-oppressive social work dilemmas in the twenty-first-century welfare regimes. *British Journal of Social Work, 44*, 1436–1453.

Saleebey, D. (1992). *The strengths perspective in social work practice*. New York, NY: Longman.

Saleebey, D. (1997). *The strengths perspective in social work practice* (2nd ed.). New York, NY: Longman.

Thompson, J. J. (1996). Social workers and politics: Beyond the Hatch Act. *Social Work, 39*(4), 457–465.

Tice, C. J., & Perkins, K. (1996). *Mental health issues and aging: Building on the strengths of older people*. Pacific Grove, CA: Brooks/Cole.

Tice, C. J., & Perkins, K. (2002). *The faces of social policy: A strengths perspective*. Pacific Grove, CA: Brooks/Cole.

Timpson, W. M. (2002). *Teaching and learning peace*. Madison, WI: Atwood Publishing.

Towle, C. (1987). *Common human needs*. Silver Spring, MD: National Association of Social Workers. (Original work published 1945)

Weiss-Gal, I. (2013). Policy practice in practice: The inputs of social workers in legislative committees. *Social Work, 58*(4), 304–313.

Weiss-Gal, I., & Gal, J. (2008). Social workers and policy-practice: The role of social and professional values. *Journal of Social Service Research, 34*(4), 15–27.

Zippay, A. (1995). The politics of empowerment. *Social Work, 40*(2), 263–268.

## Chapter 10

Academy of Social Work and Social Welfare. (2009). Retrieved from http://aaswsw.org/about-us/

Belluomini, E. (2013). Technology changing the face of social work. *The New Social Worker, 20*(2), 1.

Berzin, S. C., Singer, J., & Chan, C. (2015). *Practice innovation through technology in the digital age: A grand challenge for social work* (Working Paper No. 12). Baltimore, MD: Academy of Social Work and Social Welfare.

Bratt, W. (2010). Ethical considerations of social networking for counselors. *Canadian Journal of Counseling and Psychotherapy, 44*(4), 335–345.

Ceranoglu, T. A. (2010). Video games in psychotherapy. *Review of General Psychology, 14*, 141–146.

Dewane, C. J. (2010). Respecting boundaries: The don'ts of dual relationships. *Social Work Today, 10*(1), 18.

Dobson, F. (1997). Technology and social justice. Retrieved from http://www.psychologytoday.com

Dombo, E. A., Kays, L., & Weller, K. (2014). Clinical social work practice and technology: Personal, practical, regulatory, and ethical considerations for the twenty-first century. *Social Work in Health Care, 53*, 900–919.

Germany, J. B. (Ed.). (2006). *Person to person: Harnessing the political power of on-line social networks and user generated content*. Washington, DC: Institute for Politics, Democracy, and the Internet, George Washington University.

Guo, C., & Saxton, G. (2015). Tweeting social change: How social media are changing nonprofit advocacy. *Nonprofit and Voluntary Sector Quarterly, 43*, 57–59.

Guseh, J. S., Brendal, R. W., & Brtendal, D. H. (2009). Medical professionalism in the age of online social networking. *Journal of Medical Ethics, 35*(9), 584–586.

Hickin, R. (2017). Identity in a digital world: A new chapter in the social contract. Retrieved from https://www.weforum.org/reports/identity-in-a-digital-world-a-new-chapter-in-the-social-contract

Hitchcock, L. I., Sage, M., & Smyth, N. J. (Eds.). (2018). *Technology in social work education: Educators' perspectives on the NASW technology standards for social work education and supervision*. Buffalo: University at Buffalo School of Social Work, State University of New York.

Kuhns, K. A. (2012). Social media and professional nursing friend or foe? *Pennsylvania Nurse, 67*(1), 4–8.

Lehavot, K., Barnett, J., & Powers, D. (2010). Psychotherapy, professional relationships and ethical considerations in the MySpace generation. *Professional Psychology: Research and Practice, 41*(2), 160–166.

Luo, J. (2009). The Facebook phenomenon: Boundaries and controversies. *Primary Psychiatry, 16*(11), 19–21.

Malamud, M. (2011). It's "better to be informed" about tech tools. *NASW News, 65*(6).

McNutt, J. G. (Ed.). (2018). *Technology, activism and social justice*. New York, NY: Oxford University Press.

National Association of Social Workers. (2017). *Code of ethics*. Washington, DC: NASW Press. Retrieved from https://www.socialworkers.org/About/Ethics

Reamer, F. G. (2001). *Tangled relationships: Managing boundary issues in human services*. New York, NY: Columbia University Press.

Reamer, F. G. (2013). Social work in the digital age: Ethical and risk management challenges. *Social Work, 58*(1), 163–172.

Schuler, D. (1996). *New community networks: Wired for change*. New York, NY: ACM Press/Addison-Wesley.

Tooley, A. (2015). How the Internet and social media impacted the field of social work. Retrieved from http://www.onlineswprograms

Voshel, E. H., & Wesala, A. (2015). Social media and social work ethics: Determining best practices in an ambiguous reality. *Journal of Social Work Values & Ethics, 12*(1), 67–76.

Young, T. B. (2013). Facebook: Ethical and clinical considerations. *The New Social Worker, 21*(1).

## Chapter 11

Atlantic City: Building a foundation for a shared prosperity. (n.d.). Retrieved October 8, 2018, from https://www.nj.gov/dca/images/library/stories/A.C.report_9.20.18.pdf

Bailey, K. (1988). Ethical dilemmas in social problems research: A theoretical framework. *The American Sociologist, 19*(2), 121–137.

Berg, B. L., & Lune, H. (2012). *Qualitative research methods for the social sciences* (8th ed.). Boston, MA: Pearson.

Brueggemann, W. (2014). *The practice of macro social work* (4th ed.). Beaverton, OR: Ringgold.

Connolly, M. (2003). Qualitative analysis: A teaching tool for social work research. *Qualitative Social Work, 2*(1), 103–112.

Cox, L. E., Tice, C. J., & Long, D. (2019). *Introduction to social work: An advocacy-based profession* (2nd ed.). Thousand Oaks, CA: Sage.

Daugherty, D. S., & Atkinson, J. (2006). Competing ethical communities and a researcher's dilemma: The case of a sexual harasser. *Qualitative Inquiry, 12*(2), 292–315.

Davis, L. V. (1986). A feminist approach to social work research. *Affilia, 1*, 32–47.

Haverkamp, B. E. (2005). Ethical perspectives on qualitative research in applied psychology. *Journal of Counseling Psychology, 52*, 146–155.

Landau, R. (2008). Social work research ethics: Dual roles and boundary issues. *Families in Society: The Journal of Contemporary Social Services, 89*(4), 571–577.

Lindorff, M. (2007). The ethical impact of business and organizational research: The forgotten methodological issue. *The Electronic Journal of Business Research Methods, 5*(1), 21–28.

Link, B., & Phelan, J. (2001). Conceptualizing stigma. *Annual Review of Sociology, 27*, 367.

Marlow, C. (2011). *Research methods for generalist social work* (5th ed.). Belmont, CA: Brooks/Cole.

Miley, K. K., O'Melia, M. W., & DuBois, B. L. (2017). *Generalist social work practice: An empowering approach* (8th ed.). New York, NY: Pearson.

Monette, D. R., Sullivan, T. J., DeJong, C. R., & Hilton, T. P. (2014). *Applied social research: A tool for the human services* (9th ed.). Belmont, CA: Brooks/Cole Cengage Learning.

National Association of Social Workers. (n.d.). *Evidence based practice*. Retrieved from https://www.socialworkers.org/News/Research-Data/Social-Work-Policy-Research/Evidence-Based-Practice

Netting, F. E., Kettner, P. M., McMurty, S. L., & Thomas, M. L. (2017). *Social work macro practice* (6th ed.). Boston, MA: Pearson.

Padgett, D. K. (2013). Qualitative research: Research and evidence-based practice. Retrieved from http://oxfordre.com/socialwork/view/10.1093/acrefore/9780199975839.001.0001/acrefore-9780199975839-e-330#acrefore-9780199975839-div1-2485

Tervalon, M., & Murray-Garcia, J. (1998). Cultural humility versus cultural competence: A critical distinction in defining physician training outcomes in multicultural education. *Journal of Health Care for the Poor and Underserved*, *9*(2), 117–125.

## Chapter 12

Bass, B., & Avolio, B. (2006). *Transformational leadership* (2nd ed.). Mahwah, NJ: Lawrence Erlbaum.

Beresford, P. (2000). Service users' knowledges and social work theory: Conflict or collaboration? *British Journal of Social Work*, *30*, 489–503.

Beresford, P. (2007). The role of service user research in generating knowledge-based health and social work care: From conflict to contribution. *Evidence & Policy*, *3*(3), 329–341.

Beresford, P., & Boxall, K. (2012). Service users, social work education, and knowledge for social work. *Social Work Education*, *31*(2), 155–167.

Beresford, P., & Croft, S. (2001). Service users' knowledges and the social construction of social work. *Journal of Social Work*, *1*(3), 295–316.

Beresford, P., & Croft, S. (2004). Service users and practitioners reunited: The key component for social work reform. *British Journal of Social Work*, *34*, 53–68.

Cheetam, J. (1992). Evaluating social work effectiveness. *Research on Social Work Practice*, *2*(3), 265–287.

Cox, L. E., Tice, C. J., & Long, D. (2019). *Introduction to social work: An advocacy-based profession* (2nd ed.). Thousand Oaks, CA: Sage.

Finn, J. L., & Jacobson, M. (2003). *Just practice: A social justice approach to social work*. Peosta, IA: Eddie Bowers.

Fischer, R. L. (2001). The sea change in nonprofit human services: A critical assessment of outcome measurement. *Journal of Contemporary Human Services*, *82*(6), 561–569.

Glaser, B., & Strauss, A. (1967). *The discovery of grounded research: Strategies for qualitative research*. Chicago, IL: Aldine.

Hatry, H., Van Houten, T., Plantz, M., & Greenway, M. (1996). *Measuring program outcomes: A practical approach*. Alexandria, VA: United Way of America.

Hemmelgarn, A., Glisson, C., & James, L. (2010). Organizational culture and climate: Implications for services and intervention research. In Y. Hasenfeld (Ed.), *Human services as complex organizations* (2nd ed., pp. 229–250). Thousand Oaks, CA: Sage.

Jonson-Reid, M. (2000). Evaluating empowerment in a community-based child abuse prevention program: Lessons learned. *Journal of Community Practice*, *7*(4), 57–76.

Kilty, K. M., & Meenaghan, T. M. (1995). Social work and the convergence of politics and science. *Social Work*, *40*(4), 445-453. Retrieved from https://doi.org/10.1093/sw/40.4.445

Lindhorst, T., Mancoske, R. J., & Kemp, A. A. (2000). Is welfare reform working? A study of the effects of sanctions on families receiving Temporary Assistance to Needy Families. *The Journal of Sociology & Social Welfare*, 27(4), article 9. Retrieved from https://scholarworks.wmich.edu/jssw/vol27/iss4/9

Long, D. D. (2000). Welfare reform: A social work perspective for assessing success. *Journal of Sociology and Social Welfare*, *27*, 61–78.

Monette, D. R., Sullivan, T. J., DeJong, C. R., & Hilton, T. P. (2014). *Applied social research: A tool for the human services* (9th ed.). Belmont, CA: Brooks/Cole Cengage Learning.

Murari, N. D., & Guerrero, E. G. (2013). *Evidence-based macro social work practice in social work*. Wheaton, IL: Gregory Publishing Company.

National Association of Social Workers. (2017). *Code of ethics*. Washington, DC: NASW Press. Retrieved from https://www.socialworkers.org/About/Ethics

Neuman, K. M. (2003). Developing a comprehensive outcomes management program: A ten-step process. *Administration in Social Work*, *27*(1), 5–23.

Northouse, P. G. (2013). *Leadership: Theory and practice* (6th ed.). Thousand Oaks, CA: Sage.

Rossi, P. H., Freeman, H. E., & Lipsey, M. W. (1999). *Evaluation: A systematic approach* (6th ed.). Thousand Oaks, CA: Sage.

Royse, D. (2011). *Research methods in social work* (6th ed.). Belmont, CA: Brooks/Cole Cengage Learning.

Saleebey, D. (2002). *The strengths perspective in social work practice*. Boston, MA: Allyn & Bacon.

Saleebey, D. (2012). *The strengths perspective in social work practice* (6th ed.) Boston, MA: Pearson.

Schaufeli, W., Leiter, M., & Maslach, C. (2009). Burnout: 35 years of research and practice. *Career Development International, 14*(3), 204–220.

Schutt, R. K. (2018). *Investigating the social world: The process and practice of research* (9th ed.). Thousand Oaks, CA: Sage.

## Chapter 13

Beverly, D. P., & McSweeney, E. A. (1987). *Social welfare and social justice*. Englewood Cliffs, NJ: Prentice Hall.

Brueggemann, W. G. (1996). *The practice of macro social work*. Chicago, IL: Nelson-Hall.

Compton, B. R., & Galaway, B. (1979). *Social work processes*. Homewood, IL: Dorsey.

Cox, E. O., & Parsons, R. J. (1994). *Empowerment-oriented social work practice with the elderly*. Pacific Grove, CA: Brooks/Cole.

Cox, L. E., Tice, C. J., & Long, D. D. (2019). *Introduction to social work: An advocacy-based model* (2nd ed.). Thousand Oaks, CA: Sage.

Desilver, D. (2018). U.S. trails most developed countries in voter turnout. Retrieved from http://www.pewresearch.org/fact-tank/2018/05/21/u-s-voter-turnout-trails-most-developed-countries/

Felderhoff, B. J., Hoefer, R., & Watson, L. D. (2015). Living up to the code's exhortations? Social workers' political knowledge sources, expectations, and behaviors. *Social Work, 61*(1), 29–35.

Frunza, A., & Sanu, A. (2017). Ethical values in social work: A qualitative study. *Journal of Social Work Values and Ethics, 14*(1), 40–58.

Gutierrez, L. M., Parsons, R. J., & Cox, E. O. (1998). *Empowerment in social work practice: A sourcebook*. Pacific Grove, CA: Brooks/Cole.

Guttmann, D. (2006). Social welfare and distributive justice. In D. Guttmann (Ed.), *Ethics in social work: A context of caring* (pp. 131–144). New York, NY: Haworth.

Hepworth, D. H., & Larsen, J. A. (1982). *Direct social work practice: Theory and skills*. Homewood, IL: Dorsey.

Jansson, B. S. (1998). *Becoming an effective policy advocate*. Pacific Grove, CA: Brooks/Cole.

Jennings, P., Callahan, D., & Wolf, S. (1987). The public duties of the profession. *Hastings Center Report, 17*(Suppl.), 1–20.

Krogstad, J. M., & Lopez, M. H. (2017). Black voter turnout fell in 2016, even as a record number of Americans cast ballots. Retrieved from http://www.pewresearch.org/fact-tank/2017/05/12/black-voter-turnout-fell-in-2016-even-as-a-record-number-of-americans-cast-ballots/

Lewis, J. A., Lewis, M. D., Packard, T., & Souffle, F. (2001). *Management of human service programs* (3rd ed.). Belmont, CA: Wadsworth.

Loewenberg, F. M., & Dolgoff, R. (1992). *Ethical decisions for social work practice* (4th ed.). Itasca, IL: F. E. Peacock.

Lundy, C., & van Wormer, K. (2007). Social and economic justice, human rights and peace. *International Social Work, 50*(6), 727–239.

Mahoney, C. (2014). Effective advocacy strategies in 9 steps. Retrieved from http://www.votility.com/blog/effective-advocacy-strategies-in-9-steps

Manning, S. S. (1997). The social worker as moral citizen: Ethics in action. *Social Work, 42*(3), 223–230.

Martin, B. (2007). Activism, social and political. In G. L. Anderson & K. G. Herr (Eds.), *Encyclopedia of activism and social justice* (pp. 19–27). Thousand Oaks, CA: Sage.

Meenaghan, T. M., Kilty, K. M., Long, D. D., & McNutt, J. G. (2013). *Policy, politics, and ethics: A critical approach* (3rd ed.). Chicago, IL: Lyceum.

Miller, S. E., Hayward, R. A., & Shaw, T. V. (2012). Environmental shifts for social work: A principles approach. *International Journal of Social Work, 21*, 270–277.

Mills, C. W. (1956). *The power elite*. New York, NY: Oxford University Press.

Mmatli, T. (2008). Political activism as a social work strategy in Africa. *International Social Work, 51*(3), 297–310.

National Association of Social Workers. (1996). *Code of ethics*. Washington, DC: NASW Press.

Pak, C. M., Cheung, J. C.-S., & Tsui, M.-S. (2016). Looking for social work values and ethics in the textbooks of social service administration over the past 50 years (1965–2014). *Human Service Organizations: Management, Leadership & Governance, 41*(2), 147–161.

Polack, R. J. (2004). Social justice and the global economy: New challenges for social work in the 21st century. *Social Work, 49*(2), 281–290.

Pumphrey, M. (1959). *The teaching of values and ethics in social work education* (Vol. 13). New York, NY: Council on Social Work Education.

Rapp, C. A., & Poertner, C. A. (1992). *Social administration: A client-centered approach*. New York, NY: Longman.

Rawls, J. (1971). *A theory of justice*. Cambridge, MA: Harvard University Press.

Reamer, F. G. (1990). *Ethical decisions in social work practice: A guide for social workers* (2nd ed.). New York, NY: Columbia University Press.

Reamer, F. G. (1998). The evaluation of social work ethics. *Social Work, 42*(6), 488–500.

Reisch, M., & Jani, J. (2012). The new politics of social work practice: Understanding context to promote change. *British Journal of Social Work, 42*, 1132–1150.

Segal, E. A., Gerdes, K. E., & Steiner, S. (2004). *Social work: An introduction to the profession*. Pacific Grove, CA: Brooks/Cole.

Simmons, L. (2010). Work and economic justice: Connections with social work. *Reflections, 16*(2), 36–46.

Towle, C. (1969). Social work: Cause and function. In H. Perlman (Ed.), *Helping: Charlotte Towle on social work and social case work* (pp. 114–115). Chicago, IL: University of Chicago Press.

Walz, T., & Ritchie, H. (2000). Gandhian principles in social work practice: Ethics revisited. *Social Work, 45*(3), 213–222.

## Chapter 14

Abramson, M. (1984). Ethical issues in social work practice with dying person. In L. H. Suszychi & M. Abramson (Eds.), *Social work and terminal care* (pp. 129–135). New York, NY: Praeger.

Arnd-Caddigan, M., & Pozzuto, R. (2008). Use of self in relational clinical social work. *Clinical Social Work Journal, 36*(3), 235–243.

Brueggemann, W. (2014). *The practice of macro social work* (4th ed.). Beaverton, OR: Ringgold.

Congress, E. P. (2012). Continuing education: Lifelong learning for social work practitioners and educators. *Journal of Social Work Education, 48*(3), 397–401.

Kaushik, A. (2017). Use of self in social work: Rhetoric or reality. *Journal of Social Work Values and Ethics, 14*(1), 21–29.

Long, A. (2018). Social work grand challenges: Leaders' perceptions of the potential for partnering with business. *Social Work, 63*(3), 201–209.

Meenaghan, T. M., Kilty, K. M., Long, D. D., & McNutt, J. G. (2013). *Policy, politics, and ethics: A critical approach* (3rd ed.). Chicago, IL: Lyceum.

Miley, K., O'Melia, M., & DuBois, B. (2009). *Instructor's manual and test bank for generalist social work practice: An empowering approach* (6th ed.). New York, NY: Pearson Education.

Rooney, R. (1988). Measuring task-centered training effects on practice: Results of an audiotape study in a public agency. *Journal of Continuing Social Work Education, 4*(40), 2–7.

Rowan, D., Richardson, S., & Long, D. D. (2018). Practice-informed research: Contemporary challenges and ethical decision-making. *Journal of Social Work Values & Ethics, 15*(2), 15–22.

Williams, J. H. (2016). Grand challenges for social work: Research, practice and education. *Social Work Research, 40*(2), 67–70.

Williams, J. H. (2018). Race and poverty: Growth areas for the social work research agenda. *Social Work Research, 42*(2), 67–70.

# Index